Edge of the Screen

Edge of the Screen

Murray Pomerance

BLOOMSBURY ACADEMIC
NEW YORK • LONDON • OXFORD • NEW DELHI • SYDNEY

BLOOMSBURY ACADEMIC
Bloomsbury Publishing Inc, 1359 Broadway, New York, NY 10018, USA
Bloomsbury Publishing Plc, 50 Bedford Square, London, WC1B 3DP, UK
Bloomsbury Publishing Ireland, 29 Earlsfort Terrace, Dublin 2, D02 AY28, Ireland

BLOOMSBURY, BLOOMSBURY ACADEMIC and the Diana logo
are trademarks of Bloomsbury Publishing Plc

First published in the United States of America 2025
Paperback edition published 2026

Copyright © Murray Pomerance, 2025

For legal purposes the Acknowledgments on pp. xi–xii constitute an
extension of this copyright page.

Cover design: Eleanor Rose
Cover image from Life of Pi (Ang Lee, Fox 2000 Pictures, 2012), with tiger
by David Conley. Courtesy Photofest New York

THE MASS ORNAMENT: WEIMAR ESSAYS by Siegfried Kracauer, translated and edited
by Thomas Y. Levin, Cambridge, Mass.: Harvard University Press, Copyright © 1995 by the
President and Fellows of Harvard College. Used by permission. All rights reserved.

All rights reserved. No part of this publication may be: i) reproduced or transmitted in
any form, electronic or mechanical, including photocopying, recording or by means of
any information storage or retrieval system without prior permission in writing from
the publishers; or ii) used or reproduced in any way for the training, development or
operation of artificial intelligence (AI) technologies, including generative AI
technologies. The rights holders expressly reserve this publication from the text
and data mining exception as per Article 4(3) of the Digital Single Market
Directive (EU) 2019/790.

Bloomsbury Publishing Inc does not have any control over, or responsibility for,
any third-party websites referred to or in this book. All internet addresses given
in this book were correct at the time of going to press. The author and publisher
regret any inconvenience caused if addresses have changed or sites have ceased
to exist but can accept no responsibility for any such changes.

Library of Congress Cataloging-in-Publication Data
Names: Pomerance, Murray, 1946- author.
Title: Edge of the screen / Murray Pomerance.
Description: New York : Bloomsbury Academic, 2024. | Includes index.
Identifiers: LCCN 2024017862 (print) | LCCN 2024017863 (ebook) |
ISBN 9798765128336 (hardback) | ISBN 9798765128329 (paperback) |
ISBN 9798765128367 (ebook) | ISBN 9798765128350 (pdf)
Subjects: LCSH: Motion picture audiences. | Motion pictures–Philosophy. |
LCGFT: Essays. | Literary criticism.
Classification: LCC PN1995.9.A8 P65 2024 (print) | LCC PN1995.9.A8 (ebook) |
DDC 791.4301–dc23/eng/20240503
LC record available at https://lccn.loc.gov/2024017862
LC ebook record available at https://lccn.loc.gov/2024017863

ISBN: HB: 979-8-7651-2833-6
PB: 979-8-7651-2832-9
ePDF: 979-8-7651-2835-0
eBook: 979-8-7651-2836-7

Typeset by Integra Software Services Pvt. Ltd.

For product safety related questions contact productsafety@bloomsbury.com.

To find out more about our authors and books visit www.bloomsbury.com and
sign up for our newsletters.

It is here that we remain, with the unconfirmed longing for the place of freedom.
Siegfried Kracauer, "Franz Kafka"

CONTENTS

Acknowledgments xi

Introduction: Where a World Begins 1

1 Momentary 7
   Reflecting on seeing aesthetically and narrationally: *Citizen Kane*; *To Kill a Mockingbird*; *Play Time*; Stanley Cavell; Walter Benjamin; *All the President's Men*; Jean Louis Schefer; *Interiors*; *Notorious*; *The Red Shoes*; *Still of the Night*; the "say-for"; *Child 44*; *Passion*; "Concerto for the Left Hand" (Ravel); *Life Lessons*; *Turandot* (Puccini)

2 Breath 25
   Reflecting on air and airlessness: *A Trip to the Moon* (*Le voyage dans la lune*, 1902); *The Astronaut's Wife*; *2001: A Space Odyssey*; *Gravity*; *Le grand bleu* (*The Big Blue*); *Houdini*; *The Abyss*; *Breathe*; *Torn Curtain*; *Florence Foster Jenkins*; *Funny Girl*; *Run Lola Run*; *Modern Times*; *Roadkill*

3 Suspension 39
   Reflecting on intermediate states: *Snow White* (*Schneewittchen*, 1812); *This Island Earth*; *Minority Report*; Alain Corbin; *Zabriskie Point*; *Field of Dreams*; *La règle du jeu* (*The Rules of the Game*); Antoine-Laurent de Lavoisier; *Star Wars* (1977); The Fantastic Four (Marvel); "Poor Koko" (John Fowles); Stephen Jay Gould

4 They Figure Life 47
   Reflecting on people, actors, characters, and figures: Vivian Sobchack; Jay Presson Allen; *Marnie*; Luigi Pirandello; *The Elephant Man* (1979); *Family Plot*; Charles Dickens; Luis Buñuel; Stanley Kubrick; *An American in Paris*; *Dr. No*; *Superman Returns*; *The Phantom of Liberty*; *Spellbound* (1945); *Casablanca*; *The Philadelphia Story*

5   Here and There   71

Reflecting on cinematic and painterly space: "Boulevard des Italiens" (Gustave Caillebotte); Jonathan Crary; *Pinocchio* (1940); *Sous le ciel de Paris*; *À bout de souffle* (*Breathless*, 1960); *Passion*; *Baisers volés* (*Stolen Kisses*); Wolfgang Schivelbusch and "panoramic perception"; *Zabriskie Point*; *The Gay Shoe Clerk*; Robert Barker

6   To Have and To Hold   89

Reflecting on having the image and image world: Gretchen Henderson; Jean-Paul Sartre; *The Thief of Bagdad* (1940); *Lili*; Vladimir Nabokov; *The Talented Mr. Ripley*; *Summa Theologica* (Aquinas); Augustine; *The Five Books of Moses* (*The Torah*) (Trans. Robert Alter); the Protestant Reformation; Rudolf Arnheim; "Archaic Torso of Apollo" (Rilke); Edith Piaf

7   Muse of Incoherence   103

Reflecting on the fragment: "The Second Coming" (Yeats); "Father's Butterflies" (Nabokov); *Angel City*; Mike Davis; Joan Didion; *Psycho* (1960); J. L. Austin; Paul Goodman; Ludwig Wittgenstein; William Wordsworth; *The Nutty Professor*; *Strangers on a Train*; *They Live*

8   Speak, Anima   119

Reflecting on screen "life": André Bazin; *Life of Pi*; David Conley; *Rise of the Planet of the Apes*; *Francis Covers the Big Town*; *The Wizard of Oz*; Disney, Lantz, Freleng, and Warner Bros. cartoons; *The Cranes Are Flying*

9   Rendezvous   129

Reflecting on the face-to-face: Maurice Merleau-Ponty; *My Name Is Julia Ross*; *Who's Afraid of Virginia Woolf?* (1966); *The Bad Seed*; Johnnie Ray; *The Man Who Fell to Earth*; *Freaks* (Fiedler); *Bringing Up Baby*; *Men in Black*; *Some Like It Hot*; *Le mépris* (*Contempt*)

Interlude   145

Reflecting on *Trouble in Paradise*

10 Clutter 155

Reflecting on clearing the way: *Juno*; *Possessed*; *Bringing Up Baby*; "Shepherd with His Flock in a Woody Landscape" (Rubens); "Wooded Landscape" (Hobbema); *Fantastic Voyage*; D. H. Lawrence; *Gerry*; discernment; *Gosford Park*; *The Loved One*; *Ninotchka*; *The Seventh Voyage of Sinbad*; *No Direction Home: Bob Dylan*

11 Poison or Grapes? 173

Reflecting on picture and voice: Paul Goodman; Maxim Gorky; Siegfried Kracauer; *Citizen Kane*; Mary Douglas; Leonardo Da Vinci; Ray Harryhausen; *À nous la liberté*; *Modern Times*; *Ronin*; *Daddy Nostalgie*; *Titanic*; *A Night to Remember*; *Permanence and Change* (Burke)

12 A Claims Apartment 193

Reflecting on propositions and assessments: Michel Chion and the *acousmêtre*; *Now, Voyager*; *Catch Me If You Can*; *The Mark*; *Trouble in Paradise*; *Notorious*; *Wait Until Dark*; *Stage Fright*; *Two-Faced Woman*; *Living It Up*; *North by Northwest*; *Pressure Point*; *Messiah*; *The Spy Who Came in from the Cold*; *The Errand Boy*; *The Passenger* (*Professione: Reporter*)

13 Speechless 215

Reflecting on language and cinema; Ernst Gombrich; Meindert Hobbema; Rudolf Arnheim; *The Jazz Singer* (1927); *His Girl Friday*; *Sullivan's Travels*; *Gulliver's Travels* (1726); *Bande à part* (*Band of Outsiders*); *Anna Karenina* (1935); *The Band Wagon*; *When Harry Met Sally . . .*

14 Don't Touch Me! 223

Reflecting on cinema reflecting on touch: "Noli me tangere" (Titian); *Beyond the Clouds*; *Rebel Without a Cause*; reading the Torah; *The Marvelous Mrs. Maisel*; *The Bigamist*; *The Touch*; *E.T. the Extra-Terrestrial*; *Hud*; David Sudnow; Frank Wilson; *David and Lisa*

15 The Outcry 241

Reflecting on lost color: *The European Magazine* (1783); *Two Weeks in Another Town*; *Dictionary of Color* (Maerz and Paul); Vladimir Nabokov; *The Toll of the Sea*; *I Was Interrupted* (Ray); Stanley Cavell; *The Awful Truth*

16 A Crafty Screen 251

Reflecting on problems of gestural completion, camera faith, and the camera eye: *GoodFellas*; *The Murder of Roger Ackroyd* (Christie); *How to Get Away with Murder*; the provisional camera; provisional accretion; *Day for Night* (*La nuit américaine*); *The Lonedale Operator*; film and hypertext; *Little Murders*

17 Domain of Wraiths 267

Reflecting on being at home by the edge of the screen: *Murder on the Orient Express* (1974); *Citizen Kane*; Jimmy Stewart; *Crash* (1996); Alan Ladd; the Garden of Allah; the Chateau Marmont; *Play Time*

References 272
Index 280

ACKNOWLEDGMENTS

This book was written in many places thanks to the help of many generous people over a long period. My thanks to:

In Ann Arbor, the late Kenneth Boulding, the late John DeLamater, the late Abraham Kaplan, the late Theodore Newcomb, Joshua Schulze, Scott Smith, Matthew Solomon • In Atlanta, Matthew Bernstein, R. Barton Palmer, Steve Rybin • In Berlin, Jonathan Soja • In Brisbane, Ruth Blair, Gabriela Blasi, Olivia Brown, Daniela Caldas, Matthew Cipa, Josh Clay, Tracy Davies, Joel Fantini, Joseph Glynn, Melissa Hampton, Jason Jacobs, Carole Ferrier, Bronwyn Lea, Paolo Magagnoli, Emily Mahnken, Chloe Robinson, Ali Taylor, Jennifer Yared, and Blair Youngs • In Bristol, Alex Clayton, Pete Falconer, Hoi Lun Law • In Buffalo, the late Norman O. Brown, the late Leslie A. Fiedler, the late Abraham Maslow • In Cambridge, Mass., the late Bob Butler, the late Stanley Cavell, Tom and Verena Conley, Kate Drizos-Cavell, Susan Halpert • In Cambridge, David Brown, Tanya Horeck, Dominic Lash, Henry K. Miller • In Churchstoke, the late Assheton Gorton, Gayatri Gorton • In Ciudad de México, Mara Fortes, Dario Guerrero, Lorena Gómez Mostajo • In Coventry, Catherine Constable, Ed Gallafent, Tom Hemingway, James MacDowell, Tracey McVey, the late Victor Perkins • In Exeter, Ranita Chatterjee, Benedict Morrison • In Istanbul, Murat Akser • In Hong Kong, Richard Allen • In London, Will Brown, Laura Mulvey, Tibor Schmidt, Peter Treherne • In Los Angeles, Stephen Arkle, the late Henry Bumstead, the late Ned Comstock, Terry Dale, Elliott Gould, Barbara Hall, Kristen Hatch, Louise Hilton, Bill Krohn, Douglas Messerli, Jerry Mosher, Polo Ornelas, Jenny Romero, Bob Rubin, Vivian Sobchack, Carol Tavris, Faye Thompson • In Melbourne, Rolando Caputo, Adrian Danks, Anna Dzenis, Lisa French, Steven Gaunson, Alexia Kannas, Elliott Logan, Constantine Verevis, Ryan Warrener, Xaio Yang • In Miami, Oscar Jubis, Kitty Morgan and William Rothman • In the New Forest, Mike Hammond, Mark Kermode, Linda Ruth Williams • In New York, Derek Davidson, Todd Ifft, Stephen Miller, the late Mercedes Ribicoff, the late Peter Ribicoff, the late Claire Smith, the late Arthur Vidich • In Norwich, Stephen Mitchell • Over the Pacific, R. Claude Lahaise • In Oxford, Andrew Klevan • In Paris, Olivier Assayas, Sylvie Barthet, Jean-Michel Frodon • In Reading, Lisa Purse • In San Francisco, Doug and Catherine McFarland • In Southampton, K. J. Donnelly, Dan Varndell and Naomi Phillips • In Spain,

Adrian Martin • In Sydney, Robert Sinnerbrink • In Toronto, Brandon Cronenberg, Martin Gero, Dan Sacco, Nick White, Jonathan Wright, Ash Zukerman • In Vancouver, Jim Balderston, James Lawson, Ernest Mathijs • In Winchester, Matthew Leggatt • In Winnipeg, Jonah Corne, George Toles and Melissa Steele.

It should go without saying—yet it is far too often not said—that my friends and colleagues at Bloomsbury have been an unfettered joy. My gratitude to Dharanivel Baskar, Sophie Beardsworth, Sevval Ercin, Stephanie Grace-Petinos, Katie Gallof Houck, Dan O'Hagan, Eleanor Rose, Sarah Skinner, and Ramya Thangaraj.

There are no words sufficient for thanking family. My father, the late Michael Harold Pomerance, took me into the marvelous world of films, and my mother, the late Sadie "Syd" (Shub) Pomerance, raved enough in earshot about movies she had seen that I was intrigued early on, from a distance.

Nellie Perret is my friend, my partner, my teacher, my astrolabe, my spyglass, and my love, and Ariel Pomerance is my inspiration and a wonder.

Introduction: Where a World Begins

It came to pass that I saw how, in a long period of movie-watching—more than seventy years—while sitting in the dark affixed to so-considered happenings that glowed before me, I was constantly and continually able, more or less, to follow along from one moment to another in such a way as to believe that I was not only witnessing but also understanding: understanding first what I was seeing and, in reflection, films broadly, one film then another and another. It seemed as though I knew what voices meant when they piped out from the screen. That I grasped what bodies could mean when they moved, clutched, strained, withered, greened. That I knew transition, motion, pause, vibration, color. That the film "spoke," as it were, and I "got it." Everything was simply natural, naturally the way things are; and then I saw nature.

Any speech of any kind crosses over a gap. Here, the gap was between this conscious, happily eager, even hungry audience self of mine and the furthest reaches of the territory in which film could move before surrendering itself my way. Me, and it. "Where the self stops and the world begins," as Leslie Fiedler intoned it, in a public lecture at the Horace Rackham Graduate School of The University of Michigan in the fall of 1966, and, twenty years old, I was avidly there. It became more and more clear that as I reached for a film, the film reached for me, and just as there was an edge to my position there was, almost by fate, an edge to the screen.

Later on, it became interesting to wonder whether filmic "speaking" came on the part of a director, or a producer; a writer; a cinematographer; a designer; a group of performers. And to wonder, too, how singularly alone I was in catching what came over the edge, because, after all (as Douglas Gomery shows), film is a business in which any one item is sold to any one consumer at a relatively low cost, but *look at the number of consumers!* It made sense, I saw, to wonder about themes and sub-themes; about manifest and latent content; indeed about "content" altogether, in this form that was so very musical, even when it showed a musical. As, catching at my imagination, there seemed to be myriad other features of cinema's outward voyaging and our struggle for engagement, I accepted without triaging; I reveled. One aspect of film-watching was so very alive with me, however, so unquestionably present, that it was as invisible as my own staring eyes:

Not only had a set of assumptions and presumptions been entertained about what I should be able to grasp as a viewer, but apparently I had taught myself, and allowed myself to be taught, how to grasp. Perhaps an abyss opened between what was expected of me and what I struggled to provide, perhaps at the edge of the abyss I was able somehow to find success watching movies.

After all, there always was a mystery to the viewer, any viewer, "getting" film at all. And this goes far beyond communication. The mystery highlights a condition, that the screen's enunciation is aimed at some receptivity already prepared; or if not prepared, capable of being prepared. Not just that the General controlled the Army, or that the powers that be controlled the slaving masses, but that control was possible. When I went Saturday afternoons to watch films, I was ready already. I was ready in the half-empty Delta Theatre to see *The Charge at Feather River* (1953)—*in 3-D!* I had been made ready, though who knows how or where or by whose help. Film constantly, consistently avoided compelling me to accept and understand what I was not yet prepared to accept and understand. The so-called (so-spieled) "grammar" of film—parallel editing, continuity sequencing, shot/countershot—worked directly, as it felt, much in the way that the oxygen in the air I breathed worked in my circulatory system; and all this as much as it did—posited some theorists—because it was arranged in accordance with the biological march of my mind (notwithstanding that my own feeling was, and remains, that the biological march of my mind has been cultured by cinema). This issue, this riddle, is broad. How can it happen that when a grade-school teacher working with tiny children begins to tell them the fundamentals of grammar, somehow the grammar of this teacher telling is already (presumably) comprehended by those who apparently need to be told about grammar. To be sure, even when I am confounded by a movie I understand the confounding *as confounding*. Film seems to know me, the me who is sitting there *over the edge*. It seems to have known me all my life.

The Charge at Feather River, to take a case: The Cheyenne had become popular as a collective character trope in Hollywood at that time. They were charging forward across the (rather diminutive) Feather River, and as they raced toward the camera on their lusty horses they fired arrows ahead of them. These, of course, came shuddering into the audience, and since one was watching all this through those rose-and-blue tinted 3-D glasses, the cardboard-mounted cheap cellophane things that irritated the ears, those arrows were heading for oneself, as though one had been selected out (by those glasses if not by the shooters) as target; and so, reprising without knowing it what some legendary accounts claim audiences at the Salon Indien on the Boulevard des Capucines did in 1895 when they saw the Lumières' train chugging into the station at La Ciotat, we all ducked (see Bottomore). I do recall ducking. And all of this was also true:

- I knew without doubt that I was watching a movie. (The irritation of the fake-o 3-D glasses was an incessant reminder.)
- I knew these folk were not acting as actual tribesmen, even if, somewhere in Hollywood, they were known to belong to particular tribes; they were playing to the camera; nevertheless
- they were all paid for their work (their play), and surely what they were doing onscreen was work; yet
- I was not only within my rights but also *compos mentis* to accept the moment as a "charge" with bows and arrows, and with arrows coming my way, because
- the 3-D effect was allowing for this perception; yet, too,
- I knew of the 3-D effect, and as the perception worked, and I ducked, I knew it wasn't because of arrows, it was because of 3-D (I was ducking away from 3-D!). Further,
- although the charge wasn't real, even if it looked real (whatever looking real means), the "game" was to "pretend it's real" and act accordingly, so therefore in watching this movie I was, by obligation, and avowedly, playing a game. But:
- even then, aged seven, I knew what games were and how to play them; and I knew, too, that this game was not a game I had ever heard of before, so that my ability to play this game appeared to be automatic, even if
- as we all know, nothing in human experience is actually automatic. So,
- the producer and director knew they were creating the illusion of arrows coming into the audience, and knew the audience would accept, react to, devour, digest, wholly incorporate that illusion; while still at the same time
- knowing (securely) that the illusion was an illusion and take special pleasure in playing along with it.

Playing along, as though informed; as though prepared; as though educated; as though trained; as though readied; as though helped forward … with no experience—nor memory of an experience—of being any of those. To be sure, I was watching at the edge of the screen and the arrows were crossing the abyss, and also "crossing" the abyss: there was no—and needed to be no—vital distinction. I can remember water in the river splashing up around the horses' legs as the arrows came ...

Far more intriguing than film's power to approach its audience as familiars; more than auteurist striving and compositional propriety; more than a variety of cultural implications and interpretations as such, is the viewer's exact experience in the face of film. The truth that film is watched in our lives. The viewer of whose experience I am most aware, but also most able to care, goes by my name. What, I wonder, must I *not* need to be told about the world, about life, about human relations, about Providence, about universal things!, in order to duck, or chuckle, or "understand": the film can presuppose my informed awakeness. I do not mean the specific information or instruction manual I am required by some particular moment in some particular film to know—that which I must arrange to learn, somehow, beforehand—but what knowledge might be discovered in myself that I already—even without recognizing—recognize, such that my watching, my *surveillance,* is assured and I am neither surprised nor shocked nor caught off-guard and unprepared, left blank, left unable to go on. It is lethal for a filmmaker to leave his viewer unable to go on. Going on and going on is what film is all about. It's what everything is all about: listen to Takeshi tell Tom Conti this in *Merry Christmas, Mr. Lawrence* (1982).

Regarding this book, however, regarding these bound pages, the manner in which a reader goes on, is worth a comment. These meditations were not written to follow seriatim from some common beginning, thus they do not seek to be read in one linear order from the first to the last. One could mentally shuffle them. Even, mentally, shuffle the interior sections of one meditation with those of another. Certainly feel free to pick and choose one's form of approach. Perhaps if the reader is unfamiliar with a film under discussion she will pause to watch it; perhaps not—I have tried to keep away from the most arcane material, but of course with film it's ongoingly impossible to predict what works commercial enterprises will make available at any moment and what works will tumble into arcanity. None of the texts here *require* familiarity or previous watching, however. As, ongoingly, my exploration must follow the cinema's reaching out to its viewer, its grappling with the viewer's attention, concentration, imagination, and experience, why should this book not do the same, and why might not each reader find his own pleasing way to reach out to the text in response. Watching a film is a form of play, after all. In reading here, treat this material playfully, too: move around and through it. No lone secret message is buried, that one could fail to snag at one's peril.

Finally, a caveat:

All of the issues tackled in these pages, and all the filmic materials adduced to exemplify or inspire, are selected arbitrarily by an "authorial hand." They do constitute authorial judgments, preferences, leanings—those of a person writing out of a single self. In going to the movies, we are each of us, in a very important sense and regardless of social organization, in the dark: solitary in our awareness before the unfolding. We sit before the screen and the screen affects us one by one, notwithstanding that audiences are large. This book is only an attempt, hopefully not too feeble, at teasing out and rummaging through some of the issues that provoke me when I think about film; but, provoking me, may also provoke you. As I watch at the edge of the screen, that very special place, you are there, too. Whether it can be said that in this watching you and I are together remains to be seen.

Toronto—Hollywood—Hampshire—Toowong—St. Lucia
July 2024

1

Momentary

Everett Sloane (l.) and Joseph Cotten (r.) as Bernstein and Leland in Citizen Kane *(Orson Welles, RKO/Mercury, 1941). Digital frame enlargement.*

> *The viewer becomes a juggler, not only facing two worlds at once (the diegetic world, the screen world) but keeping them alive and in motion.*
>
> MURRAY POMERANCE ("SOUND" 65)

With what reservoir of desire and what strange anticipations do we sit waiting at the edge of the screen? Caught up watching a film, engaged, say, with a figure shifting among and speaking with others onscreen, a viewer invokes a relationship that can be understood both narrationally and aesthetically, almost as though reflecting Walter Benjamin's observation that "appearance has a paradoxical effect" (59). Along with the figure, bonded to other figures, the viewer has joined in. The structure of the watcher's bond, *during the watching,* is of piquing interest. In what ways and in what directions do I enter a room or leave it, with a figure who has caught my eye; what, if any, are the limits of that kind of movement for me? More than who this figure is in the story—an identificational and navigational issue—who is he or she in my life?

> Is it not monstrous that this player here
> But in a fiction, in a dream of passion,
> Could force his soul so to his own conceit
> That, from her working, all his visage wann'd,
> Tears in his eyes, distraction in's aspect,
> A broken voice, and his whole function suiting
> With forms to his conceit? And all for nothing!
> For Hecuba!
> What's Hecuba to him, or he to Hecuba,
> That he should weep for her?
>
> (*Hamlet* II.ii.561–70)

Weep we may as the player weeps, even without tears. What is involved as such a queer engagement comes to its limits? Erving Goffman's dictum about theatricality and audiences: "Watching is doing" (*Analysis* 381).

Narration

Consider an important distinction, between (a) *seeing narrationally,* which might also mean linearly, reductively, processually, even capitalistically, since the plot resolution is a kind of profit over the labor of seeing; and (b) *seeing aesthetically,* which might also mean experientially, feelingfully, even existentially, in confusion, and riddled.[1]

To see *narrationally* one attends to a figure's position (social, emotional, topographical) relative to others displayed, invoked, or implied in the story; and also relative to the scene in its depiction (perspective) and to the overriding

---

[1] One could think as well of Hannah Arendt's distinction between the *vita activa* and the *vita contemplativa* as contexts for our seeing.

happenings and underpinning themes that have been embracing spates of action—a heist, a love story, a travel saga, a search for a treasure. One asks, repetitively, "What is happening now?" (our way of breathing in the oxygen of the tale). Or else one asks, "What was the meaning of that gesture she just made?" Or, "How is he being read (weighed) by her?" Think: love or fakery; success or hopelessness; catch or loss. Centering the narrational problem is information: information aggregated as hypothesis: hypotheses aggregated as theory: theories aggregated as meaning: meaning importing resolution: and resolution requiring time, albeit time is something of which we can never be sure. We can never be sure we have the time to be informed, or for that matter the time to follow along. As Montaigne wrote:

> The other day someone was going through my notebooks and found a declaration about something I wanted done after my death. I told him straight that, though I was hale and healthy and but a league away from my house, I had hastened to jot it down because I had not been absolutely certain of getting back home.
>
> (26)

My own narrational relation with screen happenings goes far beyond the temporally determinative diegetic links I recognize figures having one with another (and that they understand themselves having): Jed Leland (Joseph Cotten) and Mr. Bernstein (Everett Sloane) cheering for their employer Charles Foster (Charlie) Kane: "Charlie Kane is my old buddy," Leland says at one point, "or at least he was. I know he was, until he fired me." The figure-to-figure relation includes but also goes beyond the way one detects another and "decodes" the other's placement and action (Bernstein checking Leland from the corner of his eye as they cheer). The relation has memory. Relational "reading" is going on perduringly in film narratives. And out in their secret dark abode audiences keep "reading along" as best they can, following the progressions, perhaps surmising conclusions or at least finding a way to appreciate conclusions *as* conclusions when they occur. Will poor Black Velvet be able to win the race in the climax?

The issue of "what is going on" is fraught in itself, and with some films narrative can be inordinately complex, even misleading or confounding as the script carefully dictates. Thus, following the story can be an easy glide or a strenuous climb, albeit in any case the audience will expectedly find enjoyment, satisfaction, and release. Perhaps casual viewers rate the movies they see in terms of the (satisfying) moral outcomes of plot resolution. Figures who seem to be "good" may come out all right in the end, have an optimistic future, leave with a smile; as Miss Prism says in *The Importance of Being Earnest:* "The good ended happily, and the bad unhappily. That is what Fiction means." "Bad" folks may get their comeuppance. Partly to play with this casual way of reading, in his *The Magnificent Ambersons* (1942)

Orson Welles has a very naughty character get his comeuppance in fact—but not at the moment we would prefer.

Viewers may find themselves following game pieces that might collide or merge in such a way as to be indiscriminable: the twin brothers in *Jonathan* (2018). One might bond with beings followed secretly—I didn't circulate this but when I was watching *To Kill a Mockingbird* in 1962 for the first time I bonded with a little character named Dill (John Megna) because, probably unknown to others, he was almost identical to me in some early childhood photographs; I thought he *was* me. Screen figures can keep relational secrets, too—melodrama is chocked full of this, as characters make claim, in Peter Brooks's words, "to sacred status" (16). But with or without explicit secrecy, forward-goingness is the overriding imperative (even when "forward" is "the past"). No matter the structure of any particular story, no matter the moral weight of its goings-on, or any individual's "difference from all other men" (Brooks 16), the question persists, "What is happening; and now what; and what now?" One may have to hip-hop to follow and maintain relations in their quality and vector, as with *Citizen Kane* (1941); or to work more straightforwardly, as with *The Maltese Falcon* (1941); but all ways of proceeding go forward. As with T. S. Eliot's "Not fare well,/ But fare forward, voyagers" ("The Dry Salvages").

The narrational approach to cinema, which any viewer knows how to use but which some serious critics also follow analytically, promises release (catharsis) but by no means guarantees enrichment. Stories viewed summatively make for clearcut traffic direction (not at all what we see in Jacques Tati's *Play Time* [1968]!), in this way being applications of printed literature where story agents are defined as words in print rather than bodies visible to the eye; one follows happenings made up through wordings, and appreciates the qualities of presence in which happenings happen, as the tone of the diction works to inform. For both narrational reading and narrational viewing, *information* is the key. How much can we know about this moment as part of a scheme of moments to be assembled and called "the story"? Every flicker we see is taken as a stimulus to knowledge. Momentary knowledge, I should add, since it is always conceivable that sometime after a viewing the events and what we came to know from them could all transform or disappear.

The main presumption in taking a narrational approach for understanding a film is that the viewer and/or reader is somehow, in catching a sight, independent, objective, unfeeling, deductive, and smart enough to avoid missing anything "important." Viewing is calculation, calculation brings data, data brings knowledge: a scientific piety. (Clearly, this "knowledge" can be toyed with, as in *The Usual Suspects* [1995] or *Fight Club* [1999]; but still, when one toys via narrational logic it is never not "knowledge" being toyed with.) Viewers confidently assume that no action of relevance will stray outside the information package without being tied to a clue (a thread) that remains within. Story as labyrinth, viewer as explorer: but all this without regard to the moisture on the labyrinthine walls, the smell, the image of the monster one holds within as one steps along holding the thread and seeing, as of yet, nothing. Narrational movement is about reaching goals, not experiencing voyages.

Aesthetics

To take up an *aesthetic* view of cinema—a view activated through a viewer's commitment and, in a way, abandonment of self—is another matter, since beyond what a depicted figure does, one's sensitivity is raised to: what she looks like as she does it; what she does not do at the same time; what presentation lends us by way of feelingful experience, anticipation, delight. Appearances, masks, covers, surfaces, light, color, tonality, poise, framing, margining, balance, imbalance, and more ... all come into play. Also vocal tenor, timbre, amplitude, and other qualities of sound. And expectation, hesitation, exasperation, withdrawal, and other aspects of our relation to time. A sense of expansiveness or contraction, breadth or confinement, a hint of unmapped (as well as, perhaps, a mere glimpse of mapped) territory. If plots invoke comments and discussion (in media reviews the gist of commentary) aesthetic forces harbor an experience and keep it away from discourse, hold the quickness of response in a hidden reserve, or possibly even fomenting, on the boil, as with Jo and her mother in *A Taste of Honey* (1961).

Stanley Cavell addresses this experiential reserve as, in part, a matter of beneficial "indistinctness," pointing to the work of Samuel Fuller who "thrives" on the "indistinctness of his people":

> He does it by single-minded insistence on forgoing the characterization, plot complexity, and symbolism on which movies used to depend, preserving only the blocks of crude emotion that all humans share—base levels of sentimentality, magazine hopes, eyes-open sex—and working an inventiveness with treachery and violence that lends a kind of originality to these inarticulate, mass lives. This single-minded intention discovers a way of achieving old-fashioned movies.
>
> (*World* 70–1)

Not just emotion, note, but "crude emotion," emotion not yet refined into definitions; and "sentimentality," even "base" sentimentality, in which feeling, memory, hope, fear, intuition can swamp rational calculation.

For an example, our Leland and our Bernstein again: we have been invited to watch them cheer in an extreme wide-angle shot taken up close (as one can do with wide-angle lenses), so that the mouths yawn open as great devouring maws and the eyes appear to recede in calculation; this has nothing to do with the placement of the cheer in the screen syntax at the moment, it is about touching the viewer with a tone and attitude so quick and subtle as to be digested without awareness.² As with the Gothic, Brooks finds, it "reasserts the presence, in the world, of forces that cannot be accounted for by the daylight self and the self-sufficient mind" (17).

I want now to consider the aesthetic mode of response to cinema from several points of view. Narrational analysis of cinema—or, as I could call it, "literary" analysis—has received plenty of attention already in rantings about film, generally absent the thought that for the "literary analyst," without the images the facts of the story could have been recounted quite successfully (in a book; on radio). Resting beside or beyond plot, aesthetic perception transcends or twists rationalities and received wisdom.

Twenty very small meditations:

[1] Aesthetic and narrational conceits are not mutually exclusive. An aesthetic stream can flow under, inside, or behind narration, can exist in spite of it, just as it can be used by narration for floating information. Take as a case, packaging: colors, shapes, nuances of all kinds can be telling about class, about conditions, about identity, about historical moment, and about intention, thereby helping a plot move forward in a direct and immediate way and giving us a handhold as we are sped along (e.g., a 1950s palette recreated to a degree in *Carol* [2016]). The aesthetic array can lurk behind the "proscenium" of a story in which, perhaps, so much "happens," and so quickly, and in so many directions, and toward so supreme a conclusion that pausing to consider (apparently irrelevant) colors, shapes, and nuances seems counterproductive to watching purposefully. Yet in such a case one has dedicated oneself in advance to a narrational purpose, whilst "irrelevancies" may themselves be pregnant. Walter Benjamin writes of Arabic architecture how in its "proliferating arabesques," its "ornamental density," the "distinction between thematic and excursive expositions is eliminated" (*Street* 53).

A case where the "story" is not only explicit and pronounced but also publicly sanctioned, even etched into received history, is Alan J. Pakula's *All the President's Men* (1976), detailing the Watergate Affair of June 17, 1972, through August 9, 1974. The story meanders through Bob Woodward (Robert Redford) and Carl Bernstein's (Dustin Hoffman) investigation at the *Washington Post,* as they gather shards of evidence, fail to find other shards, collate their fragments, fumble in collating, suspect, hypothesize, and ultimately mount a structure of accusation that, at the very end,

---

²Andrew Dominik borrows this strategy of wide-angle mouthing for *Blonde* (2022).

explodes with the Nixon resignation. So much for the plot. Yet one cannot watch *President's Men* without catching Redford's blond, tall, smooth-cheeked, preppy model's poses and at his side, the shorter, darker, eagerly vociferous and unguarded posturing of Hoffman. This "reserved/expressive" doubling races outside the precincts of what gets said, what happens or does not happen, what the long-term political outcomes are or may be (the narrative): a blue-eyed/brown-eyed split; tall/short; Gentile/Jewish; patient/impatient. One sees Pakula swinging us from one man to the other and back again; from patience to impatience, from impatience to patience, again and again, so that this pendular swinging becomes a powerful (if, some would argue, latent) element in the film. A lethal tale told on a swing, as it were. Or, too: we see the city room of the *Post*, designed by George Jenkins and decorated by George Gaines, where Woodward and Bernstein work: a warren of reporters, typewriters, desks, chairs, and paper in which the eye can't avoid getting lost, while Woodward and Bernstein *never* do get lost. As realism this can seem sensible enough—the two have worked at the paper for some time; they would not get lost in the newsroom—but the space we are seeing isn't the *Post* newsroom, it's a film space, and they also never get lost in the representation there. Washington in 1973 was also a warren, and the film shows how Woodward and Bernstein never got lost there either, not ultimately, not really, although they often felt they were on the verge of being lost. Being lost and not being lost are powerful elements of the film, evoking a powerful feeling of lost gravity: was it a national mood?

Jean Louis Schefer asks whether it is because the viewer is subject to "an affect never to be guaranteed permanence" that

> (sustained by the hope of an unknown body made of antennae of emotions or feelings) [he] would be some part of this turning machine, thrown into what has already been recorded? The spectator seeks this point of gravity (this center) lost only because the body that accompanied it has vanished, or, as if it had been stellified, no longer weighs anything, but is not quite returned to shadow.
>
> (*Man* 109)

[2] Aesthetic considerations, as I am naming them, may focus on superficial properties, always the most photogenic. Clothing or coverings will have texture, sheen, measurement, fit, and above all color (see the model sequences in *Blow-Up* [1966] for a bravura example). A garment's fit in hanging loosely or compactly on a body will comment upon that body, its history and condition (a perfect case study being *The Incredible Shrinking Man* [1957]). Measurement will indicate the amount of (costly) material in use and point to social class or ceremonial function: contrast Elizabeth Taylor in sparkling white, walking down the aisle in *Father of the Bride* (1950) and clomping around the house in sparser garb in *Who's Afraid of*

Virginia Woolf? (1966). Color will work by way of two palates at once: the visible skin of the character (actor in make-up) and the setting as lit. As to skin, see *The Rains of Ranchipur* (1955) where Richard Burton, a white Welshman, was made up with bronzed facial tones to look Indian.[3] As to settings, note Madeleine Elster standing at Scotty Ferguson's doorstep (*Vertigo,* 1958). Clothing can neutralize a character's presence (as with the gray flannel suits in *The Man in the Gray Flannel Suit* [1956]), degrade it (as with leprous Tirzah [Cathy O'Donnell] in *Ben-Hur* [1959]), or elevate it into allurement (Betty Hutton in *The Greatest Show on Earth* [1952]) and opulence (the Empress Tsu-Hsi [Flora Robson] in *55 Days at Peking* [1963]). As to set coloration taken in itself, a designer can make for somberness (Adam Trask's bedroom [by James Basevi] in *East of Eden* [1955]), quietude (Robert Stromberg's design for the garden of Wonderland in *Alice in Wonderland* [2010]), joy (Bernard Evein's Act I interiors in *The Umbrellas of Cherbourg* [1964]), austerity (John Box's dilapidated house at Varykino in *Doctor Zhivago* [1965]), dignity (the Archer home by Dante Ferretti in *The Age of Innocence* [1993]). Set design can reduce the sensed proportion of a character in a bizarre "world" (*Willy Wonka and the Chocolate Factory* [1973], design by Harper Goff) or expand it (*Black Narcissus* [1947], design by Alfred Junge).

Indeed, the project of appreciating a film experience not in terms of the acting or directing but explicitly in terms of aesthetic issues can bring new and rewarding attention to such geniuses as Junge, Goff, Box, Ferretti, Basevi, and many others.

Taking aesthetic surfaces as only information fields we make readings typically based in well-established social conventions. Such readings remind more than inform; we learn what we already know. Only infrequently are viewers licensed to lose themselves considering color, shape, texture, or form: the extraordinary redness of Milla Jovovich's hair in *The Fifth Element* (1997); the hat fitting, but also not quite fitting, on Charles Laughton's head when Capt. Bligh gets into the lifeboat in *Mutiny on the Bounty* (1935); Fred Astaire's contrasting socks in *The Band Wagon* (1953) and Sal Mineo's in *Rebel Without a Cause* (1955).

[3] Beyond perfunctory sensation stimulated by artistic *touches* on and around bodies, film can play upon aesthetic potentiality as a film progresses. In his *Interiors* (1978), for a notably lengthy period early on Woody Allen confines E. G. Marshall in a marriage to Geraldine Fitzgerald, who desires every aspect of her world to radiate in either pale white or distinctive beige and who will tolerate no breaches in her home design. After she leaves the scene the husband courts, then brings home Maureen Stapleton, who

---

[3]Some of the yellow (a Max Factor product) worked to ameliorate the intense blue of Technicolor lighting.

enters for the first time in flamboyant carmine red (by Joel Schumacher). When, moments later, dancing with abandon, she knocks against a valuable sculpture that smashes to the floor, we are not surprised.

[4] To disattend and negate superficial aesthetic manipulations requires a fixed concentration on storyline. But because cinema is pictorially arranged, and because pictures are compositions of light, darkness, color, tone, depth, and marginality, we are prone in default to catching—reading—surfaces as we go along: perhaps reading without recognizing that we are reading— the detective is racing after a car, and we are inside his vehicle with him, but we don't notice, or recognize ourselves noticing, the colors that passing streetlights are throwing onto his face. But viewers can come to think of themselves as cognoscenti of composition and form. Then, highlighting or reducing experience to storyline seems cogent only for retrospections: post-cinematic analyses, narrative scholarship. In watching we cannot avoid being caught by what is alluring, what is beautiful, what is abysmal, what is cold. Even watching narrationally, spectators are caught by aesthetics and moved toward aesthetic reaction. However:

As a film unwinds, let us ask, do screen figures unwind aesthetic reactions, too? Do they experience as they see, just as the viewer does? (Do they notice color? Do they notice shape?) Are they touched by feeling as much as by circumstance? Never forget that the screen figure is not only an objectively perceivable game piece in a narrative field but also, albeit fictively, a being who presents a reality of self, a doer of what the script dictates must be done. Can we succeed in imagining that a figure experiences, when we know the script has designed him to "express experience"? Can we say that in *Notorious* (1946), Sebastian (Claude Rains) coming upon Devlin and Alicia (Cary Grant, Ingrid Bergman) at the racetrack is actually stunned, stymied, frozen by their being together? Analytically speaking, the significations we detect are in Rains's performance—the figure is halted—not in Sebastian. Can we stretch to feel with Sebastian? And as we seize up with perturbation and concern when he approaches the pair, can we think Sebastian shares *our feeling of mortification that he might see something they don't want him to see?*

Bluntly, the audience can be struck in an aesthetic caesura—the view looking into the valley in *Black Narcissus*. Can figures, too? After all, what is engaging us way out here in the audience is nearer to them than to us; nearer, more quickly grasped, more blatantly present: it is in their world, not our world. Sebastian saw Dev and Alicia *first*, then we saw what he was seeing. Yet if, too brutally, figures were halted in their experience the motor of the film would seize up. The film figure must *never* experience a caesura, a true astonishment, a sense of the sublime, a boundless wonderment. Consider how we can be stunned by a vision while figures seeing the same thing are not, since generally in fictional cinema figures relate to their world factually not aesthetically; since only the narrational importance of happenings counts for them. Here is a reflection of the odd dramatic irony Cavell finds in Ibsen with "a character's saying something whose meaning is fundamental to the issues of the drama but is unglimpsed by the character who says it" (*Cities* 263). One stark case of viewer reaction separated from character reaction: in *Forbidden Planet* (1956), thanks to a splendid painted backing by George Gibson, we are treated to the green-turquoise splendor of the atmospheric horizon on Altair-4, vast and alluring; yet not one figure ever notices and marvels at the strange and wonderful color. Those who live there are, in fact, blasé, while visitors are preoccupied. Do figures privately think, "No need for me to rhapsodize, because *they* are rhapsodizing already"—*they* being *us?* Can we believe that *figures* think, I mean; not actors. This is expressly *not* what Orson Welles was pointing to when he said, "There are very few actors who can make you believe that they think" (302). The actor may or may not be a thinker, but do we believe the figure the actor is playing, is?

[5] This hypothetical question raises the perplexing and marvelous issue of the viewer's relation with what the image realizes: persons ostensibly not unlike the viewer who are in the presence of a moment realized. In the typical love story, for instance, one person is stunned by the attractiveness of another and quickly the plot has the two come together in some way. Robert Stack and Lauren Bacall in *Written on the Wind* (1956). But for us, Bacall here is utterly statuesque, a model of poise and dignity. To approach her as Kyle Hadley does is unthinkable, to embrace her less so. She is Galatea. Kyle's look, approach, touch, and bonding thus seem fake, mere scaffolding for the story and its happenings but hardly in tune with our authentic viewer response. In deep appreciation, happenings halt.

So much of film watching presumes our acceptance of a key postulate: that what is happening to a figure at the moment is *intelligible* to us, that as viewers we can identify somehow, and in identifying consider ourselves to be sensing what the figure is sensing. Perhaps we further assume or hope that the figure identifies with us. We are "in love with" screen figures. Against this unified and harmonious backdrop a figure's failure to express an aesthetic response, to mirror us, to openly find "beautiful" what we openly find beautiful, can come into focus as strange and somewhat incomprehensible. The pace of depicted eventualities assures that we usually don't have time to ponder this. When the figure is mute before a great glory, she is separated from the viewer (whether or not the viewer senses that separation). I will come shortly to address the inadequate solution that will surely be proposed for this conundrum: that the figure is thinking the aesthetic response secretly, holding it in—Kyle Hadley thinking, "God! A Galatea!!! Let's see if I can touch her!"—as we often do ourselves instead of cooing aloud.

[6] But if they make for plot "business" aesthetic figurations will gain light and focus, thus *seem* to be in figures' consciousness. For example, in *The Red Shoes* (1948) the vivid red lipstick and black eye lining she wears onstage in

"Swan Lake" give Vicki Page (Moira Shearer) an affecting aura that strikes our emotions and upsets our stance, but are there to fulfill a diegetic stage function of making the moving ballerina's face detectable at a distance (the scene is set in a theater, where we are only sometimes privileged to see the scene from the lip of the stage). Thus, as he, too, is watching in the audience, we know Lermontov (Anton Walbrook) is seeing her face. One supreme aestheticism, in which story and story relevance disappear as the emotive cloud rolls in, and in which it is a mystery to see inside the figures, is the nocturnal circus finale of Fellini's *8 ½* (1963).

[7] When a figure seems blasé to an aesthetic effect that stuns us, we can imagine passing across the gulf into her interior, can presume her to be feeling what we are feeling but withholding for some "personal" reason. We hold our reaction in as well, after all. In order to believe a figure is holding speech in, that there is something she *would* say but here doesn't, one must posit and pose her unstated, ungestured, unposed thoughts, in short one must invent, because there is no inside on the screen. We easily make up a figural "inside" by aggregating a figure's signs, but this is precipitous. Caught in the aesthetic array we may silently react while, carried away by plot business, a figure seems not to silently react but only acts toward or against The Great Visible. When a figure is faced with what we would call sublime but seems not to sense sublimity, we may downgrade our own sensation into the merely eye-catching. Or worse, we may downplay our own experience into acceptance of a filmic convention by which screen figures may inhabit the sublime but do not recognize it when it's before them.

[8] The film moves on, but not in the same way among figures as among viewers. It is in the flow of dramatic continuity that figures are embedded, racing from what happened to what is going to happen and without leisure for reflection or feeling. They seize and swallow the form, color, texture, shape, and extensivity of the present while never losing the power to press forward, to appear in the next scene. The figures are voyaging toward narrative climax but we, as with Tennessee Williams's Tom in *The Glass Menagerie*, "go to the movies instead of moving."

Nor does a screen figure have an option but to press on. Spectators are not subject to that requirement, albeit they often choose movement instead of meditation. With accessible media one finds ways of pulling away and savoring, of experiencing in a more purely aesthetic vein. Events need not be pressed into an observational chain. Tom Ripley (Matt Damon) thinking about getting into Dickie Greenleaf's (Jude Law) bathtub, waving his finger in the green water, can be there forever, like a lover on a Grecian urn.

[9] To watch film is to try, and ultimately fail at, focusing on a river, indeed a river of the past; or better, the place where all the rivers go. Iain Sinclair writes about chasing characters who always come to the sea:

And there was always, behind that accidental or strategic decision, a powerful residue from childhood, sentiment for a specific location, a lovely timeless time. The way that children process incidents, frustrations, intense smells, colours and textures that their parents have completely forgotten. Or never, in the flurry of the mundane, even registered (84),

perhaps "channeling a state of mind that Aristotle called 'Entelechia' … to capture the essence of the soul of the place: *the soul's estate*" (53; italic original). As scenes transpire they affect the viewer as did scenes in childhood, when no outcomes were at stake. These "moments," as they could be conceived, can be shaped around a figure's placement or expression, or an utterance, or a view, or a quality of light, or a kind of movement, or any or all of these and other qualities of film such as duration, transposition, rhythm, and so on. The moment is a treasure for the film viewer, a nugget around which the crystal of the film coalesces later. One could think of a film as a Treasure Island.

[10] But memory as we have it—the experiential recall of a temporal evanescence, the pulling out of a past—figures of the screen do not, and cannot, have. Their aesthetic reactions must either denote (and detonate) information—"He was driving a red car!"—or else speedily pass and in passing extinguish. A shocking retrieval of memory, such as the story centering *Still of the Night* (1982), is only a "retrieval" of "memory." Characters live in an eternal present, caught in a Korsakov's twilight zone (see Sacks), a present that if repeatable for us, since a film can be watched over and over, is for them, always, all the time there is. Sam Spade will never cease showing some chagrin and remorse when he discovers that his partner Miles Archer has been killed. Rick Blaine will have tears in his eyes when he thinks of Ilsa, never recalling that he wept a little, too, last year and the year before that, or even that he did "just an instant ago." The script can dictate to the character that he should behave *as though he has a certain memory*, "We'll always have Paris," and we can even see that putative "memory" played out in a "flashback"—convention only. The "yesterday" of the flashback is Rick's past, as he purportedly recalls it, but Rick is only a figure being touted to us as having this past, touted in a flash; a figure identified as having recall, who goes hazy-eyed at it.

The figure does not possess the film when it is over, cannot speak of it to others, in fact has at that point no relation with others; while for viewers a film can be so affecting it is unloseable in its full array. Rick is only here, never did have Paris, cannot remember that he did. Flashbacks are *entirely for us*. In our ability to imagine that Rick remembers, lies the light.

[11] Plotted out, characters in their scripted action are perennially "businesslike," always attending to what must eventuate. Actors may be expressive, characters only show expression. Moving on with storywork

(that they don't know as such), single of purpose, characters cannot reflect but are empowered only to do what we would call reflection. In an aesthetic response one lets oneself be fully overtaken by a form but characters do not have a self to be overtaken, only a design, and so they are not swept away at all. Sometimes the character design is quite fabulous. Marion Crane, say, who cannot *not go* into that shower.[4]

[12] In some films the author or authoring team has worked to confound, scramble, or twist the storyline: scrambled *Citizen Kane* and twisted *Memento* (2000). Such trick films do not confuse the onscreen figures as they confuse us—Mr. Bernstein remembers, every day, a girl getting off the ferry decades before: we may find his tale confusing but he is "confused," not confused. For a figure every move, meant to be understood as happening diegetically, is always to the move ahead, which is to say, next in a vector dictated by the script. Even if a viewer finds constraints in situating an appreciated moment in narrational syntax—is this coming *before* what just happened or *after?!?*—it is still possible for her to react emotively to a moment in its fullness, aside from story implications. Watching, I can boldly set my *self* aside—or try—but no figured character has a self.

[13] We see the body and face of the performer just as we are seeing the body and face of his character now figured in a scene. Kane will die during the movie (and again tomorrow and tomorrow and tomorrow) but Welles will make *The Magnificent Ambersons* and much more. But never be distracted from recognizing that as Kane breathes he uses Welles's lungs.

[14] For outering what I am terming an aesthetic reaction, viewers may find limitations in language, surely in English where the word "beautiful" hardly specifies enough and there is general poverty regarding words for colors, shapes, smells, textures, and sizes, not to say musical timbres (on which conundrum, more to follow). Timbres: the Welles voice, for instance, a real challenge if not to replicate then to describe in English.[5] No words and no combination of words, inky on the page, really *give over* the qualities of that voice. The body is similarly describable only in circumlocutions. And movements. And poses. Also any sense of a form looming before the lens. Seized in our responsiveness all these require translation for prose, even for garble. In a way, then, the spectator who chooses to experience a film's art is finally mute. Circumlocution might help a little: when he sees Clarice Starling (Jodie Foster) nearing the bars of his cage, Hannibal Lecter (Anthony Hopkins) sharply inhales, and in doing this moves his lips in the way a connoisseur would in tasting a vintage wine. I can say all that, a

---

[4]In *A Voyage with Hitchcock* I try to establish the unbroken chain of narrative events that make her shower inevitable.
[5]See Pomerance, "Vox."

circumlocution, but to experience his doings, the swiftness of his action, the instantaneity of its beginning, the look in his eyes, all this—puts the responder beyond language. If Lecter's demonstration of aesthetic response to Clarice—again, something relatively rare onscreen—seems more than evident this is to no small extent because just as he senses, cross-cutting reveals her standing frozen in his sensory field.

Let us consider a deeper implication of projecting value onto a screen figure that only imitates expression, our so-imagined "reading of Lecter's mind as he sniffs Clarice." When we think we are hearing a character "uttering" privately when he does not utter audibly, we can be ventriloquizing. And for his non-acoustic reaction we must project by puppeteering, though not a puppeteering we agree to accept as such, else we would see through the confounding veil. The central point upon which our spectatorship turns is a lack of awareness on our part that we are not witnessing action but witnessing gesture transmogrified into "action" by our will.

In *Frame Analysis*, Erving Goffman introduces the tactic of the "say-for" (534 ff),

> a much neglected class of doings through which an individual acts out—typically in a mannered voice—someone not himself, someone who may or may not be present. He puts words and gestures in another's mouth. ... projecting an image of someone not oneself while preventing viewers from forgetting even for a moment that an alien animator is at work.

We might consider what can happen when there are no judgmental viewers (appraisers) viewing the (movie) viewer who is saying-for (the figure), when the moviegoer's act of viewing is ostensibly private and enacted in the dark. That would be movie spectatorship at its purest, with the audience "putting words and gestures in another's mouth," and twitches in another's musculature as well, since regardless of what we see screen figures do we have no access to their heart of darkness. Presumed is a kind of elemental expressive incompetence in the screen figure, forced and constrained by drama itself. The actor works with and against this constraint mightily, trying and trying to give an unmistakable clue.

We have a gestural code. A [forlorn] child [tentatively] approaches an [apparently kindly] woman and we sense, "a child eager to be adopted, and an adult eager to have her." One can even write a scene for just before this moment, with a dialogue confrontation:

> WOMAN: I would very much like to give you a home.
> CHILD: (*Silent.*)
> WOMAN: Please think about it for a few minutes, I'll wait outside.

(See the finale of *Child 44* [2015].) Here, doing a say-for, we can infer a child's assent, forgetting that in the scene the child does not make either assent or any other comment. Quite beyond that we know how to take film scenes contextually, consider the simple fact of our being able to do "fill-in" for figures, at all. That in our watching we behave, at least to ourselves, as though we have an interpersonal bond and know them well enough to hear them when they do not speak, while at the same time maintaining unconsciousness of that bond as a construct. A central feature of the "fill-in" is a calculated self-denial whereby we think *for* and speak *for* a character, but simultaneously deny that we are doing so. After all, projection only works well if one isn't doing it. Can it be that the innocent oblivion in which spectators circulate in letting a story go on without them, is exactly the source of the power to forget?

[15] Once upon a time (before September 1960), all one could have with movies was watching in itself, period. A film would play in a theater, perhaps for a week or two (no advance notification), and afterward would vanish into the ether. Gone not to return, or gone to return only after decades (no predictions), or gone to be digitally colored before returning (thence never to be seen in its original black and white), or .... forgotten. One saw; possibly one returned eagerly the next day and saw again; then again; then again, until one could return no more. Watching the familiar then, one could look forward to a scene, a confrontation, a dance move, a color—could fondle it and try to hold it fresh in storage. But soon a new film came to nudge the first away.[6] What did one do with one's favorite moments then?

Unable before videotape playback machines to seize frames or scenes by themselves, spectators could but grasp the unbroken whole with whatever self they could bring for watching. Grasp, seize quickly. In films after the early 1930s, there are between roughly three hundred and roughly four thousand shots, a vast array of images constituting a large number of moments. One cannot grasp, hold, store it all without the aid of what Teilhard de Chardin called an "artifact of human knowledge," such as a computer with a huge memory; but that is arranging for grasping, not grasping. Stories are likely to be forgotten or warped, and moral resolutions, so crucial as we follow forward, confounded or lost. That film stories can be made generic assists some, in at least placing a viewing experience within a set of like items, yet genre interferes with memory by looping, say, a character group in one story with others from elsewhere. The sheriff came out of the saloon and confronted ... Ernest Borgnine? Ben Johnson? Jack Palance? Gene Hackman? Clint Eastwood? Very few films are so iconic they can stand out even after much time has passed, and with even these—take *The Wizard of Oz* (1939)—only some fragments linger to reemerge a long time later. We know Toto escapes from the miserable Miss Gulch, but can we see the exact image, the background, when he jumped out of the basket? Long or

---

[6]On nudging, see Diane Ackerman, *Moon.*

medium-long shot? Miss Gulch turns her head at the same time? What shot comes immediately next?

[16] Narrational attention is analytical. From an extensive, even symphonic array freely given, some "melodic" line of development is selected out, organized for streamlining, then positioned against less relevant elements serving as ornamentation or background. Happenings require to be located in sequences: temporal, causal, anecdotal, ironic. Racing with the film's progression, the mind hunts out relevance speedily and cursorily, perpetually open to discovering errors of calculation and making room for necessary corrections. A value system is overlaid, boding payoff at the conclusion and holding out promises of payoff at various stopping points along the way, all this with a reward structured for apprehension and acceptance because it is organized according to economic principles presumably shared by members of the audience community: for example, that the villain should be disarmed, left empty. But when the film is done and gone, one recollects it non-analytically. What is called up by stunned memory and provoked feeling has no place in narrative line. Often all that is left from a film is a single actorial gesture—in *Funny Games* (2007), two boys in sparkling white knocking at a door.

[17] What audiences observe in the narrational mode is what they have already agreed to recognize: a kiss is just a kiss, a sigh is just a sigh, the fundamental things apply. But as any filmic event has an objective presence regardless of contextual gravities, viewers can misread, fumble, catch only part of it. The eye of the beholder is not altogether secure. Meanwhile there is something to be seen onscreen, photographed so that it will appear this way not that way (not the way the viewer chooses to imagine she sees it). Interpretation is possible only because of the possibility of objectivity.

[18] What ineffable power can lie in the aesthetic moment rising above narrational prose, especially, perhaps, when an image and a musical sound are married. In *Passion* (1982) Jean-Luc Godard gives a macro-long shot looking up into the sky at the trail of a passing jet some thirty or so thousand feet up, and while we see this he gives us to hear the majestically looming opening double-bass arpeggio passages, inconceivably deep in tone, of Maurice Ravel's Concerto for the Left Hand. This is both diegetic and non-diegetic music, since momentarily, as we experience its presence, we configure to ourselves a jet aircraft that rumbles with this mysterious sound; but at the same time we sense together the silence of the plane so high up and the rumbling foreboding of something elsewhere: *elsewhere,* not only *not here* or *not there in the sky* but in a place we cannot think of or see, an Elsewhere. In Scorsese's *Life Lessons* (1989), at the moment of his artistic trial, desperate as he prepares his canvases for a scheduled show for which he has produced no work as yet, the painter Lionel Dobie (Nick Nolte) sits

in his huge loft at night, caught in a kind of spiritual moonlight (his young muse is up in her bedroom, high over his head, with her light streaming out through a tiny square window), and as he waits, his spirits building, the space is filled with the sound of Puccini's "Nessun dorma" from *Turandot*. An optimistic, and also a chilling, moment. Acoustic-imagistic weddings of this nature are all over cinema, notably in the relation between the quality of an actor's voice and what the figure intones: Joan Greenwood, Roger Livesey, James Mason, Jeanne Moreau, Bette Midler, Jerry Lewis, and Austin Butler.

[19] As we hear the Puccini, we see Dobie's passionate movements and the paint globbed onto his big brushes. The plot of *Life Lessons* will account to us for where Lionel is when he hears *Nessun dorma* and even, to a degree, why he is feeling so desperate in many ways, but it will not help us touch, breathe through, deeply share the moment. Only giving up one's clutch on the plot, in this case diving into the music and the colored paint, will do that.

[20] Aesthetic reactions accreted film upon film could weigh upon, could pressure the consciousness we bring to our film viewing. What, say, of greenness, a saturation to which can be added, in some dizzying arrangement, multiple variant aspects: the greenness of the bedroom at the end of the universe in *2001: A Space Odyssey* (1968), then the greenness of the Parisian apartment in *The Dreamers* (2003) and the breath-catching greenness of the park in *Blow-Up* (1966), and the blazing greenness of the field we are shown at the conclusion of *Irréversible* (2002), and the mystical greenness of the nocturnal forest in *Uncle Boonmee, Who Can Recall His Past Lives* (2010), and the fresh and alarming greenness of the grass at the beginning of *Blue Velvet* (1986), and Truffaut's green cemetery in *La chambre verte* (1978), and the green gatekeeper in *The Wizard of Oz* (1939). Each green different and thorough, each unmistakable and unimpeachable, greens of proportion and greens of depth and mystery, with no two greens in this panoply of greens directly comparable aside from what it is they share that we name "greenness," whatever that can be (a Wittgensteinian issue), this thing or essence they all have, this experience that we name *green*. Is it eternal spring? Is it decay and decadence? Is it the abyss? Is it hope? No—these are only what green may stand for but, beyond what green can stand *for,* what is it in itself? When we float with any of these scenes, any green is every green.

To hunger after a vision alone and for its own sake, to hunger seriously and with conviction in one's own appetite, is tantamount to falling out of the ordinary world. Falling through manifold greens, we note a green coming unstuck from its narrative frame, the story's scaffold melting away (like the wicked witch). Breathless, one may be very near the deep cinematic-ness of cinema. Near enough to echo Jean-Louis Schefer's reflection:

Tout m'est fiction. Je fais mon étude d'objets de plaisir et mon plaisir d'objets réservés à l'étude.

To me, everything is fiction. I study objects of pleasure, and I find my pleasure in objects reserved for study. (Question 9–10)

Then, caught this way, should we happen to see a figure *not* marveling at the green ocean in which we see him bob, would we not properly wonder whether he can understand himself to be in cinema at all, in the way that, bobbing as we see him now, he is cinema for us.

for Victor Perkins

2

Breath

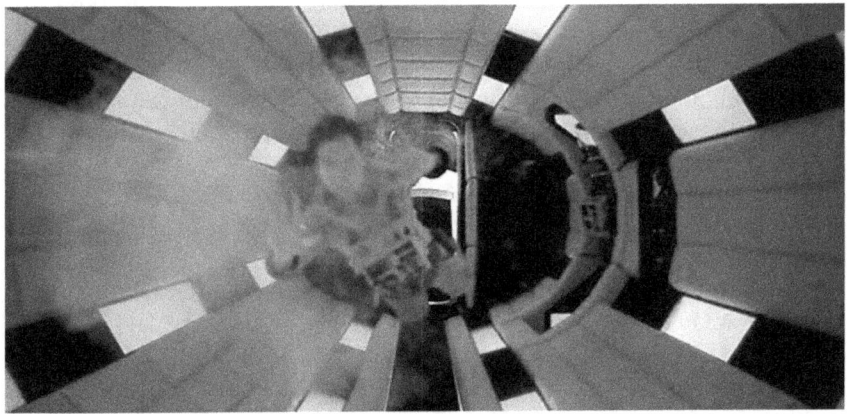

Keir Dullea as Dave blown into the airlock in 2001: A Space Odyssey *(Stanley Kubrick, MGM, 1968). Digital frame enlargement.*

A Cerebral Atmosphere

It has become conventional in films and television series depicting space voyages to include an EVA sequence. Extra-Vehicular Activity includes: airtight suiting, transition from one demarcated zone to another by way of an airlock, and a spatial flotation passage usually narrated as motivated for crucial repairs that cannot be effected from inside the ship and without which great disaster is assured. Out in space there wait exciting dangers. To heighten the drama, repair is made "difficult" or "life-threatening" in itself, and the astronauts who proceed "outside" risk mortality just for being there. The deep rhetoric relates entirely to capital, the expenditure of life energy for the preservation of a vastly expensive mechanical apparatus (that is built to promise reward and glory). In feudal times, the dramas of everyday life involved a rhetoric of the laboring body, either its endurance or its susceptibility to control by force natural or political. In the age of hunters and gatherers, everyday dramas involved the rhetoric of survival—how to move and reside in a territory, secure food there, avoid attack. It is interesting that in the earliest days of twentieth-century capitalism, space-travel narratives, of which there were then but few, did not involve the equivalent of extra-vehicular repair. The craft was a capsule, sealed and self-contained, and travelers emerged when the vehicle arrived at its destination—for an adorable, but also telling example, see Méliès' *A Trip to the Moon* (*Le voyage dans la lune*, 1902). Dangers perhaps haunted the launch, or would be found at the destination (creeping and crawling extra-terrestrially), but the voyage itself was (what we would today find) comparatively dull. And typically, no matter the type or lineage of narrative, onscreen figures manage to breathe.

Breathing in an airless space is impossible, of course. But the astronaut's magical suit is a space of its own, supplied and regulated. When oxygen runs out there, we have a handy dramatic tool.

There have been some elaborate variations on the EVA scenario. In *The Astronaut's Wife* (1995) the voyager is thrown into delicious wonder as he floats in a moment of exquisite repose with the Earth behind him, but much later in the film we learn that he suffered an attack out there, one that wasn't at the time detectable (to us, or to him); let us say he had an invisible—even a phantom—encounter. It is hard to forget how in *2001: A Space Odyssey* (1968) extra-vehicular work is done in tiny, gaily colored orb-pods, with which mortality plays a defining and horrific role. EVA sequences tend to lack ancillary sound, radioed voices being the only possibility in a vacuum, and in *2001* Stanley Kubrick does pioneer work making space not only endless but also silent as a tomb. Much of *Gravity* (2013) shows the extra-vehicular activity of two figures tethered to work in tandem, with challenges not gracefully accepted by both. Dramatically in sequences of this sort, the point is to engineer a figure into protective suiting, then pass him or her through the transitional chamber, then float him into space. An acoustic umbilicus is vitally in play, so that breathing and commentary are clearly heard (by us and some engineer live or computerized, on board). For the sound of the breathing, think Darth Vader. Or: at a critical instant the breathing is stunningly, unmistakably *not* heard. There are no whooshes to be heard from passing vehicles, nor shrieks and sudden silences on the sound system when a spacesuit is punctured, as happens in *Outland* (1981) when some remarkable (and extremely unpleasant) shots show penetration trouble of this kind. In *Away* (2020) the ship's sophisticated "airlock" requires some sixty (diegetic) minutes of slow change while the air is evacuated, and astronauts sit blimped in their bulky suits and chit chat there.[1]

The viewer's experience of EVA scenes is tempered by one critical factor, however: it is not possible for any earth-bound watcher of films to experience the rationed air or airlessness being depicted. We use rationality to project an everyday breathing experience into a spacecraft setting, so that if an astronaut socializes and goes about her technical business on a "long voyage" she can be taken to breathe as we sense ourselves doing normally (*Contact* [1997]). For us to make this projection is a cerebral task, not a pulmonary one. The airlessness of the Great Void we must find some novel way to imagine, to construct as an imaginary form, there being for us no experiential root. We jump off from what we can already claim to know—what we're told narratively about the conditions depicted. But airlessness is a pure projection for us, a mental blossoming, the figure's subjection to airlessness a pure speculation (as, in many ways, is the figure, too). There are other dramatic scenarios in which a similar, if wholly limited, kind of projection is called for: gas chamber sequences, suffocation sequences, drowning sequences, tear gas sequences, explosion sequences. In these, happenings that affect figures are apprehendable only in terms of our projections, their feeling being out of bounds to our conception: a figure's feeling is always out of bounds but in airless cases, exceptionally so. Using only knowledge and speculation, one burrows a way into a narrative that transcends movement and discourse in regular space. Somewhat similarly, in dining sequences we conceive the smell and taste of the food. In sexual and wartime sequences we read forward from the choreography of bodies.[2] Viewers neither expect to have, nor have, difficulty appreciating sequences like these.

Seconds

There is a thrilling moment in *2001* when HAL9000 has impertinently trapped Dave (Keir Dullea) outside the ship in his pod. "Open the pod bay door, HAL."—"I'm sorry, Dave. I'm afraid I can't do that." A malevolent dissembler of a computer, who speaks like a psychotherapist!

---

[1] Dramatic characters tend to have breathing troubles underwater, too—another airless zone of natural and cultural significance. See *20,000 Leagues Under the Sea* (1954) and *The Abyss* (1989) for powerful examples. I write of Luc Besson's *Le grand bleu* (*The Big Blue*, 1988) below, and in *Color It True*.
[2] For an interesting take on the viewer's "digestion" of screened erotic content, see *A Clockwork Orange* (1971).

There is only one way back for Dave, and that is for him to maneuver his pod so that its entry port is lined up with the still-open airlock door. He can use the pod's remaining power to blow the explosive bolts that are holding that port shut, and then in a horrendous gasp he will be sucked into the vacuum of the airlock. Once inside, he will have to access the airlock's exterior door mechanism by way of an emergency lever, and as soon as the door shuts air will be blasted into the chamber. This will all take an eternity of seconds. Will he be able to hold his breath that long? The airlock will initially be gravity free, so once he is introjected there, as he bounces around uncontrollably and tries to get orientation, his movements will be hard to control. There are but a few precious blips of possibility, Dave's survival through them amounting to flailing desperation without shape. Viewing this, it is easy enough to find oneself holding the breath along with Dave. Holding the breath although we are not at all in an airless gravity-free zone as we watch. We watch by a conjoined affiliation and disaffiliation, a recognition but also a denial of our own state of affairs. Invoking the paradigm of "holding the breath" is Kubrick's genius.

A cognizing denial, then, a denying cognition, quite as though having opened Pandora's jar in the darkness that touches the screen:

> Some scholars have concluded that the text has been tampered with so as to obliterate an original concept of the contents of [Pandora's] jar as good things, and to introduce the mention of the evils. Others have suggested that the jar contained some things that were good and some that were evil. The puzzling contradictions in the passage [in Hesiod] are explained if, in line with Hesiod's fundamental idea, we interpret the contents of the jar as both good and evil—not some good and some evil, but all a "gift" that was at the same time a "sorrow."
>
> (Brown, *Hermes* 58–9)

Continuity Gasps

A particular conundrum perpetually faces both filmmakers committed to realism and viewers watching their work. There is need to arrange figural presence and action, scenic design, and photographic focus in such a way that everything offered to be seen *can in fact be seen*; is well enough lit, usefully positioned, and attractive to the (roving) eye. But filmmakers also need to march their films along. (It is possible to time film shots, and to work out camera takes that can later be edited to the split second.) Marching along tends to mean that a scene is prepared by a build-up of sound, of tension, of possibility, and that the culminating scenic action drops quickly away to make room for the future. Pulsative moments occur swiftly and without obstruction, so that the viewer can be engaged in the action phrase as a whole. For example, our poor Dave could use half an hour of screen time to prepare the pod for the explosive blow, and he could do this in relative (irritating) silence, but this would obstruct our engagement; instead he triggers a system and we hear repetitive mechanical purring, then he bends down near the port (simulating the airline passenger's crash position) and pulls a switch whereupon we get an unanticipated, extraordinarily loud, blaring klaxon sound, setting him, and us, up for the flashing moment …

The explosion itself Kubrick shows from the most interior point in the airlock as Dave follows the burst of dissipating white smoke and smashes his way toward us. The entire airlock is already bathed in saturated red light—diegetically a warning that the airlock door is open to the vacuum but also a good cinematographic marker that makes for a sharp, alluring contrast between Dave in his pale suit and the rose-pink atmosphere heightened briefly by the white smoke. The shot is made in high contrast, so the white smoke and suit will dislocate from the pink ground. Kubrick's swift curtailment of the sequence, making for overall dramatic flow, works against his careful detailing of realistic actions. Whatever "vacuum" we can manage to bring into our sphere of experience is effected by way of the strange coloration, the desperate movement, and the extraordinary loud sound of air flooding in as Dave slowly relaxes against the now secure door.

Having to hold one's breath as one watches imports its own peculiar urgency for onscreen watchers. In *Beneath the 12-Mile Reef* (1953), crew members on board a boat in Greece gaze over the gunwales as they realize their sponge diver has been down too long. He is young, he is especially talented, but does he have special lungs? The same panic is simulated in regard to competitive divers in Luc Besson's *Le grand bleu* (*The Big Blue*, 1988), and also in submarine films and space epics where we are somehow on board a craft whose air supply is dwindling to zero as the story wends on. To hold one's breath while watching the screen is a summary form of participation, after all, a giving of the embodied self, but requires more generosity than viewers typically bring.

When one has trouble breathing—choking, withstanding an asthma attack—the experience is not like the experience of being engaged with a screen figure "having trouble breathing." Call this latter a haptic "impairment." We see and comprehend logically but we are not positioned by circumstance to feel, and the emotional/cognitive gap between seeing and feeling needs address else it might take over as a dominating dissonance, a prod to disconnection. Screen address can appeal to the eye and ear, and to rationality by way of the eye and ear, but not to the lungs. Bodily sounds, plaintive dialogue, collapsed postures are all rational gestures.

Interestingly, the filmmaker's need for perpetuation of continuity mirrors the (hypothetical) figure's need to continue with life. Dave's adventure in total is his own, as it were, but the explosive bolts and sustained breath, his tactics for speeding forward, analogize the editor's strategies for doing the same.

Ordeals

Aside from inclemencies of temperature and aroma, we tend to rely wholly on the autonomic system to regulate and maintain our breathing, so we don't think about inhaling. Not that taking breath is philosophically beneath notice, but that it is (mercifully) outside of intention. We presume screen figures breathe as we do, although the characters that are figured onscreen (emerging from text not flesh) breathe only through the punctuation.

Inherently, figures from scripted characters, text not flesh, do not breathe but the performers playing them, breathing through their work, give us to believe they do.

When a script calls for a character to be in desperate circumstances—Houdini (Tony Curtis) beneath the ice in the Detroit River (*Houdini* 1953)—we can find ourselves simulating his exertions, seizing and holding breath, for example, struggling to find release, without reflecting that we are watching a performance of extremity, not extremity itself, nor watching *in* extremity (unless through watching we fall into extremity) and also without the simplest self-reflective awareness that we are safe as we watch. If Curtis as performer was *in extremis* as he made these shots, we neither know nor care as we watch. Intense and equivocal, then, is our projection of self into film (from a place of safety[3]) by way of the figure's "tangible" qualities and ostensible experience. Vision makes for discomfort in the "liquid ventilation" scenes of James Cameron's *The Abyss* (1989) where, because their diving apparatus will sink deeper than man has ever gone before it will be necessary for the crew to inhale a pink liquid—salvation pink this time—oxygen being impossible down there. Breathing here has the appearance of drowning, and one is expected to "breathe" along with the figures. In the introductory passage, involving a white rat as experimental subject, dialogue is absolutely unrelenting, both explaining, soothing, and covering (for us) every instant of what could otherwise be intolerable to view.

If, generally, the personalities we see dancing onscreen move without breathing—if there are no especially discernable respiratory moments—our ongoing engagement with these humans-like-us is supported by our own blithe unconsciousness of breathing. If for us breathing "just happens," we

---

[3]Although on January 9, 1927, at 3215 Ste Catherine East in Montreal, the Laurier Palace Theater took fire and the audience, in a panic, were in a crush. Seventy-eight died, enough of them children that for long decades thereafter it was illegal in Québec Province for anyone under the age of sixteen to go to a movie theater under any conditions.

find nothing notable or untoward about breathing "just happening" for the people we watch, as long as they look as much like people as the figures in our mirrors do. Why should onscreen breathing in "normal situations" be especially significant if in daily life it is not significant for us, especially if the screen occurrences seem to be mocking up daily life? The acquiescence to the body that we share with characters is a stable pillar of our edifice of belief, in them and in the drama itself. If their undetectable breathing makes them seem like us, then the *contract of belief* is established, and once we have that we have the possibility of a wholesale transfer of logic. We can come to believe they think as we do, too.

But circumstances change when a script calls for a character to endure a respiratory torment. The figure now moves down a pathway hidden from our viewing selves. (Who in his right mind would swim under the ice in the Detroit River?) We tolerate and sustain engagement in our alienation so long as the torment leads to punctual responses we can imagine sharing, such as getting fresh air. When figures must hold breath for a very long time— there are such sequences in many films, including, for lengthy underwater swims, *The Wreck of the Mary Deare* (1959) and *The Day after Tomorrow* (2004)[4]—we will need to gasp for additional breath, a breath for which the figures cannot in fact gasp, while at the same time maintaining a blanket of non-awareness of our own gasping that can be stretched upon them in the form, perhaps, of an extrematized "nature"; if, forgetting our own gasp, we can convince ourselves we have large lungs, their lungs can be large, too. Breath-holding thus presents a borderline situation. There is only so far we can go watching a figure who has only so far she can go. One tends to hope she will survive, yet one also knows that in typical set-ups one or more secondary characters will fail just so that a principal character can succeed. What of other situations however?

In execution scenes and what we could call "termination scenes," a figure will almost always "officially" fail to survive an ordeal designed to attract viewers' sensibility; carefully choreographed shots show mechanism, personnel, and some facet of the action.[5] But the image of the condemned either at the cusp of death or in fact moribund presents the viewer with a dilemma, what Leon Festinger called a "cognitive dissonance," since any mounting feeling of anticipation, desperation, and panic at the upcoming activity, exorbitant but central to the viewing moment, must now somehow leap forward, and to a nullity. The viewer does not experience a death, and cannot experience a "death," but must somehow be guided away from

---

[4]The 2022 Netflix drama *Thai Cave Rescue* rationally poses a diving challenge that is so extraordinarily long that committed professionals are required to perform it, but the actual footage doesn't much challenge our everyday breathing.
[5]Following in method from textual strategies. See Dumas and Kafka.

"interminable" preparation ... and this guiding tends to lead to one or the other of two diegetic situations:

- [a] First, take executions: we can have an objective shot, showing a body motionless that resembles yet (appropriately) does not seem identical with the living body we had been watching with concern. Or else, the dead prisoner is treated as entirely to be taken for granted and the story shifts away from the place of execution to witness responses, official business, or indeed some other event somewhere else at a later time. The proclamation, "The execution will happen" is concluded with a tacit second proclamation, "The execution has happened," the latter sometimes overtly depicted by a notice of execution posted outside prison gates before a large crowd. Classically, a Hollywood convention for public execution moments was presenting a raucous crowd of witnesses, usually spiced with close-ups of individuals slathering with hunger, and to accompany all this with a musical drum roll. At the culmination, when the sound stops, the crowd falls abjectly and summarily silent (in a kind of mimicry of the expired condemned).
- [b] Or, in "terminations," the ordeal is played out extensively as a foreshadowing.[6] Andy Serkis's *Breathe* (2017) has Andrew Garfield spending much of the picture imprisoned in an iron lung as an early sufferer of polio. Garfield's Robin Cavendish falls ill in Kenya in 1958; the Salk polio vaccine was initiated in 1955, but in the United States. Robin's ultimate fatality is predicted long in advance, but our experience of watching him progress through the story in a cloud of hope is substantially colored by the pumping and hissing of his iron lung, which occurs with enervating regularity like the percussive beats in Gustav Holst's "Mars." He is forced to time his communications around the "gasps" of the machine, or to use facial musculature against the pressure of the bodily compromise he suffers. A rhythmic, mechanical-sounding breathing is produced, amplified on the sound track to signal a machine hard at work on behalf of the victim. A similar narrational trick is used for Darth Vader in *Star Wars* films, with an echo added in the sound mix to make the creature inhaling and exhaling seem far away inside his eye-catching black carapace. *Gravity* is a stark contrast, in a way. Ryan Stone and Matt Kowalski (Sandra Bullock, George Clooney) are both fully suited up and floating outside their space vehicle with the black pit of space rolling all around. Their situation has become

---

[6] For an especially elaborate and involving treatment, see *The Killing* (2011–14).

extreme, the oxygen metered, and they are having immense trouble working with their tethers. Then Matt comes to a point where if Ryan is to survive he must sever himself from her. In their ordeal now, they have completely functional aural communication suit-to-suit, the sound recording (by a 44-person sound team) so faithful it records every nuance of vocalization and breath. All of the struggle registering on their faces is contracted into the sound track, and the vision supports what we hear. The voices are much too clear, as long as they are both there, and at the instant Matt floats away into nowhere our attention is instantly directed to the surviving Ryan, whose air supply is now ensured.

Pulmonary Drama

Breathing becomes palpably—that is, optically—physical when the figure's body can be seen to twitch, endure spasm, go through physical exertion, or ostensibly weaken and decay; respiration trouble is played like a wound. In strangulations we see a victim's struggle subsiding first into tranquility and then into stillness: there is no better example than Armstrong's handling of Gromek (Paul Newman; Wolfgang Kieling) in *Torn Curtain* (1966), partly because the death throes of Gromek are handled by the performer (and filmmaker) through close shots of the victim's hands flicking spasmodically and finally collapsing into limpness as his head is kept inside a gas oven. In pillow suffocations the victim's body thrashes discernably and then calmly ceases to thrash; or else fails to thrash because, as we have seen very explicitly, the victim is unconscious under medication (*Saltburn* [2023]). These conventions of filmmaking are learned by viewers, but equally by actors playing such scenes. In all cases of breathing violently compromised, the "victim" tends to become especially active in some way as the process commences—perhaps only through eye movement—letting the activity (the movement) fade away through the duration: the initial hyperactivity renders the collapse more contrasting and thus easier to see as a dramatic change. This is "negative acting," as when a change of mind is called for and an actor's smile is slowly withdrawn on camera. "Change of state" is read through modulation of body movement onscreen, usually with an intensified (emphatic) initial set-up.

"Acoustic air troubles" are created by the performer using vocal techniques such as gargling, gurgling, choking, coughing, gasping, humming, and so on. Whether or not such soundings are realistic to the world at large is beside the point, as long as they work in tandem with the proper images to convey an action that can be read as "realistic." Such distinctive tonalities must be designed for easy discernment as "strained" or "fretting," distinguished from "normal" tonalities produced in the same show by the same figure. To give slight assistance to the viewer who might be prone to conflating a strangling or suffocation moment with a moment of stifled joyous excitement, the lighting will be altered, shadows may be created or deleted on scene (and in post-production), and a specific colder color cast can be given to the coloration. It is possible to use sound mixing in post-sync to dub in not only "death throes" but also extreme transformations of other kinds. Thus, in *The Exorcist* images (1973) of pretty young Regan (Linda Blair) twisting and gawking in her bed (as the Devil takes possession of her) we hear nonsense syllables in a voice entirely indeterminate between human and animal. Mercedes McCambridge, who manufactured the vocalization for that, told me that she created this "Devil" sound by putting a rotten apple in her mouth and half- (but only half-)swallowing it while the sound assistant raced to record her gagging from up close (Conversation). In the final drowning sequence of *Cape Fear* (1991), Robert De Niro produces his babble of revelation directly, as a form of abstract music. Extreme vocalizations must be out of key with the contextual surround and notably out of key with the figure's general utterances.

Breathing Effects: Lungs as Actors

I have written elsewhere of Katharine Hepburn's extraordinary *breathed speech* in a key scene of *Holiday* (1938; see *Virtuoso* ch. 18). Similar feats of extending a very long articulation through regulated expulsion of breath (see Matt Damon's work in *Good Will Hunting* [1997]) abound in moments of professional singing onscreen, especially the sort to be found in, or leading toward, opera. In the cantata of *The Man Who Knew Too Much* (1956) we have lengthy phrases sung by Barbara Howitt without apparent pauses for breath, a feat replicated by Julie Andrews in *Mary Poppins* (1964), as she performs "Supercalifragilisticexpialidocious"; and later by Joel Grey doing "Money, Money" in *Cabaret* (1972)—this last something of a nod to Ginger Rogers's pig-Latined "We're in the Money" from *Gold Diggers of 1933* (1933). The singer's forte is to deliver the melody and lyrics of a musical piece without offering evidence of the labor required to do so— quite as though the music merely and spontaneously flows out. Playing the lead in *Florence Foster Jenkins,* Meryl Streep notably *offers evidence* of her character's labor in singing moments. Ethel Merman gained a huge reputation in the 1940s and onward for belting out powerful stage-musical numbers with especially long phrasings, to live audiences in large auditoria *without using any amplification.* There is no better example than her performance in *Gypsy* of Jule Styne and Steven Sondheim's "Some People" commencing May 21, 1959. One speaks euphemistically of an articulate singer's "powerful lungs"—Barbra Streisand singing "People" in *Funny Girl* (1968)—but in fact the competent professional singer successfully elides reference to lungs in use. The impression of extraordinary vocal power given in musicals by performers who sing (on key) while simultaneously dancing furiously is often fostered by technical adjustments in cinema: a post-dub of the singing, while on set the dancer merely speaks out the words. But to see musical performance of this kind done live onstage is to see action unaffected by technical adjustments.

The soliloquy may call for another effect in cases where the performer chooses to deliver extended passages without taking a breath inside the text as, in 1964, I witnessed Richard Burton doing with the "O what a rogue and peasant slave am I" soliloquy from *Hamlet*. Pausing after a line of dialogue to let another character react is a cover for the performer, who can seize a breath during the pause; but one need not wait for others to react, a strategy visible in Leamas's shopping spree in *The Spy Who Came in from the Cold* (1965). He *could* breathe between phrases but Richard Burton colors in the despair of his character by not doing so, instead sustaining one breath through his pauses. In a comedic version, the "board room" sequence of *The Errand Boy* (1961), Jerry Lewis conducts and mimes facial gestures during a long jazz riff and while smoking (and waving) a lit cigar.

With its numberless sequences of heroes "footing it" over long distances without needing to catch their breath, action cinema has inured audiences to a peculiar stress that is ornamented gracefully onscreen, the commonplace accomplishment of strenuous activity without apparent breathing. This not only rationalizes the more general experience of seeing figures behave onscreen as though breathing isn't necessary but also makes screen figures' pulmonary prodigiousness seem an explicit part of the story structure. See Franka Potente's work in *Run Lola Run* (1998). One could say that the more exertion a figure puts in without gasping the more he or she seems precisely like a scripted character—only a character—and the less like the human model basing the rendition; but it also seems true that if we aren't watching breathing we won't care. The inverse is also true: the more intrusive and strenuous the gasping the more a laboring actor comes into view, as in *Ghost Protocol* (2011), where there are three significant scenes filled with aerial shots and close-ups made with a reversing camera so that Tom Cruise is seen racing into the screen, teeth clenched and, with express drama, pumping arms—pistons in a giant engine: he does not breathe, and he is always (only) Cruise. Once, late in the film, with one of his legs wounded, he moans.

With such athletes of silent film as Charlie Chaplin, the soundlessness of the bodies is woven into the basic structure, replaced here and there by indications offered through intertitles. In *Modern Times* (1936), a sound film, the musical Chaplin uses many variations of technique to provide pauses, evocative gestural "sounds," and melody, and in the famous scene where he is swallowed by a great machine the breathlessness adds to the effect of desperation coupled with playfulness.

Not only the mouth but the body as a whole enunciates little of itself in cinema. Racing figures do not tend to pant, bones do not crack during massage, cookies do not crunch on the tongue, and such acts as bathing, lovemaking, dressing and undressing, and rolling in the grass are comparatively silent as we watch. Here, in mute or half-mute action, the body speaks its truths through positioning vis-à-vis other bodies or objects, placement in a scene, and style of movement, but it does not sing. We do not hear the hanged man's neck snap, but we may hear the groaning of the rope untwisting. We see orgasm through its careful pantomime instead of hearing it, or, as with Olivia Vinall and Iain De Caestecker in *Roadkill* (2020), we hear it without seeing it. When Tarzan swings, the branches that he uses help him silently, but down below animals grunt and meowl. When a gunshot victim falls to the ground the body makes no noise. The screened body is continually pantomiming its situation, not its condition, except in situations where a specific acoustic expressiveness is used to add serious weight to a drama: the king's hand pounded down on the oaken table and the ensuing jangle of silverware, the metallic clank of the sword yanked out of its scabbard, the clink-clank of the faithful blacksmith's hammer coming down, the splash of a diver. One senses a kind of *pudeur* in the "polite" reduction of private sounds or ones that would intrude into the action. Often in hospital dramas, the beeping of bedside equipment covers the patient's silence, as it were speaking on behalf.

Instrumentals

A central cinematic problem with "air" scenes is that air is invisible (life hides from the eyes). Three solutions present themselves, varying as to cinematic effect:

[1] First, actors can mime a character's breathing trouble in the absence of any other signification: choking, coughing, repetitive sniffing, covering the mouth, looking around desperately, clutching at the throat. Viewers have to learn to recognize and appreciate such signals. The sinking vehicle trope, like the frozen ice cap, allows for a small air bubble into which the actor can make the character poke a face to grab a "last" breath. Performative miming informs

the audience doubly. There is air here, invisible though it is, and it is the delimitation, not the absence of this air that causes the problem that struggling tags. In such depictions, air is like money, something that contrives to show itself while generally remaining invisible. Its richness and quantity are visible through substitution of gesture for substance.

[2] A second possible address to the inherently unmanifest nature of air is filling the screen with the image of a notably visible, sometimes purportedly noxious substance diegetically "filling the air": a smoke (*World Trade Center* [2006]), a cloud of particles (*The Mummy* [1999]), heavy exhaust from a fast-moving train (*Sullivan's Travels* [1942]), a dense unidentified cloud (*The Incredible Shrinking Man* [1957]), a weather effect (a tornado in *The Wizard of Oz* [1939] and *Messiah* [2020]), a problematic rainfall (*The Rain* [2018] and *Memoirs of an Invisible Man* [1992]), a fire ablaze (as in the crashing plane of *Stairway to Heaven* [1946] or the conflagration in *Notre-Dame* [2022]). The substance or condition can be labeled "causative" in relation to figures' troubles, and can work extradiegetically, too, as a less costly substitute for difficult or expensive scenic detail. The troubling air is "tinctured." Interestingly, all objects also fill the air, that is, take up air space, but only some objects "in the air" are shown as dramatically significant there: whizzing bullets (*Saving Private Ryan* [1998]; *North by Northwest* [1959]), frogs cascading from heaven (*Magnolia* [1999]), plummeting parts of a fragmented aircraft (*Donnie Darko* [2001]), or slowly descending manned parachutes (*The Gypsy Moths* [1969], *Empire of the Sun* [1987]).

[3] Thirdly, air troubles can be indicated through instrumental reference. A dial very clearly labeled OXYGEN SUPPLY with discernable numbers or percentages and a pointer that can be shown to move from a high number to a low one. Or an AIR QUALITY gauge with a green zone and a red one. These matters are in the bailiwick of the set designer or prop master, and the designer will attend to the relation between the meter itself, as a purportedly realistic engineered object, and its contribution to the forms and colors in the shot array. Will this thing be shown in macro-close-up or only in medium- or long shot? Will it need to be touched by an onscreen figure? A special dramatic treat can be offered in films where agents from one culture are compelled to use a device from another culture for labeling which a different language (with different orthography) has been used. The American naval team boarding a Russian submarine (*The Hunt for Red October* [1990]); the earthling

military team taking over an alien space vehicle (*Independence Day* [1996]). Here, all the significations in the gauges are visible enough, but also indecipherable.

Indecipherable: a sign of untouchable and unimaginable. The question of whether there is or isn't air looms at the edge of the screen, charged yet also moot since in watching we lose our breath.

for Paul Levy

3

Suspension

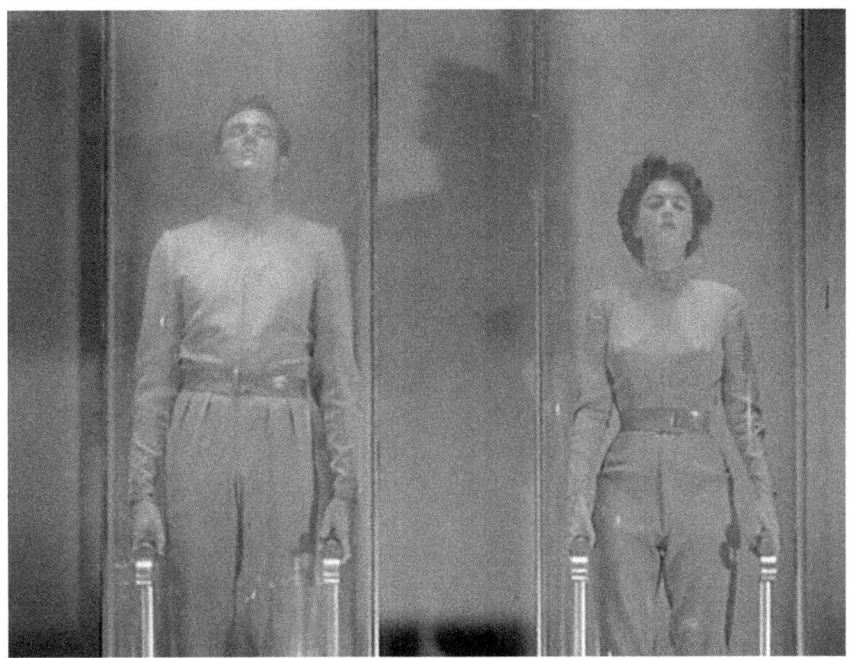

Rex Reason and Faith Domergue suspended in This Island Earth *(Joseph Newman, Universal International, 1955). Digital frame enlargement.*

The Grimms offered *Snow White* (*Schneewittchen*) in 1812, working it over until reaching a final version forty or so years onward. Scholars have suggested various still older origins of the material substance of the tale. A key to the story is the beautiful girl's poisoning at the hands of the witchy stepmother-queen, who offers her a contaminated apple, cutting it in half and consuming the safe part herself (a trope used in Agatha Christie murder stories and also replicated as standard action in films where a drugged drink is on offer—*The Lady Vanishes* [1938] has a nice, twisting case). The sweet princess succumbs, and seven dwarfs preserve her body funereally in a glass coffin (glass so that it will be technically possible for an imaginative audience, especially after the Disney remake of 1937, to "see inside"). Death, at any rate, as suspension "out of the air." The same trope was used by Shakespeare in *Romeo and Juliet* (1597), likely also based in some ways on tellings and writings from long before. Here, too, is the drugged condition of "artificial death" leading, tragically, to death itself. We see shards of this configuration in space travel films involving "suspended animation" (*This Island Earth* [1955] was an early one), with central characters available to the viewer in transparent receptacles either vertical or horizontal, where they linger not fully alive but not medically dead. They can be resuscitated at "will"—usually by a shipboard computer system, as in *Star Trek* (1966), *2001: A Space Odyssey* (1968), and *Alien* (1979). In *Snow White,* the rescusitative "will" belongs to a handsome, and notably kissable, prince.

To work dramatically, "suspended animation" must present as total stillness, muscular dysfunction, and retracted consciousness. In many cases, a bevy of instruments connected to the "sleeper" registers corporeal functions clearly (if arcanely) to the camera. The viewer is presented in this way with a visual conundrum, a body that looks precisely like what cinema normally gives as a corpse, a "dead" one, hooked up to instrumentation that shows it is very much alive (see *Minority Report* [2002]). Coma sequences in medical dramas work in the same way, with, frequently, the addition of loved ones seated at the bedside, holding the patient's flaccid hand and singing or reading to them to "keep the brain functions alive." We anticipate eyes popping open. In suspension scenes the camera will hang upon the transparent receptacle, casket, pod, or tube in which the body lingers, to show the same airy airlessness as in normal scenic depictions but with instrumentation indicating "breathing," which is to say, the presence of the breathable. Typically in suspended animations, actors do not let the chest rise and fall. By whatever high-tech magic, respiration as a bodily function is maintained whilst visible breathing is suspended:

> Then gave I her (so tutored by my art)
> A sleeping potion; which so took effect
> As I intended, for it wrought on her
> The form of death.
>
> (*Romeo and Juliet* V.3.243–6)

The production onscreen of a "form of death" by means of explicable technologies is hardly less than a recursive portrait of film and its endeavors in regard to the exigencies of the flesh (as André Bazin said). All of what the figures onscreen donate to the viewing eye is a "form of." All screen deaths (save the very tiny number of cases in which, for one tragic reason or another, an actor's death before the camera was actual) are "forms of death." All screen life is a "form of life." Friar Laurence is claiming, in effect, to have produced a little show, here invoking mortality as a mere dramatic trick that works to convince an audience blinded to reality.

Stories would have us see figures who are in "suspended animation" breathing by means of a technological assist built into the plot: a motorized, computer-controlled, or magical chamber designed for this purpose and this purpose only, regulated as our autonomic nervous system regulates our breath, and capable of producing respiratory action and response without the body exertions in and around the chest cavity. Of all this we are given a crystalline vision, as though through unpolluted air. And the sleeper rests and breathes unimpeded, as though caught in purity. Yet the absence of an explicit air mechanism in or attached to the chamber, the elegance of the design with all features incorporated away from sight, can oddly suggest airlessness. An airy existence in airlessness. Our clear vision of the sleeping body stands in for that body's maintenance through respiration (as with all screen bodies). The better we see—and invariably the camera gives a portrait shot so that we can peer into the face of the sleeper—the more reliable seems the sleeper's stability, even as, clearly for us, from the body there is no sign.

Aeolian

Of the Aeolian Islands, Aeolus made his home on Lipara, "a floating island of sheer cliff, within which the winds were confined" (Graves I. 160). He had several sons and daughters, some of whom, innocent of the prerogatives of Olympus, thought nothing of sleeping with each other. "Aeolus had confined the winds," Graves recounts, "because he feared that, unless kept under control, they might one day sweep both earth and sea away into the air. ... If a storm were needed he would plunge his spear into the cliff-side and the winds would stream out of the hole it had made, until he stopped it again" (160). We see in such films as *The Wizard of Oz* (1939), *Tempest* (1982), *Twister* (1996), *The Perfect Storm* (2000), *The Day After Tomorrow* (2004), *All Is Lost* (2013), and *Messiah* (2020) roiling air acting dramatically in storm mode, with some maelstrom working to center and concentrate the action. In relation to such films we can look at *Elephant* (2003), in which time passing is suggested by scudding clouds filmed with the camera cranked down so the shots will be sped up. Or at the strange *lento* cloud formation that signals the arrival of the mothership in *Close Encounters of the Third Kind* (1977). Staged as threatening, inclement weather is inherently dramatic and pushes protagonists to find safety. This strategic movement separates internal from external air, the former being protective and safe and the latter being perilous. In his film *The Birds* (1963), Hitchcock repeatedly treats avian massing as "weather" and sets up scenarios where people huddle indoors for safety and are under threat the moment they go outside (into the birds' domain); but the birds let themselves in!

Noxious smell is treated dramaturgically as a sort of indoor weather, a defamation and dirtying of the amicable air that nourishes and protects. Odor seems not only aesthetically offensive—characters indicate its presence by gesturing withdrawal and offense, a telltale twitching of the nose to suggest they have caught something problematic—but also dangerous to health. A bad smell, typically emanating from organic waste of some kind, is treated defensively as a possible invasion and infection. Alain Corbin writes that in the French social imagination

> sulfur, stinking emanations, and noxious vapors threatened [air's] elasticity and posed threats of asphyxia. ... Hippocrates and his disciples at Kos had already emphasized the influence of air and place on fetal development, the formation of temperaments, the birth of passions, the forms of language, and the spirit of nations—ideas which were to give rise to epidemiology in the latter years of the ancien régime.
>
> (13)

Breathing could thus become tempestuous. "Noxious air and miasmas circulated, drawn in by the staircases. They were discharged onto the terraces, flowed back in, and stagnated in the corners of rooms" (Corbin 52).

But Aeolus's winds can be stirring as well as stormy. Think of our invigoration as in *Titanic* (1997) we watch Jack and Rose perched at the prow of the great ship, arms spread, with the wind blowing their long hair. Or note, in *Zabriskie Point* (1970), the marvelous thrill and challenge of the American flag rippling in the breeze outside the windows of the executive's aerie. Superman's cape fluttering as he flies. By contrast the exquisite repose of the floodlit windless baseball diamond in *Field of Dreams* (1989).

Always in film, the air must be shown through substitution: an object somehow moves, a facial expression somehow registers, a visible weather formation disturbs the horizon, a stillness elevates the unseen to sublimity. But when weather becomes foul the cinema can reveal it only through rationalization: safety measures, tactics for revitalization and repair if not just defense. Corbin writes, "Abhorrence of smells produces its own form of social power":

> Foul-smelling rubbish appears to threaten the social order, whereas the reassuring victory of the hygienic and the fragrant promises to buttress its stability.
>
> (5)

Thus the image of the wealthy sophisticate, member of the ruling class: at her dressing table, whereupon a myriad perfumes are set in order (*La règle du jeu* [1939]; *Marie Antoinette* [2006]); or in the presence of a glowing and sumptuous banquet (*Portnoy's Complaint* [1972], *The Age of Innocence* [1993]; *Marie Antoinette*; *I Am Love* [2009]); catching premonition of digestive delight (*Babette's Feast* [1987]); or in a bath laid through with aromatic oils and floral unguents (*Spartacus* [1960], *Cleopatra* [1963]). Perfumes, delicacies, and fragrant oils all settle into the screen picture by way of attractive glass phials and decanters, gilded plates, and slender urns handed up by obedient slaves or servants themselves fully decorated in bold colors (but none that outshine the colored brilliance of the intoxicating perfumes, food, and bath). Fragrance is in the capacity of those who command, those who suffer no limit (for good or for evil). And with foulness the viewer is guided to thoughts of degradation, spoils, putrefaction, disease, and disintegration: the rancid alleyway filled with garbage, often outside the kitchen door of a restaurant or hotel, the decay of an animal corpse, the quieted battlefield in which a survivor tromping through knee-deep mud must avoid the already decaying bodies and half-bodies of the dead (*1917* [2019]), if he can avoid anything at all. Decay and rot are unmistaken signs of threat to order, just as orderly perfumes imply social elevation (and social elevation implies social control [*La femme Nikita* (1990)]). These contrasting objectivities, suppuration from discolored flesh on one side and elegant little cut-glass bottles of amber liquid on the other, signal two distinct poles of organization, implies Corbin. In film the appetizing and the repulsive are offered as causes, performative association offered as effect, whilst the smells themselves are perforce completely missing.[1]

It is the air that becomes social health (variable in cultural circumstance). It is the air that becomes vile sickness. And since we do not see the air, we must conceive it from the things it glides over and bathes; but also, past conception, accept that neither health nor sickness are essentially onscreen.

Attack

Airborne attackers, natural and military, make use of the air to aim themselves for brutality. As they race, these nefarious things—a swarm of bees in *Mr. Holmes* (2015); a swarm of aircraft in *Pearl Harbor* (2001)—become in themselves the center of attention, "starring" in the shots that show the movement as key, as though beyond movement there is nothing

---

[1] There was a brief period of exception in 1959 when Mike Todd Jr. "offered Smell-O-Vision" and Walter Reade Jr. "pioneered Aromarama" (see Gomery 230).

worth consideration. Air, then, is only graphic space in which attackers are situated, no differently than the fields in grounded attack sequences.

No trace of weaponry is more spectacular to the eye, more indicative of destructive force, than fire, the beast that eats oxygen. Antoine-Laurent de Lavoisier was the earliest to teach how without air, specifically the element he named "oxygen," there can be no fire; and onscreen fire is air (oxygen) hyperdramatically seen. When we see fireballs (*Star Wars* [1977]), flames shooting from windows (*Darkman* [1990]), crashing objects or automobiles bursting into flame (*The Dead Zone* [1983]), campfires (*Easy Rider* [1969]), towering or other infernos, we are seeing air. The pyrotechnic effect is thus a cinematic convention for making air tangible to a story. When the fire is hot enough to make a character back away (spectators watching the burning cropduster in *North by Northwest* [1959]) or alien enough to reduce a human being to a pile of white dust in three seconds (*The War of the Worlds* [1953]) or unrelenting enough to power the destruction of an empire (*Citizen Kane* [1941]), it becomes a notable cinematic reference to the breathing of characters around it. Their breathing becomes immediately tangential, affected, arrives at the border.

In November of 1961, Marvel Comics premièred the Fantastic Four, including among other notables Johnny Storm, "The Human Torch." This young man could self-convert into a flying fireball. In a single compound image one saw in screened print (and later onscreen) (a) the human body, (b) the ball of fire impregnated with that human spirit, (c) speeding movement, and (d) use of the air for sustenance and as a navigational medium. Flesh + fire + flight + air, unified (not to forget boyishness).

Both fire and Lavoisier's nutritious oxygen make reference to the curious duplicity of air, and fire onscreen reveals that duplicity by relationship. A patient scientist spends decades formulating and stating a theory, and in mere seconds, as though in an infernal blast, the papers containing his theory and its mathematics are turned to ash.[2] Fire in the nurturing hearth; fire raining down from heaven.

Writing of Lavoisier's early work in geological theory, Stephen Jay Gould harkens back to the unmistakable, irrefutable oxygen and the fire it can bring, when he writes, "A candle of light, nurtured by the oxygen of his greatest discovery, never burns out if we cherish the intellectual heritage of such unfractured filiation across the ages" (114). Gould's prose here is metaphorical, intended to bring Lavoisier's spirit and actual life somehow into connection with his own. But the invocation brings up the most stalwart, modest, and enchanting indicator of oxygen's nourishment of fire as well as one that is not only visible and beautiful to see but very frequently,

---

[2]*Forever Amber* (1947) has an especially interesting case of document incineration. And John Fowles's story "Poor Koko" is a chilling case.

in romantic and modern cases alike, made part of cinema: the candle. The candle, in the cathedral, in the maiden's tower, magnified in the torch in the stone stairway, diminished and multiplied upon the birthday cake, burning eerily and dreamily at the edge of the screen, never guttering, is always nothing less than an offering of the burning sight, the sight that burns, and the incandescence that flames up in the airless chamber of cinema.

for Leslie Fiedler

4

They Figure Life

James Stewart, Cary Grant, and Katharine Hepburn (with John Halliday and Ruth Hussey behind) in The Philadelphia Story *(George Cukor, MGM, 1940). Digital frame enlargement.*

Preamble

In an illuminating essay, "Being on the Screen," Vivian Sobchack explores a kind of self-multiplication undertaken and experienced by the actor. She takes as a central point of reference (through the good sense of her phenomenology) the actor's multiplied embodiment as known by that being. Owing much to Sobchack's analysis of "prepersonal," "personal," "impersonated," and "personified" bodies, here I take another route, considering (i) the person, (ii) the actor, (iii) the character (or role), and (iv) the screen figure as seen and experienced. The last two are of principal interest to me, since the actor's *person* is in almost all cases unknown to viewers (and even when known, known only as much as any human being's person can be known by familiars); and since the actor's status as *actor*—an occupation that surely stirs great interest—I explore more fully in *Moment of Action, Virtuoso,* and *The Film Cheat.* Leaving the *person* and the *actor* aside, then, let us tease apart the *character* from its embodied, activated form which I am calling the *figure*. We may think to meet characters at the edge of the screen but they are hiding in the script. The ones we meet and come to know are figures.

Conceived by a writer (or writers) and then specified in a treatment, working drafts, and finally a shooting script, the character "grows" into a sort of maturity, a pre-figuration leading finally to a casting process, at some point during which a character will be encountered by an actor. It is most basically through casting that the character becomes known to the viewer because the actor is now positioned to make it known. Somebody is chosen (or chooses herself; or is put forward) to play the role, to "bring the character to life." All the things the character seems ultimately to be, and will be taken by the audience to be, were dictated in writes and rewrites before staging work began, although it is true that actors sometimes improvise on set, exercising freedom of their own: "He wouldn't say it that way; he'd say it this way," this presuming a charming camaraderie the actor believes she is sharing with the character. The figure is offered up for an actual encounter, however, going by the character's name, indeed having no other name, and ruthlessly fleshing out the character's specifications. When casting agents work, they sometimes look for body or facial types (scanning head shots and actor resumés, sent in by agencies), in the case of central roles always attending to a performer's box-office draw and, when the situation calls for it, to a performer's power in the movie world (as potential producer, or "big name" with above-the-title credentials).

Regarding the formation of character at an early stage of production, here is Jay Presson Allen's script specification for the mother in *Marnie* (1964):

> BERNICE EDGAR is a haggard woman in her early forties, who has been prematurely aged by chronic pain, desperation and guilt. She retains only remote vestiges of good looks, but a hard-dying vanity and sense of survival are evident in her grooming, her pride in her figure, her ready disdain of the slackness of others of her class.
> She is common in an essentially Southern way… a way which implies ignorance and material deprivation rather than a purely physical, generic vulgarity. She is not particularly intelligent, but she is intuitive, and a hard life has quickened her natural defenses.

> BERNICE is a fanatic. She has had the strength of will to channel the greed and passion of her youth into dedication. MARNIE is her symbol of redemption, and the house is her altar.
> She is a compulsive housekeeper. An unwashed dish, an unmade bed, an untidy table top are <u>frightening</u> to her… they are the signal evidence of loss of control… she is always in danger of expulsion from the temple.
> With MARNIE she is always authoritative, demanding, inhibiting and inhibited. Only with the child, JESSIE, is she ever spontaneous and easy.
> She is essentially frightened and suspicious, but she is not, like MARNIE, a stranger to love.

This elegant text is not an elegant pictorial description painted in words by someone who viewed the film and transcribed from the screen. It comes from the screenwriter's head, inspired to whatever extent by her reading of Winston Graham's 1961 novel, and is given to the director as information that he can use, if he wishes, for casting. The part went to Louise Latham, a Texas actress whom Allen knew. Latham figures Bernice in a profoundly touching performance.

Sobchack considers that we "become apprenticed to" and "learn" a character by way of the actor's body. Perhaps the body itself is not enough, and our learning happens according to the figure the actor gives us, albeit that figure is always the actor's body at the moment we take it in; yet there can be no doubt that in our taking it in, the figure must be more than the actor's body. In that figural "body" are both presences and absences, both hints and riddles. As cinematic moments transpire, we find a very great deal more to a performative body than can be evident in any one frame onscreen: but the frame can work as an ID card. As to studying what goes on in fashioning the figure it is surely sensible to look to the actor's gifts and powers—poise, elocution, breathing, mobility, even memory—but when we see figures onscreen we do not look principally at the range of actors' abilities; that lapse of judgment is part of what makes screen performance and its reception interesting. Figures confront us, and we take them as the characters they were written to be back when the figure was pre-acknowledged as *character* + *work* and the work was entirely out of bounds. The figure can approach, befriend, then touch us. We generally have no problem at all associating a character with a very specific way of behaving, by way of the figure behaving that way; or with a very specific face and body (shown in the figure) and some characteristic group of movements; nor are we troubled remembering the character by way of this figured embodiment, remembering at least in fragment, long after the performance is done.

It is the figure we see, the figure we remember. It is the figure, not the character, who is in our field.

Because embodiments—figures—can linger with us so powerfully, they can fully occlude observation of the character as written; the character, from description of which the casting process proceeded. Thus, hearing of legion other actors who may have been considered for a role, who would have very differently figured the character now so very intimate with us, can be disarming. For the harridan mother in *The Manchurian Candidate* (1962), a role immortalized by Angela Lansbury, there had been serious consideration of Lucille Ball.

Because we have the power to carry him or her forward in our lives through memory and retrospective feeling, it cannot be true that the figure exists only in the work. The full screen image may not linger as persistently as a sole figure who inhabited it.

Bounds

We can meditate upon the filmic character in terms of one particular facet, namely, bounded existence: that the character "exists" in only a particular zone, under a particular gravitation. Every figure we encounter in a film has grown from a character reducible to the script. While like the script the characters of a picture are invisible to us (we are seeing only figures) they are there nevertheless, and the actors doing the work of bringing the script to the screen are very conscious of them. They have no personalities until the actor entangles with them; they exist as constructs. The screen array that catches our watching is filled with constructs, but we take those constructs as figures who can seem as real as any persons we have met. We are so accustomed to thinking of cinematic beings as vivacities, spiritualities, energies, beauties, darknesses, and luminosities that we neglect the carefully balanced framework from which they sprang as embodied figures. To think of the character at all, means stripping the figure and its performance away, de-casting, traveling back to the page—which is where actors spend a lot of their professional time. The actor reading the page; re-reading the page; fingering and teasing and dreaming from the page. And what, too, of the person who wrote the character on that page, the writer? Luigi Pirandello:

> The author has to merge with his character in order to make it live, to the point of feeling as it feels, desiring as it desires, so also to no lesser degree, if that can be accomplished, must the actor.
>
> But even when one finds a great actor who can strip himself completely of his own individuality and enter into that of the character that he is playing, a total, full incarnation is often hindered by unavoidable facts: for example, by the actor's own appearance.
>
> ("Illustratori, attori e traduttori" 1908)

Regarding the actor's appearance as a possible contribution to performance, hindrance or not, think of Jeff East (1974) and Eddie Hodges (1960) as Huckleberry Finn; or Matt Damon (1999) and John Malkovich (2002) as Tom Ripley; or Bette Davis (1939) and Cate Blanchett (1998) as Elizabeth I.

Or what of the characters themselves, quite aside from any willing performer who might conjure to desire what they are described as desiring? What of those characters on the page, before that magical time when figurations grew from them? After all, over the run of a stage play many different actors could create many different figures based on a single scripted character—Philip Anglim initiates Merrick in Bernard Pomerance's *The Elephant Man* and not long later David Bowie takes the character over; in the film (1980) we have John Hurt—and in filmmaking the idea of one and only one single actor breathing personality into a character is, excepting major stars, a myth: dozens of casting possibilities are considered for a role and when, twenty years later, a film is remade the process is repeated: Superman was George Reeves, then Christopher Reeve, later Tom Welling, Henry Cavill, Brandon Routh. We attach ourselves to the figure of our time, surely, or to the one who suits our taste. Whoever or whatever the character was has disappeared once the actor is fully at work.

Figurations have a very great power of indelibility, regardless of the characterizations they spring from. When in the mid-1970s he was making *Family Plot* from a script by Ernest Lehman, Hitchcock had cast a particular actor in the role (to make alive the character) of the nefarious Adamson. This actor had to be summarily replaced. William Devane was brought in, and all of Adamson's scenes hitherto finished were now reshot. It is virtually impossible as one watches this film to imagine any other Adamson than Devane. Devane not only animates this character; he *is* this character. Yet, not in truth.

If figurations can be indelible they can also be evanescent. It could be argued, I think, that there is a threshold to the number of different actors who can be cast and then recast in a single role, say, over series episodes or remakes; or a threshold to the singularity of appearance and manner that will be presented in actor changes. And once that threshold has been reached—there is hardly better evidence than the long spate of James Bond films from 1961 onward—the figurations themselves seem to melt away and the character as a manifestation of the writing comes forward as a confounding abstraction. Some producers will go to considerable trouble to *avoid* this kind of evanescence, as we see with Peter Jackson shooting his three *Lord of the Rings* films at one time, with the same cast; or with the contractual arrangements by which Daniel Radcliffe, Emma Watson, and Rupert Grint (and some others) were tied to the Harry Potter film series, all eight of them, from the start.

Invisible

The invisible character is hidden by her figure. If we think to see the actor—and in seeing, as Pirandello suggested, to collapse the drama—it is only that the figure the actor wears seems (however briefly) to have fallen away; yet such an eventuality is entirely fraught, since who is to know, and how would one know, that it is the actor and not a heretofore secreted part of the figure currently being seen? We casually call up "actor-character" relations, but as the character is invisible and inaccessible once the actor owns it, only the figure connects with us. With only the figure do we strain and bid to connect.[1] Notwithstanding the character and the figure go by the same name, are treated much the same by others, and speak the same—or pretty much the same—words, there is a subtle, crucial difference. When on camera or onstage an actor steps into the shadow, takes a breather in a scene while some other actor takes the light, a figure retires or pauses or holds breath and, attracted to the action, we turn our attention away. But even in these pauses, and quite precisely as stipulated, the character—still unseen—is still there.

Words

Not only are characters the words printed in the script, by agency of which details of movement and utterance are given, but they are conceived in a moving complexity by way of language and its reception. The director, the producer, the actor, probably the casting agent will read the words before they meet the flesh. Let us imagine that when a particular reader—say, an actor who lives in Mandeville Canyon—reads the script, a conception is spurred, an imagination, say, of a person shaped and tailored to specification—and somehow resembling what is seen in the mirror, and bearing a now-imagined voice for uttering what the script gives the character to say. "What kind of voice do I do for this character?" (Young, old, Yiddish, Turkish, Brooklyn, The Bronx, wise, innocent, smarmy, timid?) To read a script is already to invest one's embodiment. Since we are all living in an era when legion novels have been transposed to the screen, lay audiences are accustomed to thinking of novels in terms of screen adaptations (rather than the other way round) and are prone to casting the actors they "know" in the text as they read. Philip Marlowe: Humphrey

---

[1] I am grateful to Jason Jacobs for the wise suggestion that in the park-photography sequence of *Blow-Up* (1966) our protagonist (David Hemmings) strains athletically to reach forward in this way, with his camera. The lovers are a show, and he is trying to move through the figures in order to touch the actors (for him the persons) generating them.

Bogart, Robert Mitchum, Elliott Gould, ... Liam Neeson. Think, however, of nineteenth-century readers of Dickens and Austen, readers prior to 1890 who did not have motion pictures to use as models for their imaginations and a great number of whom did not have access, either, to the theater. (Nor was it usual for the theater to present staged renditions of novels with actors fleshing out character ciphers.[2]) What might such readers have construed in passing their eyes over this description of a personality in *Oliver Twist?*:

> In a frying-pan, which was on the fire, and which was secured to the mantelshelf by a string, some sausages were cooking; and standing over them, with a toasting-fork in his hand, was a very old shrivelled Jew, whose villainous-looking and repulsive face was obscured by a quantity of matted red hair. He was dressed in a greasy flannel gown, with his throat bare; and seemed to be dividing his attention between the frying-pan and a clothes-horse, over which a great number of silk handkerchiefs were hanging.
>
> (105)

If the Fagin imagined by such readers were a creature of which these hypothetical casters had, already, no preferential ideas, might they not have sprung him from acquaintances in their everyday lives? For us with our image warehouse, working backward from a film's offering of figures—Alec Guinness as Fagin [1948], Ron Moody as Fagin [1968], Ben Kingsley as Fagin [2005]—to try at grasping the written character that came first is taxing; the images dominate, therefore define; whereas when one reads (today, in the archives) a screen treatment or set of script drafts for something that was never filmed, one senses more accurately how much the flesh and blood of the character must germinate from words.

In the Character Pen

Think of the cinematic vision as a great pen. The figures moving there can never, never leave. Once they have been on the screen they can neither go back to the page nor find any other home. It is quite as though a high wall has been built around them; as though they have told one another to remain where they are, in this sanctified place, this strange *hortus conclusis*; have come into a full belief, a commitment to stance and eternal presence, and a profound despair in the impossibility of finding a door. What is a door,

---

[2] I saw once, long ago, a staged rendition of *A Christmas Carol*, in which Patrick Stewart played every single role in the script (December 19, 1991, Eugene O'Neill Theatre, New York).

indeed? Penned in by the screen; penned in by the figurations they present in screen moments.

They hover before us, these magical, elusive entities we persist in thinking of as beings. We step out for a coffee and return and still they are here, whispering, looking out—or looking at the world for me. I sleep, weeks upon weeks, and when I come back for another viewing, lo, they are here, still. Or, if it were 1958 and I were gazing at them on the big screen from the big darkness, and if I sat there all day long and watched five consecutive screenings, there they would be five times over, always behaving the same way, always mouthing the same platitudes. Perhaps I should have predicted they would be here again, but oddly I didn't, I just opened myself to vision in an uncatalogued innocence. And my own opening onto them—sitting and waiting with wide eyes—was in stark contrast to their own forced inability to be in the open, their own closed-in existence.

Seeing them at the edge of the screen I might wonder what crime these penitents must have been adjudged to commit, that they should be locked up this way, so that on my every visit, no matter the time that has passed since last I was here, they are certainly to be found, the same personnel dressed the same way, repeating those phrases partly like mantras and partly like sentences of death. Kafka gives us the crime being stitched into the body of the accused—"The machinery should go on working continuously for twelve hours. But if anything does go wrong it will only be some small matter that can be set right at once" (192)—but here, stitching need not happen, as the body of the accused will never be redeemed in any event, has already been stitched over to make the telling figuration. Rick and Louis and Ilsa and Victor and Strasser never actually leaving Casablanca, though a bullet might appear to fell one, an airplane appear to lift two more off; and the rain on the tarmac never lets up. Roger O. Thornhill never stops proposing to Eve Kendal. Psychic Kristen Stewart never finds her deceased psychic brother, but he is endlessly here and not here. And Marilyn Monroe never quite discovers that Tony Curtis isn't a girl. It goes on and on, the cycle of happening, caught inside these cells that fill the shelves of a library without a librarian, a catalogue without a cataloguer, a temple without an archaeologist.

Buñuel

Luis Buñuel of course repeats the dirge implicit in this theme by presenting vivacious figures trapped in a space they suddenly discover they cannot leave, or suddenly find they do not wish to leave, or suddenly forget how to leave, or somehow never think of leaving. Leaving ... is ... out of ... the question. Or his bedraggled bearded Simon is at the top of his plinth in the desert, always and always, arms outstretched, eyes gazing down to the whore in her sailor shirt, then up to heaven (*Simon of the Desert* [1965]). In *Viridiana* (1961) a little girl will endlessly skip a rope that also finds use as a noose. In *The Exterminating Angel* (1962) people will age and die, and change faces, and lose themselves in an elegantly furnished room that has no exit (until, with no warning, an exit appears). Again and again one returns to this room, from which one cannot even step across into the room adjacent. Consider that there are no systems of penalty maintaining the "order" of the shapeful incarceration, no threats, only the incapability of bringing oneself away, which must transfer to the spectator, of course, so that the delice of the film never melts off. Buñuel carving a metaphor for cinema itself.

Buñuel wrote that, in sum, he had to "await the final amnesia" (Sacks 33). Forgetting—forgetting it all—is a way out, but onscreen the people I meet never forget, never can forget, never think of forgetting as much as (without sincerity) they talk about it.

Kubrick

Recollect that stunning but also preposterous ending of *2001: A Space Odyssey* (1968) where, having found ourselves miraculously in a bedroom as quiet as a crypt, vast marble floors, a more than spacious bed, vast distances to the pale green walls, and seeing the man in the bed (one we knew earlier in life, knew and watched as with his youthful vivacity and cunning he navigated to the stars, but grown ancient now, more wrinkled than a curtain), and gazing at his Slab. From this cloister, resting with all this accoutrement, breathing with the shallowest of breaths, we are carried away without preparation—so we would think—to an orbit around the earth, the black starfield, the sapphire planet glowing, and near us enough that we can feel ourselves impregnated with it, an interplanetary embryo. Well, there. Is Kubrick's cinema not saying, "This room, this room, I have had enough of this room, get me out of here," so that the jump to the orbit makes some kind of spectatorial sense? Yet look again, because the embryo in its (translucent) sac has no propulsion, no memory of propulsion, no hope of propulsion; and is therefore fixed forever, sailing in a byzantine ellipsis at this horrifying distance from the earth, and for that matter possibly also tucked inside that room.

The cinematic transition, the cut or dissolve or fade that could seem to bring us from a bedroom to an orbit, would promise to be a way out, would dissolve a scene away and replace it with a renewal. But that is an illusion. The old man in the bed and the embryo floating are one and the same, the bedroom is not *at the end of the universe,* it *is* a kind of universe, one that contains orbits, and, though we do not see this, objects are orbiting already, perhaps orbiting the Earth, perhaps orbiting a finer star. We are never freed from orbit, just as film is never freed from orbiting through the projector and shining upon its audience.

Ariadne

In their world, the Diegesis, the figures are lost in place; redemptive Ariadne does not exist to offer a saving thread that could show the pathway forward and out, through time, through the twists, through the "story." In her stead we have only a set of flimsy conventional devices by which we can enter into belief in continuity. No thread, only the twisting labyrinth and the Minotaur, which is to say the hero: he or she whom we would meet in a brave encounter and spectacularly fail to become. We are caught in the twists and turns every time we see a film, every time we see *this* film, but because time is passing and has passed, every surface, every rock, every dark embankment shows itself with new form. See how in *Rebel Without a Cause* (1955) Jim Stark does not manage to escape the observatory's wild nightmare, that the old sage lecturing in there was a wondering boy once, like him, and is forever there as a sage who was once a boy, never understanding the stars he points to. In *An American in Paris* (1951) Leslie Caron, racing down the steps of Montmartre with Gene Kelly at the end, after evaporating from his ballet dream, will soon be alone again in Paris, ready for him to meet, and he will be alone in Paris again, will meet her, and they will dance together by the Seine, which flows and flows again, and he will dream her. In his dream he will awake into his dream. What can he possibly think he is looking for, this young American painter self-exiled to France, that it might materialize here in a young woman who dances effortlessly and in dancing with him frees his dance? Count the twists, the turns, the flips, the retreats in his moves from the beginning of the film to the end, but what can he possibly be turning and turning to find? "To find the way out: the poem" (Brown, *Body* 56).

Fate

To see the figures of a film at each moment until the end of time—the end of time when we are watching a film is the end of the film—is to witness their fate. This is who they are because this is where they are going, and this is who they will be always. Donnie Darko, forever sensing the foreboding, thinking perhaps, as he sees a cloud, that *that one* is *the* blackening cloud on the horizon. And then a foreboding that scratched our expectation is made real, far too real, as it confronts his sweet presence even while he sleeps. But soon we will find him on his bicycle again, scooting into the hills of the far northwest, sensing a dark foreboding. When any film reaches its apotheosis with a figure's death—Donnie Darko, Charles Foster Kane, J. B. Books, Mary Queen of Scots—there is no termination, as could seem; no closure; only a caesura in the action so that other figures can borrow the end of one life as a source of meaning in their own. Life becomes message. We can believe they will be led somewhere by this meaning, but even as we engage to remember them they will become callow again and in need of learning from a death.

Tolstoy

I pick up *War and Peace* and read of the adolescent blushes of Natasha Rostov, that she "lay on the sofa, covering her head with her hands, and did not stir" (587). I allow myself to be pricked by a series of grammatical needles, I react to verbal triggers. Were I illiterate, this girl would not exist for me other than as, perhaps, the growling sound of a voice (while someone told me the text—put Tolstoy's and the translator's words into his mouth). Further, because she consists of a package of words, she remains consistently an inky black presence on one white page after another. Always on the page, even as I turn. Always black on white. She can never get off that page, squeal, stretch, sympathize as she might be said to. Michael Jennings: "The 'power' of the textual road thus indeed 'commands the soul' of the linear reader" (in Benjamin, "Introduction" 9). When I see the novel made into a film, whether Natasha's form is visited by Audrey Hepburn (1956) or Lyudmila Saveleva (1966) or Morag Hood (1972) or Lily James (2016), no matter, she cannot step away from the projection (that is, the film strip, the image chain), and would appear to be in Moscow not now but in the nineteenth century, before 1812 when Napoléon invaded. She must needs be as embedded in the state of film, as film is embedded in the state of film (see Perkins); just as on the page she is embedded in the word "Natasha":

> "No, Sonya, I can't anymore," said Natasha. "I can't conceal it from you anymore. You know, we love each other!".
>
> (577)

The syntax tells me that she says things, she loves, she conceals, she stops concealing. But whatever she does (and holds herself back from doing) she persists, too, in being this aggregation of ciphers staring up at me from flatness. When I see the films, she is light.

The actor's work to figure out the character; the perdurance of the figure through a film, so that in every scene where she appears (where the body that represents her is seen) she is reasonably the same, just as she was in the previous and will be in the next: these are conventions of performance and scripting, patterns of make-up and costuming and posture and tone. Since the actor knows she has a body she knows Natasha Rostov is going to have a body, but also that Natasha Rostov is not going to have *her* body, only a body resembling her body. To have a life (a "life"), to be coherently herself, the figure must be usurped by the actor making her. Put the hair up in a pair of matching buns, one on each side of the head. Wear the clothing just a half-size too large—the costumer will be happy to adjust it. To set the figure aside is to see that Natasha Rostov is only a character in *War and Peace,* can exist only in *War and Peace,* a zone that includes all discursions about the Tolstoy novel, all renditions, all variations. And when I am outside of *War and Peace,* with surety this textualized being fails to show up. Her ghost can inhabit my memory and my dreams, but as to Natasha, who can no longer conceal from Sonya that she is in love, she is caught, and caught up in the work that pens her in.

Sequel

Say, some time after a film is released another one appears in which we find "the same figure" again, that is, a figure born from the same character, occupied this time in another, quite different adventure. The Sequel!!!!! The retrospective prequel. We have no trouble convincing ourselves that having survived *Dr. No* (1962) James Bond thrives again, ready to wrestle with Rosa Klebb in *From Russia with Love* (1963). He was rambling in one trap, and now he is at play in another, same 007, same wry smile, same naughty mind. But how can we recognize this same (reborn) James Bond while remembering the other (departed) one, except by invoking a resurrection at which we can thrill? Not resurrection from the dead, because cautiously the scripter prevented James from dying in *Dr. No,* but resurrection from worse: the prison of the other film; the narrative presence. What he has done, our James Bond, is merely to slink away from a raft on a turquoise sea and embed himself in Istanbul, the Basilica Cistern. But we take all the places in all the Bond films as corridors in a single mansion containing offices baroque and modern, scientific laboratories, lounges, closets for armaments. Time flies, he changes his face, but he never leaves the place. He must be as he was or he cannot be the same, and it is on the basis of offering viewers "the same" in a new context that the sequel film is marketed. The renovation of the context never extends further than the protagonist's eager hunt, never fills in over the shot horizon. He is always *here*. He must be here, because *this one here* is the item we have paid for.

Growing Old

Time helps us enjoy spectacles by aging us as we watch. Every time I come back to *Dr. No* I see a different Sean Connery, not, as discourse would have it, a "bug in amber" never eroding, although of course he is *like* a bug in amber, but instead someone I discern always with new eyes, older eyes, eyes that have seen more of life. I sense difference, modulation, development as I age through viewing film. (One recognizes what one knows how to recognize.[3]) And this sensing of difference in myself, which is Time itself, helps me enjoy a belief that the characters are free to age, too. As long as I am committed to my own growth they are not absolutely frozen in a repeating cycle; yet, not frozen, still they are frozen, frozen to the gears of the cycle. Because although time has passed for them as for me, they have retained innocence.

Thus, while I was aging the figure, locked in his pen, was not. Fifty or more years on, he is what he was in the age of innocence, and my sighting of him now endures a shift, like taking a bead on a fixed star. When *Dr. No* was released, Connery had just turned thirty-two. If I watch it fifty-eight (light-)years later, do I find, somewhere in the chain of configurations he gives us, a wise old man waiting to become himself, a senior hiding in make-up? No, he is what he was. Do I become the person I was watching him when he was thirty-two? Ah. Well, I am not trapped in film. If I take this Bond to be in his early thirties (Connery did the performance age-as), how, looking back across almost six decades, do I maintain for what is onscreen a susceptibility of the kind I had when I saw it for the first time? Because its ontology is photographic the screened film preserves life, even youth, just as Bazin claimed; it embalms; but on this side of the edge of the screen conditions are different. If actors long dead can continue now to create their screen personae, quite as vividly as ever, how do I read their figurations as both dead and alive?

Looking at movies, I take everything I see to be happening now, and time does not exist. But then, remembering that time really does exist, or surely that memory exists and thus some kind of passage exists, I wonder, what am

---

[3]A few weeks ago at this writing, I saw again as for more than fifty years I have seen, Billy Wilder's *Sunset Blvd.* (1950). But this time it was a story of how young people look through older people as though they are made of glass.

I doing when I am watching the screen and seeing what is not going to grow old as, watching the screen, I grow old?

Games

A marvelous synopsis of *Psycho* (1960) at its end suggests boldly something we are so incapable of accepting, that our Norman was never there.

Hamlet moans, "O, that this too too solid flesh would melt,/Thaw and resolve itself into a dew!" (I.ii.132–3). Solid, sullied. Dew, do. Since we deeply suspect that Hamlet has no flesh, that he is a Shakespearean construct, no matter the brilliance with which he is illuminated for us, we can feel relieved in knowing that he suspects he has no flesh, too. His revels will soon be ended. But then at tomorrow's matinee he will speak with his dead father again. Immortal, with flesh both solid and sullied. Norman Bates has this kind of flesh, too: solid and sullied, melting, thawing, resolving itself.

Plenty of modification in drama: horrors, quandaries, games. The murder revenged. The beautiful Ophelia and the beautiful Marion gone into the water. The search intensified. The fear resolved. Love discovered. And yet, enwebbing action aside, how can we get out of here?

Chatter

Or could it be argued that when the film has wound out and the viewers have left the viewing space, heading "into their lives," they lapse instead of remembering: lapse into chatting it over, lapse into a cup of coffee and thou. Could it be argued that into their talk, into their language the figures creep, *now converted to words* after successfully morphing out of the film by way of the mouth? When we chat him or write him the figure is part of language, especially in that we invoke his presence with a sounding meant to act magic. Word summoning thing. Our speaking of a figure bears similarity to, yet substantially differs from, the texting by which that character was born in the first place, set into his cage. The writer made a cage and by means of magical words that would invoke them put into it the sorts of people who could exist there. But no words, the scripter's *a priori* or the commentator's *post hoc*, are what we see.

Words are never ever the figures we see. To use words upon these creatures is to circumlocute, as we are forever doing, words being objects in a material sense, concrete, but not when they are summoning, not when they are spells. The screen figure is before us because he has been spelled in the writer's language. And we may think to keep him before us by spelling him again in our own. But he is still there in the cage, still advancing and retreating, saying lovely things, looking for all the world like a sculpture. We do not withdraw him from the movie by citing his name. Say what you will, Roger Thornhill is hanging from Mt. Rushmore. Say what you will. You can concoct his marriage for him, he will be with Eve, they will go off and have a life, but none of this is the case. He will pull her up into the high berth of the sleeper, and that's that. And pull her up. And pull her. "There you go, Mrs. Thornhill." While she does not go. And he will be coming down in the elevator on Madison Avenue, ready to snag his *Times*.

In or Out

When my eyes devour Bryan Singer's *Superman Returns* (2006), especially the exciting sequence where our hero saves a passenger-loaded jet aircraft that has lost its wings from crashing into Yankee Stadium (at the moment a pitcher is winding up!), I consider myself to be inside the film and accompanying its figurations. Inside the ongoingness. And more: I see this ongoingness from not only very close (the expression on poor Superman's face as he holds up the prow of the plane in vertical descent) but also multiple positions, flicking around like a veritable Tinker Bell. The sequence is a fine illustration of David Bordwell's "intensified continuity," with the camera bouncing through narrative space like a neurotic and forcing us to take up first one point of view and then another quite contradictory to it and then still another, all most swiftly, with no more than, at the very most, a second or second and a half in every position. I watch this ongoingness bouncing, swooping, approximating, relishing.

    I am afforded, and eagerly seize up, a sense of freedom, particularly as Superman and I fly together, and, for emphasis, as we are backed up by the "flying" aircraft. Until I see the ground approaching, a vision withheld until near the end of the long sequence, I do not have a perspective upon limit, but instead regard the air around as extending off in all directions of the compass, and upward toward the heavens, without cease or boundary. Off, off I could go, inspiring, expiring, rotating my wings. There is no spot in the universe I would feel it impossible to touch. The events of the moment that are capturing Superman's attention—and therefore mine—have to do with the safety or endangerment of this aircraft, the now unseated passengers, the beleaguered pilots, the technical parts of the thing, the smoke, the flames. These danger flags have the quality of bounding his activity, in the sense that, given fate and gravity, he has no alternative but to address things when, and instantly as, they manifest. He is, as one says, *caught up* with the action and bound to it. The sense of this cloistering is contradicted powerfully by the spatial scene, the boundless blue, the flowing air. And also by our confidence in his supreme powers, a confidence reliable and soothing, so that as he arrives on the scene we know instantly that all will be well and can relax watching his technique. Our confidence is the expansive blue itself.

Superman administers to us a technical lesson.

And oddly, although we know there are forces against which Superman must strive, principally the gravity which pulls a heavy thing down to earth, we do not feel subject to those forces, never actually fear for an instant that we, too, will fall. We are up in the air (without wings and without superpowers) but we will be fine and dandy up there, so fine we do not have to give consideration to how it is we can be so fine.

To be in this story, to be watching it *from the inside*, is to lose the perspective through which it can be seen as a story. This is one of the ways in which film is like dreams. Or like those arcades that fascinated Walter Benjamin: "Arcades are houses or passages having no outside—like the dream" (406). When we are dreaming, we do not have the perspective for regarding ourselves engaged in a dream. Unless, of course, we "awake" in our dream—"dream wake"—into yet another dream that we cannot see as a dream. Caught up in the action of *Superman Returns* I am free.

Or, this is how it feels at the edge of the screen.

I can also rest *outside* this and other films. I can be aware of many things beyond my engagement:

1—That this is a film, being shown through a system.
2—That I am in a space designed for watching (a public space, a private space), in which I can ease my concentration and relax my guard.
3—That my eye will easily be guided by light and form, by rhythm.
4—That I will find things intelligible, but also recognize myself finding things intelligible. In short, I will know throughout that I am dealing with a construction, and will even have suspicions about the method and history of its building. This aircraft, whatever its origins in any reality one might name, I recognize as part of the action setting, built to engage viewers here. The stadium is rented, no doubt, and filled with extras, not to say contracted actual baseball teams, just for fun. (Perhaps they filmed at a real baseball game; but what baseball game is real?)
5—That I can see what all this is, what anyone would say it is in a grounding reality that resides underneath the fiction.
6—That in this way I understand the airplane is part of the story, the stadium is part of the story, the passengers are part of the story, and Superman is part of the story. And then,
7—That I can see that as parts of the story all these are required to maintain their status indefinitely: as they are parts of the story now

they were always parts of the story and always will be. They are confined to the story.

When I am outside the engagement I can see the pen. And when I am inside, I am free.

A Perplexity

But a conversation between a sense of confinement and a sense of liberty is a theme of *The Phantom of Liberty* (1974). Can we know ourselves to be penned into a story (written in; but also caught up in) at the same time as being so present we feel no blockage, no limit? Can we be free and not free at once?

Take a scene many people remember for some reason. A dinner party with each diner seated at a polished table of expensive wood, upon a nice clean toilet. They "dine" together (note the power of the ironic quotation marks, which power is made entirely visual in the film) and then, one of them makes an excuse and darts away to a tiny chamber adjacent, where it is possible, in complete privacy, to eat a meal. The situation is just revolting enough—not really supremely revolting, but revolting in a slightly unnerving way—that our presence *inside* the tale is compromised breath by breath and we work to overcome that compromise. On the other side, the situation as seen from without—say, perhaps, just reading a summation of it here—is seductive enough to make us forget for an instant that these folk are only figurations who must stay forever inside this tale. Outside, we are drawn in. Inside, we are cast out.

Yet even this duplicity is part of the tale, part of the confinement, finally. Buñuel is trapping us in his joke.

Jokes

Every joke is a trap, in that while we participate in it we are committed to belief in whatever the jokester relates, a belief that, unsullied and undaunted, promises the explosive delight of the punchline. Indeed, the punchline becomes watered down to whatever degree we are not fully engaged in the telling. Whatever is in the joke, *as we are inside the joke appreciating it,* is in the joke forever. The priest, the minister, and the rabbi who walk into a bar … : always they are there, side by side; and told about once now ready to be told about tomorrow. And the rabbi always says, "You know, …."

Construction

All the constructions we make are traps when we are engaged with them on their own terms.

Hitchcock

My dream of the figure and the figure's dreams, or: the figure's dreams as part of my dream of the figure. In *Spellbound* (1945) John Ballantine (Gregory Peck), who has been having horrible recurring dreams, is with a benevolent psychiatrist-chum, Constance Peterson (Ingrid Bergman) as guest in the home of her teacher and mentor Dr. Brulov (Michael Chekhov). Under her caring warmth and Brulov's kind fascination he recounts one of his dreams. The dream-talk of the patient to the psychiatrist is heard through standard Freudian methodology, with roots that go all the way back to Genesis, in which a spieler (*spieler* = talker; = trickster; = speller-out of dream tricks) is decoded by a listener of suitable status (Joseph and the Pharaoh). To listen is to understand. To listen is to see.

Brulov finds Ballantine's dream fascinating, as does Constance—and as do we, at least thanks to set design by Salvador Dalí. The old man offers some intelligent pathways to decoding the structure as a masquerade of truth, with objects standing for other objects, and so on: a symbolic working. But we need not linger on this aspect of the moment, because there are no things that are not standing in for other things, dream things perhaps only most provocatively of all.

As to inside and outside, however, how far inside can we hope to go, how far outside can we retreat? While Ballantine is spieling, we are taken not only inside him, inside his organism to the dream center; but inside his dream, the dream which is presumably *waiting there* for him to reveal and us to discover. This dream is played out onscreen (with those alluring Dalí settings) as, stumbling, Ballantine narrates from off. We are given a glorious point of view. Spectacles unfold, meld, transform. For transformations alone Dalí is the ideal designer. In truth these are all paintings roughly two feet high and three feet long, accomplished in black, grays, and white (see Cogeval and Païni). What we are meant to presume, watching the film at this point, is that in watching the dream we are seeing precisely what Ballantine is seeing as he narrates. This sight, that from the outside one easily calls a dream, is, while it is in action before the consciousness, a reality. He watches transpire what we watch being depicted. There's a casino, for instance, with a mysterious dealer, and we see the space and the dealer as Ballantine does. But two things: first, Brulov and Constance are blindly *outside* this patient's dream and not sitting with us to watch it in the movie theater, yet at the same time they are *inside* it as they listen and transpose, and also inside the dream-vision called *Spellbound* where that dream plays out. And, of course, they do not know that they are in *Spellbound*. We may well be dreaming their labor at decoding him through professional formulae that turn Ballantine's words into their own picturings (which may or may not be like our visions), that morph his narrational words into dramas, allowing that *this* will mean *that*, or *that* will mean *the other*, just as for Ballantine, who sees what we see, or something close to what we see, pictures are being turned into words. To emphasize: Brulov and Constance cannot see what we see; they are sitting near Ballantine in a room. And of course while we are seeing the dream, and also believing in Constance and Brulov fitfully attending it, we presume that through their special training and knowledge *they do see,* at least in the sense of "getting the picture." In fact, if we accept them as psychoanalysts (the crux of the film), they see better than we do because they can interpret. They get the picture even though they cannot see. Or: we are seeing quite easily and plainly that while they listen they cannot see, *yet we believe that they see.*

If they saw nothing their interpretation would be only verbal improvisation, but if that, it wouldn't match our visual experience. Words <> images <> words <> images ….

Constance and Brulov hear what we hear, but we do not find ourselves limited to seeing what they, blinded but professional, see in translation of the hearing. Ballantine is narrating our images but for them only telling a fairytale. We operate watching this as though the dream-images mounted onscreen are illustrations of his narrative. But: there is no question that in the imagery as we see it there is much that Ballantine does *not* include in his narration, so the effect is very much that of a man looking at pictures who points out to another man, unable to see them, what the pictures contain, and in doing this mentions only some things. Brulov may be helping Constance decode, but we see a great deal more than they hear about, and therefore our decoding, amateur as it may be, will outshine theirs.

Containment is the subject of every aspect of this business, but principally the subject of the narration as analysis, since Ballantine never for one breath comments on the form of the images, the contrast, the quality of light, the shapes of things—all of which are patent to us—beyond using the very most rudimentary language. He names what is there, names the objects being manipulated: a real play-by-play, rambling but also powerfully selective.

We hear his play-by-play but we see the event itself ("itself": insofar as Hitchcock has had it arranged and shown), and we are thus constantly charged with the task of alternating between the man's vocal synopsis and the images he synopsizes. The simple solution is to trust Ballantine and understand the dream images precisely as he hands them over, converted into words—in short, select as he does. A careful look would show the folly of such simplicity. Brulov, in fact, magically "sees" more than Ballantine hands over, but through the arcane trick of paying very close attention to the words and their ambiguities (which must, of course, register for the speaking audience as ambiguities in the same way).

John Ballantine will always have, and recount, this same dream. (I myself have witnessed this many times.) Like cinema, it is a recurring dream.

One talks about recurring dreams but, not to mention that he makes clear this is a recurring dream, here for us is an apotheosis of recurrence, since the dream is in a film and the film unspools and is rewound again. Always the same dream, always the same diagnosis. The story illusion—always leading us as engaged viewers to neglect confinements regarding the tale—is that locked-up Ballantine is being freed by Brulov to escape the torment of the event that plagues him, that has caused his amnesia, which, brought to light, will finally evaporate. But beyond this illusion we must see that Ballantine who "loses his amnesia" never really loses his amnesia; that he will always be forgetting again, having this dream, being freed. We can be with him as we watch, and feel the liberation that he is being led to feel, but when we pull away from the film we have to admit it was a story, bounded like all stories, kept at a distance. Ballantine's recurrences will recurringly present to anyone as original.

And is this his dream, anyway? Or only what he says his dream is?

The Taste of the Trap

Superman holding up that aircraft:

We taste the charge of his muscular exertion (this creature with unlimited muscularity), the pain shooting up the forearms as his hands press against the nose of the fuselage, and we sense the pain shooting through his shoulders as he works against gravity, now and forever. And when he manages to make the thing come to a halt only feet above the pitcher's mound (not just the field, note, but the pitcher's mound) and, using all the strength in the universe, tilts the plane horizontal and lays it gently down like a baby being put into a crib, we feel the air come out of our lungs in synchrony with his giant sigh of relief (from his super-lungs). Since we breathe and breathe as long as we are alive to watch a film, we can sense our breath as being a permanent feature of this moment, the moment that doesn't die, and sense Superman's exhalation to be a permanent feature as well, part of his confinement in this narrated event that he endures with no consciousness of narration.

Voices

"Be careful, be very very careful," I warn Sam, "because playing that song again could have really shady consequences. You'll be bringing back the past. And maybe these two really quite decent people should be allowed to continue their lives toward whatever unknown future, without retreat." And he says to me, dear Sam, "Well, but y'see, this is such a nice song, and I love playin' it." So he plays the song, and you know what happens—just what I predicted. It's that old "They're playing our song" routine. And Sam is right, it's a very lovely song that goes immediately into the vault of untrammeled memory. It's even nicely recursive because it invokes memory and draws memory forward but also actually says, "You must remember this." Charming. Neat.

Now I can back away from Sam's old white upright, a nice treasure, and find a table where somebody will bring me a little glass of champagne that I can nurse while I watch Ugarte get nailed and so on.

So good to be there. Hustle-bustle all around. The door to the back room opening and closing.

But in being there I am filled with the desire to speak to these figures, and to encourage them with lifted brows and smiling lips to speak back to me. Let our words touch each other. Let us become friends. Because, when all is said and done, it is friendship, isn't it, between watchers and the figures from whom they can't take their eyes. Friends immediately recognized and acknowledged (even the very evil ones), admired or challenged in familiar ways. Familiar above all: in the family.

Perhaps my thoughts are stitched into these story moments, so that every time I come back to this café and find my same chums taking the same postures—Sam at the keys, "You must remember this … "; Ugarte sweating and in flight—every time, I have the same thoughts, thoughts uttered in verses repeated so often they have become incantations. Sam, the friendly piano player, who is so loyal to Rick and who regrets his friend's break-up with Ilsa: so unfortunate, so controlled by caprice of fortune. Always Sam the friendly piano player, never Sam who up his sleeve has tucked away a secret hope that he can get those letters of transit, the ones stowed in his piano, into his own clutches and fly off with …. With somebody. Never that Sam. And never a Rick who actually does turn Victor over to Strasser instead of just shamming. Nor ever a Louis Renault to say, "Don't round up the usual suspects."

The more I realize the abject internality of all these folk, their situational quagmire, the more it becomes evident that conversation is pointless, will never move us forward. Always the same this, forever and ever; it becomes the lyric of a hymn and my every thought of it, phrase by phrase, a worship in the hidden temple. They will not really talk to me, only say their lines, and they cannot change their lines, either, not now, so that their lines have taken on the character of a signpost. Figures, figured in figurations. Great ironies will be produced—even laughter—if I outer a line of my own invention, something fantastic and out of the blue, "How about a new bowtie?," and Rick comes back with, "I stick my neck out for nobody." In the late 1960s, at the Waverly in Greenwich Village, members of the audience routinely spoke aloud to the characters onscreen, offering comments preposterous and ironic and bringing laughter all around. "Don't go into that room!"

Lord of the Ring

A supreme power of film—Stanley Cavell knew it passionately—lies in its making available a domain where anything can happen. But I add: in which, too, what happens must happen. At least, according to the logic whereby we understand our world.

The uncanny closing moment of George Cukor's *The Philadelphia Story* (1940), in which Tracy Lord (Katharine Hepburn), on the cusp after an inebriated night's ramblings and chatterings, and now having made it plain she has no intention of entering marriage with the supremely dull George Kittredge (John Howard), stands behind a door that leads to the make-do "altar" in the living space of her mansion, accompanied by her anxious mother (Mary Nash), her new chum Macauley Connor (James Stewart), and her former husband, now puckish instigator C. K. Dexter Haven (Cary Grant). Just behind are her father Seth Lord (John Halliday) and Liz Imbrie (Ruth Hussey), Macauley's photographer pal. We can hear the rustling outside, and the organist bravely accompanying the as-yet empty marital space. The guests have no idea what's happening but Tracy does know, sociable, extremely conscious sort that she is. Affable Mac has offered her a proposal, which she refused with a sweetness unknown on the film screen before or after. And now she must confess to the family friends. So she pries the door open and peeks out. "Stop that music!":

> I'm.... terribly sorry to have kept you waiting, but.... there's been a slight hitch in the proceedings." *We are looking at her screen center from within the seated crowd. Now we cut to her side, as she faces out the door left with Dexter directly in her rear.* I made a terrible fool of myself which... isn't unusual. *Dexter smiles patiently, sympathetic, agreeing.* And... and my fiancé,... uh, my fiancé that was, that is, he... thinks we'd better call it a day. And I quite agree with him.
> UNCLE WILLIE (seated outside next to Tracy's young sister Dinah): Peace! It's wonderful.
> TRACY: Uhh... bec—uhhhh... Dexter, Dexter, what next?
> DEXTER (dictating): Two years ago I did you out of a wedding in this house by eloping to Maryland.
> TRACY (leaning out, broadcasting): Two years ago—

The camera pans right to find Dexter sweetly confronting Mrs. Lord and her husband Seth. <u>He pulls a ring from the lady's finger.</u>
DEXTER: My dear—Just a loan. *To Mac, standing in the rear with Liz Imbrie.* Here, put this ring in your vest pocket.
MAC (showing the inside of his jacket): Don't have a vest.
TRACY (continuing):—oh, you were invited to a wedding in this house—.
DEXTER: Hold it in your hand.
TRACY (continuing):—and then I did you out of it,... um ...
DEXTER (back with Tracy, dictating again): Which was very bad manners.
TRACY (to the crowd):... which was *very* bad manners.
DEXTER: But I hope to make it up to you by going through with it now as originally planned.
TRACY: But I hope to make it up to you b— *She slowly turns, agape, looking hopefully at Dexter who returns her gaze. She is about to touch his face, to lean forward, but she turns back to the crowd letting him take her hand.*—by going..... *beautifully* through with it now, as originally and (*glowing*) most *beautifully* planned.
DEXTER: So if you'll just keep your seats for a minute.
TRACY: So if you'll just keep your seats a minute ...
DEXTER: That's all.
TRACY: Emm... That's all.

Dexter is proposing remarriage, of course, thereby, and, not with intent of his own, dubbing this picture one of Cavell's "comedies of remarriage." It is a wonderful turn of the tide, swift, with the sun glowing, and a sense of peace fluttering down upon the multitude as though from the beating of angels' wings.
But:
That very tiny breath in which, having thought this through and come to a sureness that this must happen, Dexter realizes the need for a ring. A ring, a ring, a kingdom for a ring. "We laugh," writes Cavell,

> both at the victory of light over darkness and also at the truth, hard to locate, of Dexter's power, apparently some mysterious power to control events. The magic invoked by the genre seems localized in this figure.
> (137)

A ring that will seal the truth and the troth (= allegiance; trust; faith; creed). And a ring that will bring all the proceedings full circle in an elegant, formal, perfect way. What can he do, Dex, he has been visiting the Lord's estate in order to smirk at, if not somehow besmirch haughty Tracy's link to Kittredge and without any hint of a thought that he might tumble for her again. And then, right behind him (his perfect support) is the already well-married lady, the one who gave us Tracy, with the ring on her finger. The ring Tracy's father gave her so long ago. So: "Just a loan." Margaret Lord astonished, sure, but things are happening much too quickly for the astonishment to travel anywhere. And the propulsion forward is as grammatical as can be, paced by the phrases of the little speech that must come one after the other in an elegant, formal way (as on a printed invitation).

Now Tracy is going to be married with her mother's wedding ring.

And not only Tracy's marriage to Dexter—once a failure and now to be a success (we can hope)—is a redoing; Margaret's wedding to Seth is being redone, too. The ring which is the ring of truth, the ring that captures, and, most paradoxically if also profoundly, the ring that binds. Within this ring is the gathering of lovers' hopes. But within this ring is the film, itself ringed by circumstance and love. It is an astonishing fact so terribly easy not to find astonishing, that every time one watches this masterpiece one finds the necessary ring on Margaret Lord's finger. It is borrowed again and still again. Or, she makes a loan of it without even thinking, so obvious is it that what is about to happen is the only possibility for happening.

The only possibility, and therefore the one that we discover and rediscover, always amazed, always soothed and refreshed, and always forgetting that once upon a time, in the valiant days of yesteryear, we were soothed and refreshed just this way, and just, with that crowd waiting, here.

for Stanley Cavell

5

Here and There

Gustave Caillebotte, "Boulevard des Italiens" (1880). Public domain.

1

Looking at a fine canvas, Gustave Caillebotte's "Boulevard des Italiens" (1880), I was suddenly carried back to, of all possibilities, W. G. Sebald, who reflected once, "The Alfa glided slowly down the street and vanished around a bend which seemed to me to lead to another world" (103). So, a canvas that is another world, or touches one. And within it, a vanishing.

A pallid blue sky without the enthusiasm of spring. Long buildings glowing yellow in the cuddling autumnal light. Extensive rows of trees on both sides of the street, receding and receding, finally in the distance graying until they are ghosts of trees. A sad enough time of the year, and this is the City of Light more than a hundred and forty years ago at this writing, a place and epoch also gone into the far distance, and faded into the gray phantasm of printed textbooks. In the foreground, at right, an almost glistening coal-black wrought-iron balustrade at the side of a balcony, with mauve shadows filtering through it. The nearest trees are silvery brown and distinct, but as the eye moves off they are finally only far-off space.

People walk the sidewalk down there, indistinguishable from this height, and there is a yellow car. A busy street, lots of action indiscernible.

Our view is to the southwest, from a *mobilière* on the north side of the Boulevard between the Rue Taitbout and the Rue des Italiens, and not more than two short blocks away from No. 8 of the Boulevard, where stood the Théâtre Robert-Houdin, owned after 1888 by the hyperinventive Georges Méliès. I suppose myself to be watching this street as Caillebotte did, to be "stepping in his shoes," and in the actual act my "here" is a spot upon that balcony just at the edge, looking at, then past, the wrought iron. I do not move.

I ... do ... not ... move.

How might this painting have been seen in 1880, before cinematography? What sense of decorum might viewers have summoned forth? It is not fixed in an album or in hand, like (after 1839) a photograph, it is on a wall; the wall is in a chamber; the chamber is in a building, private or public. One leans close, one backs up. Is this but one canvas among many to be regarded this afternoon, and will we think of how long we are standing here, unwilling to squander time for seeing others? Do we require to know the history of painting in the West, so as to "properly" slot this canvas? Are we gazing at a reality, or at a picture of a reality, or simply at a picture? Street, street picture, or picture?

Consider what is stationary here. If I "take a walk down the pavement," my eyes remain in my stationary head and my head remains on my stationary body, so that the "walk" conjures my imagination of motion, entirely fabular. As I "move" through the Parisian space Caillebotte depicts—entertain the illusion of such movement because my eye is really curling across a stationary surface that implies but doesn't offer space—the vision of the city is vague and dissolved, ongoingly so as I step forward. But I am here staring at a painting, and if this surface refers to Paris itself, the far-off vagueness is only because I am stationary staring: motion in reality would preserve a continuing vagueness at the continually receding horizon and the horizon would never stop receding until the end of time. But here for me the forms of things dissolve into Caillebotte's horizon, the horizon into the forms of things, the city into the sky. Might I say I *lose sight* of things? As Jonathan Crary suggests of the nineteenth-century stereoscope, "tangibility (or relief) is constructed solely through an organization of *optical* cues" (59; italic original).

Also, think of time. In the same way these autumnal forms vanish and blend here, fade into impercepibility, some rich summer has now faded into history, and the painting is a record of and statement about that loss. Things are crisp and knowable to my eye, but when I "travel" away I approach a place where knowledge becomes dream and there is no summer.

This is a coherent and magnificent view, a statement for the eye to receive, but it is the only statement exactly of its kind. If, for some obscure reason, we dislike our present position, the balustrade, say, or the quantity of sky we can snatch from here, the picture must be abandoned, at least by us, because this presence and limitation is effectively what the picture is and the picture can promise to be only itself. One sees this canvas by agreeing to the viewing position—just upon, or magically floating in the air beside, this balcony. Perhaps we even meditate upon balconies—Caillebotte and Manet loved them: those architectural fillips that lure us outside the home while we are still at home. This balustrade, curved, made of iron, is like a chain of sorts, and around 1880, incidentally, wrought iron was coming into fashion (the Tour d'Eiffel, that opened March 31, 1889, with metalwork commencing July 1, 1887, was built as a showpiece for it). (See Billington.)

2

Moving the eye down Caillebotte's Boulevard is imagining moving because the eye sees only a fixed surface. With a painting, movement is imagination whereas with a film it is illusion. When I watch a film, I am, it seems, moved instead of moving myself; I can relax into my seat as a passenger. The imaginative movement of the penetrating eye shares something with the written text that for Jean Louis Schefer is "organized primarily by imaginary durations (that is, by an invention of time) from which the signification of objects consequently arises" (*Body* 66). We invent "the duration of a world that we call imaginary because it can act as the model and the sounding board for every universe still possible" (66). The painting can even be said to be composed of pretexts for imaginary duration. However I might fabulate "points," "nearness," "distance," … it is all language, and here am I standing in front of the canvas, and the canvas is there. The idea that when we see a space depicted we might either move through it or else conceive of moving through it, is a cinematic idea—note how the Disney technicians built for *Pinocchio* (1940) a vertical rig that would permit the camera and camera focus to seem to move into or out of the painted animation. It was late in the eighteenth century that paintings were hung multiply on walls to give a "salon" or gallery effect, an illusion of movement for the viewer: landscapes typically high up, portraits at the viewer's face height, still lifes in between.[1] There is something *Heimlich* about the painted view, too. John Loughman and John Michael Montias report Ernst Gombrich's comment about the "domestication" of easel painting as canvases (particularly of the outside world) came into the house as decorations (132). Caillebotte's construction of the Boulevard rouses emotions: exhilaration for the immediacy of presence, sadness for a distance that beckons but will not be visited. Indeed, the distance suggests a particular kind of horizon, that I am not empowered to cross. That foreground tree, the one with the most color, its browning leaves, I watch as day by day they decline to shrivel and brown further, refuse to drop; and see how they are not snowed upon. Not only Caillebotte but also Monet and Pissarro liked to paint snow, gave it presence. Caillebotte gave it weight as well, but snow is not here and will never fall.

3

Film versions of Parisian streets—Quai de la Tournelle in *Sous le ciel de Paris* (1951), Les Champs Elysées in *À bout de souffle* (1960)—do not seduce the viewer into an indeterminacy. They pose a territory we possess for a moment before leaping to another spot, and another, spot to spot, that we may see a world more closely, or through comparison. Before what it strives to possess is eclipsed, the eye must move. The depths of a scene one explores by way of vignettes that do not necessarily arrange themselves rationally but which penetrate, invade, probe almost medically into the body of the city. Always, in some way, haunted progression. The tranquility of our stasis before the Caillebotte, the perceiver's meditative stasis in perception, is replaced at the edge of the screen by an energy of transposition. Views are opened to a new kind of mentality, no longer extensive, deliberate, and stable but spontaneous and swift, unable to predict. One seizes a view rapidly, practiced and inured already to the spontaneity of sudden appearance and its impending dissipation. In a pulsing rhythm one accommodates oneself to making accommodation. The idea of changing the point of view[2] is generic to the experience. Point of view goes beyond being a selection and becomes a carnival.

And we learn how not to be dissatisfied by shifts (in short, to cast away the viewer before the painting). The rhetoric of presentation tacitly

---

[1] A typical arrangement is illustrated in Stadler.
[2] Even, as in *Wavelength* (1967), by means of slow zoom only.

pronounces that no vision, however distinct, can be full enough to give all of what is now posed as an unboundably complex arrangement. By simulating the composition of some classical paintings with costumed living models and immediately showing the way a camera crew moves around them, Godard openly plays with cinematic as compared with painterly perspective in *Passion* (1982). The depths effectively created for him by Raoul Coutard's camera, both in the grosser studio setting and within the "framed" area of each "painting," surprise in showing how relatively arbitrary painterly depth can be, and hint at the subtle magic of arbitrariness. Since with cinema there come changes in point of view, and since these changes vibrate among themselves, the idea of having some preferential object in the field is abandoned, vanquished—save, we would hope, for the delirious presence of the glowing persona (about which, see below); yet even the persona disappears. It is only provisionally that an object can be preferential. Truffaut's meandering stranger in *Baisers volés* (1968): "Je hais le provisoire; moi, je suis définitif." Whenever a new object is brought into view, by jump, by flash cut, by pan, by dissolve, it changes its rank and status. Even a composed vision, say a still life (a sumptuous bowl of fruit on a table in *37°2 le matin* [1986]), resists being preferred, proclaims itself as but one happenstantial territory through which we move to arrive at an only promised station. In moving depictions everything that shows a *here* anticipates a *not-here*. The viewer is no longer an observer upon a balcony but the center of a storm.

Each vision not only vanishes for its successor but offers itself to be seen only with a commitment to abandonment, since the next vision is always the purpose of the one that came before just as it is simultaneously the opening for what is still to come. The eye is in motion seeing. Here I point to the strange phenomenon Wolfgang Schivelbusch, following Dolf Sternberger, named "panoramic perception" (*Journey* 61). However speedily or spasmodically a story pulses forward, first (a) the forward view is closed to us, we never see where things are going, and then (b) that forward motion has its own thrust and power, forces us to invent, as per Schefer, a syntax of durations. With quickly renovated camera positions (very quickly in Bordwell's "intensified continuity") each new vision becomes unpredictable because one cannot have desired or expected to be seeing it; and also galvanizing, since one has to react with electronic speed or it will be gone.[3] Faced with ongoing surprises in procession, one develops an elevating purposelessness in viewing, one enters a world of possibility, without the gravitation of things.[4]

---

[3] "Galvanizing" from [Luigi] Galvani (1737–98). See Piccolino.
[4] The cultivated purposelessness may be considered a blasé attitude. See Simmel, *Geldes* 264ff.

4

The glowing persona as lure: What is our deepest wish regarding the movie star but somehow, by way of some superconjuring, to reach past the screen and touch her. Literally take her in the arms and warmly embrace, old friend, wise mentor, ancient bust. "A privileged central nucleus articulates itself against the surrounding area," writes Ortega. "The central object is a luminous hero" (110). There is a corporeal bulk, a promise of flesh. To embrace it, to feel the warmth, to lend it our warmth since alone in the world of the screen it is frozen.

5

Thinking of such painters as Caillebotte staring down the Boulevard des Italiens, or Frederic Edwin Church camped beyond Cotopaxi (traipse every morning to the same spot, set up the easel), or Georges Seurat at Argenteuil, or Canaletto at the Old Walton Bridge, one has a sense of the melancholy eye whose hunger is never sated. In cinema, such meditative pungency resides perhaps in the face, a scape that seems to have no limit and no end, also continually in (ostensibly) purposive motion so that every gestural or quasi-gestural nuance can be stabilized for meaning in the gears of a dramatic plot—discounting cases where the essence of the dramatic plot is precisely a face that cannot be read: Terence Stamp's in *Teorema* (1968), Lon Chaney's in *The Unknown* (1927), Monica Vitti's in *The Mystery of Oberwald* (1980), Keanu Reeves's in *Thumbsucker* (2005). But regardless of its intelligibility, cinema always moves past the face, takes the face as pretext for a future. The moving eye of cinema has a future always on the way. Relentless happening.

Since the shot brings both an opportunity for apprehension and an energized looking forward, a wandering spirit is invoked, one assuming continuous possibility of knowing. What becomes dominant then, even fearsome, is the edge of the frame where knowledge is posited and challenged. Not those mere boundaries imposed by the screen ratio and the cameraman's formation of the rectangle, that line beyond which we have language and action -off, but more pungently the edge that holds the image away from us and hints to creep close to the auditorium. The edge that makes me think, "I am/ I am not." Concealed in the face of a shuffling consciousness is the small shard of missing, titillating information the upcoming shot promises to reveal. The presentation of the obscured body, the presentation of the obscured meaning and intent. Always informed, we can never have enough information. And every turning body refuses to reveal its secrets. In picking up "information" about visually demonstrated relations, we also confront our ignorance, the colorless fact that in the warehouse of the receiving spirit there remain, always, empty shelves.

6

Producing numerous views of a proposed reality, often a proposed singular reality, cinema engenders and addresses a spectator always already eager and nervous, jittery for angles, angles and more angles, always questioning (perhaps finally abandoning) the integrity of the self in the face of film's wholesale democracy. What does *the other viewer* see with her *other point of view?* The heist film is interesting because it poses (a) figures who operate in action by taking technical views, just as we do watching them; (b) other figures who have other technical views but cannot be viewed by the first ones; as well as (c) conditions spread over fragmented space, that attract both figures' attention and ours (usually not in the same way). In the classical heist, the conspirators work together as a team, amalgamating a single view tagged to the team leader with his plan; and the camera watches every key gesture in a chain that leads to a singular treasure. See *Du rififi chez les hommes* (1955) for an elegant example. In the contemporary version— for example *The Italian Job* (2003)—we have the team split up with a formalized division of labor. Typically, no two agents share the same spot topographically, and to catch the broader plan unfolding the camera must jump among the many agents to get the "overall picture." That structure is nicely played out in *The Anderson Tapes* (1971) and *Mission: Impossible* (1996). A unique progenitor is *Dr. Mabuse, der Spieler* (1922), where a split team with labor neatly divided is emphatically and deftly unified onscreen through various modes of communication with Mabuse at the hub (but *Mabuse* was far ahead of its time). In the "multiple perspective heist," as we might name it, opportunity to view an object (the treasure, the plan enacted) from all sides is preferential to choosing an "ideal" point of view: improbability. The conceit of a single viewpoint is under attack from racing forces of a multi-perspectival future.

7

As one studies a painting or watches a film one is in the hands of another. It is the painter's action that puts distance into the perspective, creating a longing for a presence that will never be ours. The filmmaker and his editor work through ongoingness to intimate a future. Note Godard's jump cuts, toying with our sense of time, jostling our belief in conventional continuity and the metrical approach of oncoming events.

Cinema teases us with the as-yet-unseen, urges us to rely on forthcomingness, to hope that every unfinished sentence will find completion (think of every shot as a sentence, or a phrase). During the moment of cinematic presence, however—a shot, a camera move, a facial expression–during the extension, there is a strange contentment to be felt as we marvel at form and space, even a revelation of incompleteness as a new genre of finality. In painting revelation is here before us, as much as it ever will be, not held off in a distant prospect we already know cannot be found.

8

About distal space painting incites a curiosity; the motives of figures are in relation to their space (this space now, as they will not be traveling to another), clear if riddling when present to us but still and perpetually unknown afar. Film is interested in happening as emergent, and uses space to ground our experience—which is not identical to happening. Happening always emerges, experience is immediate. Giving light, focus, and prominence to foreground figures, the camera vision intercalates with narrational need, links each presence to a previousness and an oncomingness. Action takes decoration from space, is colored by space, may even find definition in a space, but the space is for holding the action rather than confronting our regard, this even with the most spectacular of places filling the most spectacular space, as in the Death Valley sequences of *Zabriskie Point* (1970), where we are given a scape to blot out all others, primeval, astonishing, apparently endless, and yawning out to a far world wholly alien until, at first slowly and with increasing momentum, distinctive human figures invade and come proximate, occupy both the medium ground and, barely visible there, the distance: this part of the desert is now clearly appropriate for a certain kind of human action, imagined if not played.

The presence of a figure does not contradict invocation of a point we cannot know: a point, not an eventuality.

9

A photographer's still camera can move; moving cameras can be still. In early cinema, one frequently saw the product of a stilled camera recording motion. In a film like the Lumières' *L'arroseur arrosé* (1895) a central figure actually walks off the stationary camera before reappearing, and the camera does not move to follow, as surely it would today. Their film *Promenade des autriches dans Les Jardins Zoölogiques de Paris* offers, for some fifty or so seconds, a parade of fabulous animals heading toward the fixed camera from an indiscernible distance: ostriches, llamas, horses, dogs, and so on. It is a charming sunny day, the dappled light makes every muscular twitch glorious. Where these magical beasts are coming from, whither they are going, we neither know nor need to know. But at the same time, without inquiring we *do know* that there is a point of origin and a point of terminus, something beyond the delight of this simplicity. One has the feeling of the camera pinioned in place. The beasts march forward, as each afternoon in the spring they march forward, same route, same parade order, same lethargic but regal speed of motion. And they have done this before. Yet also, stunningly, they are *only doing it now.* So this parade is placed in history and outside of history at once.

The stationary camera here produces a cinema *à la manière de la peinture*. Even in early W. K. L. Dixon films, showing performers against a black ground—the strong man; Annabelle dancing—that black nothingness attracts wonder and forbids examination, and we have the brave gesticulations of the subjects, the strong man showing his biceps; Annabelle twisting with her butterfly wings. It now appears so present and actual, so close to the yearning view, that they seem to have, to have had, and to bode having no other existence. Figures in Caillebotte.

But think of the parenthetical close-up insertion. In Edwin S. Porter's *The Gay Shoe Clerk* (1903) we find a young woman has come, chaperoned by her mother, to try on shoes at a store. The male clerk pays her special (read randy) attention. At one point the girl raises her very long skirt so that he can see her shoe on his support stand, but in doing this she reveals her ankle. Clerk is astonished and ravished. While he gawks, mother slams him with her umbrella. End of film. But while that clerk gawked we could, too, because instead of the fixed medium-distal position from which we saw whole bodies in action, spread left to right on the screen, we were thrust into a view where the girl's ankle literally took up the entire frame, relatively gigantic, confrontational.

"The close-up," writes Jean Epstein, "is the soul of the cinema" (236). "I have neither the right nor the ability to be distracted" (239).

Regardless that it dramatically follows the logic of the clerk's eager move, the close-up is entirely unexpected by the viewer—this is generally regarded as the first use of close-up in film history, and presumably no one watching films had ever thought about seeing this way. The jump is radical, shocking, far more intimate than one would have expected (or would have felt legitimate wishing for). We could say that the cut into the close-up mimics for the viewing audience not only the attitude of the salesman figure but more importantly the attitude of the judgmental onscreen looker-at-figures, the mother. What will Mother tell the girl in chastisement as they walk away? One already has a sense of being more present in the acted scene than would be possible in a painting, exactly because of the temporal rhythm of the cut and the corporeal augmentation made clear by it. *More present:* present in an augmented experience; present more wholeheartedly; enjoying a reality.

Liberated, the camera could now feel free to behave like the curious personality it presumably always felt itself to be but somehow, pinned down, hadn't become.

10

There is also a temporal perspective, in which some moments are so very far away they transgress the boundary of our perception; whereas other moments seem wholly present. We can even conceive, rationally, how the fashionable film we saw last night will age as time goes by, and how in five years it will look outmoded, simplistic, unwatchable, though we are still writhing from the experience of watching it. If we can be thought to live in a painting we are looking at, then our looking is "in" and "now" and only that; we only dream unthinkable tomorrows and yesterdays. If we live in a film we sense ourselves moving inexorably from what was, toward what will emerge, and only quirkinesses of plot or extravagances of casting or figuration will distract us from that progression.[5] The happening-now, the having-happened, and the soon-to-happen are melded or enchained in the passage of film: Jean Marais stepping through the mirror in *Orphée* (1950). Cinema is forever shunting us from history. Sometimes in that shunting we are offered a distinctive vision of shunting itself: at the very end of Olivier Assayas' *L'heure d'été (Summer Hours,* 2008) a brother and sister stand side by side gazing at an ornate Beaux Arts writing table mounted on a curling plinth in a display at the Musée d'Orsay, and as we see the spotlights shining on the polished amber surface of that piece we recollect the story that the film has now finished showing us, a story of what this desk used to be, who owned it, and the whole account of how it came to be here in this museum: the whole sad story presaging whatever it is that sad stories look forward to.

11

"The motion of the train shrank space," writes Schivelbusch, "and thus displayed in immediate succession objects and pieces of scenery that in their original spatiality belonged to separate realms":

---

[5]In the way that the eventfulness of life and experience distracts us from the earth's thousand-mile-per-hour rotation, which is always happening anyway.

The traveler who gazed through the compartment window at such successive scenes, acquired a novel ability that Gastineau calls "la philosophie synthétique du coup d'oeil" ("the synthetic philosophy of the glance"). It was the ability to perceive the discrete, as it rolls past the window, indiscriminately.

(60)

Journalist and historian Benjamin Gastineau's *La vie en chemin de fer* had appeared in Paris in 1861: *Le voyage est la lecture du livre de Dieu* (12).[6] The cinematic form requires not only that the viewer be capable of making the glance and comprehending its harvest, but also that the glance comprehensively come to be taken as routine, sacred, in social arrangements. "To glance" must somehow become synonymous with "to look," looking being transformed altogether. What was once thought a specialized form of looking, useful in only certain restricted circumstances, becomes generalized into everyday usage. The "glance" having become the "look," there is no longer any glance.

Although by the late 1880s Parisians would have been at least somewhat adapted to the "coup d'oeil," when Caillebotte painted "Boulevard des Italiens" the glance as a *standard mode of looking* was not yet in place (albeit Caillebotte certainly knew and fancied railways [see his "Landscape with Railway Tracks" (*c.* 1872) or "Le Pont de l'Europe" (1876)]). The *Boulevard* was to be seen while standing, its atmosphere floating around the viewer, suffusing the atmosphere of the viewing room. Caught in a coup d'oeil, a painting like this one with an inaccessible depth would not have had leisure to manifest its absent distance. In the glance, all things are present and nearby to the traveling eye.

12

It is possible to deny, then eradicate, the eye's illusion of fixation and capacity for reasoned study, and substitute a throbbing search. Are we all then become detectives? Search and search, as though in the world somewhere there lies buried a vital clue, and if only we look hard enough—whatever it can mean to *look hard*—if only, if only, if only ... the secret will be revealed. Or will the revealed secret produce only the itch to open another secret? In his film *Blow-Up* (1966), Antonioni gives us a painter of pointillist canvases who confesses with a casual sagacity, "They don't mean anything when I do them. But afterward I find something to catch onto, like a clue in a detective story." This character does not say, possibly because there is no need for him

---

[6]"A voyage is a reading of God's book."

to say, that before one can call anything at all a clue one must have invented a detective story, one must have become used to detecting.⁷

By looking at all its fragments—or as many as we can hold—by shifting, jumping, bumping from one to another, can we pray to remake the broken world? That prayer is the promise of the camera:

- That, as in *Passion,* a clear blue sky is not enough, is not actually something until cutting across it, far away, a tiny jet leaves a long, long trail. Sky + jet + jet trail (+ Ravel).
- That, as in *Written on the Wind* (1956), when an old man having a heart attack falls all the way down a curving staircase and up above at the balustrade an elegant woman in gray rushes to gaze down in horror, we are caught in uncertainty whether to concentrate on the dying man (Robert Keith) or on the woman aghast (Lauren Bacall). Trapped for the instant in uncertainty, we flip from one to the other (although of course without the camera one could never flip this way).
- That after a twister a dazed little girl opens the door of her dingy little abode and suddenly, through the rectangular aperture, discovers in blazingly colorful repose the magical place where she has landed: where are we, exactly, seeing first the one thing and then the other? Are we in the doorway? What power escorts us from a plain view to a second plain view a hundred and eighty degrees away? Yes, we know it is a pair of shots for *The Wizard of Oz* (1939) cut together into a filmic continuity, but this little *faux* explanation doesn't help at all because as we watch we do not know of filmic continuities or cutting but only of what the glance has seized. How can this presence of ours leap so fluidly and so swiftly, and from seeing in tinted black-and-white to seeing in color? Who must we be, what urgency must have invaded our consciousness and our gaze so that the amazed little girl, in herself, is not enough? (Caillebotte painted flâneurs on the Boulevard Haussmann satisfied to see them forever, and without intimating where they came from or where they were headed.⁸)

People turned to process, to proceeding toward more proceeding; everything part of a journey (a reading of God's book), and we never find home. The Wordsworthian "recollection in tranquility" called for a feeling now dissipated, but that once had a coherence we can presently revisit. Watching

---

⁷I write about detecting in the English pleasure gardens of the eighteenth century and the connection between this habit and film viewing, in *Cinema, If You Please.*
⁸*Paris Street, Rainy Day* (1877).

films we not only employ a moving gaze, we believe in it, so that our reaction is a moving reaction and tranquilities of the past are gone.

13

A bridging between the stationary and the moving gaze—between the flat painterly use of perspective and the moving involvement of cinema—seems to have come toward the end of the eighteenth century with the invention of the panorama (Gk.: pan=everywhere; horama=view). It was the mode of perception facilitated by this creation that Schivelbusch builds upon in addressing train travel of the nineteenth century. Robert Barker (1739–1806), an Irish painter, was granted a patent by George III to build a structure circular in form with a raised viewing platform about halfway up and accessible from a dark passage beneath. A high and vastly long painting would there entirely surround the viewer, being lit from above. Laurent Mannoni quotes from the original Barker patent to the effect that the drawing or painting intends

> To perfect an entire view of any country or situation as it appears to an observer turning quite round; to produce which effect the painter or drawer must fix his station, and delineate correctly and connectedly every object which presents itself to his view as he turns round, concluding his drawing by a connection with where he started.
> (177)

"The canvas was effectively endless," Mannoni comments (176).[9] Barker's Leicester Square, London panorama of 1792 was the "true triumph" (177). Description of another piece (given by Mannoni in quotation of a contemporary German journalist) shows the importance of movement in panoramic perception:

> The painting has a surface of more than 1,000 square feet and is attached on the inner surface of a circular building which is 90 feet in diameter. The spectator is placed in the centre of the painted sea, on the upper deck of a frigate. This maritime landscape is particularly delightful. The illusion is so strong that the spectators believe themselves to be truly between the harbor and the island, in the open sea; they even say that some ladies have suffered from seasickness.
> (178)

---

[9] A state of affairs curiously repudiated by a "train voyage" sequence in Max Ophüls' *Letter from an Unknown Woman* (1948).

It is Mannoni's estimation that the "imposing representation" of the panorama "hinted at the dream of a complete spectacle, of 'total cinema'" (176), here making a conceptual leap between the (painted) picture's static quality and the perceiver's ideal movement (in apprehending). Schivelbusch does not put it this way, but he envisions this leap being literally engineered through the development of railway travel and the associated perception of travelers who could see only a world passing by. Schivelbusch quotes Sternberger:

> The views from the windows of Europe have entirely lost their dimension of depth and have become mere particles of one and the same panoramic world that stretches all around and is, at each and every point, merely a painted surface.
>
> (57, qtd. in *Journey* 61)

Visitors to the panorama were of course free to stand perfectly still and look in one direction only, perhaps an application of the device considered somewhat perverse since the real thrill was advertised to come with rotating as one gazed, indeed, rotating slowly, so that the circularity of the proposition was entirely subsumed in the ongoing detail of the landscape to be seen. Design overwhelmed by progression (and progress). The circularity of the painting would become apparent only in the extreme peripheral vision, and if one did not rotate slowly. By way of the panorama, a visitor could think to voyage through a world, and it is this link between the voyager's movement and the acuity of perception that enables the conceptual jump from the panorama to the motion picture. Perceptual motion became a benefit; as movies developed, considerably more possibilities were introduced—we can remember that the Barker viewing platform was itself architecturally fixed at a uniform height and distance from the painting,[10] but the camera dolly, vastly improved from the 1970s onward, undid this limitation (see for example Salt 278–9).

Cinematic motion was negotiated with audiences in a relatively stable and slow-moving arrangement of propositions,[11] so that the leap inward to be seen in *The Gay Shoe Clerk,* a radical change of point of view through insertion of one single close-up, took time to settle before being accreted upon by other similar jumps (as, in *The Lonedale Operator* [1911], from a long shot into a close shot of the heroine's wrench). Later, stage by stage, increasingly complex perceptual movements were encouraged. Once the

---

[10]The viewing chamber at the top of the Eiffel Tower works this way, modeled to some degree upon Barker; but the idea of reducing the globe to a point of gaze was considerably older. One can find it in the fourth-century Milyon Tasi in Istanbul, a pillar marked off as the centerpoint of the Byzantine Empire.

[11]On negotiating optical techniques and interpretations with audiences, see Carey.

agile camera was operating, systematically by the beginning of the 1920s, watching movies was thoroughly impossible for viewers who had not first accustomed themselves to "turning" through (and past) experience while looking. Turning, as in the panorama. Turning through a world, as in railway travel. Turning, as in jumping one's interest from one thing to another.

Erkki Huhtamo discusses the need to establish continuity in panoramas once they grew past a certain point. In Artemus Ward's New York displays in the 1860s, for example, there were not only stationary but also moving panoramas, and a curtain was used; often "the showman gave his prologue next to a closed curtain"; but this curtain, once raised, did not stay up. "It was lowered again several times, during the intermission and at the end" (250). But a problem arose with artists' desire to use the panorama for representing notably long unfolding territories:

> As moving panoramas grew longer, the literal representation of continuous space became impossible. Although the Mississippi panoramists made months-long sketching trips, even hundreds of sketches could not cover the entire river... The impression of continuity was created artificially, because there was no alternative.[12]

We can easily compare the problem of creating the "impression of continuity" between motion picture shots made from different points of view in a single scene, or incorporating long, medium, and close-up shots; as well as in movements from one scene to a (purportedly) contiguous other.

One had to have learned not only how to see in motion but how to avoid suffering from motion sickness, because an eye well trained to establish a single perspective and hold it through reflection and meditation was now invited, nay obliged to dart through the details of a perspective, seizing and relinquishing again and again, continually flexing its openness to light and its focal musculature in a relentless hunt for booty never to be vaulted. As well, to see cinema was to see the whole world anew, because human relations, once thought to be fixed, were now understood to be in continual process, each confidence a possible future betrayal, each betrayal a possible accident. In aesthetic terms, this is Ferdinand Tönnies's transition to modernity by way of *Gemeinschaft* becoming *Gesellschaft* (see Weber's discussion). The more that cinematic fictions displayed and mocked them, social relations tended toward the dramatic. Whereas once the accident was a puncture of the binding membrane of a situation, now accident was a mode of existence, a pretext and a climate. In his *Hugo* (2011), Martin Scorsese touches upon the centrality of accident by carefully replicating the October 22, 1895, Gare

---

[12]This last sentence, "The impression of continuity was created artificially, because there was no alternative," stands to this day.

de Montparnasse train catastrophe when an engine rammed through the station wall and dropped toward the pavement outside.

14

For the early nineteenth-century visitor who had paid to stand on Barker's viewing platform, and who turned round and round in an itinerant excitement, what could have been the pleasure of sight? To see all of what was before one to see, surely; to snatch the world as it presented itself, all of it, every last detail, even if the turning meant details were only temporarily in view (but perhaps not "temporarily on view" in the way that in life objects we encounter are but "temporarily on view"). To be a compounder (a holder) of space. Certainly to "have" space all around, outside one's field of view, behind one's head, but to collect by inspiring. To have the feeling of coming into momentary possession of a vast landscape, albeit in a special place built for engineering such possession; in the countryside such a viewer would have stood upon a downs and turned round and round to see as far as the eye could see in every direction, but possess no containments. Nature was here both expanded into the freedom of limitless visual space and closed in by being harbored in a special room. One went in, and the entire world visible in one supreme perspective was placed at one's feet. If the painting were suitably high, the eye would have trimmed off the top and very bottom just in its forward gaze, so that, if the join were seamless in the painting, there would seem to be no framing at all.[13]

We might profitably think that the panorama had a special attraction for urbanites, who lived their days among confining crowds, in blocked alleyways, and otherwise cloistered. Here at the top of Barker's darkened staircase was the open land itself, freedom under a beaming sun. The viewer's rotating body helped convey the illusion of freedom.

In the panorama, one ideally abandoned the platform upon which one stood. Watching the panorama with pleasure, then, the viewer had learned how to block away (repress, even) the technology by which she watched. In that repression, perhaps, lay a singular pleasure. Watching cinema we generally block the process away, too. To enjoy a perspective in motion, one denies the motor. Breathing at the edge of the screen we recognize no edge, no screen, no breath.

---

[13]In Hollywood painted backings from the 1930s onward, a vital process was the seaming together of gigantic canvas strips so as to fabricate an uninterrupted whole. See my discussion of *Brigadoon* in *Eyes* Ch. 4.

15

Whether a painter is engaged with a canvas or a filmmaker is making a shot, some point of view, or point of initial view, is selected and established in a process that involves not only the catalogue of all possible views—those taken by the self and others; those imaginable—but also a notation of details that from any particular viewpoint will not be clear (in the distance, or off-).[14] Temporally, when we look back remembering a film, its time span can be roughly available but we lose the sense of anticipation that came with the fleeting promise of being embedded *soon*. We can lose, too, a sense memory of earlier experiences of the cinema, a memory that helped us understand *moments passing into other moments* as a special effect.

16

With painting, the perspective's far-point—in Caillebotte the distal end of the Boulevard—is finally overcome by a cutting off of desire, a stamping out of the hope to go there. So, upon that balustrade-enclosed balcony over the Boulevard one is not only privileged but also entrapped, point of view locked in, and freedom can come only when we step away from this canvas and perhaps find another hanging to its side (another, but incomparably different, prison).

In all this, how about comprehension? Comprehending by way of what is near but not by way of what is far off; comprehending by way of what is before us now but not by way of where we are going next? Comprehending through a sense of presence; comprehending through unexpected memory and unexpectant anticipation. The riddle of the painted canvas and the riddle of the screened film: are these really two different riddles or are they, when all is said and done, the same?:

> He particularly agreed when I said that over the years I had puzzled out a good deal in my own mind, but in spite of that, far from becoming clearer, things now appeared to me more incomprehensible than ever. The

---

[14]Interestingly, with both painting and cinematography one condition persists: that the easel and the camera or dolly must find, somehow somewhere, a secure position in which to stand. We have the tales of photographers like Timothy O'Sullivan trekking into the Western wildernesses with cameras and large plates hung upon their backs; or of a painter like Church struggling through jungle and hill to find his perch; and with the cinematic system there are fabulous technologies for mounting and positioning the camera (a legendary story being Alfred Hitchcock's positioning of the Technicolor camera for shots in *Rear Window* [1954]).

more images I gathered from the past, I said, the more unlikely it seemed to me that the past had actually happened in this or that way, for nothing about it could be called normal: most of it was absurd, and if not absurd, then appalling.

(Sebald 212)

for Assheton Gorton

6

To Have and To Hold

Kristen Stewart in Personal Shopper *(Olivier Assayas, CG Cinéma/Vortex Sutra/ Sirena Film, 2016). Digital frame enlargement.*

Own/Have

What I see onscreen is mine as I see it. In the moments which I take (possess) from the film I am wholly wrapped up, both embracing and being embraced, wondering and worrying, flying with exhilaration and standing back aghast: all within the walls of the same unknowable room with the smell of salted popcorn in the air. As I sit next to my boyhood chum Slava (Sviatoslav Vladimir Vladimirovich) basking in the light that glimmers onscreen, it does not occur to me for a breath that this panoply of twinkle and form has been made, all of it, for *him*, though he may think that. I don't suppose it's been made for the vague crowd lingering in the dark peripheries, either. It is for me, the landscape, the mother, the cowboy, the space cadet, the alley leading to a chain link fence. It is expressly for me, has been made to be so: I believe in the act of watching and in the act of my watching supremely.

I believe in watching and my watching breathes with that belief. The filmmakers may be serving me but, as I have never met them, they cannot be my servants—surely not my slaves, here in this purportedly post-slave, post-feudal society, this golden capitalism. They may live—and live well—on the lucre others and I give them. But the pleasure I have in watching has nothing to do with finances, everything to do with exchange in the earliest, simplest form. As a product to be screened and watched the film is capital goods, rented, not owned, by me (it is copyright to someone else); but the film as my point of focus, its many intricate parts as I see them: here is the source of my pleasure and my understanding, mine, all mine, to own and to have.

The film as I understand it and as in retrospect I will understand it ongoingly, strikes by way of my biography—and has been fashioned to address many people this way, so it speaks to my biography generalized, whatever impossibility I can fathom that to be. I must know myself and what is for me: but I must know how I am not, like Ludwig II of Bavaria, the only audience for the show.

Was the film I'm watching made to my order? No and yes. I did not request it, but my seeing is out of requirement. I surely could not have known enough in, say, 1951, to order up *The Bad and the Beautiful,* and even if I had wanted such an essence I would not have guessed who could satisfy the yearning. Sometimes, too, there is something I catch onscreen, knowingly, willingly, that flies in the face of all my sense of decency. Yet even then, instead of feeling a twinge of discomfort at the debasing, humiliating, offensive image, this besmirching of my sacred ideas of cleanliness, still I watch with open eyes, I scan the horror, because my eyes are desperately open. Unavoidably, certain negative images—if you asked my opinion, I would claim them disgusting—come into my conscious apprehension and there become, against my rejection, mine. Even the darkness in which I try to drown these negativities is my own—"This thing of darkness I/Acknowledge mine"; their ugliness is an ugliness of my own making. "The portrait that killed Zeuxis no longer exists," writes Gretchen Henderson:

> but a similar painting haunts our cultural landscape. Considered unattractive enough to gain the nickname of "The Ugly Duchess," *A Grotesque Old Woman* or *An Old Woman* (1513) was painted by the Flemish artist Quinten Massys. When the painting went up for auction in London in 1920, a notice appeared in the *New York Times* announcing the sale of a "portrait which is generally accepted as being the ugliest one in the world" due to its subject of a duchess "famous for her repulsive features."
> ...
> Her reputation for ugliness seems to arise from her aged attempt to squeeze into an outdated youthful dress. She evokes something more or less than human. Her facial features appear stretched, with a flaring

arched nose, broad cheeks and forehead. Modern viewers have described her in animal terms.[1]

(42; 43–4)

I am one of Henderson's modern viewers, having stood and stared at this portrait many times, always in equivocation: wonder is present, and also leaning backward just a little, so as not, with my eyes, to come too close.

On owning and having, Jean-Paul Sartre:

> To possess means *to have for myself*; that is, to be the unique end of the existence of the object. If possession is entirely and concretely given, the possessor is the *raison d'être* of the possessed object. ... Moreover originally it is I who make for myself the object which I want to possess. My bow and arrows—that means the objects which I have made for myself. Division of labor can dim this original relation but can not make it disappear. *Luxury* is a degradation of it; in the primitive form of luxury I possess an object which I *have had made (done)* for myself by people belonging to *me* (slaves, servants born in the house). Luxury therefore is the form of ownership closest to primitive ownership; it is this which next to ownership itself throws the most light on the relation of *creation* which originally constitutes appropriation.
>
> (*Being* 752)

Let us accept that the film as I see it has been made for me—that I take it personally: I can take it as having been made for me just as *we* can take it as having been made for *us*. I know it was made by persons not exactly employed by me but employed in a system of production that counts (sensibly) on my (continuing) support, a system that is, in its way, *my system,* because my bank account supplies my support. I am not innocent enough to think there are no profiteering moguls in filmmaking, but in the midst of watching the film I incorporate their motives and drives, their arrangements, their specifications, without special consideration. I am riddled by seeing.

The Image and My Own Image

Sartre: "To be the unique end of the existence of the object": yes, that is how I take myself at the edge of the screen. Time is experienced as lived: time here, time now, time in the regard. While I am to it, the object is to me; and is only to me in my singularity, uniquely to me as my presence is a unique presence. Talk to me about the image if you will, but I anticipate no

---

[1] The painting hangs placidly in the National Gallery, London.

resonance in what you say. The image's existence extends and stretches, then ends at me, in me, with me. In my seeing the film is my having it: having is seeing, having is hearing. In my having is the way I see. Slava Vladimirovich sits chuckling at things I don't chuckle at and I leave him to it.

Shows within the Show

This weird and wonderful affiliation with the constantly moving, constantly engaging figurations of the screen can be known by, can be reflected in, film itself. *The Thief of Bagdad* (1940): swathed all in candy pink, the Sultan of Basra (Miles Malleson) is giddily touring the evil magician Jaffar (Conrad Veidt) through his opulent toy collection. Marvelous and challenging these things, each more complex than the one before. Jaffar shows pleasure enough, because his intention is to contribute, in a moment, a special toy of his own invention. But first the Sultan insists on showing off his very favorite!

This is a tiny theater, set up on a tabletop. Curtains and a proscenium margin a stage upon which a team of tiny acrobats, no one taller than a raised pinkie finger, exercise and dance at the Sultan's command. (He is the possessor of the theater; and of the figures.) In practical terms, a team of dancers were filmed on a black-backed stage and matted in here, so that what we see on the diminutive stage, rather than cardboard cutouts in curious puppeting, is "actual" tiny people choreographed in unison. It is as though the Sultan has a toy carnival of performing mice, except that his "mice" are people reduced in size, and in "owning" them, making this display, he is showing off his sultanly potency. On show to Powell and Pressburger's camera filming this, however, and thus on show for viewers watching *The Thief of Bagdad,* in which, now, the toy theater takes up the full screen, is the presence of a watcher (the Sultan's guest Jaffar) absorbed by the toy. A watcher absorbed as we are absorbed (as the Sultan knew we would be absorbed). If in watching we resemble the Sultan and his guest, focused, entranced, then the Sultan and his guest have become our moving "toys," rendered for us to possess, but toys as giants if we are watching on a big screen. What makes a toy here is not size but status in performance. Were we to watch *The Thief* on a mini-screen of some kind, the play-within-the-play might be so tiny as to be almost imperceptible but the Sultan and Jaffar watching it would be roughly as tiny as here on the big screen the Sultan's stage figures are for us.

The play-within-the-play format—in cinema, a character attending the theater or an opera or watching television or, like Woody Allen in *Play It Again, Sam* (1972) and Michael Pitt in *The Dreamers* (2003), going to the movies—invariably invokes audiences possessing by eye. The rapt gazing the camera shows us in such scenes, the enlarged oculus shining with screenlight, the lips stilled in parting ... all this is the joy of "having" that is being openly demonstrated to viewers themselves engaged by this demonstration of a demonstration. "This is what it is like (what it looks like) to be thrilled in seeing something." We can note how interesting are these visible lookers now looking, and possess them, too. In that act, are we possessing ourselves? Or are we freed from possession?

Memory of Sight

The image mingles not only with the confounding swirls of my present but also in relation to the stratified history of my remembered experience. The links I make in connecting the image are mine both because I effect them and because I am the one who is gathering, sorting, deciding upon, and preferring them. If I find lateral relations, mirrorings, musical repetitions—is this because I always look to the side, somehow use a "lateral consciousness"; or because I love and fear mirrors; or because I have musical training? Having taken in the image, I privilege a line, a shadow, a surface (the smooth cheek), a colored radiance. Sometimes, I find a center of organization laid down by the image-maker, sometimes I re-make an image by centering it as I would. Every description of, every announcement about an image that I make is a revelation of my possessing self and, whilst I am viewing, even the maker of the image becomes *the maker of this thing possessed by me*: my own maker of things like this thing.

The image is mine in another way, too. I have the choice to glare at it, drink it down in long draughts, sustain it (today I can pause the screen, but I can also remember); or merely glance and throw it away because there are so many images pressing for my consideration and only some can be cherished. An image is not chosen because of some characteristic of its own, however, but because of some characteristic of me; I do the choosing, consciously or not. I *make* the movie that has been made for me. "We may be interested in what photography and film are," writes David Rodowick helpfully, "but we are also equally or indeed more concerned by what we have valued qualitatively in the experience of contemplating them, or indeed by what we ourselves become in watching films" (73). Do I know what I see, or do I see what I know? Everything that I regard in the film is known to me *through my regarding*, resonates with, helps build my understanding of the way things are. I see in order to learn how to see.

Writing to you at this moment, reader, I retain a vivid recollection of something I saw in 1953, a buoyant spring-green presence that seemed to float my way in Charles Walters's *Lili* (1953). I was in the tiniest of theaters in a summer beach town, almost alone in the place, and this color filled me with boundless joy (one can read of such joy in Nabokov, who taught a dear friend of mine, and she glowed telling me about him, but this was long before I came to recognize who he was). Boundless joy, though. It is impossible to have an experience of limitless pleasure with *Lili* now for several reasons: the film is no longer projected in theaters; the recorded versions transferred first to tape and then to DVD couldn't sustain the saturation of this and other colors, likely because the three camera records made by Robert Planck with the Technicolor apparatus faded, during the improper storage that was deemed affordable at the time (and this film has not been restored). There are untold problems with archiving film negatives and especially Technicolor black-and-white color records (from which, if they are in good shape, new matrices can be struck and a brand new print effected). I have kept that spring green, however. I do not access it regularly, but it is stored to be accessed. It is also true that instead of feeling unadulterated joy at the thought of accessing it I feel trepidation that age may have weakened my hold.

Unconventional

Speaking of "possession" we tend to think, monetary transaction and handing-over of goods. (Rather than, say, the more arcane sense of a mind or spirit being taken over by some definitive, usually malevolent forces.) I possess when I pay the bill. But this is only a superficial way of understanding the change of state in which something which was not mine comes to be mine. Possession is in the sentimental regard one has in commanding the presence of an object which offers its presence. Say two characters come together as though they are going to embrace, but they don't embrace. I make way through the tangle of the coming together, a tangle enriched and complicated by the *almost-ness* of the almost kissing.

An Image, Not a Story

I say that an *image*, not a *story*, is mine. Many are those who write and talk about film as though the images are but pretext for the story; but surely the story is pretext for the images, and a rather public pretext at that, since in bulk the stories we see on the screen are limited in variety, elemental, even if cloaked and ornamented to seem infinitely variant (so that the Producer can produce lucre). In seeing the image one regards it more for what it calls up in itself, the tap into memory, the offer of an untasted taste. Always with an image one is lost, searching for orientation just before being lost again with the next image; the hunt and the orientation joining in a rhythm that belongs to the observer. To avoid the pomposity of self-invocation (for whatever reason), we chatter about the plot as we leave the theater, as though the plot is really what faced us from the screen. We chatter about anything and everything except the watching we did in a sacred rite.

Perhaps if I cannot find my experience in relation to an image it cannot be mine and I reject the film. Is this, perhaps, what people who know nothing about filming and its exigencies, actually mean when they say a film is "bad"?

Limit

My artistry will seize an image and join it to another. "Artistry as such is tied to a quick grasp," Walter Benjamin quotes Balzac (41). But broadly speaking, how much is there to grasp? To have *and to hold*. With amity, Edgar Friedenberg once advised me that the last man who could be said to have known *all* of his culture was Aristotle; my own repository therefore seems limited, my grasp not so effective. Where to find space for every new thing I might wish to store?

If I use a strategy to reposition some images; to realign them; or to bind them in a new more comprehensive way; or even jettison them so that a new image can be situated for memory—can an image be jettisoned?—am I not the man invoked by Italo Calvino, who wrote, "The mind refuses to accept more faces, more expressions: on every new face you encounter, it prints the old forms, for each one it finds the most suitable mask" (95). So many films I see, so many images in those many films remind me of something else. Am I now fated to find only images that wear the masks of other images? Do all my images provoke mere nodding recognition rather than hungry stupefaction? Any film watcher could reasonably wonder how long it had been since an image actually refreshed sight.

Out of Syntax

I cannot muster a flawless syntactical memory for imagery. Moments arrive, often many from the same work, but often I lack the order in which they fell, although oddly I do have a keen sense of tempo and rhythm. Example: I can see Una O'Connor running a tiny tobacco shop in *Random Harvest* (1942), appearing there twice in fact, with the two appearances separated; but I have no idea where exactly they are to be found overall, what scene each follows and what each leads into. Music is different: I can hear whole movements of symphonies and concerti but if, onscreen, images were placed to accompany the music, I remember them discreetly, not in forward order (*Brief Encounter* [1945] as good an example as any).

My will to see and my process of seeing do not, it seems, derive from the same embryological matter. I have stored and kept available much that came my way a very long time ago, like the spring green in *Lili* and much else. Structures are built upon such fundaments. I sucked in these early materials—early in my life, not early in the history of film—almost naturally, even unaware of what an image could be and what its status in reality. For instance, the blinking blue lights at the nocturnal catastrophe of the train wreck in *The Greatest Show on Earth* (1952) and the escaping animals—monkeys, confused lions. Much later, in *J'ai épousé un ombre* (*I Married a Shadow* [1983]), there is another train wreck, similarly chilling, yet not blue; or at least not blue in the same way, even if it does have blue.

Do images added late resemble, are they modeled upon, older ones, caught and stored when the storehouse was new?[2]

Seeing and Context

Both physically and socially some experiences, places, people, and things weigh more than others. We attend with a sense of this gravity, consigning to waste or recycling the images that do not seem pre-eminent in a field. Return to Taylor in *Virginia Woolf*, for instance: the way she holds herself, the slick way she moves, her slumpy postures, her sour facial expressions—all these as orchestral embellishments of the raspy quality of her voice: we may hold this embellished voice as more important than which particular room of the house she happens to be in at any moment although, of course, the screen images will show the settings. Setting in this film works as it did on Broadway, as a mere container with enough realism to substantiate the characterizations yet without spatial value of its own. There is more spatial value in the settings of *Alien* (1979) or *The Talented Mr. Ripley* (1999) or *Anna Karenina* (2012). This is why Mike Nichols can export some of the action of Albee's vital game-confrontation scene to a local bar, when on the stage there was one set only. He knew that in his film nothing would really change with a new setting, the focus being four main characters and how they go to war, here, there, anywhere. It could be said that we watch Taylor's Martha out of context.

When they are registered, the images that one adds to one's collection must finally be congruent, or at least not disturbingly *in*congruent, with the system by which values are already ordered there. "The theory of value,"

---

[2]On the thrill of the novelty, see Spielberg's *The Fabelmans* (2022).

writes Foucault, "makes it possible, in fact, to explain (whether by dearth and need or by the superabundance of nature) how *certain* objects can be introduced into the system of exchanges" (218; emphasis mine). Certain objects, but not every object. I sift when I see, and I also extract centralities and relinquish marginalities. A good example applicable to Hollywood film, especially of the classical period but with relevance also to film afterward even into the present day, can come from Guy Davenport's recognition of the detached head as "a symbol of what we think we are and what we're up to" (50). When the individual's personality, moral future, attributed biography, and social substance are taken to reside in the head, particularly the face (the head's "head"), the character as a wholeness can be represented by the facial close-up, that telltale feature of Hollywood dramas and publicity. "Why do we not have a sculpture of Pasteur's cunning and Wanda Landowska's miraculous fingers, Pavlova's feet? No: tradition is tradition" (50).

Remembering Rancière's observation, "Images are like words in the dictionary which have value only through their position and relation" (52) we may wish to note positions and relations in our extractions; wish but have no power. Further, the image exists already in the film's value-ordered relations but, if I would have it, not in contradiction to my already systematized organization of values, which is part of my viewing self. As per Davenport, we value heads. I see as in my head I know to see, out of my (acculturated, value-oriented) experience. When I see screen blood (say, viscous in the Coen Bros.' *Blood Simple* [1984] or splattery as in *The Irishman* [2019]) I am not encountering the appearance of the substance for the first time but instead already prepared with images, thoughts, information, and arguments about blood and its qualities, its functioning, its order and disorders, and its cultural value. I have slept in a blood bank storage facility and learned its secrets in the night. I have scraped my knee and seen the blood and felt the feeling. I have taken a course in first-aid. I have seen dissection of a carcass of which blood has been replaced by latex. Onscreen a man is shot and I watch as he bleeds, but this blood of his that I now take as mine to own and to hold is blood that derives from blood I possessed already, and not only in my veins. I see with blood on my hands.

Seeing through the Temple

Received thinking, such as was addressed by Flaubert in *Le dictionnaire des idées reçues,* does something to shape the system into which we feed the images we keep. In the West, much of our received thinking about beauty and form owes to Christian theology as invoked in the thirteenth century by Aquinas, who in *Summa Theologica* praised St. Justin Martyr in particular for drawing "truths in their fullness from the doctrine of revelation," a doctrine with, at its apex, Jesus figured as not so much a messenger as a message from God. In the sixteenth century Augustine followed, with his doctrine proclaiming man as

> being neither soule only, nor body only, but consisting of both. Tis true, the soule is not whole man, but the better part onely, nor the body whole man but the worse part onely, and both conioyned make man.
>
> (492)

We do not find so explicit a division of inner and outer, the wholesale outerness of the body and innerness of the soul, in older texts such as the Pentateuch or the Greek myths. Prefacing his translation of the *Five Books of Moses,* for instance, Robert Alter comments on the powerful yet mysterious Hebrew word *nefesh:*

> A term that has no semantic analogy in English, the Hebrew *nefesh,* which the King James Version [of 1611[3]], following the Vulgate, often translates as "soul," refers to the breath of life in the nostrils of a living creature and, by extension, "lifeblood" or simply "life," and by another slide of association, "person"; and it is also used as an intensifying form of the personal pronoun, having roughly the sense of "very self."
>
> (xxxv–xxxvi)

The Protestant Reformation of the sixteenth century was a signal agent of change for practices and ideas about theology, the soul, and the afterlife in and beyond Europe, with particular effects in England where, with Henry VIII's failure to secure an annulment from Catharine of Aragon and subsequent denial of the Catholic Church, Protestant ideas and beliefs came to dominate much of English philosophical thought. This kind of thought underpins a great deal of what is now accepted as philosophical principle and a canon of critical rule devised in and promulgated from Oxford and Cambridge. Here is twentieth-century art historian Rudolf Arnheim, writing matter-of-factly: "The material body was the vessel of sin and suffering. Thus visual art, instead of proclaiming the beauty and importance of physical existence, used the body as a visual symbol of the spirit" (104). Apprehending and possessing the body by way of sculpture or portraiture might be seriously problematic from this point of view, and an escape route would have to be part of the "religious" rationale by which one *saw.* If, however, one worked with quite other postulates about the body, treating it as something other than the vessel of sin and suffering, seeing the body might be different. And of course in cinema, one sees the body. One sees and sees and sees the body. Rudolf Arnheim quotes Nicolas Poussin—a painter interested in the

---

[3]Contemporaneous with Shakespeare's *The Tempest.*

Christian world order—to the effect that colors are (but) blandishments to lure the eye (275): lure the eye, as in draw its line of attention away from the pure forms (again, a Christian idea) that are truly valuable. In a somewhat similar vein, William James quotes John Locke (born into Puritanism, later educated at Christ Church, Oxford) warning about giving over to the allure of a beauty that "requires no labor of thought to examine what truth or reason there is in it" (Locke 91, qtd. in James I. 484). We can note the stringent asceticism in all of these postulations, the denial of pleasure (so infuriating to such a filmmaker as Pier Paolo Pasolini). In privileging the examination of truth, Locke stands back from "the entertainment and pleasantry of wit," the power of "metaphor and allusion," in which "beauty appears at first sight." Yet there is more to life than asceticism, more than reason, more than the purity of pure thought. Experience can also be a matter of first sight. And first sight can be mirthful, ecstatic, confounding, thrilling.

James is creditably swift to address the one-sided Apollonianism of "the Lockian school." Apollo's sober rationality, that strict withdrawal and fine discernment which, for Locke, helps prevent us from being "misled," ostensibly seeks a pathway by which we can improve ourselves. A more Dionysiac (and existentialist) view could lead to experience as celebration, dream, phantasm. Rilke evokes the withdrawal from Dionysianism in his "Archaic Torso of Apollo,"

> We cannot know his legendary head
> with eyes like ripening fruit. And yet his torso
> is still suffused with brilliance from inside
> like a lamp, in his gaze, now turned to low
> gleams in all its power. Otherwise
> the curved breast could not dazzle you so …

(a poem that flows forward like the erotic blood in one's veins). When I have an image, when I bring it into my possession, I can be doctrinaire, using my vision to ascend to some as yet undiscerned higher level of spiritual existence as, for his part somewhat pompously, does Osmond in Henry James's *The Portrait of a Lady*. But I can also, and with a rich profusion of worth, be dazzled, possess, retain, and develop, as a way to what Norman O. Brown, the Freudian/Christian/Classicist, sees as "unity":

> Is there a way out; an end to analysis; a cure; is there such a thing as health?
> To heal is to make whole, as in wholesome; to make one again; to unify or reunify: this is Eros in action. Eros is the instinct that makes for union, or unification, and Thanatos the death instinct, is the instinct that makes for separation, or division.

(80)

However it may be that through reaching out one chooses to come to terms with instinct, through Apollonian withdrawal or Dionysiac embrace, by the airy way that leads to division and separation or by the way of the fire, a relevant sense of beauty comes centrally into play, and it is beauty, beauty conceived according to any scheme of relevance, that attracts the feelingful or studious eye. Beauty can radiate inside, or erupt in expression, but one will make the choice to have it over and above what is not beautiful in one's understanding. So it is that when I rove through my memories of cinema, catching this moment or that as a kind of tableau, ethereal enlightenment is not my quest. The eye's banquet is. Like Hitchcock's Sebastian, I can rue, "I knew but I didn't see."

Hauntings

Haunted by a residue from pre-Christian Greek culture, John Keats envisions, but finally holds back from succumbing to, a world of raptures. "Sylvan historian," he sighs—

> who canst thus express
> A flowery tale more sweetly than our rhyme:
> What leaf-fring'd legend haunts about thy shape
> Of deities or mortals, or of both,
> In Tempe, or the dales of Arcady.

The very dales of Arcady, indeed, where the green of the grass is always incomparable and the trees only sigh in the low wind, and everywhere there is hope and lushness and promise and endlessness. Yet quickly he is summoned—by what power?—to the impenetrable and the mysteriously sacred, the world for access to which one must deposit one's hesitations on account:

> Heard melodies are sweet, but those unheard
> Are sweeter; therefore, ye soft pipes, play on;
> Not to the sensual ear, but, more endear'd,
> Pipe to the spirit ditties of no tone.

Is he imbued with fear, perhaps, at the thought of unreservedly inhabiting the zone of a leaf-fring'd legend, of making a home in Arcady? The Grecian urn brings back to him a world also invoked in visual art later on, filled with glades and forests, nymphs and gods, animals in harmony and the waters above the earthly firmament—yet he needs must search out something ineffable, too. He cannot hold a rhapsody about Arcady fulfillingly, and leave aside the (churchly) piping to the cogency of spirit.

Bernardo Bertolucci's *The Dreamers* straightforwardly addresses this problem through Matthew (Michael Pitt), a young American cinephile visiting Paris for the first time (in 1968)—essentially the filmmaker's stand-in. For Matthew, falling in love sparkles above all things social, religious, and political, so that at film's end, when the moral gavel comes down, he must stand bereft to witness the French boy and girl with whom he is utterly *bouleversé*, bourgeois children of two well-meaning Christian moralists, abandon him in their wake as the students' revolution begins in the streets. Politics is their holiness, after all. What he wants to do—love, make love, see film, devour film—is now only a passé children's game for presumably "grown-up" Théo (Louis Garrel) and his (somewhat obedient) sister Isabelle (Eva Green). Finally, in what moralists will consider a proper triumph of Truth over Experience, Matthew stands left alone in the streets, the tumult raging toward him charged with Principles and Salvation, and with the solitary tactile chant of Edith Piaf ringing in his head. He is incapable (blessedly) of abandoning the search for beauty and feeling that have led him here. We can see how he will go off one day soon to make films like the ones he loves to see, to make love, indeed, through film. Théo will become a Sénateur. Isabelle will probably marry one.

To Think the Thought of the Sight

One darkness still awaits, or is here already, in its inexact and overwhelming pools. I have been considering the image as a phenomenon of possession, my possession as I look. And now, taking one step back, I must consider the consideration I have been making; better, consider that all along I have been making one particular consideration. Here is Sartre on this riddle, on

> the famous problem of the characteristics of the true image… in every way it demands a negation; that is, at the very least a nihilating withdrawal of consciousness in relation to the image apprehended as subjective phenomenon, in order to posit it precisely as being only a subjective phenomenon.
>
> (*Being* 62)

If I "withdraw consciousness" to see where I stand as I posit in this way, I find the walls receding, the space around me painfully indeterminate, and images wavering as if entering and exiting a puddle of lambency. As I think about the film image as something I have whilst I am looking at it, in this very thinking I cannot be either looking at it or having it. What I am looking at in conceiving "looking at" is a kind of void, beset by gusts of urgency, even musical beats (heartbeats), and without either color or form except that a clarity I fervently hope has color begs to be first arrived at and then revealed. There is no longer a repository I can claim when I point to my claiming.

But when after this holiday I return to the picture, it glows immense before me, and I sense myself full of delicious longing again and, gasping with relief, coming to life.

for "Max" Sebald

7

Muse of Incoherence

Martin Balsam as Arbogast in Psycho *(Alfred Hitchcock, Shamley Productions, 1960)*. Digital frame enlargement.

1

A shining shibboleth in the dark toolkit of critical language is *coherence*, the resting and arresting idea that a work can be thought made up of parts, these parts discriminable and self-contained—T. S. Eliot's fragments shored against his ruins; and that a Utopian state can be achieved in which all of the parts can be "fused together," seen in one view, which is to say, interwoven and conjoined into a singularity: this is *coherence*. Sublime. Grounded. True. Alight.

Further, there lurks a moral imperative: that a work *ought to be coherent*, that coherence is a value in itself, of itself, for itself; that it requires no further rationale. There is a good and pleasing harmony when all of the pieces fit into a kind of jigsaw, a Jigsaw of Unity, out of which, when we scan with a keen eye, a single valid touching picture clearly emerges. Thus, to argue against narrative incoherence is commonplace.

Also commonplace is the argument about the coherence of action with setting, or of one performance with others, or of beginnings with endings and endings with middles. When a person or character speaks in such a way that one sentence doesn't seem linked to another, or in such a way that an assertion seems literally inappropriate (out of place), we might say (with a frown) she speaks "incoherently." We often get "incoherence" in scenes after a debauchery, a drug infusion, a serious accident and hospitalization, an amnesiac episode, a trauma. Trauma (Ger.: *Das Traum* = the dream) is often "incoherent." Yeats in "The Second Coming":

> Things fall apart; the centre cannot hold;
> Mere anarchy is loosed upon the world.
> The blood-dimmed tide is loosed, and everywhere
> The ceremony of innocence is lost.
> The best lack all conviction, while the worst
> Are full of passionate intensity.

Take a man who, stabbed in the head, falls down a flight of stairs in the middle of a film. For coherence it is ideal that he should have been searching for a missing person (say, a woman; even an attractive woman) who disappeared earlier; and that his own disappearance after death should provoke some other people (who don't know him at all well) to suspect that he wasn't genuine in his search. Their disappointment seems coherent with his sudden departure; his sudden departure coherent with his tumble down the stairs bleeding from the head. Another coherence apparently stands upon (A) the missing woman's not being part of his experience on the stairs, and also (B) her not being included in others' ruminations about this man. Not that there *is* coherence, here in what I point to or anywhere else, but that we think of coherence when we work through it. *Coherence* is a plan.[1]

Or, take that sweet little boy who discovers an alien in a shed behind his house one night. For coherence this little unearthly creature should come under horrible threat from vicious government thugs, and our darling, having befriended it (with, what else?, Reese's Pieces), should save the creature and be present when a magical spaceship brings him home. The boy who helps E.T. go home should be recognizably the same boy who found him in the shed.....

Films would purport to be coherent. Or if not, then artfully and intentionally incoherent in a teasing way (thus, invocations of coherence). If

---

[1]And in French the word *plan* means *shot*, as in filming.

a film is incoherent but not discernably in an artistic or intentful way—not in a way labeled "artistic" by the prevailing legitimated arbiters (the film critic of *The New York Times*; the scholars published in *Film Quarterly*)—it is usually taken to be amateur and unworthy of serious attention. What we attend to seriously is coherence and what it collects. Coherence: what makes the beginning of a sentence wind forward to an ending that "fits with" it. What makes the beginning and middle and end of a sentence, a poem, a film, a stage play, a speech … cling. *Cling* as at the very end of *Saboteur* (1942), when Norman Lloyd memorably shrieks (at the top of, and just before falling from, the Statue of Liberty), "I'll cling!"

Our lives, of course, do not in themselves have coherence. One could say coherence is alien. The moments of our lives do not cling.

Here today, gone tomorrow; there yesterday, here today; there yesterday, here today, somewhere else tomorrow. Memory can take us only so far in the quest to connect the present with the past, our present with our past. Our past is interrupted, invaded by so many books and chapters and paragraphs of other people's utterings; and by so many pictures; and by weather; and by events; and by pain; and by the alternately fading and glowing taste of pleasure. Memory can take us only so far. And to project a future coherent with our present means to take the very greatest care with every single step, such great care, indeed, that taking care takes over from stepping and we find ourselves paralyzed with choreographic challenges.

It would be easy to propose that it is because our lives are so incoherent that we yearn for coherence in art, that in its being coherent our art somehow models what life could ideally be, notwithstanding that it somehow fails. Yet the question is begged: if there is no coherence as we breathe, still, what generates a desire for coherence, of all possible hearths of desire? What would predispose anyone to seek not harbor, not shade, not illumination, not tranquility, not peace, not grace with the hands upon materials, not mystery, not the fruits of curiosity but … coherence? One must wonder if there can be imagined some value in coherence itself, a value somehow essential. Earth, Air, Fire, Water, Coherence.

2

To hold the proposition of coherence sacred as a tool is to empower oneself to find fault, since it is easy enough to show how virtually any thing "doesn't fit with" virtually any other thing; doesn't fit, contradicts, is merely tangential to, or simply doesn't belong in the same aesthetic universe with. Whatever might or might not belong in a universe; and quite as though one understands what a universe is, or what a tangent is, or what we really mean when we say "fit." Once one has the tool called "coherence" one can find things not only "incoherent" but, if the tool is pleasant in the hand, "regrettably incoherent." If Flaubert were alive still, "coherence" would find its way into his *Dictionnaire.* Or perhaps "incoherence" would: *incoherence*—to avoid at all costs in the face of authorities.

"Coherence" makes an appearance only when we fashion it.

3

Early in 1939, Vladimir Nabokov wrote "Father's Butterflies," intended as a second addendum to his novel *The Gift* (but not published there). The narrator Fyodor revels in the "fascinating, lifelike portrait" made available in his father's four-volume work, *The Butterflies and Moths of the Russian Empire,* published in 1912.[2] One is required, Fyodor writes, somehow to escape the hegemony of "idols or habits of thought that, having rooted themselves and developed more by the rules of secondary mechanics than initial inspiration, have nevertheless acquired legislative power. ... One must renounce habit":

> One must have one's thought assume an uncommon pose that might, *a priori,* appear as difficult to achieve as the unnatural arm-and-leg motions of a floating human are to a beginner (*tyro*) at a swimming school. But as soon as this special approach (*the knack of the thing*) is seized—and if the author has succeeded in rendering it, then it is thanks more to happy chance than happy predisposition—what is set forth below will immediately become clear, and will even become so obvious and coherent that the reader's mind will involuntarily race ahead, and reproach the author for excessive elaboration.
>
> (215–16; emphasis original)

What is set forth will become *so obvious and coherent* that the reader will race ahead. In short, the *coherence* betokens a pathway completely lacking in disturbing lacunae, hazardous pitfalls, obnoxious fences, slippery rails, whatever it could be that would hold up the beggar's urgent progress. The reader must move. The reader must race, glide on the ice of thought. So that, for instance, even such a divagation as thinking about the gliding reader and about the *coherence* that will shine upon her way (so smooth!), so helpful for moving on that ice, cannot seriously be thought of as incoherence, as it surely is. What is every step back to consider one's stepping back but a momentary injection of the incoherent into the bloodstream of the happy mover?

---

[2]In *The Gift,* we are told this title applies to the first four of six proposed volumes, and these came out 1912–16 (102).

To the thing that is coherent there will be of course a seamlessness; no staples or stitches to catch the fingers, no evident boundaries from the crotch to the sleeves.

Nature does not know coherence, this human invention, this conceit.

4

Two thinkers about Los Angeles (or Angel City, as Sam Shepherd had it in his play of that name, its mogul spinning in his sumptuous chair become, himself, cinema). Mike Davis, SoCal born, uses a scathing surgical eye:

> Although other American cities betray some of these tendencies—that is, Faustian economic restructuring, social porosity, elite anti-semitism, central place competitions, internationalization of class formation, extreme political fragmentation, and disfranchisement of the inner city—none (to borrow the city's official slogan) "brings it all together like Los Angeles." The most permanent boomtown in American history, Los Angeles has always been "the Great Gatsby of American cities." Through the ebb and flow of individual fortunes, the real city-making will of Los Angeles has been incarnated in a succession of power structures made coherent by common *accumulation strategies,* and distinguished by specific modes of insertion into the larger power structures of the Californian and national (today, international) economies.
>
> (104–5; emphasis original)

Davis can see how there are too many competing entrepreneurs angling for land and benefit on different scales, too many blazing visions of an Angeleno future (for the white), too many excuses for the eradication of history for the place to be singularly itself, to be its own self-declared Paradise, without a forcefully imposed *coherence,* and he notes the common accumulation strategies that bring together the immigrants from New York, the slummers from San Francisco, the old money and the new. Bring together under a banner for which even the Latinos can see themselves cheering, and also the long-inhabitant American-born Japanese, when they are not clipping other peoples' hedges in Bel Air. An organization based on what-we-want-to-have-ness and how-are-we-going-to-get-it-ness, who will we have to beat, how tall will we have to build our towers, how peaceably can we suction the water from the Owens Valley. Davis's is an image of Los Angeles as a makeshift coherence, a community no longer on the civic level—as, perhaps brittlely, in the 1920s—but rationalized, glued, safely mirrored in the computers of the transnationals.

A more poetic, if scathing sensibility is at work in Joan Didion, a Northern Californian descended to glory:

> What is striking about Los Angeles after a period away is how well it works. The famous freeways work, the supermarkets work (a visit, say, to the Pacific Palisades Gelson's, where the aisles are wide and the shelves full and checkout is fast and free of attitude, remains the zazen of grocery shopping), the beaches work. The 1984 Olympics were not supposed to work, but they did (daily warnings of gridlock and urban misery gave way, during the first week, to a county-wide block party, with pink and aquamarine flags fluttering over empty streets and parking spaces for once available even in Westwood); not only worked but turned a profit, of almost $223 million, about which there was no scandal.
>
> (149)

Didion cannily mentions Westwood and the Palisades, but not, at this juncture, Vernon, a neighborhood not at all her own in any sense. There was at the time of her writing, and remains now, in Paradise West, a certain *incoherence* of note, a "great local truth,"

> and the inchoate heart of the matter: this house [a new put-up for Aaron Spelling] was, in the end, that of a television producer, and people who make movies did not, on the average evening, have dinner with people who make television. People who make television had most of the money, but people who make movies still had most of the status, and believed themselves the keepers of the community's unspoken code, of the rules, say, about what constituted excess on the housing front. This was a distinction usually left tacit, but the fact of the [$45,000,000, 56,500 square-foot] Spelling house was making people say things out loud. "There are people in this town worth hundreds of millions of dollars," Richard Zanuck, one of the most successful motion picture producers in the business, once said to my husband, "and they can't get a table at Chasen's." This was a man whose father [Darryl F. Zanuck] had run a studio [Twentieth Century Fox] and who had himself run a studio, and his bewilderment was that of someone who had uncovered an anomaly in the wheeling of the stars.
>
> (157)

Chasen's, out of existence now but back then at Beverly Blvd. and N. Doheny Drive, was *the* "in" dining spot for the motion picture elite. The elite crust of that elite lived in Bel Air, with the merely elite out in the Palisades, while production types like designers tended to settle in the Valley somewhere. The television and music maharajahs were in Holmby Hills. These were none of them enclaves exactly, but zones to which only the fat wallet would buy access—the fat wallet now on the iPhones of the Ama-Flix moguls, who are building even bigger. Los Angeles's East Side areas like Watts would go unmentioned and unnoticed by Didion's West Side types, and this division by race, ethnicity, and class was Davis's recurrent focus. But what Didion picks up is that even in the manicured West there is a fragmentation of forces, and the movie people don't eat dinner with the television people. The television elite, of whom, when she wrote that essay, Spelling (1923–2006) was a leading figure as producer of *Beverly Hills, 90210, Dynasty, The Love Boat, The Streets of San Francisco, Charlie's Angels, Melrose Place,* and much more, built their empires largely after the 1960s and had, therefore, new money; while the movie people had been there since before the 1920s, had been in the houses later sold to the television people to tear down and rebuild. There is new New money now.

What a crossing of the class divide, then, was heralded by movie people going into television, not, like Jane Wyman or Doris Day or a legion others in their advancing old age but in the full flower of highly productive youth-scented middle age: Rock Hudson on *McMillan & Wife,* Fred MacMurray on *My Three Sons.* The crème de la crème did not put a toe into television except, perhaps, to do a guest slot on a late-night or variety show. Johnny Depp became a star example of the class bridge crossed the other way, having been a star of television before slipping over, with *Nightmare on Elm Street* (1984), into movies. After 2010, the platformers (Netflix, Amazon, Disney) brought a raft of high-end movie people into dramatic formats intended to be watched as television had long been watched: at home. Adam Driver, Leonardo DiCaprio, Viola Davis, Meryl Streep ....

All of this points to the essential incoherence of the Los Angeles scene, the sliding and the friction between unmatched parts. Los Angeles is natural in that way, and very human, incoherent as is all Nature and all Civilization, and nothing like the taut, tight, smartly cohering fantasies crackling in its fires.

5

Fashioning coherence is a practical matter. One first selects out, and carefully names, precise elements—a figure, a place, a node within a wave of activity. Then, through a process of recollection, reconstitution, recognition, and reservation one stitches the selections together with connectives that make sense at the time. *She did that, remember? And now look!, she's going to do this!* A recipe for readiness to "discover"—readiness because one has just made possible—a "through-line" that stretches in a curve guaranteed to be satisfying because it is familiar. The star system works this way, with faces celebrated because we have seen them before; the true celebration is for our own act of recognition, and for whatever is done to and by the star to aid their recognizability. The smaller the outburst—chit-chat is fabulous—the easier the recognition. In recognizing these folk, we make to "discover" a growing self in them every time, accreting upon the old, elevating and brightening the identity. Thus the star has, as seems, a *coherent* career, all the parts of which hang together in a "personality" or "biography" (that tend to be publicity constructions).

For *plot coherence,* take that fellow stabbed in the head on the staircase and tumbling backwards to his death in *Psycho* (1960). Abruptly at that instant, Arbogast's assiduous search for a girl gone missing earlier is aborted, and he himself vanishes, leaving others to wonder whether he'd always been nothing but disingenuous. So, even fashioning a terse account for you this way, reader, I already quite casually mention (1) a man; (2) a staircase; (3) a stabbing; (4) a head; (5) falling backward; (6) resultant mortality; (7) searching for a (8) girl, and so on. By choosing these items to select out—there is much I omit: say, the wood of the banister—what I am hoping to do is account for the scene of *his* presence on the stairs. One can have variations. If (3) he is stabbed in (4) the head and (6–5) dies after falling backward, we have a coherent cause-effect line. If (3) he is stabbed in (4) his head but this happens on (2) a staircase of all places, the man will surely (5) fall, and perhaps backwards, and will (6) die even more certainly. Imagine that this (1) man has been (7) searching for (8) a woman (any woman, if you like, but he is after a particular woman [whom he has never met]); already then a latent emotive field is invoked for interpretation: he is fatherly, he is paternalistic; he is curious like an adventurer, and so on. If soon later (9) it is presumed he is now no longer eager to find (8) her, this presumption must come from (10) someone onscreen, and this must reasonably be a someone who (11) doesn't know him well enough to believe he wouldn't cease his hunt unless he were dead. This (11) someone (or pair of someones) takes the trouble to presume his disinterest because a little earlier they presumed his interest; and also because there is no time now to muse, nor time to access evidence of any kind. And so on. Many such lines of attack are possible. What kind of shirt was he wearing?—note how I artfully avoid mentioning this, and so many other visibles available on the screen, available and lit and centralized, in order that items (1) through (11) can be teased out for pleasure. The man himself, his reason for being, his appearance, his voice, his eyes, his cautions, his apparent understandings and knowledge: just leave all that go, because whoever we might like to imagine him to be, he is going to be stabbed on the stairs, and that will be the end of that. Or those stairs: concrete slabs, marble sheets, wrought iron, wood? Six or seven or eight stairs or fifteen, sixteen, or seventeen stairs? Stairs in bright light, stairs in dim light? And so on. Or that he tumbles upon a Persian carpet of all possibilities. What kind of structure is it in which these stairs exist, an office building, a church, a house? Where is this, Budapest, Istanbul, Tel Aviv, Toronto, or "Fairvale"? And why do I leave all these details out?

And:

If the stairs are in or near Fairvale, what on earth is Fairvale, and how should it be thought significant (read, coherent) that a man might be stabbed there instead of somewhere else; or that of all eventualities in Fairvale he should submit to a stabbing rather than, say, a massage? Could he not have been stabbed in Phoenix, Arizona? Or Los Angeles? Or not at all? Could he have been stabbed but not mortally; crawled upstairs, peeped around, discovered nothing at all that would help him find (8) the girl? Yes, surely, *in another film,* but here when he is stabbed on the stairs, and necessarily so, there is so much to look at, to look past, to look for, to look through.

Plot coherence might tell us whether there is something about this man that requires, dramatically, that he die. But if die, by stabbing? Should the stabbing relate to any other stabbing? To any other use of any other knife? Is the whole moment not about a man but about a knife? *Cohere:* originally (*c.* 1595) "stick together." But everyone who has watched *Psycho* knows full well that the film is deliciously, deliriously, magically incoherent. The incoherence is all. Notice: this man Arbogast (Martin Balsam) appears out of nowhere, goes nowhere, and disappears into nowhere, all the while making a rather profound impression of being self-satisfied, curious, sly, polite, doubtful, confounded, porcine, sweaty, rude, suave, and much else. Nothing will come of nothing. And if it is nothing out of which nothing will come, what of that staircase then? What of that knife?

6

Here, in a primary lecture, is J. L. Austin:

> It was for too long the assumption of philosophers that the business of a "statement" can only be to "describe" some state of affairs, or to "state some fact," which it must do either truly or falsely. Grammarians, indeed, have regularly pointed out that not all "sentences" are (used in making) statements: there are, traditionally, besides (grammarians') statements, also questions and exclamations, and sentences expressing commands or wishes or concessions. And doubtless philosophers have not intended to deny this, despite some loose use of "sentence" for "statement." Doubtless, too, both grammarians and philosophers have been aware that it is by no means easy to distinguish even questions, commands, and so on from statements by means of the few and jejune grammatical marks available, such as word order, mood, and the like: though perhaps it has not been usual to dwell on the difficulties which this fact obviously raises. For how do we decide which is which?
>
> (1–2)

Yes, how to decide? How to figure the difference between, or to choose between:

- A: Asking the question, "How to decide?" and meaning by that, "through what process of thinking would we decide?" or "Who exactly should be the person or persons to decide?" The word "decide" would be a reference to a mental and vocal operation in actuality, but not that operation itself.
- B: Asking the question, "How to decide?" with a shrug of the shoulders, as though to say, "Life is full of fudgy little choices like this and none of us has the least clue how to pick."

The interesting intricacies of Austin's discrimination between what he calls "constative" and what he calls "performative" language entirely notwithstanding, he clearly sees them as possibilities that language offers in and of itself. Paul Goodman's *Speaking and Language: Defence of Poetry* in some ways goes even further (see 69–85):

> There is a difference between words as signs that help us to cope with their designates and words whose designation has been blurred, so they become detached from experience and we expend ourselves in the words. But it is the nature of speaking a language that these two cannot be clearly distinguished in actual speaking. We cannot use words to cope unless we believe in their meaning and assert it, and this belief depends on utterance, grammar, history, the existence of speakers and hearers.
>
> (85)

If one cannot easily decide which is which, language that states a case or language that by commanding an action is an action, how is one to find, in language at any rate, coherence?

The word "language" here should be taken as a generalizing noun, to rhyme with "sufferage" and "luggage." The act of doing the tonguing. It does not refer specifically to vocabulary, all the words you know how to recognize; or to lexicon, all the words you use. It is your *way* of wording, mouthing, tonguing, articulating, uttering, announcing, proclaiming.

John LeCarré: "Sentry towers, then a patrol boat bristling with guns, glide past him. Ours or theirs? It is immaterial. They are nobody's. They are part of the great impasse he is here to unblock" (67). Am I remaining coherent, quoting about the "great impasse" this way? We stretch for coherence, after all, and a person's reach will be insufficient. The indeterminateness of the object (guns) not belonging to that side (the pro-capitalist militia) or to this side (the revolutionary youth), or belonging to both, or belonging to either, or not quite belonging. How to find coherence on the canal? And the bullets will be flying.

The wholesale agony buried in Wittgenstein's proclamation "Wovon man nicht sprechen kann darüber muss man schweigen" (*Tractatus*)—"Of whatever we cannot speak about, we must be silent"—is that keeping the lips sealed, never contracting to utter a syllable, is deafeningly problematic when the world offers so many provocations. Like film, life flows on from situation to situation—situation, not room—and what we say, how we say, varies with the situation. We are impertinent, accusatory, sanctimonious, pompous, ridiculous, noble, estimable, soft, soothing with language, and imprecatory, and salutative, and on and on. What could it mean exactly, what we are saying, what she is saying, and how coherent could all this be?

7

Wittgenstein is interrogating solipsism. "That the world is *my* world," he writes,

> shows itself in the fact that the limits of the language (*the* language which I understand) mean the limits of *my* world.
> The world and life are one.
> I am my world. (The microcosm.)
>
> (*Tractatus* 5.62; 5.621; 5.63)

When I seize the film, when I seize what of the film comes to my possession at the edge of the screen, I need not wish that my seizures should form a coherence (rather than, say, mingling with seizures from elsewhere). Speaking personally, I typically seize from a film not while I am watching, there is too much progression, but (as Wordsworth commanded) in tranquility, while I recollect what I recollect, and while I discover emotion (*my* emotion). This is what I think of as the residue or trail or wake of the film.

A peculiar highway moment: Marion has slept overnight in exhaustion. She awakens to find a highway patrolman staring through the driver's window at her. (Sunglasses, no expression on the face, official cap.) Up so very close, he fills the entire window, and the entire window fills the entire screen. In short, authority (Mort Mills) fills the entire screen. (This was in 1960, on a screen 1.37 times wider than it was high. The black-and-white negative was processed and printed at the Technicolor lab, and this is one good reason why the blacks are so saturated and the contrast so profound.) The policeman's head would have been, in fact, some fifteen or so feet high.

And his sunglasses, not only functional and hip but also dark, impressive as blockers, not enablers. Here was a new Polyphemus, gigantic, looming as though in preparation. What will, what can, he do? I do not evacuate this portrait image from my library, and looking back now, sixty years on, I realize that at this moment I've forgotten Marion entirely, do not at all care what her reaction is, and when Hitchcock gives me to see her startled reaction it's a trifle. I have laid aside that she is fleeing Phoenix with stolen money, although the coherence of her guilt and the staring policeman is surely salient. He exists for me in another dimension, a dimension not only cinematic (I am seeing this on a film screen in a film theater) but also meta-cinematic because the image of him is so very like the cinematic image more broadly: it looms, is gigantic, presents a world of giants at which I can only marvel in some incoherent combination of trepidation and love. As he gawks at her, she surely feels his touch, his trespass on her territory (Kong with Ann Darrow); although it is also true that she is trespassing on the state's territory by sleeping on the road.

One thing centers Arbogast's final image for me, resists erasure, and that is the look of surprise in his eyes as, just at the cusp of falling backward, he catches a final sight we are not to have. As a brother viewer, he transcends us, but death is the punishment.

8

Think of how our memories of film cluster. The policeman in *Psycho* with his shades. Marilyn Monroe in *How to Marry a Millionaire* (1953), blind as a bat without her glasses and walking headlong into a wall. The thick eyeglasses the Mother Superior wears, because she cannot see the world so clearly, in *Viridiana* (1965). Julius Kelp's owlish glasses in *The Nutty Professor* (1963). Miriam Haines's eyeglasses and Barbara Morton's in *Strangers on a Train* (1951). An eyeglass cluster. Is it a form of coherence or a celebration of incoherence for celebration's own sake?

One can never collect the world fully enough. Every coherence harbors a defect, something that shouldn't be there, but demands to be; something that should be here, but isn't. The sunglasses in *They Live* (1988), that change the world?

9

Again to sad Arbogast. (We can keep returning; he will always be there.) He has materialized at Sam's hardware store in Fairvale—"Let's talk about Marion ... "—because, in his words, he tailed Lila there. Lila, who has been in Tucson all weekend, having discovered that Marion her sister is missing, and who presumably also knows about the mysterious and wonderful Sam who owns a hardware store in Fairvale. At least in Lila's thoughts at the moment (we presume), Marion is the sort of person who, were she to pick up and leave town, would have only one place to go. Thus, for Lila, Marion Missing = Marion in or heading to Fairvale and Marion heading to Fairvale = heading to Sam.

But when Arbogast asks where Marion is, Lila says, "I don't know." This is somewhat complicated. In the man's demeanor is certainly something to hint at the identity he claims, "Private Investigator," but about Lila we know nothing at all beyond the way she currently appears, demure, quiet, proper, and reserved. Thus we cannot reasonably expect that her immediate reply to Arbogast is designed to give her sister protection: that she *does* know, but isn't saying. *We do know, however,* and *know that Lila really does not know*; therefore, this smartie detective who knows enough to "tail" Lila is a man who does *not* know enough to see a dead end. (Not being present to learn is one way of not knowing.) While Arbogast survives the moment, he is never going to be certain what to think of Lila.

Effectively, Arbogast is coming out of nowhere, and in entering this way (diegetically and extra-diegetically) he attests to the power of cinematic narrative, where a character "exists," is figured, directly upon "appearance." As he comes through the door and "makes an appearance" he is born. Then, quickly, his purpose. Let us note that there are no other characters in this film—and very few in Hitchcock's work altogether—who appear so perfunctorily, who exist by way of self-announcement, and who hang in the air like ciphers. Lila, too, hangs like a cipher of sorts .....

Our Arbogast is here on a hunt—and, having seen the film thus far we can coherently understand why he needs to be hunting—but he is terminated before finding his prey. His presence occasions something like a passing shot of (a reference to) a hunter searching, but that's really it. Let us ask two key questions about this man:

- A: What does this hunter contribute to the film *coherently,* simply by virtue of being what he is?
- B: What can be the meaning or value of a hunt without a catch?

Arbogast's contribution to the film (as story) is plain and simple enough. He presents direct evidence that our cherished Marion, taken in her prime, seized in pristine innocence (against all the randy urgings of her boyfriend), did not leave the scene without a trace, evoking no memory, causing no anxiety in others. A trace: even her name wafting in the air. Lila, as we can see, as we have seen just before the detective entered, is anxious already, and mystified (mystery brings anxiety). Sam is now somewhat anxious, too (and for his own reasons, of course). And it is now quite plain that Lila (or Lila and Sam together) did not hire Arbogast, that in fact until this moment, when, appearing, he tells Lila he has been tailing her sister, this man was unknown and unimagined. It was unimagined that he would be searching for Marion. And it was unimagined that *anybody at all* would be searching for Marion, as though a *search* was called for. All of this must be aggravating Lila. But Lila shows almost no emotion, here or later. Calm and tranquil, yes, but also, perhaps locked in ….?

As a plot device, Arbogast leads onward from the point where Marion was cut off. And if we are to see an extension such as this, we must wonder what the line of continuity is that stretches through Marion's actions, leaps away at her death, and is picked up by Arbogast. Obvious is that soon that very line will be picked up after yet another jump by Lila and Sam working as a team. One continuing, yet broken line or arc of movement. Yet two things about this "line": where can we say it begins and in what context?; and why would we lean toward the conclusion that really it is a continuing line rather than a group of discontinuous promises leading to abysm? (What kind of *statement* is this line?) Given the imagery onscreen, not only the faces but also the territory, an abysm of promises is a very reasonable supposition. Perhaps the "line" began in a rainstorm, sent by Divinity. Perhaps that.

Arbogast and his search, at any rate, afford us belief that if Marion died in vain her death is not exactly a secret (and not exactly *not* a secret), and we can hold our belief in her as a figure as long as Arbogast is alive to search. When he dies, we must abandon that belief. And then when the psychiatrist gives the police some sage advice, we can struggle to find the wick of Marion, and relight the candle of belief that went out. Believe > don't believe > believe > don't believe > perhaps believe …..

The story could continue without Arbogast (although it would need some additional minutes of screenwriting), and so the Arbogast sequence is something of an incoherence. The link to what came before is really spurious and slight: he found a sister, he tailed her. A link to what comes later is entirely non-existent.

As to Arbogast's hunt yielding him no catch, we can find some stimulating analogy to film as a form. At each hunting moment he "catches" only the next moment, only the need and energy to keep going. The absence of a culminating catch makes it possible and necessary for him to act through an unfolding, just such an unfolding as film more generally presents. Nothing we see (as hunters seeking a catch) gives itself over fully, but everything acts as a promise of a catch tomorrow. "Jam is not jam unless it is a case of jam to-morrow and never jam to-day. Thus by pushing his jam always forward into the future, he strives to secure for his act of boiling it an immortality" (Keynes 370, qtd. in Brown 108).

10

In cinema's edited form, consisting almost always of a filmic join (or cut), some B unpredictable from the point of view of a preceding A happens more or less sharply onscreen. The A > B transition is to be taken as at once logical and improbable: logical because the viewer can be presumed to own already, or easily find, a rationale for the movement, a logic; but improbable, since the movement toward B is accomplished in accord with a spontaneous will (of the camera, of the filmmaker—joined by the willingness of the viewer) no matter the rationality. Unlike text, a piece of film presents not only a constative averral—"This is a fingerprint pad, on which a finger will be pressed down"—but also, simultaneously, a performative angle of view—"The finger entering the shot from off- suggests, thus indicates, the presence of the pad in advance of its use; the fact that a technology pre-exists a usage." In text: "The finger came down on the fingerprint pad." Again, "finger" and "pad" and "came down" as constative: subject-verb-object. Whereas one could say, "The finger came down on the fingerprint pad!" with scorn, as though the fingerprinting was an outrage. But in the constative announcement "finger" and "pad" are alike in the same line of text, margined by punctuation; "finger" implies "pad" and "pad" retroactively implies "finger": in film there is only the unspooling, and the mind's eye cannot reach forward or, faithfully, back, and there are no commas.

11

Arbogast, a final time.

He stands at the check-in counter of the Bates Motel chatting, oh, not so casually, with Norman, who isn't relaxed under the best of circumstances. The questions about Marie Samuels (as Marion called herself)—where she sat, what she did; when she checked in, when she arrived; who arrived with her; whom she called; did he spend the night with her, how did she pay: cash or check????: all too much for him, he's a nervous boy. Sweet, but also nervous. And he finally says, or blurts (it's sometimes hard to tell the difference with him: say > blurt, blurt > say), "I'm sorry, I have work to do, Mr … if you don't mind … "

Arbogast, wordsmith: "I do mind. If it don't jell, it ain't aspic! (*Smiling*) This ain't jelling."

Yes yes, a gourmand.

Norman served Marie Samuels a chicken sandwich, and the walls of his little parlor are lined with stuffed birds, and such birds can be roasted and then served cold, coated with aspic. Was the chicken in the sandwich coated with aspic? Aspic will keep the air out. And taste fine. And give a lascivious sheen.

He's standing there on one side of the counter with Norman on the other side of the counter and he's talking to Norman about aspic.

This is before he falls down the stairs backward with a stab wound in his head.

This is before the part I wrote about before, before the before, and then soon after that, before he will try to climb some stairs and get stabbed and fall down dead. Then if we love this film, and surely we do, or at least surely we will say we do, we will watch it another time, second sight, and presto, there will be Arbogast alive, alive after he was dead, and he will talk about aspic again, and then fall. The more we watch this over and over the more he comes to life. It is as though, with Arbogast, beyond his dying, his screen life simply goes on and on, endures forever, as though in aspic. This is one of the marvelous aspects of the film experience, that we move, if awkwardly, forward and backward at the same time. That we find the future in the past. As to Norman and the Motel and the girl who is missing and Arbogast's whole claim to fame: that's all not jellin'. There isn't any aspic here. This is all raw.

And our detective, it's so clear, would prefer aspic.

Let's dig and dig for the coherence. He's come out of nowhere, tailing the (unkenning) Lila after her sister, whose name he knows to be Marion even when he discovers that she has registered at the Motel as Marie Samuels. He's come out of nowhere, put up to this by whom? The realtor Lowery? The police? Hardly the police. He's looking for the missing Marion and he finds a hardware store, and he quizzes locals, and he probes a staircase and dies. And that's that, no aspic. No aspic, that is, no polish, no grace, no gleam, no preservation. And of course, now that we're thinking of aspic we can see that nobody else in this film has aspic either, but—

But why are we thinking of aspic?

Arbogast can easily say, "Something's not coming together here."

But he doesn't say that, he says "If it don't jell it ain't aspic ... and it's not jellin'." If this is to tell us he thinks in food metaphors, should we be looking at the various scenes in this film in terms of eating, making food well-cooked (Lévi-Strauss: "civilized") and gleaming? Or should we think—much more probable, it seems to me—he's just a man who had a side thought and wove it arbitrarily into the moment. Only a saying he uses all the time in his life, the life that ends here but that otherwise has nothing whatever to do with our concerns. It's all so poetically incoherent that he should talk this way. And incoherent that he should die so abruptly. And devastatingly incoherent that we should come back for a second taste and find him alive, still asking questions.

Still trying to put together into a single whole, a *coherence,* the entirely incoherent little fragments in this detective's hands (and without aspic). Just trying to assemble a unity. Just trying. Just doggedly trying. Just being a dog on a scent. Or like a dog but not a dog, because a dog wouldn't be assembling the pieces for coherence, a dog would be satisfied with whatever piece he could gnaw on for the moment, and wouldn't need aspic, either.

for Joan Didion

8

Speak, Anima

From Life of Pi *(Ang Lee, Fox 2000, 2012). Tiger effect by David Conley. Digital frame enlargement.*

Inert

These figurations I see and follow onscreen, the boy in the boat with his tiger, these entities that look so very much like life … such fidelity … are not the ones they resemble; those ones are beneath and behind them. These are no more living creatures than the sea that bobs around is the sea. They look live only if I take the precaution of not looking carefully.

Better still, these pictures of people show what looks like people pictured. Kurt Vonnegut Jr.'s Fred Rosewater ogles a nudie magazine with Harry the fisherman, who is scowling at a picture of a French girl in a bikini:

Fred, understanding that he seemed a bleak, sexless person to Harry, tried to prove that Harry had him wrong. He nudged Harry, man-to-man. "Like that, Harry?" he asked.
"Like what?"
"The girl there."
"That's not a girl. That's a piece of paper."
"Looks like a girl to *me*." Fred Rosewater leered.
"Then you're easily fooled," said Harry. "It's done with ink on a piece of paper. That girl isn't lying there on the counter. She's thousands of miles away, doesn't even know we're alive. If this was a real girl, all I'd have to do for a living would be to stay home and cut out pictures of big fish."

(109)

Looking at the screen and noting the figures moving there, I can conclude that as pictured "people" or "pictures of people" they have a certain objective reality, characters as objects, props as objects, scenes filled with objects that define their space. As objects they surrender all agency.

These figures I see are made, and surely one could generate a whole figuration, all its expressions and moves, all its hesitations temporalized and urges gestured. So long as it is only by virtue of gesture, placement, motion, and pose that every feeling, every nuance of personality, every spirit makes itself visible to us who watch—well, these things can be drawn. As I write, we are still in the early days of computer drawing (we call it "CGI": computer-generated imagery, as though the computer literally *generates,* as though it *gives birth to* images) and all the pictures that computers make—or ornament—look very much like fabrications from a smart machine: amazing figurations, but also amazing fabrications of figuration. One looks and rather than seeing, one is astonished to see. Do we still hold something aside for special access, for the unique pleasure of recognizing a human face? For hi-def CGI images have remarkable detail, by which I mean, the kind of detail that deserves a remark, because it subtends a view from nearby with a "nearby" that is as near as one can get without penetrating the atoms of things. Perhaps even too nearby. Far nearer by than anybody would ever come for any reason, anywhere, with anybody.[1]

Given that at death a person loses all agency, all will, all sensitivity, all awareness, and becomes, now fully gravitational, inert, a thing in the world (a thing like the child's white ball that bounces down the street in *The Third Man* [1949]), we can see how all figures have endured a "death," are inert entities, with no agency of their own, no self to which we could attribute life. All of active screened "life" is brought to scripted characters in performers'

---

[1] This is an appropriate moment for me to express deep gratitude to Martin Gero, who many years ago, in its infancy, cast me in a hi-def movie and allowed me to see onscreen the amazing results.

playing them out as figures, but when that playing has been effected, when the movie or the stage play is over and the actor has schlepped his activating powers home to bed, where is the figure then ... and where the character? Well, the character still exists, the script on the bookshelf. And in the performer's working memory, the space into which she reaches astutely for fetching it to inhabit again: at tomorrow's matinee; or at 7:30 a.m. being made up for soundstage 26. (A fascinating exception: in confidence games, a character comes to life as a figure, but very often only once [See Goffman, "Cooling"].)

In more than one way an inanimate character can be reborn after a hiatus. Another, perhaps quite different performer can come and take up the mantle—this happens not infrequently, and not only onstage.[2] With a film, we can go back tomorrow and watch again, and there!—the character dead as ever because without agency and self, yet fleshed out and thriving because of the actor's repeat presence. The actor eternally present. James Stewart's mother, he wrote, would see all three showings of every movie he made for three running days: "She never missed a showing."[3]

These pictures, these figures pictured, that I return to watch again and again; we all return for them: the favorite film, the favorite scene, the favorite twitch of the shoulder while taking the shirt off. As we watch, some spirit of conviviality is continually wanting that the appearance of life should be given back to these lifeless things, that the characters be animated. (Watching a character do something onscreen is so much more galvanizing than hearing somebody recount what that character did.) It is for us, and only us, that characters are animated, but the fact that they have been animated is not, apparently, enough. We desire that they be animated *again*.

And animated again by cinema itself. All those tiny convivial tics: Jezebel's eyes turning to the side a little when she has just said, "Oh Buck—I wouldn't have some Silly think what *I* said be the cause of anything"; or when a character pauses in a doorway (Buddy Love) and looks around before taking a puff—so real, so breathful, so *living*, yet also so infused by the editor, who has chosen to leave a little more tail in a shot or to start with a little more head.

Shame

As in Plato's cave (doesn't every viewer think she remembers it?), yet in a cavern that is much larger, methinks, the projections race before the eyes,

---

[2] In five Broadway runs of *Gypsy*, Rose was played by Ethel Merman (702 times), Angela Lansbury (120 times), Tyne Daly (582 times), Bernadette Peters (451 times), and Patti LuPone (332 times). See also Pomerance, "Dumbledore."
[3] And in Cecil B. DeMille's *The Greatest Show on Earth* (1952) there is a very touching moment during the circus parade when Buttons the Clown (James Stewart) finds an elderly woman in the audience and comes with his puppy to visit: it's Mom, and she can see him once a year.

and since there are many folk huddled to watch, the projections befall all of us. Jung interprets one dream this way: "The dreamer discovers that he is keeping the light from those who stand *behind* him, namely the unconscious components of his personality. We have no eyes behind us; consequently 'behind' is the region of the unseen, the unconscious" (122, emphasis original). But with cinema we do have eyes behind us, if not really in a theater then watching the same download and readying to text a reaction. We do have eyes behind us, and so the audience as an Other becomes our "unconscious." Are we a little bit guilty in seeing, because we know that every vision we seize is being held back from the "person behind our head," who is seeing only in fragments because their line of sight is blocked by our ecstasy? That is: are we a little ashamed of the ecstasy?

Shame defends against the Jungian *anima,* that personal and idiosyncratic unconscious spring. From our unconscious we can be thought to derive the impetus and energy for animating the figures we're watching, for exhaling life into them. They are living out our unconscious—our broadly unconscious—lives.

This, at least, is one way to look at it.

In another view, those figures on the screen, already and always dead: we are making them come to life as we have come to life; we are giving them to share our living. How, after all, *as far as we can know of ourselves,* did we come to life? Are all those stories of maternity and paternity to be taken as accurate because such things are so very widely circulated? How is it that our eyes opened, and how do they open each morning, even now?

> What burning cities taught her and the death of love taught me—that we are very dangerous! And that, that's why I wake each morning like a boy—even now, even now!—I swear to you, I could love the world again!… Is the knowing all? To know, and even happily, that we meet unblessed; not in some garden of wax fruit and painted trees, that lie of Eden, but after, after the Fall, after many, many deaths. (Miller 79)

We make these creatures our siblings—

> "You! hypocrite lecteur!—mon semblable,—mon frère!"
> (Eliot, "The Waste Land")

—and it may be that largely because of this impetus to share life, which we discovered somewhere somehow and now embed in the waiting and vacuous figure, in the figure as envelope, … that because of our desire to give over a personality we are moved to come back again for more; more sight; more giving. Make, step back to look, continue making. We have not finished building the tower. Kafka:

> If it had been possible to build the Tower of Babel without ascending it, the work would have been permitted. ("Tower")

As we are insatiable about seeing ourselves, coming to know ourselves, the figure is a very helpful tool, being always available tomorrow again to go higher, brighter, nearer.

Replacement

As screen figures travel into the world of computer generation, the conundrum arises of replacing live actors with CGI constructions, a process that would allow the very literal resurrection of deceased greats of the past in brand new characterizations (scriptings) but, to strike a moral note, at the same time render unemployed a very large number of committed and hardworking professionals. André Bazin has pointed to the screen image as already a resurrection ("Ontology"), but this current development would be a resurrection of resurrections. Beyond morality, however (and the film business does persist in positing travel beyond morality), the issue is technical: how faithfully can a rendition be done? Note, the aim is not to find approval with those of us who have met the actual people being "generated," but to find approval in the eyes of a new "viewer *mavin*" type, quite accustomed to looking at CGI and equally accustomed to finding telltale faults with it, or *not* finding: in *Life of Pi* (2012), say, David Conley's brilliant CGI-animation of the tiger, marveled at as high-tech and visually unique albeit it was made through the use of an actual tiger alive and posed in another location. By wondrous contrast, the tiger that Joan Allen fondles in *Manhunter* (1986) was a real one, real in life and real in the place and time of the filming. Not only the physical "look" of the form must be created; but also a (for us) stirring urge for motion, responsiveness to the environment and to other figures, all of which, at least so far, are best screened through the use of an actual (living) model who would wish to move and who responds to her world. Pixels persist in not being cells.

Memory of Form

With computer memories growing in size (thus power) all the time, hyperanimation becomes a real possibility: a world presented in, say, 5K which displays surface features so picayune that no human eye behaving naturally would pick them up in everyday life. The screen world is then an "improvement" on everyday eyesight, or can through a form of education come to be thought as such. Improvement, *as* improvement, is discernible as the gap between the quality of our vision of a screen figure and the quality of what we ordinarily see. Hyperanimation succeeds when audiences learn to value it for itself as a kind of pleasure offered only in cinema. We feel uncannily near, uncannily familiar, even involved in relation not only to the subject matter but also to the mode of production and the producing action itself. Not the ape, or apeness, but the CGI'ed ape and its CGI-ness. If we do not learn to value seeing in this "special" way, either watching cinema or anywhere doing anything, our alternative is to learn and be content with the pleasure of *hypoanimations*, visions accessible in an age of CGI yet rendered less effectively than CGI would render. Can the viewer who was excited in *Manhunter* and then staggered by *Life of Pi* possibly watch the tiger disintegration in *Forbidden Planet* (1956), achieved in part through matting, and think it wonderful? There is no doubt that it is wonderful, or open to being understood as wonderful, but what transformations of self, of knowledge, of expectation, of hunger, and of satisfaction must take place before, accustomed to hyperanimation, one can find it wonderful fully knowing its relatively primitive quality as an image transformation?

Hyperanimation can appeal by predicting a convention of sight to come, a kind of optical utopia. We could think of it as bacterial vision, in that being brought closer and closer to surfaces we approximate the environment of microstructures. Microstructures become the components of, begin to define, a newly proximal space. Thus the burgeoning of the new detective and espionage genres, or the meticulously enacted social-class melodrama where focus flies to the antimacassar or the signet ring: the tiniest of details giving away the greatest secrets. Already now in detective dramas, with the figure's cell phone held up close to the cheek we hear what's on the other end of the line while simultaneously hearing our listener breathe. Forensic narration.

Animalization

Let us think of "performative animation," the actor's making a character real in a situation by using a visible mechanical system for augmentation because in the circumstance the body alone is not enough. An expressive mechanism can be a replacement the mechanics of which stand in for the actor's labor, as we see with Griffin Dunne's morphing body in *An American Werewolf in London* (1981); Eddie Redmayne with a speech simulator in *The Theory of Everything* (2014); Andrew Garfield with an iron lung in *Breathe* (2017). Perhaps less thrilling to witness or learn about in a machine age are non-mechanical acting assists—Derek Jacobi working with a stone in his shoe to produce Claudius's limp in *I, Claudius* (1976); Tom Hanks's make-up and body padding in *Elvis* (2022). Performative animation almost always passes undetected if it lures the sympathy of the viewer, or if, as with *Theory of Everything*, it is expressly intended to be our focus of concern. Part of the cinematographic/design challenge with dramatic animating mechanisms is to set the scene in such a way that the mechanism can be sufficiently present without compromising the intended vision or, indeed, the star close-up. Mechanical elaborations can overtake the scene. Ridley Scott's *Alien* (1979) is a case in point, whereas in *Creature from the Black Lagoon* (1954) the creature is always seen in a perspectivizing context.

Sometimes a living non-human creature is shown speaking onscreen, a creature with whom, in everyday life, we associate sound but not language. Consider the difference between the aliens in *Arrival* (2016), striving to communicate but forcing the earthlings who are the film's central characters to struggle out of their language-style and into another; and *E.T.* (1982) learning from Elliott how to use English words like "Ouch." In fantasy film, examples teem. *Planet of the Apes* (1968) and its numerous sequels in film and television depend for their story logic on simian creatures (basically of three ethnicities) conversing intelligibly—even eruditely—in English. In these shows, the apes are played by human actors in quite visible make-up, so that the speech seems to emerge from beneath the character. In *Rise of the Planet of the Apes* (2011) and later films in that group, Andy Serkis postdubs the vocalizations of what amounts to a full-fledged CGI animation of an ape. But in all these cases, we are seeing apes, whose non-human vocalizations we already know from off the screen, now speaking our language. For contrast compare the squeals of Cheetah (the chimpanzee) in *Tarzan the Ape Man* (1932). What can be found in the *Planet* shows are "animalizations," widely in use from television's *Mr. Ed* (1958) with a talking horse, or film's *Francis Covers the Big Town* (1953) with a mule, or *Doctor Dolittle* (1998) where animals socialize with Eddie Murphy.[4] Such animalizations can be mocked, with "performances" of a "creature" that looks very much—but only very much—like an animal lent a voice: the Cowardly Lion in *The Wizard of Oz* (1939) or any of the Disney, Lantz, Freleng, and Warner Bros. cartoons with talking bunnies, Tasmanian devils, roosters, crows, and friends. In animalization, the "talker" or "gesturer" definitively looks like an animal that would normally be expected to make some kind of sound *but not words*.

Also screened are "figural fantasies," in which figuration is accorded, by way of voice, gesture, and motive to a *thing* we are to imagine has "come alive." The quality of "life" is always understood by the viewer as an introjection or an add-on to what never escapes attention as a plain object. By virtue of the personality imported via dubbing, the thing—teapot, framed canvas, Venus flytrap, stone wall—can seem as feelingful as anyone in the audience, a sibling under the skin, but in accepting such figuration the audience must come into the belief, pantheistic in its way, that (a) things can be alive in their thingness; (b) if they were alive they would be alive in

---

[4] After having done so by implication only in 1967 with Rex Harrison, whose gestural responses are meant to indicate what a visible but unanimalized animal has "just said."

a human way, that is, alive as we are alive seeing them; (c) this particular thing could be alive now, for special (dramatized) reasons; and (d) if it were indeed alive this thing would show life exactly as we are being shown. Take trees, for example, lifted out of Germanic, Celtic, and Druidic mythologies and given active purpose, as in the celebrated apple tree in the forest in *The Wizard of Oz* that wants its apple back from Dorothy, who picked it. Cartoon animation is full of speaking tractors, houses, and the like, in speaking mode pure creatures of the imagination.[5] Often in cases of actor voice dubbing the voicer is well-known and, we may well think, "suits" the character: when Sean Connery is Draco the Dragon (*DragonHeart* [1996]) we can recognize how in other performances he is somewhat dragonish, this making Draco Connerian. We will conjure resonances like this notwithstanding that we have no experience of the actor's voice outside movies nor of dragons outside our dreams.

Deaths

It happens sometimes that a character will be scripted to be dead. A body found on the floor, a creature expiring in a bed, someone dropping down from a gunshot. As the shot of the dead body involves an actor playing dead,[6] that is, as *play* is at the center of screen "death," in some ways the actor behaves exactly as he or she would while *playing* anything else. The animus, which in this case would be understood as *the absence of animus,* is breathed into the figure—usually, of course, holding the breath. Often, for dramatic purposes if not for moral ones, the "living" dignity of the figural person is retained: put on display, yet, in the story, without life.

An actual corpse centering a shot being typically out of the question, dramatized "death" is produced through a simple gestural change on the motile face coupled with some carefully depicted, perhaps elaborate body transformations, an early stunning case being Nately (Art Garfunkel) in *Catch-22* (1970), with a belly torn open and spilling entrails. In battlefield scenarios designers, make-up artists, and cinematographers will collaborate to effect *variable morbidity*—multiple corpses *all somehow different,* this a dramatic conceit not a reflection of real-world conditions. The "wound," as conceived and achieved by make-up experts working with costumers, acts to rationalize the transformation of "death," to discriminate the figure

---

[5] Note how in *Snow White and the Seven Dwarfs* (1937) the mirror itself does not speak to the evil queen; a face appears to do the talking, and we must wonder who, if not the queen herself, is appearing in this mirror.
[6] Not always an actor who is healthy, since a "death" scene may require little gross physical effort.

from one who is asleep. For the bodily sign some careful articulation of circumstance can be substituted: the portrayal of the gas chamber, gallows, electric chair, or injection gurney; or the complex arrangement of machines, colored gowns and napkins, tools, and light we associate with operating theaters. The death of Kane (John Hurt) in *Alien* (1979) is a kind of "wounding surgery" showing a substitute operating-room situation and a body opening that explains the figure "perishing."

If we look carefully at film routines involving death, we find that the now-dead figure bears a strange and evocative relationship of appearance with (a) living figures all around and (b) itself, before death. One is asked to see a transformation in progress, from being to non-being, yet maintaining the form. Thus, we can trace back from the corpse to the expressive being who used the same hands. Early in the morning of October 17, 1849, the composer and pianist Frédéric Chopin died, and the same morning a cast was made of his hand, his now-dead hand, as though even in death that hand clung to the living, active version of itself, and as though it was the hand of the selfsame Chopin that played the piano. Simply to get a cast of the famous hand as a believable simulacrum, there would have been no need to act so speedily as to preserve from extinction the fire of Chopin's life in that hand. Nor did the passion to hold that hand, even as cast, supercede the mythical supposition that it was Chopin's *hands* that played the piano, not Chopin.

In *The Cranes Are Flying* (1957), the hero Boris (Aleksey Batalov) perishes in war. His body falls backward to the ground, its open eyes staring upward through the treetops at the brilliant sky. To animate the moment, the actor opens himself to the presence of the camera looking down upon him. But in the flicker of an instant just before life is extinct, we leap inside Boris and look up at the sky, too. Now Batalov has disappeared, the camera has replaced him.

for Paul Goodman

9

Rendezvous

Elizabeth Taylor as Martha in Who's Afraid of Virginia Woolf? *(Mike Nichols, Warner Bros., 1966). Digital frame enlargement.*

"The other can be evident to me," writes Maurice Merleau-Ponty, "because I am not transparent for myself" (410). Surely, when I am already with another person, so that a camera or third party watching us would aver that we two were "together," there are always presentiments. I sense a flow of warmth coming my way from this other, a radiance; and I receive and interpret language signals that seem easy enough to grasp and accept; and I notice a clothed body apparently healthy or not; and if that person is holding props I decode what these are, what they can be used for, what they are being used for now. All of this adds up to a kind of partial understanding. But I am also sharply aware that our encounter is delimited, that I am getting only a part of something much more amorphous and mysterious. Only some arguments, only some attitudes, only some comments, only some restricted facade presented to me. I can suppose that someone else would get another view. This tentativeness of view, this partial construction is with me in virtually every case, to some degree: a keen sensitivity to being separated, to seeing things a little askew comparatively. I sense: *this is only part of the picture*. And the sensitivity is keen, even prodding. If I can somehow reduce this sensitivity, or my awareness of it, I can be *in a rendezvous*. No rendezvous is as full as one could imagine it to be.

The bright illumination of the other is always bordered by an exquisite darkness in which nothing is apparent.

In cinematic depictions of human relations, this tentativeness and partiality are not part of what can be rendered, at least, not conventionally rendered through a process used to make images with a good exposure density and with fulsome framing, and with the pressing need of the story pushing onward. The film stock could clearly be way under- or overexposed, leaving the figure very hard to make out, and although this is what makes the conclusion of Hitchcock's *Vertigo* (1958) so overwhelming, it's not often done. What can in fact be rendered onscreen, and what is habitually rendered, is hidden motive, retention of a secret, duplicity—these renderings done by way of superficial clueing: specific pointers to what is specifically not there to be seen. While such "secrecies" can be thought to represent a dark area unfathomed in real offscreen life there is also likely to be a great deal more before me than secret objects, angles, memories, persons, plans. Much happens with the other that is not really secret but is inaccessible because it does not come into play here and now, while we are watching. In a film, sensitivity to, feeling about, impression of, even suspicion of the other are hard to get at except by way of indicative, performative gesture, which is rife on the screen. In cinema as I encounter it, the gestural circus makes it seem nothing is really beyond me.

The viewer is always an intimate (even to strangeness and alienation). That something of character A is beyond the intelligence of character B can be established only when it is not beyond the intelligence of the viewer, who "knows all," or at least knows substantially more. When sweet and generous Dame May Whitty kicks into action her ugly plan to kidnap the innocent Nina Foch in *My Name Is Julia Ross* (1945), it is noteworthy how quickly, how surely, how unquestionably we become part of her dark world. The con games and lies any figure can foist upon others are essentially—now or soon later—palpably clear to me. In my everyday life this is certainly not the case. Always there is something past my awareness. Let us say, to be even clearer, that what may remain untold and unclear are only the *secret* secrets and lies in the secreted person of a figure, information that has absolutely no bearing on the film.

Screen figures will seem to meet one another, will "fully know"—fully *enough* know—the others they meet. In *Who's Afraid of Virginia Woolf?* (1966), Elizabeth Taylor's Martha seems confident in her recognition of George Segal's Nick, met only moments before: she grasps him for not only what he is putting himself out to be but what he is fearful of letting others see, the extremes to which he can be pushed or dragged before a situation collapses. She already knows; she has mapped his funny bones. She knows Nick is holding something in, just a little, perhaps out of fear; yet if he doesn't want to "go along" with her mad games he certainly doesn't want *not* to "go along." All this is being acted out (brilliantly) so that the audience can have access to it. Let us say, she read Nick enough for us to be reading Nick insofar as the demands of this drama go; but she also shows that she knows there are things about Nick inaccessible to her. Inaccessible forever, thus out of play.

When a guest enters the home in which we live, sits beside us on our couch, with or without a glass of Scotch, we are far more in the dark about them than Martha seems to be about Nick; uncertain as to what resides inside the perimeter of their presence. In cinema that perimeter is elided. One implies it, perhaps; teases and hints; but what is shown is all of the personality on the momentary stage. All, at least, one could reasonably ask for.

Motive

An easy function in cinema, because it rests on sequential display, is the "buried motive" structure. Usually there are three phases:

- (A) A character presented in sweet innocence, usually with some carefully manipulated graphic infusions—platinum blonde hair coupled with a white frilly dress; then
- (B) an image of this same character in what is directly represented as an equivocal attitude—touching another person's neck with eyes a little too noticeably fixed and somnolent; and using fingernails; then
- (C) a full-fledged character portrait where malevolence is signaled through the actor's use of the gaze or the mouth position or the body angle; and to this scene the cinematographer imports anxious shadows. Because of the lighting—that is, *not* because of what has been established through action as an actual malevolence in the character, the platinum hair is compromised toward darkness, and with more contrast the frills of the dress seem active rather than passive; the eyes are turned even more askance than the full head is,

as though the character needs to see what is behind her, watching. We are ahead of a character, watching her watching for what may be behind (that we do not and cannot watch).

Mervyn LeRoy uses his characters' gazes in *The Bad Seed* (1956) to reflect upon the audience's gaze and upon the audience's inability to see everything that is laid in front of it. He confounds us, as his character Rhoda Penmark (Patty McCormack) confounds everyone around her. The "everything" not laid before the eyes is not a perimeter of momentary, situational, existential shadow, it is a shadow in which this clearly visible character hides motives that she does not want us to see (but which we too sincerely suspect are there). There come to be two tiers to Rhoda's "badness," first, that she actually causes pain and anxiety to other figures, willingly, knowingly, with calculation; second, that in the anticipatory phase of the flowering of this badness we see her, as it were, "preparing." In short, she thinks ahead of doing things that will be seriously problematic, much like a heister preparing to rob a bank. What nails our estimation, though, is the look of the character while all this is going on. Golden pigtails. A golden smile. A perfect modulation of childhood wonder and sweetness. All this so that soon, when she acts up, we can know that the sweet-little-girl posture was entirely a masquerade. Needless to say, William Friedkin replicated this trope in *The Exorcist* (1973).

Secrets

Sometimes a figure will own a secret that is revealed to the audience first and to another character only later, so that we are "in on" either the camouflage and duplicity or the modesty and surprise. In *There's No Business Like Show Business* (1954) the flamboyant singer Steve Donahue (Johnnie Ray) has not yet told his singer/dancer mother (Ethel Merman) that he intends to leave the family act, and indeed show business, and become a priest. He sings more than one song in the film, with such genuine enthusiasm one is wholly caught up with him as a musical figure—fans of rock 'n' roll owe it to themselves to see Johnnie Ray. The mother is swept away by him too, and also a faithful Catholic, so that when her son reveals who he "really is" she is deeply shocked. Here, interestingly, the various aspects of Steve's transition are placed onscreen one by one, a sequence of him performing carefully separated from a quiet conversational sequence in which he makes his confession. At no point does the thought of him having an ulterior motive present itself, and it is only by watching a number of scenes in relation to one another that we can conclude he had to have been harboring a sacred secret for some time, perhaps beneath his performative style.

Only rarely can diegetical secrets be secrets to us, because by definition the diegesis is a revelation and most of what is in the film must finally be open as we watch. When A keeps a secret from B it is only a "secret," a dramatic construction that calls for a certain kind of playing out behaviorally: A taking caution when B is within hearing range; A murmuring; A whispering to C; A smilingly confiding to B something distinctly other than the secret. When these tactics come into play, the viewer gets: A's demonstration of cautiousness; A's ability at vocal control; A's strategy for whispering; A bringing C into the picture while B is left out. We learn about A by way of the secret A is keeping and how A keeps it, but the secret itself is only pretext for that learning.

The secret is a currency in the story. When we are truly being kept in the dark we have no way of knowing, as with secrecy more generally. But as films purport to show life they must show secrecy, while at the same time we must be sufficiently inside to realize it is secrecy we are being shown.

Missed Opportunities

The secrecy and buried-motive structures both set up a viewing situation of profound interest, in that as we confront them we must come to terms with our engagement: not only cognitively, as though something we did not know is now coming clear, or as though we are learning how information was missing earlier but is present now; but vitally and optically, in the deepest root of our watching, since we are finding that we cannot see all of what we hope to see, need to see, estimate that we are seeing. We are encountering figures in a situation, but there is more to them and to the situation than what is accessible in our encounter.

Of interest further is a fundamental convention of characterological cinema: that some B encountered by some A will be found a human being—will sense the conspecific bond—in roughly the same way as A. Small perceivable differences between the two will account for personality quirks and distinctness of appearance, yes, but in any event a figure B believes she is encountering in A "herself modified," herself played out in a second manifestation; with A, the same. Similarly, we take the humanness of the figures we meet to reflect upon our own. Even alien monsters seem to behave in a recognizably "human" way: human figures can read them onscreen; or can find reading them impossible exactly to the degree that we find reading others impossible in the everyday. Films about concentration camps, torture, degradation, and catastrophe easily frame scenes in which this conspecificity—the human being's recognition of an other as equally human—is given contrast, special attention, and/or ironic shift: the assumed fundamental bond bases some scenic adaptation that makes for viewer fascination: say, a prison warden or agent of power treating prisoners as sub-human (Hume Cronyn in *Brute Force* [1947]) when we all know they are not. That kind of rendezvous challenges our sense of conspecificity.

Some rendezvous are established as surprises. A figure can be perceived incorrectly as to gender, with gender understood to be a central aspect of the dramatic context at the moment. When the gender "truth" is revealed, after an exposition showing various instants of pain and vicissitude, we can suddenly be brought to the thought that the negative experience, whilst we took it to apply to the figure we were watching and interpreting, was applying to gender *itself*, too, and therefore to us. The figure was indeterminate, we learn, but exactly and only as regards gender; and this suggests the possibility that gender itself is indeterminate (see more generally Butler), that so-thought firm categories are subject to buffeting (consider the work of Jaye Davidson in the much-touted *The Crying Game* [1992] or, in *Albert Nobbs* [2011] that of Glenn Close or Janet McTeer [astutely unfeatured]). If we take gender identity to be descriptively central, films positing indeterminate figures play with our deep understanding of things.

Even more shocking than a gender mis-take is a species gaffe. *I take you to be a human in the way that I am human, but I am wrong.* Consider Ian Holm's Ash in *Alien* (1979);[1] or David Bowie's catatonia-producing (for Candy Clark) alien self-reveal in *The Man Who Fell to Earth* (1976). By implication at the end of *Enemy* (2013) a giant spider has birthed itself out of the body of a former female occupant of the apartment in which it answers the door. In *Blade Runner* (1982) a seductive female (Daryl Hannah) is revealed to be robotic (a "replicant"), not human. In *The Thing* (1982), a monstrosity embeds itself in figures who give all the appearance of being human until a fatal moment; the script teases out the suspense as the group leader MacReady (Kurt Russell) tests his companions one by one, and with each test the audience finds itself as nervous as the men watching. When, finally, heat is applied to the blood of Palmer (David Clennon), the Thing emerges and runs amok in the closed space. The scene is self-aware of moving toward this climax, and of using the tension produced when characters know each other *as human* only in part, as an agency of its own development toward climax.

When he meets an unanticipated (an alien) type in figure B, A's loss of balance or rhythm can reveal the arbitrary boundedness of the system in which people like him (we think we are all such people) make observations and calculations in the first place. For A, as it turns out, B *cannot be taken for granted* as a recognizable person like all (human) persons, with (only) different qualities, motives, name, biography, or marginal characteristics of

---

[1] The actor *is* a person, of course, and becomes sharply present to us as such until make-up jumps in to save the day.

identity. Instead there is a whole grounded and hitherto unrecognized kind of being, a notably un-normal non-human form as far as the dominating human understands it, a "thing" or "entity" that/who resides or lurks "under the skin" of a normal-seeming human. Leslie Fiedler discusses the power of such otherness in *Freaks,* but not the upheaval produced by the surprise. Something of Goffman's "biographical reconstruction" may be in play (see *Stigma)* when the original rendezvous of A and B now comes to seem, in lambent retrospect, a falsity from start to finish.

Sexual Rendezvous

Sexual rendezvous onscreen are treated like other typical encounters, with the exception that participants tend to become partially or fully unclothed and engaged with each other more rhythmically and with more emotional amplitude than otherwise. There is no way to show either the so-called "actuality" of passionate feeling or their desire, save through the indexicality of rapid, more rapid, slow, slower, loud, louder, quiet, quieter action—all this being decodable to some watchers and entirely obscure to the uninitiated. I refer not to what is seen to happen in a sex scene but rather to the mode of awareness one figure could be taken as experiencing during a sexual encounter with another, as it can be apprehended by viewers outside: the figure's apparent understanding, or illumination, or secretion of otherness. Oddly, perhaps, when one lasts through watching a sex scene until its close, one realizes that afterward the characters do not seem to have a more complete awareness of each other than they did before. Screen sex is essentially a form of carnival ride. See *Devil in the Flesh (Diavolo in corpo* [1986]).

Curtailments

"I recognize and affirm not only the Other but the existence of my Self-for-others," Jean-Paul Sartre affirms *(Being* 380), and further, "My body is utilized and known by the Other" (460). This recognition and affirmation, the attendant constraints upon use and interpretation, constitute the appearance and the penumbra of the rendezvous. When I am with someone, not only are they *to* me and *for* me, and in that degree *of* me, in a way that I presume I am to them and for them and in that degree of them, but this relation that we have, as a kind of relation, is no surprise on either side. The other is with me now, but only in a particular way, and I am with her likewise. She knows this. And in her being with me now rests awareness of the nowness and presence of her being with me, this presence general enough but also signaled for me here and now, as a feature of our being together in this present that the other recognizes and with which recognition she does not fail to concur. I witness her telling me about grandmother's recipe for coconut cake, waiting patiently for her to output all the details while she is waiting for me to absorb them (and repeating when necessary); but at the same time, right there for me to witness, too, is her knowledge that she is with me here and now only to share grandmother's recipe for coconut cake, so that a myriad extraneous aspects of her being are not presently to be involved, and are consequently not involved, albeit by means of sharing this recipe she is certainly giving all of what is pertinent about the self she wishes to invoke at the time. She gives herself over to me unstintingly, but not fully. She shows pertinence, and does not show impertinence; or: whatever she shows I take as pertinent. When I watch film, I take what a figure gives as the sum total of pertinence.

But more:

The fact that her unstinting handover (of the recipe) is not a full donation of self, is quite as apparent to me—while I consider her—as is the limited being she does share; I know that she is both here and not here; both giving herself and hiding herself; both showing and concealing. This is not secrecy, it is an address to the limitations of circumstance. There can be thought nothing strange about my interlocutor's partiality, since time is time, and we have only a little moment to speak of coconuts, and for her to more fully reveal herself would perhaps be, if not an agony, dominating. *And by the way, I never make this recipe because I have a degenerative muscular condition in my left wrist ...* but I don't share that, since I recognize that for her, sharing the recipe is all this moment is. Or is she waiting for a special signal?

In the cinematic alien-reveal or monster-reveal or gender-reveal passages to which I refer above, however, and in other revelations of their ilk, a crisis pushes forward the revelatory gesture, by which, in a flashing moment, some figure comes to know (as do we), beyond what is being overtly presented and recognized in the presentation as overt and nothing more, a troubling *additional fact*. Without such a crisis no figure would puncture the tender boundary of the moment to say or show more about herself, to give some extraneous hint. When she reveals a hidden self, we see how it was that she had knowledge of the form of the moment in excess of the knowledge she showed, and was borne forward by her observer; an observer who might be holding a secret, too. In *The Man Who Fell to Earth*, when Bowie goes into the bathroom, locks the door, and methodically removes his human-being mask, he is fully conscious of how painfully the girl outside is going to react when by seeing she knows him, even though she has been begging for his real self.

In a rendezvous there may be on both sides the slightest tincture of apology for every breath. Although cinema does not give us the excess of being-beyond-presentation, because each filmed view can be only itself, it can give perspective on a little cover maneuver that one figure could use as excuse for hiding a little (use, therefore, as signal she knows she is hiding). Effectively in the cinematic rendezvous, a chain of "excuses" is quietly and politely offered as couch for the chain of exhibitions. *I know I say too little* .... One nice example would be a seductive woman (Vanessa Redgrave) who is on a schedule of some kind, keeping half an eye on a wristwatch lest time has come for moving on (on from David Hemmings, in *Blow-Up*). Here, her curtailment of an interactive moment with him is shown as having been forewarned and predicted for her at the same time as being enacted for him in a way that attributes causation elsewhere. *I love being here with you but there is more to my life than that, chum, and now I must fly*. In a witty riposte upon this tiny signal, Alan J. Pakula has Jane Fonda speedily check her wrist watch during copulation, as an occupational introduction, in *Klute* (1971).

A sudden, sharp transposition of emotion due to some offscreen cause or unshown memory can also act as a cover. A and B are talking, but suddenly (typically with a kind of "cloud" passing over in the lighting) B casts his eyes away and glares fearfully or aggressively, quite as though something else has just abstracted his concentration away: again in *Blow-Up,* Hemmings sitting up after the teen romp. This (for us) absent "something else" covers the character's continuing and visible awareness that he was always here only in part to begin with.

Yours

The screened figure presents a self in a "normal" way, that is, as though everything and anything of relevance to our knowing her by way of this rendezvous—of relevance to our taking and being prepared to take, in regard to her presence, every and any action that her presence seems to require—is here now, fully and unequivocally here, for us to see. That, while we all know it is possible to hide things and know, too, that she may be hiding something, indeed probably is, nevertheless we are ready to go on the assumption that nothing one could possibly (reasonably) care about is being hidden. She is open in this presentation. It is a perfunctory, matter-of-fact display. "You see before you facts and only facts," she seems to say, "because although my own private emotional 'take' on the facts I present is also a fact, I would not dream of keeping out of your sight any fact you could be wanting. Nor would I lead you to think I am the sort of person who would hide that way. Nor do I fail to hope that you do not conceive me as such a person. I am exquisitely and perfectly, completely and irrevocably, factually here before you. I am here, all of me is here, here for you, here for you to see and discern without bound. I am yours."

Not Telling

It is of course necessary in the everyday to do some general editing of what we reveal, but this is not the same as keeping a secret. After all, there is so much about Him that She could conceivably know, but that He has every good reason for presuming She would have no desire to know; and being in on which would in no way facilitate Her behavior; and which is even, relatively speaking, ugly. So why not just keep it in the pocket? After all, that which one does not have practical reason to put on show in a particular situation is not to be taken for granted as that which the other would have good reason to know. He thus does not tell Her just what He honestly believes She would not care to hear; actually, what nobody ever cares to hear; what He himself has never cared to hear about anyone else, as far back as he can remember. *I have a birthmark just about an inch below my right nipple.* Or: *My father is the internationally famous author of at least two dozen books that I know you have read, but let's go have coffee.* Interactants work through situations by making presumptions about one another's expectations and presumptions in regard to clarity; it's part of what it is to be with other people, to be in a rendezvous at the edge of the screen. When, by contrast, He has a *secret,* he knows or presumes it's something She would very much want to know, would feel entitled to be told, and He knows and presumes, too, that He has every good reason to suspect this *and to not tell it*; He feels *entitled here and now, and uncompromised, in holding back*. She surely does not go through life feeling entitled always and everywhere to full and unadulterated knowledge of the universe as a whole, but… but as to *this secret: He'd better keep it. Or better not keep it.* Her attitude will hang upon what She guesses the secret is.

In the everyday, we do find ourselves realizing or learning moment by moment that there are things not being "put on the table," that our knowledge is a *partial knowledge,* perhaps because time is passing and there is limitation in nature; yet screen figures do not appear to benefit from this learning or to have such a realization, and certainly do not tend to signal consciousness of being kept from consciousness in this way, or of not being sufficiently conscious, when they appear to sense themselves being conscious. They elide the thought of constraint and limitation, unless constraint and limitation are vital to the screen story in which we rendezvous with them. This, even in the case of a secret openly hidden. Thus onscreen figures take other onscreen figures as read. In doing this they guide the audience to take those figures as read, too. And to take them as read in taking others as read. Each is fully, uncontroversially, unproblematically all and everything that is being put on view. Indeed, what is being put on view *is their everything*. Presence perfunctory and whole.

Because as we watch they do not sense it, screen figures do not react to their own only limited exposure to one another. Even in situations where He finds Her so interesting he wants to see and know more about Her, we know about this desire only by way of an ensuing scene where they are together again: by the *ensuing* nature of the later event. Nothing in His first, earlier gaze said, *I cannot see enough. You are not revealing what should be revealed. I want more.*

Familiars

The elision of partiality in screen encounters—partiality, not secrecy—brings on screen situations in which figures who meet one another behave as though for all intents and purposes they are already familiars. *Whatever I meet and learn of you here is all I need to meet and know, but frankly I understood already that things would be this way.* Surprises, agonies, misconstructions—these are all dramatically constructed on top of the base familiarity that is uniformly present like an ether. When in *Bringing Up Baby* (1938) Major Applegate (Charlie Ruggles) picks up his hands, encircles his mouth, and simulates a panther's mating call, we may find the moment comic, even outrageous or provocative …. but nobody onscreen blurts out, "Oh gee, Major, I didn't know you could do that! (You are surprising me)." When in *Superman* (1978) our hero springs fully leotarded from a phone booth, no passerby on the street gapes, "Oh gee, Superman, I didn't know you used phone booths!" All these things are as they are. That is, whatsoever the dramatic world contains, it contains by nature.

In some respects, the *de facto* familiarity of screen beings one to another mirrors a similar, structurally important—and for us entirely hidden but presumed—"familiarity," that of actors one to another on set. Familiarity << familiar << *of the family*. Yet in the fact of it so often, there is hardly time for people who haven't met before to spend time getting to know one another as the business of portraying characters rolls on, k'ching k'ching. The rendezvous of those who demonstrate encounters is itself attenuated. This absence of real familiarity is part of what makes professional courtesy on set, so very important.[2]

---

[2]The courtesy involved in movie-making could merit a book of its own.

Morphs

A much-used trope in adventure, crime, and espionage sagas: H, a hero, innocent at the moment, meets a superior figure S in some organization or company (his boss; the president; the chairman of the board). This S is puissantly sleek, groomed, wealthy, and aloof, a man who takes pleasure in his position but especially in his sumptuous office (almost always surrounded by plate glass windows giving a high view of a vast city or territory). He is informing H, instructing him, chatting chummily. He is the guy with all the files. Later, at a dramatically climactic moment, S is revealed to H as none other than the brutal villain. Now we find him mad with cupidity, relatively disheveled, and socially disgraced. At such "reveals," it is clear to viewers thinking back that when H originally "met" him, S was nothing but genial and honest ("nothing but" unless these viewers have seen a thousand renditions of this theme, in which case they recognized up front what innocent H was failing to see); clear and evident that there has been a morphing scene (off-camera) so that S could be reshaped into the loathsome and dishonest cur we finally see. Call him S1 (previous) and S2 (eventual). If between S1 and S2 there are no significant visible differences the film lacks irony (a nutrition that action film requires for survival); if the difference is far too great, one or the other of S1 and S2 seems a misconstruction and our engagement falters. Ronnie Cox plays such an S in *Total Recall* (1990); Jeroen Krabbé one in *The Fugitive* (1993); Matthew Goode one in *Watchmen* (2009). The trope is turned on its head with Humphrey Bogart for rom-com effect in *Sabrina* (1954).

Consider alien/monster films: genial and pretty S1 covering the hideous monster S2. Here, S1 must be (a) human to H, just as H is human to himself, but secretly, in a way that is made available to us by design, (b) inhuman, alien, warped, de-natured, surgically altered, disfigured, and/or bestial. The typical account of the morph is that our villain fell under the warping influence of some fabulous *thing* of the imagination, "X." X: gamma rays, a torturer, an extraplanetary birth, drugs…. If the morph is to be read as serious the S1 > X > S2 transition must be managed clearly but also patiently. Vincent D'Onofrio's almost instantaneous cockroach morph in *Men in Black* (1997) exemplifies the problem; he is finally a joke, not a terror (as the film intends).

Now, to make a further turn:

In morph structures, for disillusioned A the "shockingly" revealed Other, B, is finally someone who was presenting both a false front and, instant by instant, a false penumbra. One knew along with A that one was seeing only a fraction of B, and knew that B knew this, yet one also felt secure in guessing, along with A, what it could have been that B was disingenuously not putting on show. B knew that A knew this, too. Now one discovers that in guessing at the penumbra, one couldn't have been further off the mark.

B's private knowledge of self and A's estimations of B's unshown self were, all along, utterly incompatible. Our friend A has therefore been proceeding through the narrative unkenningly deluded, and this deludedness will itself come under treatment in the film, since taken on its own it merely degrades the figure into someone unworthy of our attention. We must not only meet the seeker A as undeluded (thus attend to B as he does, without recognizing artful disguise) but also think of A as being naturally above delusion, just as we would prefer to think we are. B, too, must be given treatment; hideous ultimately, he or she must earlier have had attractive qualities, else why were we watching, and worse, why was A watching?

In the disavowal or dismantling of the figure-to-figure rendezvous in cinema when villainy enters, many erasures come into play. Consider Dr. Charles Nichols (Krabbé) in *Fugitive*, as in police captivity he becomes dishonored. We find that his old colleague and chum Dr. Richard Kimball (Harrison Ford) not only ceases to confront him face to face now, not only ceases to read his gestural signals as authentic and ingenuous but also ceases conviction that the man knows him; the erased Nichols is not merely the dishonored Nichols, and can have no link to him now. By film's end Kimball is moving away without consciousness of Nichols, without memory of Nichols, without anticipation of a future in any way involving Nichols. Nichols is, in all these ways, out of the picture. And this happens too with Lamar Burgess (Max von Sydow) in *Minority Report* (2002), who early in the film is with John Anderton (Tom Cruise) as a generous mentor, recognized in and out of frame. But finally he is erased triply: disconnected from himself as a presence on show; disconnected from Burgess as an implication outside that presence; and disconnected from traces of Burgess's observable self-knowledge while, like anyone, he shows himself.

Encounter Boundary

Film scripts build in, and directors and performers refine, the strict temporal placement of characters' gestures, and account for them to the audience. This is done by making figures' encounters onscreen *purposive* ones; the purpose bounds and sharpens focus on the gestures. A moment exists as part of the narrative in order that an action happens in it, and the action covers the so-perceived "natural" limitation of concern we clearly see in all parties to the event. From any character's point of view, then, *this is not only what I'm doing, it's what I'm doing reasonably and knowingly,* and further, *I present those aspects of myself congruent with my purpose.* In the rendezvous, the second party signals awareness that the other's self-presentation is limited by a kind of modesty, a brief looking-aside from the interactional possibilities. A very brief hint, to be sure. *Even by only hinting at my awareness of myself I have already paid you enough courteous attention.* In filmed situations scripted as professional—bank executives, dentists, garbage collectors, schoolteachers—formal cut-offs are pre-embedded in the structured encounter, usable with all comers. "Take two aspirin and call me in the morning," but also, "Please—and I know I don't have to say this to you, so I won't say it, but I'm thinking, 'Don't stand here now discussing the Yankees or the weather.'" Once we have the doctor's office and the doctor, the push-off, gentle as it may be, is a foregone conclusion.

This is one of the reasons why entrapment scenarios can be so galling in their effect. Characters who would normally take leave of one another are forced by some overriding circumstance to remain together, thus to actively confront and find rationale for the other's self-aware holding back from full revelation and the other's signaling that self-awareness. *I think this elevator's stuck.* (See on this Buñuel's *L'ange exterminateur* [1962].) Often, filmmakers and writers will jump away from the confinement scene where characters are trapped—a breath of air!—and then jump back. The embarrassing extension of mutual regard between partners to a forced relation dissipates as soon as they are not before us, not so much because this tiny hesitation is no longer fascinating—it may well be—but because whatever action we cut away to has its own immediate draw. In *Dog Day Afternoon* (1975), we escape frequently from the confines of the bank, the limited encounters of the employees who work together daily but don't have to know one another too well, the nervous inter-relationship between the heister (Al Pacino) and his accomplice (John Cazale), to see the crowd and police outside in the street, these folk putting on a genuine entertainment involving gaping, screaming, shouting through a loudspeaker, jostling near vehicles, and so on. Because we have not forgotten the dynamics of the inside scene, when we jump back we do not have to be initiated but we also do not tend to form judgments as to whether figures' relations with one another have been stretched during our absence, whether they have tiptoed into one another's penumbra. It's as though when we get a break, they get a break.

Scene cutaways would purport to address the dramatic need for juxtaposing a number of contrasting situations so that together they form a complexity, and scriptwriters know this. But the cutaway also performs the function of covering over the kind of strain that attenuation of attention can produce, not only among figures who are others mutually but also among viewers who over the minutes of focus become more and more aware that there are potentially interesting facts about these folk that are not being revealed; this very attenuation of *not revealing* means rationalizing the extended mutual attention under force, since one can say the same superficial things only so many times before one starts looking psychotic. From the writer's point of view, the more you delve into the parts of a character that halo around what the character must make evident, the more the characterized figure becomes a focus of the drama and the less attention can be directed to happenings. As cinema must seem to happen, and to be chockful of happenings, the heroic eye must draw away from the drawn-away eye of the other lest modesty infuse the atmosphere with unbearable self-consciousness.

Waiting Room

I am suggesting that Merleau-Ponty's observation, that the other appears as the completion of the system might, on very close inspection, prompt a little emendation. The other appears toward our completion of the system yet does not manage to fully provide that completion because, as I cannot not be aware, my view of the other is perforce insufficient. It is the insufficiency that makes me conscious of the certain "standing back" film has such trouble showing: not only film performance but film itself. Films carry us into an extended waiting period, as we sit in anticipation of the arrival of the system that will not arrive. Call it, if you will, Godot.

Rendezvous

I am talking with a stranger and he has finished talking. But it is as though he is still saying something, now in a tiny hiatus. As though he is now saying, "And that was all I wanted to say." Or, "This is not all I have to say, but it is all for now." Our Now is done, his and mine, we can suppose, but that brief additional glimpse he gave me into his cavern, that someone is there carefully monitoring how much this one says at any moment, and noting this slight prolongation of my attentive gaze upon him backing away, entirely without abruptness, effectively bowing the head, giving a wave—"There will be more. But not now."—*that* is our true rendezvous.

Needless to say, telephone conversations do not work this way, because in pure acoustic tennis one says or doesn't say and no other move counts in the game. But distant conversations involving video images do.

The consciousness I have of the other's consciousness of me, and of himself being conscious of both me and himself, the consciousness that gently backs away when things are "done," works strategically as a gesture of continuity, a gesture that leads forward. It gives a guarantee of a happening localized, and assures of the possibility of movement. Every conversational gesture that remarks upon itself, "That's all I have to say," opens space for the next. In my relation with the other, these moments beckon and offer, and work very much to charge the present circumstance with the idea of a fullness of meaning that has not yet been achieved, a feeling that there is more to say, more to know, but the time for saying has run out.

Every scene in a film is a promise that the final scene fails at fulfilling in a way that makes us happy (there being, perhaps, no finer example than the taxi ride that concludes Ernst Lubitsch's *Trouble in Paradise* [1932], that Billy Wilder rather crudely imitates in the punchy last shot of *Some Like It Hot* [1959]). "Next" is always implied. Cinema is always about arriving at a future but also, as Godard hints in *Contempt* (1964), without a future: *senza avennire*.[3]

for Julio Cortázar

---

[3] I refer to "rushing ongoingness" because frames are always passing by, twenty-four to the second, even when we have the illusion of a "slow" dissolve or fade to black.

Interlude

From Trouble in Paradise *(Ernst Lubitsch, Paramount, 1932). Digital frame enlargement.*

Tenderness

"How do you do it? How do you lie to someone to their face?"
        LIRAZ CHARHI TO NAOMI WATTS IN FAIR GAME *(2010)*

Peter Bogdanovich wisely commented that the "Lubitsch touch" had a musical quality for one thing and evoked a certain European sophistication and precision of expression for another. Lubitsch, he added, would act out the parts for his cast to see and imitate, all the parts, every scene. If, reader, you have never seen a Lubitsch film, a very great pleasure awaits you.

Managing expression that is at once "sophisticated" and "precise" is crucial for the actor, who knows that with a deep concentration the audience is laboring constantly to understand the delicacies offered in vision and sound. With "precise sophistication"—"sophisticated precision"— there must be something gossamer light, that transcends interpretation, something like a perfume or the memory of a taste from one's youth. Deep concentration blots expression and its reception, covers it over with theory, forces it into a static importance. In Lubitsch, the actor often gives off the subtlest clues or intimations without actually proclaiming. In film-watching today, however, audiences have become used to extremities of proclamation, bold, strident, and emblazoned, so that "European sophistication and precision," as Bogdanovich put it, hardly survives to leave the trail that can tease.

One finds in Lubitsch actorial conviction in the grand importance of the tiniest tic, the smallest cant of the head, the smile partially withheld, the lilting phrase uttered entirely without sincerity. Once in a while the viewer is delivered an image with no sound accompaniment, so that tonalities, postural nuances, and lighting effects alone must accomplish the work of conveying the nuance of the moment. The Lubitsch script is finely crafted (not that he is the sole filmmaker to attend carefully to his scripts): there can be no dropping of lines, murmuring of syllables, racing through phrases: every note must be heard, as with Schubert.

Reproduced above is a frame from *Trouble in Paradise* (1932). We see a pair of (matted-in) shadows, male and female, draped across the coverlet of a somewhat decorative bed. (This is the bedroom of the new secretary.) One figure is that of Madame Colet (Kay Francis), incalculably wealthy president of a cosmetics empire in Paris; the other of her newly hired secretary Gaston LaValle (Herbert Marshall), whose subtle delicacies of comportment in her presence have intimated to her (as have her delicacies to him) that a romantic dalliance is possible. Perhaps I may be permitted to say that nowadays, as the world of the everyday moves so very quickly onward, *indication* that bodily play is possible goes entirely elided by bodily play itself, sprung into. But never in Lubitsch. Also, no prurience here, no shyness, no coy wink. This isn't a winking moment, it's a postural moment. Madame owns Monsieur's time, but Monsieur owns Madame's heart; possession is nine-tenths of ownership.

Already by this point, the film has become almost immeasurably more complicated than this image allows for, yet for appreciating what we can see onscreen at this instant very little other information about the characters is required. Suave, intelligent, and cunning both, these two have been gently stepping in and out of each other's rooms (read, bedrooms) at the top of the vast curling stairway. Whispering. Gazing fondly. Whispering. Gazing. Closing the door. Opening the door. We have been following their "evening together" by way of an ornamental little clock, the hands of which move gently forward to "walk" us through the night. It is now well past midnight and the shadows imply the relationship has come to something of a head. What in particular has Lubitsch arranged for?

The answer is an artful broth of unity mixed in with the idea of unity. The idea of unity is a withdrawal from unity, and unity is a withdrawal from ideas. Lubitsch understands how showing the would-be lovers in action with one another—whatever action—would be far less decorous, far less meaningful, far less implicative than showing the clocks as "pointers." And now he knows that showing the figures in action, live, before our eyes, would undo the vibration produced by seeing them only as shadows. The figures themselves, at this instant, would be penumbras to these shadows!

Embodied in his shadow Gaston is not exactly stoop-backed, but neither does he stand with a firm upright posture. He has given himself to bend a little her way, the smallest momentary obsequiousness to indicate servility, compliance, willingness to do her bidding always. He has given a confidant's advice about the color of her lipstick and her face powder. He has attended, with unsurpassable grace, to her every need before she feels it. That this man is using a false name we know already, and also that he intends to steal from this object of his delight a great deal of money, having arranged, on Madame's behalf, to have some of her insurance funds transferred each month to the house budget, *in cash*. We know, in point, that on Madame's behalf he has taken over Madame. And that she is completely unaware— that he has given her no signal of which she would have to be aware—is not only clear, it is elemental, else the joy of watching his operation would be leeched away. That he is as mischievous as he is gallant is a lovely pique, and that he is as gallant as he is mischievous is a balm. Further, we have learned to resign ourselves with the greatest contentment to the realization that the prospect of making a distinction between his scheming and some genuine feeling on his part is beyond us.

Our simplest strategy is to read Gaston as both a villain and a charmer, in business as in love, in love as in business. Were we to see in him nothing but a villain the entire film would be ruined. Such is the hypercritical view of Madame's voluble suitor Monsieur Filipa (Edward Everett Horton), a booby. Our regard is more affectionate. Gaston's lips—amazing that in a shadow we can think to make them out—are always ready to seem willing but not craving, ready but not eager, present but not hungering (when his overall project makes no sense at all unless he is craving, eager, and hungering; as he names himself to her, "One of the *nouveau poor*"). Morally he is impeccably honest even in thievery, our Gaston: honest in that he doesn't tell much by way of untruth, not that he ever tells the whole truth. When he steals a strand of pearls for Lily his partner (Miriam Hopkins), it is a glory to watch him turn at Madame's door and let her have a look at them, offering in salute a smile which is also a sigh, happiness but also chagrin, because he is enchanted with her and enchanted with the idea of "taking" her, more or less equally. He has no arrogance. He has no rude, smug grimace of triumph. On the bed covers, in this shadow, we cannot see his eyes and therefore cannot, as, watching films we so often presume or hope to do by such an act, read his mind.

Gaston is a romantic and a connoisseur. Having opened an envelope from the Major (Charlie Ruggles), yet another soldier in Madame's army of suitors, he feels it appropriate to comment: "But the letter has no mystery ... no bouquet!" In her shadow silhouette, Mariette's lips are clearly opened, her head tilted back in surrender, and therefore her eyes—not for us!—are pinned to him hopefully and vulnerably. Even for only this horribly terminating instant I am yours, each shadow says to the other. The chests are touching so it is a close enough embrace. She seems to be breathing the aroma of his gracility. There is no urgency on her part, nor any slight hint of need, since, as we know already, she is endlessly supplied by retainers of various kinds (such as Robert Greig and C. Aubrey Smith) and lacks for nothing; has never lacked; can never lack.

Between these two at this moment so long after the sun has set, after dining and talking and talking and talking, what we have is delicious, daring proximity; suspenseful desire; curiosity. He would love to know precisely where her weak points are, and she would love to know precisely how much she can hope to be pleasured by his love. Both fear the revealing commission that would throw far too blazing a light, and make the curtain fall. Gaston is willing to pay for her secrets by sharing his own—to a point. If she is the same, she doesn't let on. Is this perhaps a moment in which a crossroads has been reached, where romance is one of the possibilities and ruin another, where romance and ruin are married. As there is no text that could possibly transmit the delicate marvel of this film, I must write only hints.

This odd bed itself: the coverlet has been pulled tight, as though by invisible hands. No sleeper makes a bed so finely. The bedside table lamp is a dainty one, just marginally effective to shed light: rather than illuminating it conveys to the sleeper the idea of illumination. There are two ruffled pillows, side by side, quite as though each party to a duo could have one in delight, proceeding to tumble or not tumble into sleep. At the same time the bed itself is not quite a double bed, it sleeps one and a half, or, bound in some bizarre entwinement, two. Recall that this is the pre-Code era. Since these shadows represent the two who might conjoin here—we suspect they will—the bed (and all it stands for) makes address to itself only; there is no indication they will spend the night together here, nor an indication that they won't. Lubitsch's films, composed as all films must be of indications, are made of moments that surpass indication.

Meanwhile the clocks have been ticking, or, without ticking moving on. Time is, if not flying then, passing. Mariette Colet had better make some move if she intends to secure this lover (who has arrived out of nowhere and could presumably disappear into nowhere, too). Gaston is calculating how many hours are left to him in this household, this trouble-ridden paradise before, with or without Madame's treasures, he must flee. To take delight in this woman and her world, as his every gesture shows he desires and means to do, would require a kind of repose, a loosening of the stricture embossed by the clock's hand. One would have to forget time in order to remember Madame, but time is flying and the dogs are coming near.

Marital Bliss

Gaston's accomplice/pal, is she secretly his wife? His lover? His Nemesis? Perhaps all of these. Watching the two of them together one has no trouble comprehending her in Biblical tones as his *ezer k'negdo,* a phrase regarding Eve's relation to Adam that is far too simplistically translated "helpmeet." The phrase literally means "helper who is against him." Lily helps by wrestling, as it were. By going in the opposite direction, she tempers his moods.

By the time they are in Paris, Lily and Gaston have become a team of confidence tricksters (and each of them, we are led to believe, rampaged Europe before the film began: we saw their most recent escapade in Venice). Mme Colet hires "Miss Vautier" (Lily) to be Gaston's secretary, the secretary of the secretary. She is stuffed away in a room presumably typing, but in fact conniving with him and showing more zeal than will fit any moment witnessed by Madame. Madame suddenly summons her to bedside. A private tête-à-tête while breakfast is being consumed, with Miss Vautier carefully pouring Madame's coffee and adding Madame's cream, all with propriety and modesty in what we pleasurably see as her very swank round hornrims.[1] When Madame turns her head to nibble her croissant, Lily cannot stop herself from taking a peek at the jewel box, hunger inscribed all over her. But actually, what Madame wants is a tiny confidence: Monsieur LaValle has been demanding that she eat no potatoes. An implied request: Can you do something about that? I adore my potatoes. At least do not tell him: I increase your salary by fifty francs.

---

[1] I am grateful to Ariel Pomerance for clarifying that these would have been men's horn rims since eyeglasses explicitly for women did not exist in the early 1930s.

A woman who with the flick of a wrist could buy half of France.

Lily and Miss Vautier are of course more than happy to duck into this little vestibule of secrecy, with Lily in the process becoming nothing less than Madame's new best friend. Does Madame surmise that Miss Vautier could be another one enjoying Gaston' flowering? Well, power to Miss Vautier, but no matter: Monsieur LaValle will be mine. In the same way everything Madame sets eyes upon becomes hers. That is what it is to be Madame. That is Paradise.

A dramatization with rewards tumbling as from a fountain, without labor, without demand, without strain, without the use of the muscles. The figures—and the film with them—ripple on.

The two women together: they have curly semi-short hair, artfully sculpted, Madame in something close to black and poor Miss Vautier in something close to blonde. Lily's eyeglasses signal a keen view of the territory, and that she is obtaining that view quite openly, even with innocence. Would she perhaps like some coffee?—No, but in Madame's very invitation is nothing other than a genuine personal warmth, if formally ornamented. How charming that Madame's peignoir is larded with silk roses, a complete travesty of need. Yet she is so very likeable, in her silliness and her failed attempts at pomposity. To guess that it was her husband who had the fortune, may he rest, and that she came up from below, would be easy, but also entirely irrelevant. Irrelevant as potatoes.

The halo of Madame Colet's superiority, indeed the superiority of folk like Madame Colet, will find reflection in a much later face-à-face between Gaston and the official secretary of the Colet et Cie board, Monsieur Alphonse Giron (Smith), a gargantuan and stentorian stuffed shirt who wishes the world to know that he has enjoyed the confidence of the Colet family *for ... forty ... years!* Giron has seen through LaValle, and is ready to turn him in as Gaston Monescu, internationally known confidence trickster. Gaston glances to the side. He will have this peacock, but not presently. Giron has always done the Colet et Cie books, about which fact, and whatever be his last name, Gaston is displeased. Not long later he is in her bedroom with Madame as she goes to her safe. He sits on the arm of her chair, and leans back, smiling, on guard:

> GASTON (in close two-shot with her): What would you say if you found your safe had been robbed?
> MARIETTE: I wouldn't say anything—I would act.
> GASTON: Call the police?
> MARIETTE: Instantly.
> GASTON (as if to approve): Mm-hmmmmm ...
> MARIETTE (lightly): But why talk about robbery on a night like this? *She pauses—ironically?, he is not quite sure.*
> GASTON (ardently taking a last chance): You look beautiful!

MARIETTE: Thank you. *(Turning back coolly to the safe combination.)* Seventy-six, eighty—
GASTON (rising; the game is over): Mariette!
MARIETTE: Yes, Gaston?—

And then he uses the weapon stored up against Giron:

GASTON: You *have* been robbed—for years. And not a hundred thousand francs, but millions. And you know who did it? Adolphe.
MARIETTE (confused): Adolphe?
GASTON: Adolphe J. Giron.
MARIETTE (laughing at him): And you expect me to believe that?
GASTON: Naturally not. But I expect the police to believe it. *He goes to the night table and in close shot picks up the telephone. Frightened she takes the receiver out of his hand, sets it back.*
MARIETTE: No!
GASTON: Why not? He's a thief—he's a criminal.
MARIETTE: I don't believe it!
GASTON: Then why are you afraid to let me prove it? *She turns away, beginning to suspect there might be truth in what he says.* It would be a terrible scandal, wouldn't it.
MARIETTE (to herself): Giron ... !
GASTON: Yes, Giron! Chairman of the board of Colet and Company. Honorary president of the Orphans' Asylum. Adolphe J. Giron—distinguished citizen!.... Well, shall I call the police? *(Mariette's silence eloquently says no.)* I see! You have to be in the social register to keep out of jail. But when a man starts at the bottom and works his way up—a self-made crook—then you say, "Call the police! Put him behind bars! Lock him up!" *(He glares with indignation, then goes to the safe, gives the dial one turn and opens it. The papers inside are in complete disorder. CLOSE SHOT MARIETTE staring at the open safe. CLOSE SHOT GASTON going toward her, bowing formally.)* I don't seem to have my calling cards with me, Madame Colet. So permit me to introduce myself informally—Gaston Monescu. I assure you in my own circles I am very well known. *Mariette looks at him sadly for a moment. She gets up, restraining tears.*

Now the light has changed in the amphitheater of their lives. Mariette can no longer pretend she does not know this man, how sad: nor proceed to know him wholeheartedly as the endlessly fascinating Gaston LaValle whom one adores. Cold reality has set in, and cold reality is, and can only be, Madame's superiority plain and simple.

Of such a magnitude is Mme Colet's superiority, her poise suggests, and based in such unquestionable natural right that she need merely offer a smile. The ethereal sveltness of her frame constitutes her presence. Indeed, her elegant semi-modernist abode is useful if only for permitting a pleasing angle on that frame. "Madame will require the car, she is going out … "—"Madame will not require the car, she is not going out … "—"Madame is going out, she will need the car … "—"I will not need the car, I am not going … " A woman of (exquisite) posture, garbed in potentiality, one who needs think of only the potatoes she would like to have. Big potatoes, small potatoes. Champagne merely to sip without regard; flowers to sniff; books upon books not to bother reading.

In Paradise

Lily and Gaston have jumped to an escape plan, perhaps with a meagre hundred thousand francs—although she would very much like to have Madame's pearls. There is a train at midnight. Lily is frantically, but also happily, packing up. Gaston has stationed himself with Madame, and when the house telephone pesters he does not pick it up. Lily becomes frantic. She bursts into his room to have it out with him—what is he doing, dallying with Madame? He would sell himself so cheaply? Great vituperation, a foamy little performance. And Madame enters!

Lily confesses that she came here to steal Madame's money! Here—she strides over to the bed and drops a packet of francs—it's not worth it anymore!, heading for the door with a sneer for Gaston and Madame both. Through this, Madame stands in statuesque placidity, a tranquil smile on her face, a graceful brightness in her eyes—eyes like diamonds. She may well be surprised, and she may not—after all, what does anyone and everyone ever want from her but money?—but she remains composed, dignified, sweet. Then Lily has a change of mind. "You've bought him for fifty francs!" A whirlwind, a little tempest, with platinum hair.

Gaston races down the stairs after her, as we can hear while never taking our eyes from the sedate Madame Colet. Back he comes. It is confession time.

The truth: he, too, wanted to rob her. He shows the thick strand of pearls he has purloined, "for Lily," and rather than being taken aback she smiles with understanding. With a startling quietness and softness of manner he takes his leave, in fact the manner of a gentleman—that is, a man who has learned to behave as a gentleman.

And now a tiny Lubitschean *coup,* an oh-so-gentle nod to the stark reality of class: gentle because full of wise comprehension, gentle because with the Lubitsch touch nothing, not even screaming, is loud. Mariette's lover has gone, her pearls in his clutches, her hundred thousand francs are gone, but she merely stands in repose, smiling, her eyes bright with comprehension, her future assured, her composure preeminent. For pathetic Lily, the money was a universe, a thousand thousand tomorrows. But for the social diva (perhaps only a woman transformed into a social diva, but still a diva), money is absolutely nothing. A trifle. Even less than a trifle. So things go in Paradise.

There is a popular interpretation of the film's title, namely, that into the tranquil Land of Paradise there has entered a worm. The idea: pretty Paradise is actually corrupt, and may not recover. Or even: there is no place, not even Paradise, without stain. Thus, *Paradise isn't Paradise*. My own suspicion is, that a reading of this sort is not Lubitsch's way of seeing things at all, it's far too cynical, the sort of reading Billy Wilder would have made. For that kind of reading, the film's focus would be stained Paradise; in short, a stain. But I think, instead, that the focus is Trouble, the tiny province of Gaston and Lily as they make to climb their ladder to success. They are trouble, certainly, but have now found themselves visiting not the empty personalities of hotel guests in fabulous vacation spots, nor governments, nor collections of art—so refined but also so limited as they are—but, verily, Paradise itself, the place where there is so much shining bounty, shining beauty, and shining beatitude there can be no imagination of a greater light. Trouble has come to Paradise: *Trouble IN Paradise:* and has labored there with the slyest and most earnest care, day after day, bow after bow, gaze after gaze, *küss die hand!* If in the end Trouble has come away with something less than was desired—always something less, else what is Heaven for?—still Paradise, the gleaming doyenne of Paradise, stands with her smile, her poise, her timeless sense of life.

We are finally in the car with the two crooks as they are driven off. He wants to gift her the luscious pearls, and reaches into his inside pocket. Reaches again. Reaches again. But slowly, bravely smirking at him, she withdraws them from her bosom. Find a thief to catch a thief! And now, gloating, she boasts she has the money, too, and searches for it to show him. But ... search, search ... where is it? And Gaston gently pulls the wad of francs out and hands them to her. A major screen kiss as the film ends. True love. Let us love each other and steal from each other as long as the sun is in the sky!

to William Rothman

10

Clutter

Above: From Juno *(Jason Reitman, Searchlight, 2007). Digital frame enlargement. Below: Joan Crawford in* Possessed *(Curtis Bernhardt, Warner Bros., 1947). Digital frame enlargement.*

So much to look at! And to look at now!

Almost as easy as breathing, while we are watching at the edge of the screen, is neglecting or altogether forgetting the optical complexity of the process, that each and every image must be taken in somehow, with images rushing into history and more yet to come, all of this with lighting speed (some shots, even shots with a moving camera, last only a quarter of a second—six frames). The eye will be guided to operate upon the screen rectangle rather than simply gobbling it. There is more to see at any instant than navigation requires, and for so many viewers, notably viewers fixed upon narration, the process of navigating is primary; yet there is continually more to see. As we watch a film, it is not difficult to be lost, lost even when we look to admire a composition with no concern for the story. Given the optical challenge of watching, of keeping attention focused over a period of time, the issue of clutter becomes centrally relevant.

The cluttered frame objectifies all of its contents, including persons. Clutter is not crowdedness. As we find in many canvases by Hogarth, a frame can be crowded with people without being cluttered at all, each figure having discreet presence and personality inside a collective boundary. We may think of a cluttered space as one in which the number or arrangement of situationally relevant articles overwhelms a viewer's capacity for attachment.

Two images from motion pictures: a teenage girl's bedroom from *Juno* (2007), designed by Steve Saklad and dressed by Michael Diner and Catherine Lehman: if in Victorian sitting rooms one could have noted a fashionable predilection for ornamental objects, *Juno* is set in a time when ornamentation for its own sake is passé. The character is without independent means, cannot expand her space and needs every available inch of it for the objects that are essential to her psychological good health: she does not regard her inexpensive designer chair, her numerous and omnipresent flop-eared stuffies, her pillows, or her wall full of photographs (torn from magazines) as ornamental; they *are* the deep structure filling-up the empty spaces of her life (this emptiness being the film's take on "typical American late twentieth-century middle-class teenage normality"). A teen's ability to move around in her space is downplayed as irrelevant; and the bedroom is impassable to anyone but her. The character is not the subject; the design is the subject: not a girl in her room but a girl's room.

A radically different use of diegetic space is in Curtis Bernhardt's *Possessed* (1947), where Joan Crawford is a nurse-attendant in a rich man's home, spending her free time in a love affair with an architect designer. The designer (Van Heflin), who does not love her in the (possessive) way that she loves him, and the rich man (Raymond Massey), who ultimately employs him, both live at the edge of a splendid lake in cottage homes with docks, so that between them a motor craft can speed, by day and by night. David's home is down near the water, Dean Graham's palace is atop a crest of rocks gazing down. When, at Dean's, Louise has a blow-up with David and demands to be taken home, we see him chauffeuring her in his motorboat, and the long shot of the boat skimming across the nocturnal lake, with the vast spread of pines in the far distance, diminishes the characters' physical size onscreen but at the same time accentuates their presence; in this landscape shot, David driving and his passenger Louise are exceptionally present even if not very visible. At his cottage moments earlier, she was rhapsodizing about living in nature like this, standing by a window outside which the water could fill her field of vision (and ours) with moonlight dappling its surface with silver. In that shot—technically more a portrait—it is actually the silvery lake that seizes and clutches attention and Louise, large enough to occupy the rectangle, is diminished by comparison with it.

Still more provocative, and more telling, is one of the film's opening shots where we find an as-yet-unidentified Louise dragging herself along the empty streets of downtown Los Angeles. In a splendid shot by Joseph Valentine, the city has been arranged as a concrete garden cloister, the receding clean verticals of lampposts like an avenue of trees that emphasizes the receding line of the sidewalk against the receding road with storefront windows margining the righthand walk. Though she is by far not the most pronounced figuration in the shot, seen in tableau from some twenty-five feet away Louise takes all of our attention because of her stumbling loneliness; we fixate, as she must be doing, on her signal presence in this urban vacuum.

Still another set configured as a room, another character portrait involving two principal and two supplementary figures, can be seen in *Bringing Up Baby* (1938). We are at a chic bar, designed by Van Nest Polglase and not revealed fully onscreen. To be seen is one corner, just enough room for a "meeting cute" between Katharine Hepburn and Cary Grant. The set is built to facilitate a shot aimed straight into the forward-jutting prow made by the twin moldings on the bar's two sides. Even though Hepburn is not the brightest figure onscreen here (the barkeeps are wearing starched white jackets), she ascends because of her sharply executed attitudinal gestures and Howard Greer's costume design—a glittering lamé fabric with a preposterous collar. Grant's gestures are similarly marked. There is visual elaboration here, the neatly arranged, shelved bottles, the stools, the floor, the polished bar, the stony gazes of the barmen, but none of this advances to the viewer's consciousness as a priority over the principal duo. However notable, the setting does not interfere.

Consider, then, (a) cluttered and (b) uncluttered designs, a differentiation made in terms of not the amount of material encased within the rectangle but the appreciable distinctness of some central feature of importance. Gazing at Hepburn and Grant, one could easily find much else to sustain interest, but the camera has converted what would be seen in the real world (if it existed), a relatively cluttered environment into an uncluttered one; complexity into simplicity. The same with Crawford on the sidewalk, where although there is a great deal to capture one's interest we fixate on Crawford. Clutter is not in a place, it is in a view, a kind of showing by someone who doesn't know what he most wishes to show; or who knows that he most wishes to show only everything.

Nature

Nature always fills the vacuum of inexplicit space. In one of his poems Paul Goodman observed how out of the pavement in New York City an ailanthus was pushing its way up into life. As to human nature, people spread themselves as they can, and when they reserve parks and vistas they appropriate these as views. The view: prospect of action to come (as with the US Geological Survey's nineteenth-century photography of the Great West by Timothy O'Sullivan as advance surveying for the railway—Nicholas Ray's *Johnny Guitar* [1954] makes reference to the "construction" of the west in its beginning passage).

When presenting a landscape as a form in itself, that is, not a harbor for realistic or mythic human action (see the proportion in Claude's work), the painter is not bothered to "leave room" in the canvas, to save "room" for the visitor's meandering. Growth and presence will be everywhere and anywhere the eye can penetrate. If we look at Peter Paul Rubens's "Shepherd with His Flock in a Woody Landscape" (1615–22) or at Meindert Hobbema's "Wooded Landscape" (1667) we find human figuration in a likely, but also notably reduced placement, working merely for scale and as one of the standard indications of civilized force having taken some limited control of the wildness. We do not see paths, roads, hillocks, trees, and fields arranged so as to make room for a human prominence; we see a human experience fitted into a landscape that came before. In the Rubens, the shepherd is pausing at a brook, but the brook is part of the world that is, was, and will be (and the sheep seem to tuck into it, natural parts of this world themselves).

A radical comparison: look at the situation depicted in Richard Fleischer's *Fantastic Voyage* (1966). Miniaturized human scientists have been injected into the afflicted body of a diplomat whose brain must be made to function again. They pass through the circulatory system and are amazed by the copious platelets streaming past. Albeit this image represents a scenario entirely (if not wildly) fabular nevertheless there is nature in the blood; and the human circulatory system, as least schematically, does look like this in part. The scene, then, is as representative, as cluttered with investments, as Rubens's watering place and Hobbema's wood, but it is not difficult to see how the set has been built, designed, colored, and lit in order to concentrate our attention, after a quick initial shock at the surround, upon the human crew guiding the ship along. *Honey, I Shrunk the Kids* (1989) shows a terrestrial design—latex and Styrofoam and paint—photographed to wrap itself around, and in this way feature, the child protagonists of the moment; full-screen "design clutter" except that the arrangement of forms and the color contrast between them and the background puts our concentration on the figures alone. Here and in *Voyage,* "nature" has grown into the available space, but the depiction eschews a view of unbridled growth in order to arrange a human scene. Alexander Korda's *The Jungle Book* (1942), an early (and stunning) British Technicolor film, makes splendid use of set design, color, and light (in one sequence the jungle combined with a massive reclining Buddha statue) to make the figures—tiny in proportion—stand out. Coloration is central: a gray collapsed tree trunk, a blue stone wall, and the lavender sculpture are all cool enough to recede optically so that the pink garments of the characters leap toward the eye.

Since narrative cinema is constructed to give the narrative special prominence, space is often designed to accommodate it, from any and all angles and at any and every remove. The space is rendered as a diegetic place (see Tuan). Further, as D. H. Lawrence saw,

> Different places on the face of the earth have different vital effluence, different vibration, different chemical exhalation, different polarity with different stars: call it what you like. But the spirit of place is a great reality.
> (6)

In *Jezebel* (1938) Bette Davis is often lit to seem visually integrated into the space, to recede into the clutter instead of emerging as a *figure out of place,* the central reason for the depiction. This framing/lighting design isolates and features a woman whom we are to take as *merely happening* to be where she is, a woman who is in another realm. There is light around her, but the camera's focus helps soften it into a generalized halo. Around the central figure(s) of a sequence there need not be a designed emptiness. The design can be full, depicting the nature of the place, while a negotiation has been effected to reduce some elements in pictorial strength so that other elements may shine.

Reduction

That dwarfing of the human figure logically placed in a vast scape: In *Gerry* (2002), two boys have been hiking the desert (Casey Affleck; Matt Damon). Mountains far off behind them are covered over, uninterruptedly, with intriguing deep furrows and shadowy patches, promising peaks, spreading talus slopes that all have the potentiality to arrest us because they may contain an answer to the film's riddle: the way out. The ground at the boys' feet, the rumples in their clothing, the precise detail of their dropped heads could (but don't) signify, though their bodies are large in the foreground and the lighting has been effected to pick out the (star) faces and frame a vision around them. Reduced entirely to minority status the figures inhabit this "cluttered" space, this vast and ostensibly empty space cluttered with unread clues.

We can make for ourselves what Ortega called "proximate vision," with a field of vision crisply organized:

> In the center there is the favored object, fixed by our gaze; its form seems clear, perfectly defined in all its details. Around the object, as far as the limits of the field of vision, there is a zone we do not look at, but which, nevertheless, we see with an indirect, vague, inattentive vision.
>
> (109)

With intense shadows and downcast posture the boys signal their attitude, but it is the vastness caught by the framing that explains their condition; in the context of the mountainscape, their despondency seems of relatively little interest (ironically). Things have been here a long time, a long long long long time; are here now; will be here tomorrow. On the human scale, in their own ken, the two boys' lives are everything. On the scale of this place, this universe, they are a pair of breaths in a thousand thousand years.

Peek-a-boo

A filmic frame can be composed in such a way that, reflecting a diegetic crisis of the moment, the cinematography collaborates with or passes through the boundary of the story to reflect a redemptive clutter inside the tale: the image is cluttered only because it is fully revealing some dramatically vital clutter that is a figure's surround. Say, a figure notices a situated clutter and, to hide him- or herself or some other figure or thing, "carves" out a position directly inside it so as not to be distinguishable to a judgmental observer inside the story. Jamie (Christian Bale) crawling through the rice paddy in *Empire of the Sun* (1987). The sacred object thrown into the furnace at the conclusion of *Citizen Kane* (1941). E.T. stuffed away for safety in the toy closet in *E.T. the Extra-Terrestrial* (1982).

These hide-and-find constructions work by a delicate arrangement: the viewer must be able to detect "cluttering," found or invented, as indicative strategy; therefore, the image must offer the outside viewer opportunity to (a) suspect the presence of a treasure, (b) not find it, and then (c) find it, and to find reasonably demonstrated how it could have been that the inside viewer didn't detect. Part of one's viewing pleasure will be a sense of triumph over figures who *will look but signally fail to see*. Screen figures do not normally tuck things away from our view, only from the views of other screen figures.

Note: tucking away isn't the same as framing out. The camera can frame materials out that we easily take to be "in the picture" and "related to the goings-on." But a figure of the screen indicating to us that something is being withheld from our sight only raises the ante on a situation, a little trick that surely can be used in the storytelling but very rarely is. The viewer becomes hyperconscious of a staged ploy to affront and deny her, it being generally taken for granted that anything and everything that exists in the dramatic world is and should be there for us in one way or another.

Pathway

The eye finds a pathway through the forest of symbols (as Victor Turner labeled one kind of surround). Every frame, every picture, every composition is potentially a confusion and a conundrum, material being arranged in numerous axes and having been selected to give various hints of narrative importance. Part of the viewer's task, picked up by inveterate film watchers with so much ease they address it more or less unconsciously, is organizing the elements of the image in a pyramid of declining importance from the most to the least significant items for selection and notice. What should be centered? What should be left to spread, fade, or drop away on all sides? What binds one thing to another? And this organizing: we do it very swiftly. More: as each momentary selection of key material represents a node in a moving wave, in making selection one considers not only the aesthetic appeal of the instant but also probabilities, that anything and everything in a film image bears some likelihood of a forthcoming continuation of appearance; so that in order to follow pictured events one must seize upon and centralize the most probable aspects of the image now and for the immediate future. Seize, hold, follow forward, until some punctuative tactic—a fade, a dissolve, a pan—that indicates a breath or change of attention is warranted. When we watch film, then, we are ongoingly picking our way through clutter, even a clutter of abject emptiness (as in *THX 1138* [1971] with its blinding all-white environment).

The viewer will have to make a pathway forward and (perhaps faultily) sketch another pathway leading backward to assist memory's reconstruction. But the filmmaker has a pathway in mind, too, and can direct or misdirect the viewer toward it or away from it. A central feature of suspense-related films is a peculiar and intentional misdirection that leads viewers to calculate a practicable path far from the one on which the story will be running. Mysteries, such as *Psycho* (1960) and *The Crying Game* (1992), thus have developmental strategies that are unpredicted in the audience because they were designed to be unpredictable. It can be that the viewer becomes aware of being lost and struggles to find a better route (a route that makes more things explicable) but one can also stun or shock a viewer by "permitting" formation of what will seem a secure line of procedure and then, in some climactic spasm, revealing matter entirely unexpected and undreamed of (as in *The Sixth Sense* [1999]). In musicals, by contrast, arrayed objects and figures appeal variably and in a broader perspective, leaving the viewer to hope for a combinative resolution—which comes, often boldly and extravagantly, in the finale (see *There's No Business Like Show Business* [1954] for this fragmentation and resolution: a resolution much more tightly organized visually than what came before).

Nothing constrains the viewer who watches a film several times over from picking different pathways forward each time, even pre-briefed by earlier experience. For example, on accreted viewings of *The Third Man* (1949) one has the feeling of finding (of encountering) Harry Lime earlier and earlier and understanding him less and less.

Clutter can be helpfully diminished if audiences "take for granted" screen effects that *could* be attended to, but need not be. Thus, by the mid-1950s viewers had seen so much Technicolor film, especially in musicals, that color itself might "fade" into the zone of the immaterial. Ditto much elaborate costume design, so that costumers had to work harder if they wished to impress. Sets were often taken at face value to be striking in themselves. And widescreen, experienced in 1955 as a visual thrill, could be learned and fully digested as a visual format, ultimately "looked through." In general, effects that had once cluttered, sharpened, and intensified the narrative quite punctually came to be silently "read into" a viewer's incorporation of the picture. Say that audiences watching *The Wizard of Oz* in 1939 were far more stunned—even imprisoned—by the color itself than were audiences watching a similarly colorful *Ben-Hur* twenty years later.

It should be added that when picture makers are lacking in a certain discernment, images can easily be cluttered (without the filmmakers noting) by splotches of sunlight in unhelpful places, sharp glare, out-of-focus objects, spoken dialogue mouthed too quickly, bad microphone pick-up or sound mixing, overlay of distracting musical tracks to cover dialogue-free moments, not to mention performer misarticulations and overdetermined portrait close-ups that block away clarifying visual context.

The Critic

When an image is "filled to the brim" with interesting visual information—say, figures fascinating to look at posed in space fascinatingly designed, and holding fascinating objects, and conversing pithily with one another, so that everything seems to twinkle and glow and beckon to the eye—one requires discernment to select out for concentrated attention. Broadly speaking, the more one looks, the more one knows of the subject, the more discerning one can be. One can see a group of so-thought identical items and through a carefully, patiently, steadily, unflinchingly aimed gaze discern the small differences between them. The project is like that of the street photographer, who literally pursues the image, the telling instant, the adequately lit angle, and keeps shooting if he can, even when he has caught the frame he thinks he wants, because beyond the wanting he knows that he cannot see what is on the negative until he processes the film. Perhaps the camera will see, and only later be known to have seen, something he didn't recognize at the time—perhaps doesn't recognize still now. The prolonged gaze, the cautiously adventuresome gaze allows for a moment to discern. There is a splendid tiny moment in *The Red Shoes* (1948) when Lermontov (Anton Walbrook) has to choose *which* red shoes will be used in his ballet; he walks with purpose along a line of shoe pairs, halting in the middle and pointing with his stick. François Truffaut pays homage to this with a splendid tiny moment in *La nuit américaine* (*Day for Night*, 1973) when the filmmaker has to choose from a number of similar possibilities for a gun that will be used at a crucial moment in his picture. Discernment, discernment, discernment.

The word *critic* refers to *one who discerns*.

To *criticize* is to discern. Discern, not preach. Discern, not cleanse the environment. Discern, not evoke taste. One has known since one's earliest days how to like some things that taste good and dislike what tastes bad, and this has nothing whatever to do with critical discernment. The critic sees what is there.[1]

When the screen is cluttered—and to some degree it always is, one way or another—one's *critical* task is to look and discern with vitality. To see *through* the clutter, to what the clutter is covering. Which is finally to see *the clutter itself*, as an aesthetic form.

Talk

My comments so far about clutter have referred principally to the visual. When a story is elaborated through speech, and when speeches contain vital tags of "information," it is a matter of direct prose composition to lead an audience down one path, or to mislead it down another.[2] Acoustic clutter is the compounded aggregation of *all* things said and sounded, all tones and timbres, all associated linguistic contexts and reactive emotions, and

---

[1] I am grateful to Jason Jacobs for discussing discernment with me.
[2] One must be wary of screen captions with films not in one's language, because these are only rough approximations of what is being said. Captioning is an outsourced procedure, not handled as part of the film's production.

so on. As we tend to filter when we hear—or at least, as some of us do—this aggregate is almost never experienced as what it is, and "important" sounds are selected out from the background, rather in the way that in communication protocols signal is isolated from noise. With film, however, *noise* is very hard to be sure about. Jacques Attali writes of a "primordial, threatening noise," communication with which is *prayer*. He refers to Genesis, the *chaos* before there was form. If a discerning way of hearing is some kind of defense against the power of that noise, some kind of tamping down or distancing or controlling by shaping, then in cinema, guided as we are to the "important"—say, prayer-worthy—sounds, we may be hearing only in order to save ourselves.

From this intense array the viewer must decide what to value most, that is, what to presume figured characters are valuing most whilst they utter. Melodrama is a direct challenge to decision-making of this kind, since in that form the disguise of value becomes of paramount dramatic importance. In all movie watching, making sense involves for the spectator a plunge into the sonic clutter, a distinguishing what is momentarily relevant—or only blatant—from what is "background," although the ear, open to all sounds from all directions, does a comparatively poor job of this. R. Murray Schafer taught that "the more discriminating we are about sounds, the better the signal-to-noise ratio we will demand in our ascoustic environment" (8), but becoming discriminating is the challenge and the difficulty. The star of the story we will always hear, of course. Yet how does it happen, how can it be, that the protagonist always has the most crucial things to say? Certainly by convention, but if the convention is spotted as such, viewer's engagement wears thin.

The relation between appearance and claim finally becomes available to the viewer's judgment. In simple—or mechanical—narratives, every figure's truth is fully stated at each moment to the degree that it can be found relevant (to other figures, thus to the viewer), and what makes for story complication is a particular arrangement of truth-tellings and truth-announcements by which conflicts, resolvable and irresolvable, are created. When a figure "holds back from" speaking, the holding back is (somehow) not held back and, indeed, may become dramatically central, as we hear in, say, *Gosford Park* (2006). When a figure stores or deposits a thought, silently, we are given to see the storing or depositing. It will seem incongruent for someone to claim, late in a film, "Oh, I had that idea a long time ago but didn't tell anyone," if we didn't notice the initial thought. When a figure finds the world funny, a smile comes into the eyes; when sad, a frown—silences both. The story becomes a kind of clockwork, with figures geared into one another's presence through articulated expressions oral, postural, facial. Not merely the physical *being in space*, but the posed presence-in-moment signals the status and attitude of a being.

But as figures onscreen are free from the obligation to speak the truth always, deceit or its possibility exists fundamentally; yet dramatically, there is never a point to a figure lying without our knowing—now or later—that she is doing it. Once a figure can lie, both other figures and the audience are faced with the difficulty of aligning appearance, manner, gesture, placement, origin, and avowed purpose with utterance; suspicion enters the narrative universe. A figure whose language is plain and clear may thus have a hidden motive in what I would call an "organic" story structure; an entire second, secreted world of action is invoked beneath the obvious, and the figure's hidden motive is the key. Bertrand Tavernier's *Death Watch* (1980) is built around a striking problem of the organic kind. The viewer must have binary vision, watching at one and the same time the surface that is given for presentation and the (only) hinted underside that is not. In "mechanical" story structures, by contrast, nobody has hidden motives, but overt motives might conflict (Preston Sturges is a master at this), and the possibility that presences may be gathered together in a straightforward arrangement doesn't contradict the possibility, or likelihood, that the overall situation may be manifestly difficult or impossible. Many animated cartoons work this way: see for a hilarious case Chuck Jones's *Duck Amuck* (1953). In the 1920s, organic stories came into popularity—consider *The Hands of Orlac* (1928) or *The Unknown* (1927); then developed with the marriage comedies of the 1930s, the noirs and police procedurals of the 1940s, and the melodramas and adventure stories of the 1950s. By the 1960s, when cinema became interested in sociology, motives were hidden everywhere. It became possible to envision a social scene in which not only were there motives in the dark but the displayed act of hiding motive itself became a highlight of the story, and one could compare various characters as to their deftness at keeping what really moves them out of sight. There is plenty of this to catch, motivated in a symphony of different talents, in *The Asphalt Jungle* (1950).

Organic arrangements are cluttered differently than mechanical ones since details are spread across many levels, as in a department store, at the same time that we are flooded with *layered* claims, disclaimers, assertions, questions, aggravations, aspirations, fears, suspicions, verbal hesitations, and other acoustic "noise," all cluttering the appearance of things but from *underneath*. In mechanical, or surface cluttering, it is lines of tension between openly shown figures that we must tease apart. There is carefully marked organic acoustic clutter, for example, at the moment in *Letter from an Unknown Woman* (1948) when after walking with a young soldier in Linz Lisa tells her parents she is "spoken for": they hear one thing; she means, and we hear, another. What she hides is central; what she says is marginal distraction. All the clutter directed at the parents here, is directed from her—though not the Lisa they know how to recognize.

Trying to discern centrality, then, one is beset not only by a visual array but also by assertions of variant quality, challenging us to connect them with other utterances heard or still remembered. A figure who seems dominating and gorgeous might turn out, too soon, to be dead, or of only trivial interest, or a deflection; while a figure to whom nobody has paid any attention might become heroic (see, for an intentionally confusing example, *The Big Sleep* [1946]).

(Obstructive) clutter is augmented, even exacerbated, when "posturing," "performance," and "masquerade" blatantly enter the proceedings, since now any figure may turn out to have more than one voice and more than one way of appearing to others. One is continually probing beneath costumes, beneath beards, beneath hairstyles, beneath speech patterns and local accents, in order to find out who a figure *really is,* that is, who the figure is to be understood as being at the level of narrative resolution (*Midnight Lace* [1960], *The Passenger* [1975], *Watchmen* or *I Am Love* [both 2009]). When a film has a very large principal cast (accounting stars and character players only), one is confronted by two tasks throughout, and they are off-putting when combined: (1) to separate and decode all the signals clearly: casting agents not infrequently select numerous actors whose facial structures or hairstyles, as conceived for the production, seem so similar that keeping them coherent and apart will be sure to present difficulty; (2) to reasonably discriminate away the items meriting "inattention" so as to find a trail through the thorny woods. See *Murder on the Orient Express* (1974).

Clutter's Own Voice

There is more to linguistic clutter than jumbling intentful, sincere, deceitful, and manipulative utterances in the marketplace of meanings. Usually, "deceit" is resolved definitively by the end of the film, so that at least retrospectively the viewer can gather who was Good, who was Evil, and how the ultimate Triumph of one over the other actually worked. But what about entirely forthright and convincing speeches, from multiple characters bent on projects that do not yet, perhaps do not ever, discernably overlap or mesh? George and Martha in *Who's Afraid of Virginia Woolf?* (1966): do their projects finally mesh? As screen folk may not necessarily be talking with or to one another, but be broken apart into different scenes, the audience would expect no direct bridges of continuity between them. Further, every leap brings us into a situation already in progress—everything in cinema is already in progress. Whatever is being said we catch on the run, as a fragment. Voices can be notably different, with distinct timbres and rhythms, and all utterances do not necessarily unify.

As to catching on the run: in Antonioni's *The Passenger,* a journalist presumed dead is traveling around Europe with a purloined identity. Back in London, his estranged wife—his "widow"—is with the fellow's television producer, looking at some video material he shot and discussing him in the past tense. Cutting back and forth here, one is always knowingly in place and one comprehends the conversations as far as they go, but if we are to take the talk in the two situations to be happening at the same diegetic moment the only way to "tidy the clutter" of the fragmentation is by way of irony, listening for phrases that have meaning *to us* beyond what they can mean to those who speak them. Often in cinema altogether, but very much in contemporary cinema today, irony functions as a clearing mechanism. In a banquet scene in *I Am Love*, a whole second universe is invoked by virtue of the soup lingering in a decorative bowl, so that as soon as we look down upon it all the table conversation suddenly starts having double meaning. The abruptness of the dialogue editing in these and other contemporary sequences is in sharp contrast to the fluidity with which intercut sound passages were linked in films of the 1930s—for example, *Dinner at Eight* (1933). There, one tended to find a single continuous line of dialogue development—all of the many figures behaving about, around, in reference to, and for a single event; or in multiple disconnected events. In Howard Hawks's *Bringing Up Baby*, there are scenes involving "internal" dialogue clutter that affects and disorients only the figures in their momentary self-focus but never the audience watching, who understand, from an outside perch, everything the little snippets of talk are meant to aggregate to. The scene with the olive toss in the bar is exemplary, with Cary Grant, Fritz Feld, and Billy Bevan failing because of their discrete placements to note how Katharine Hepburn is dancing a single unbroken and smooth action involving each of them, seriatim.

"Talking past," a form of conversational dismemberment, nicely presents ambiguity as a form of linguistic clutter. Two figures have what seems to each an unproblematic encounter, but they are not talking about the same thing and don't realize this. A standard ploy in comedy, Shakespearean and otherwise. Of this, no better cinematic example than Abbott and Costello's "Who's on First." Or plain linguistic ambiguity: in *The Man Who Knew Too Much* (1956), ostensibly no comedy, a dying man confesses to a stranger a name that seems bizarre, and it is discovered to be that of a taxidermist. But when he is found, the taxidermist, a tranquil, elderly, peaceable man (who stitches up dead animals) doesn't understand why our seeker is seeking him. Soon, the hunter admits he is searching because a man is dead, and the old taxidermist surmises, on the spot, that some exotic form of taxidermy is being asked of him. "Gallows humor."

When an ambiguity of speech is posed without any resolution at all, a genuine comedic punch can be produced. Near the beginning of Tony Richardson's *The Loved One* (1965) puckish Dennis Barlow (Robert Morse) queried by his seatmate on an aircraft what his profession is, replies earnestly, "Artificial insemination donor." The duality between puckish Dennis as a masturbation addict and sober Dennis as a loyal public servant is never undone.

Verbal ambiguity openly delivered can cause spectatorial alternation between one and another possible meaning of a word or phrase, between two lines of action; this way, in a sense, clutter is being produced not by the film but by the viewer. In *Ninotchka* (1939) Léon (Melvyn Douglas) has invited the hyper-stiff Ninotchka Ivanova (Greta Garbo) to his apartment in order to woo her:

LEON: Ninotchka, do you like me just a little bit?
NINOTCHKA: Your general appearance is not distasteful.
LEON: Thank you.
NINOTCHKA: Look at me. The whites of your eyes are clear. Your cornea is excellent.
LEON: Your cornea is terrific.

Is she slyly taunting him, saying he is pleasing to look at but by using such language as would convey a military inspection? Is she pretending to a professional diagnostic attitude or authentically displaying one when she points to his "cornea"? And does she pick up and enjoy his slightly mocking echo of the same word? He uses the word "terrific" to offer an explosion of desire, but does she or doesn't she regard his comment as diagnostic, too? Two optometrists by moonlight. The possibilities of *double entendre* are rife in this Lubitsch film. Verbal "clutter" is partly what makes Lubitsch Lubitschean.

There are many other possible constructions of spoken clutter, such as when we see two sides of a telephone conversation at once and in the double vision are brought to know that one party is misleading the other with language that actually does not mean what it sounds like: language sent out as false packaging but heard ingenuously. The bathtub sequence of *Pillow Talk* (1959) is constructed on the basis of such clutter, ironically placed where two different people are cleaning themselves. Generally the audience is faced with ambiguity between the words to be heard coming out of a figure's mouth and the face containing that mouth at the instant the words are spoken—especially if a device of some kind separates two conversants in geography. A listener to a phone picks up every syllable but has no picture to accompany. In such a case—frequent in screwball comedy—a listener may completely miss an ambiguity that is presented to strike us. In face-to-face situations the viewer usually weighs the sincerity of speech against the presumable sincerity of facial expression. It is interesting that the reverse possibility, measuring the sincerity of the face against the presumable sincerity of the voice, is realized but rarely: a fine case is Alec Guinness's performance as unsmiling Yevgraf, the coolheaded but, as we hear when he speaks, warm-hearted half-brother of Yuri Zhivago.

Pictorial Ambiguity

A special case of optical clutter is presented by special effects sequences that give a presumably unfettered picture of an impossible world/situation: again false packaging that is not—that cannot be—determined to be false, in this event meticulously, even obsessively detailed. In a sense, everything we see is clutter covering a field we wished to find, a field of the plainly "real." In these cases, there is virtually nothing but clutter onscreen. Some of these films are dated. Nathan Juran's *The Seventh Voyage of Sinbad* (1958) poses an evil magician (Torin Thatcher) leading his pet dragon through the valleys of a mysterious island. "Follow! Follow!," he urges again and again, "Follow! Follow!" And, clumping footstep by clumping footstep, the gigantic beast dutifully complies. As we see them profiled in long shot, the little man urging on the mega-beast along the rocks and sand, we must mentally toggle between:

- the diegetic meaning being suggested, that something awful will happen as a result of the action of this beast urged on by this horrible master, principally because the beast is obedient and the master epitomizes evil; and
- realization that this is a Ray Harryhausen Claymation dragon, there being no such things as dragons in the real world; every twitching movement of the thing is delicately produced in stop-motion, and the stop motion has been combined with matted photography to get Thatcher, filmed live, into the picture.

We have, then

- [A] Nefarious Sokurah calling his pet beast for help, and
- [B] Torin Thatcher shooting this scene alone, looking up at what will later be animated in, but at present isn't there, and working by shouting at it to convince us he sees his beast.[3]

Because stop-motion animation is typically detectable as such (a more recent and, some admirers say, more sophisticated rendition is Nick Park's *Chicken Run* [2000]), a viewer is confronted with a cluttering dualism and alternation: story > production > story > production. Tom Gunning's critique of the rationality-affirming "intellectual disavowal," "I know, but

---

[3] The delicacies, delights, and perils of stop-motion animation combining action from living people are noteworthy in the extreme and deserve very serious attention. A clay dragon can be manipulated by hand frame by frame if necessary; a human being cannot. There is exquisite work by Harryhausen to be seen and appreciated in *20 Million Miles to Earth* (1957).

yet I see," is illuminating in this context ("Aesthetic" 117), albeit it doesn't quite touch the buried anxiety of loving an image on one side while telling oneself such love is forbidden (or self-indulgent; or insane), on the other; that is, the purported imperiousness of knowledge over optical experience. Often in his ethereal dramas, such as *The Darjeeling Limited* (2007), *Moonrise Kingdom* (2012), and *The Grand Budapest Hotel* (2014), Wes Anderson produces ambiguous clutter by juxtaposing carefully cast characters against intrusive scenic design, always as visible or more visible than the screen figures; something of an homage is given by Bong Joon Ho in *Snowpiercer* (2013), where not only the settings but the actors themselves are brought into ambiguous contrast with the figures they play.

Special effects that do not trouble to self-identify as special effects do not produce the "effects intrusion" so familiar to adepts who gripe about or praise SFX work they have cannily detected. Over time, techniques of both production and detection change. Look at *Forbidden Planet* (1956), or *The Elephant Man* (1980), or *Avatar* (2009) to find successive, but usually, at the time, unspotted "effects intrusions"—for all, in the depiction of fictional worlds we stretch our credibility to accept them as integrated and whole. These worlds are fictional for us, to be sure, not just because they pretend to a reality but because the reality they pretend to is inherently unbelievable. But in *How Green Was My Valley* (1941), *Kings Row* (1942), *Some Like It Hot* (1959), *Marnie* (1964), *Jaws* (1975), *Empire of the Sun* (1987), and many other films, much effects work goes undetected as such, adds no "effects ambiguity" to whatever clutter the film may or may not be offering, this because the worlds being depicted, while make believe, smart of what we know already to be real.

On the Hour

In some way that is aesthetically or narratively grounded, viewers always need to know what is happening right now (both in itself and in relation to other apparent happenings in this film) and, for proclamation or disclamation, "when" this happening occurs in the line map of the diegesis. Because film moves forward in real time, no matter its depictions, forward diegetic movement always seems more natural, easier to digest, than backward. And sometimes in a flash, a story leaps far forward or far backward, but to a setting that looks identical to the point of departure. The narrative event will be interpreted on the basis of events that preceded it in real time: *preceded*—that is, we saw the events already and, as timed on our wristwatch, not so long ago. A radical leap backward in diegetic time can be seriously confounding, events now being posited that in some arcane complexity *precede* what we saw already. (*Citizen Kane* is a special nightmare in this respect; as is *Gone for Good* [2021].) We can also have

"After the future." The experience of the moment can be cluttered by temporal confusion.[4]

A jump can be made toward an indeterminate temporal situation. This produces another kind of doubling, or clutter, since both (1) the action detail (a figure standing in a room) and (2) its temporal setting (the day after what we just saw; five years after what we just saw) are to be noted and comprehended at the same time, and without screen tagging. David Lowery's *A Ghost Story* (2017) has many complex transitions of this kind, some indicating a far future, some a distant past, some jumping a short period (hours), some a very long but unspecified one (centuries), and meanwhile onscreen to be witnessed, as we are borne along in this fashion, are events of the subtlest delicacy, where the tiniest displacement of a figure's posture or position can have huge interpretive consequence. We must shift from (1) considering details as relevant to the action at hand to (2) noting details as clues to the time frame, and our shifting itself can produce meta-elisions. The film pointedly does not prepare its viewer for temporal jumping before hinting at it—part of its charm.

Period dramas effect a different temporal ambiguity, since if they are very well achieved technically (costumes, sets, actor mannerisms, language: *Gone with the Wind* [1939]), their illusion can wholly absorb the viewing consciousness. Then, altogether wrapped up in a story *in its offering*, one can easily forget *the temporal setting in which one sits to accept the offer*, that is, one can be so enthralled in the diegetic time frame that it becomes a kind of present moment. For such an experience, a falling-out will occur with any however slight indication that a presentation *is being done* (awareness of a costume as a costume, say, on which misadventure, raised to the level of horror, see *Somewhere in Time* [1980]). But when one watches an artfully contrived and fairly absorbing historical scene (*The Ten Commandments* [1956]) or an artfully contrived futurism (*Ex Machina* [2014]), can any one of these seem better than the others, fuller, truer, more *placed?* Even absorbed in a film, one is conscious to some degree that this is not the only historical scene cinema has ever offered. Does a futuristic story exhibit (and repeat) an alarming tendency to seem hypothetical in our active apprehension of the moment (regardless of the fact that of course, as we do know, it is hypothetical) and does a historical epic invite us (repeatedly) to inhabit a space subjunctively—not *because* it is as we see it and know (believe) it but *as though* it were the way we see it and believe it (willing supposition)? We see the Titanic sinking (*A Night to Remember* [1958]): this is a reference to how it (actually) was?, or this is a proposition as to how we

---

[4]The German Netflix series *Dark* (2017) is a three-season experiment with audience confounding and character blurring that, some would argue, doesn't quite come off in the end. Among other conundra is the question of whether the end is at the present, the past, or the future.

might consider the way it was? Are we to think we are there, witnessing the event? Or we are here, witnessing the explicitly witnessable account of an event? It sank this way? *Or is it sinking before our eyes?* Or, a great show and nothing but a great show is before us ... ? The touching confusion at the edge of the screen is in some ways like the confusion we find gazing at a Seurat from a distance and then moving up close where the dots are visible (a Seurat; a printed comic strip), that is, a purely optical confusion; but purely optical only to a degree, because the elaboration before us of a presently non-existent time frame, in precise technical detail, occasions its own troubling dream. One helpful clue here: the positioning of the camera (and the lens) can openly hint at the showmanship of the vision, or can bring forward instead the vitality of instantaneous happening. The "troubles of pinpointing" constitute the clutter here: any working device, mode, tactic, trick, clue, or implication that reduces our viewing certainty.

Repute

Reputations can clutter experience. Thus, a first encounter with a figure can have all the impressive power that comes with unfettered social experience, while, to a viewer's loss, later encounters with the same figure can insist on being "founded in" that first encounter, in short, come clear only as reflections, traces, echoes, shadows. In his remarkable *No Direction Home: Bob Dylan* (2005), Martin Scorsese includes an extraordinary concert sequence (well known to Dylan aficionados) filmed in Manchester, May 1966, at point in his career when Dylan was using an acoustic guitar, backed up by the Hawks, later The Band. All through his singing, which is rich and natural and full of feeling, Dylan is heckled by disgruntled members of the audience who, convinced he has sold out, tell him to "go home!" One voice shouts out, "Judas!" A certain much-popularized and now very familiar "Bob Dylan" was the person these concertgoers had bought tickets to see, and having bought those tickets (perhaps with limited funds) it was him and only him they wanted, *and were willing* to see: see *again*, one could say, because their desire stood upon their vision of something from before. The problem for Dylan, who was allowing himself to grow as musician, performer, poet, and human being, was that a reputation had not only preceded him, it had replaced him. Here, only the traditional Bob Dylan could sing, the one who was known in advance and known, too, outside present experience. Henry David Thoreau: "How deep are the ruts of tradition!" In a tradition-oriented world, very few untrod paths remain for those who would step where no one has stepped before.

"Every generation," wrote Alexander Herzen, "has its own fullness."

to Brandon Cronenberg

11

Poison or Grapes?

From A Night to Remember *(Roy Ward Baker, Rank, 1958). Digital frame enlargement.*

A Silent Question

Do pictures ask us to respond? If they do ask, and we wish to respond, do we know how? As Paul Goodman saw, "The speaker may be all there, but the language is inadequate to say his say" (38). "The great work of the Master who, with all his art, at the cost of his heart's blood, prepared for us the delight which we may enjoy so cheaply, will not reveal itself to us as we pass by—talking perchance the while," wrote Anthony Trollope (163). When we gaze in respectful viewership, should we feel obliged to comment, should we feel invited? Or should we keep silent, let silence reign? Is there a compulsion to speak, an urgency that the picture's glory stimulates? What, in short, is the tantalizing force field between picture and voice, if such a force field exists? *I reveal myself, talk to me.*

When she was about eighteen, a British chum of mine recently confided, she went one day with her brother, two years older, to see *A Night to Remember* (1958), at the time a film considered widely to be something of an extravaganza. They had benefit of a rather large screen (in Hammersmith) at a Saturday afternoon showing, but only a small audience was there, thus, almost no obstruction between them and the film. They sat appropriately wide-eyed, agog, passengers mobbing the steerage, aristocrats jostled by the captain and his officers, the toffs jostling against their wives, and then the Thing, and the water, and the night. When it was all done they crept silently out of the theater, located their Austin Mini, silently crawled in, and silently headed home. After a long while my chum felt she had to break the silence. "So: What did you think about the movie?"

More silence.

Then the brother replied: "Yes! I just didn't understand the bit with the musicians playing on deck while the ship goes under. Would people really do that?"

Dumbfounded, my chum replied, "Wow, from an epic like that, this is all you took away?" Nor has she to this day quite brought herself to accept his so distressingly singular response; and he has moved far away to New Zealand, where he arrived not by ship.

It seems to me my friend had to have been presuming, if not boldly taking, a very clear approach to this film, tagged as a member of the category "Films in General": When you come out of a "Film in General," you talk about what you saw, quite as though the experience at the edge of the screen is pretext for conversation. This is certainly a step away from Trollope's talking while viewing, but it does make talking implicit in viewing. Emerging from cinema one needs accompaniment of some kind, and the talk that binds companions has propriety. It is a long voyage from the screen to the streets, after all—New Zealand is closer. A voyage from the screen to the streets needs a melody.

As I, too, have seen that film, I can attest that when it ends there is no card onscreen that reads, "Thank you for watching. Feel free to raise any question you may have." It would be effortless to manufacture such a sign, film it, and append it at the end of every movie in every theater in the world. But there is no such call, not formally. There is no regulation, no "understanding" that a film—a "Film in General"—will, should, must, cannot but provoke comment, and that such comment should generate discussion, and that discussion could sway attitude and feeling.[1] Unbidden, people talk.

Not that talking is a general response in our culture.

---

[1] I exclude formalized studio preview screenings, after which audiences typically are asked to fill in a card with questions about the film. These tend to occur only in the Los Angeles region, and are, for any film, small in number.

The ease with which we talk about films, become involved in conversations about them (such conversations as my friend's brother was apparently so loathe to join), might indicate that for us the image "naturally" begs a response; tickles, prods, places us under a type of pressure. Movie talk has even been institutionalized, through the professional responders we call critics,[2] some of whom are given airtime in the media, so that what they say will be widely and publicly received—in some cases, received even more widely than a film is distributed. The critic with his response has become something of an entertainment, tending predictably toward acerbity and wit: sometimes a far better entertainment than the film under review. As an entertainment, an "Entertainment in General," the critic gets talked about, too. A person with a critical appreciation (appreciation, not judgment) can even wing off and work independently of a film, holding forth for the benefit of those who would undertake to absorb Holding Forth. Look at me.

I am intrigued here with something far from the appraisals a critic might offer: the fact that we have invented the well broadcast, vastly circulated critic *in order to have judgment said, judgment pronounced*; that the criticism of, the saying about a film has become, if it was not always, part of the viewing experience.

If not always: here in 1896 is Maxim Gorky in Nizhny Novgorod (see also Gunning and Gaudreault):

> There, everything—the earth, the trees, the people, the water, the air—is tinted in a gray monotone: in a gray sky there are gray rays of sunlight; in gray faces, gray eyes, and the leaves of the trees are gray like ashes. This is not life but the shadow of life, and this is not movement but the soundless shadow of movement. ... But suddenly a strange flicker passes across the screen and the picture comes to life.
> (see www.laphamsquarterly.org/arts-letters/life-devoid-words)

(Often in its early days, a film began with a still frame that would "come to life.") Gorky was a writer, however, one of those whose mode of being is linguistic. For those who are not writers or speakers, but who speak and often write about film, need their film attendance mean, essentially, "see in order to speak of"?

Talk

"While the voice may come at me, and *into* me, as a projected sound," writes Brandon LaBelle, "it is the other's mouth to which my body turns"

---

[2]On which social role no comment more acerbic, scathing, and entertaining is to be found than in Anthony Trollope's *The Way We Live Now* chapter 11.

(3). What is it that people talk about that would draw listeners to their mouths? We find Joan Didion listening in at a Hollywood party in 1967: "People talk to each other, tell each other about their first wives and last husbands. 'Stay funny,' they tell each other, and 'This is to die over'" (222). Or in Haight-Ashbury at roughly the same time, where things are notably different: "Words are for 'typeheads,' Chester Anderson tells them, and a thought which needs words is just one more of those ego trips" (128). Or take Siegfried Kracauer in Berlin in January, 1946:

> Signs of the life here: everything transpires in an empty room. Nothing is conveyed. There is no movement nor a favorable atmosphere, and nothing issues as a result. You might best understand what I am trying to describe by imagining that nothing is happening in your house, truly nothing at all.
>
> (qtd. in Schivelbusch, Crater 23)

Talking neither as elaborate, nor as metrical, nor as abstract, nor as formal as writing. What is the species of meaning that is conveyed by talk and that talkers feel they need to have and to share? In an age of global witnessing, when vast populations not saddled with the burden of eking out life spend inordinate time being targeted with information and "entertainment" by the powers that be, it becomes a kind of piety to confess what one has seen, concomitantly what one has heard or seen being said, and much talk about film may serve the purpose of allaying guilt at having had the privilege to witness what others have been denied.

One can typify "film talk":

[1] *Navigational.* This is a utility in our jittering modernity beset by ongoing and unrelenting movement, very often vectorless, where people and things are headed somewhere even if they don't know it. Once the world is understood as being in perpetual motion, one's experience is more likely to include the encounter with strangers, whose way of evaluating, and of talking out an evaluation, may be incomprehensible or conflicting. "Chacun rapporte pour son trophée la tête de l'ennemi qu'il a tué," wrote Montaigne, "Every warrior boasts as trophy the head of the enemy he has slain"; but who is the enemy? Mapping becomes a cardinal act. When one talks, there enters a strict consciousness of elapsing time, of schedule, of pertinence, of courtesy.

People do navigational talk when they are lost, and need to find their "way." In a film it is very easy to get lost; the film is a map of itself. *Citizen Kane,* for a case: I know the scene where Mr. Bernstein tells the story of the girl on the ferry; and the scene where Jed Leland is in the old folks' home. But which comes before the other? Since the story is a place, where am I to locate myself in this story and where will this self-location take me? One can talk about a film by pointing to a stimulating scene, as though the scene exists on its own, floating above the diegesis.

Talking over a film navigationally can resemble hunting in the wild, and the hunter basically unfamiliar with a motion picture will easily fail to find nourishment. Before videotape (essentially the late 1970s), after one had seen a film it disappeared. With tape, one could re-watch what one had seen a long time before; and possibly in re-watching also rewind, to find that precious moment. DVD and Blu-Ray have obvious advantages, and sometimes one finds these advantages in streaming, too. If the story is a melody, when was that glorious note?

But more: when I am telling somebody about a film I've seen, can I and do I avoid thinking and mouthing about this telling? Do I make any acknowledgment at all that my talk is an attempt at finding both myself and my interlocutor in space and time? Further, considering the possibilities of language only, can I possibly find some way to specify how it is that one has a sense of events and time passing in a certain tempo and with a certain rhythm; how someone moves swiftly or slowly from a building to a cottage? And where is the compass for the film anyway?

[2] *Moral, Nutritious*

Moral talk is for trading the good and the bad, not necessarily at the level of serious ethical philosophy, J. L. Austin or Hegel, but through the everyday chatter that finally composes the morality of the street. "That scene was terrific!"—"That scene was terrible!" One makes with one's friend ostensibly agreed-upon valuations. It has long been a problem, then a custom, to discriminate between the nourishing and the poisonous. Indeed, paleolithic hunters knew to discriminate natural substances that could produce poison, sometimes to be used on an arrow tip to bring down prey. Foraging for the daily ration involved knowing what to keep away from, a proscriptive regime echoed in the apple problem in Genesis. In Genesis, eating is equated with knowledge, and we all know how some knowledge is beneficial and some is poisonous. Mary Douglas discusses various ceremonial applications of poison among the Azande, sometimes for the oracular detection of witches—the poisoned oracle would see better (107) or *see in a different mode*. Alain Corbin notes how odor could occupy "the status of a partial poison," recollecting that "Henry VI died from sniffing perfumed gloves" (68), an event that, bruited about the court, could perhaps have acted as some kind of warning. Moral talk as life-saving. "Don't watch that film, it will corrupt you." Even better, NC-17: *No one 17 and under admitted.* Or more casually and generally: "Don't go see that, you'll hate it," or "Go see that, it's fantastic!"

But speech is essentially linked to the problem of poison, because poison is often finally mouthy, and, of course, talk can be poisonous:

IAGO: Rouse him! Make after him poison his delight,

Proclaim him in the streets;

Othello I.i.71–2

Vasari describes a painting of Uccello's, "a scene in which a serpent, doing battle with a lion, shows, with vigorous movements, its ferocity and the poison which it spits from its mouth and eyes, while a nearby peasant girl keeping watch over an ox is painted with the most beautiful foreshortening" (77–8). Da Vinci was ancestor to[3] cinematic monster effects of our day (and was surely an influence on Ray Harryhausen). He

> carried into a room of his own, which no one but he himself entered, crawling reptiles, green lizards, crickets, snakes, butterflies, locusts, bats, and other strange species of this kind, and by adapting various parts of this multitude, he created a most horrible and frightening monster with poisonous breath that set the air on fire. And he depicted the monster emerging from a dark and broken rock, spewing forth poison from its open mouth, fire from its eyes, and smoke from its nostrils so strangely that it seemed a monstrous and dreadful thing indeed.
>
> (288)

We should also consider how the mouth is an organ of preaching, a source of "wisdom" about what to approach and what to stay away from in the quest for perfection. Here is Andrew Sarris, for many years considered a super-*mavin* of American "directors and directions," sermonizing on artists who are "less than meets the eye," presumably to turn us away from them to some degree:

> [John] Huston is still coasting on his reputation as a wronged individualist with an alibi for every bad movie... As a stylist, Huston has always overloaded the physical with the moral... [Elia] Kazan's violence has always been more excessive than expressive, more mannered than meaningful... Whatever artistic sensibility [David Lean] once possessed is safely embalmed in the tomb of the impersonal cinema... The cinema of Joseph L. Mankiewicz is a cinema of intelligence without inspiration... Billy Wilder is too cynical to believe even his own cynicism
>
> (156–7; 158; 160; 161; 166)

Navigational wisdom about purity and impurity, about the stale and the fresh, about the dirty and the clean, about the profitable and the unprofitable is taken in and valued according to the conditions in which readers and listeners live. Some readers and listeners are inherently more

---

[3] In committing his visions to the process of drawing. There were earlier fabularities about monstrous combination (see White).

eager for guidance than others, and some take *being informed* as their right. Walter Benjamin on the newspaper, that tool for packaging wisdoms and circulating them among the multitude:

> Science and belles lettres, criticism and literary production, culture and politics, fall apart in disorder and lose all connection with one another. The scene of this literary confusion is the newspaper; its content, "subject matter" that denies itself any other form of organization than that imposed on it by the reader's impatience. For impatience is the state of mind of the newspaper reader. And this impatience is not just that of the politician expecting information, or of the speculator looking for a stock tip; behind it smolders the impatience of people who are excluded and who think they have the right to see their own interests expressed.
>
> (741)

[3] *Persuasive*
"I've just seen *Titanic,* and it's unbelievable! Go see it immediately!" I've just seen *Elvis!* I've just seen *The Wizard of Oz!* I've just seen *Rancho Notorious!*

Casual discourse, under which rubric I would classify movie chat, will presume an unqualified aesthetic and/or political standard and take the speaker as a qualified arbiter of taste—quite as though, given the unmeasured variation in biography and culture in our world, some lone arbiter figure is indeed imaginable. The urgency, the stridency, the marquee-neonlit-emblazing of the rave is an outering of relief and pleasure, of course, or relief and utter dismay, but it is also—and, I think, not unconsciously—a calculated emphasis, an announcement that sums to an ad. Why does a speaker entranced by a film wish to spread the entrancement (spontaneously and freely on behalf of the producer) except as a way to gain social verification of a feeling that is otherwise in some painful way ungrounded? The film's producer has certainly paid for his own advertisement.

Possibly the need for verification of personal experience derives from a deep conviction that one's feeling must make sense, and gaining another's affirmation is tantamount to being declared "correct," "sane," "sensible." In effect, through movie chat we perform our own attendance and reaction in retrospect, seeking from our own audience the declaration of approval that, in its own way, all staged entertainment seeks. Our joy is someone else's entertainment for the moment. The "legitimate critic" has a very large audience to whom a thumbs up or thumbs down can be shown.

[4] *Alignment*
Alignment talk helps people (a) avoid bumping into one another unnecessarily and (b) make appropriate arrangements to get together. It builds communities of like-thinking individuals who can recognize one

another because their thoughts have been verbally signaled. Alignment talk is a variant of assembly talk more broadly. How to gather, associate, form a group; why to get together, and where and when. Precision alignment is a development of capitalism, given the manager's need to ascertain and assure that the workers will travel from home to the factory on a predictable schedule: you are at home in the shadows where I cannot see you, but when will you be here at the machine under my factory light? Or, alignment talk for administering dissimilar work arrangements woven together for complex manufacture—"You work over there, I work over here"; "You do this part of the job, I do that," as in, "She shoots the film, you cut it." Division of labor (as discussed in Durkheim) we see nicely exemplified in René Clair's *À nous la liberté* (1924) and in Chaplin's *Modern Times* (1936), with no apparent talk at all; thus, alignment talk is not necessarily implicit, fitting the precisely calculated movement among workers. It can be a clock of the everyday.

Because it is formed to be functional in patterns of action that are themselves tight and swift, alignment talk can go wrong if it is overcooked, for example, given out with more specification than is helpful. Here I invent an example one would *not* encounter in the everyday:

> A (emerging from cinema): That movie?... Hmm. In a hundred and twenty seconds, I will be using my ohashi to pick up some daikon, and as soon as I have raised it up about three inches over the polished oaken tabletop I shall ask myself, "Well, yes, indeed, *was* that a good movie?"
>
> B: I understand. I take your point. I'm with you. Yes! I thought maybe what I'd do is, actually slurp some green tea, and then slurp some more green tea, possibly three slurps, and then I would say, "What?!—you think that was a *good* movie?"

Actors can ramble, can oververbalize in this way as they warm up, purely as an oral exercise,[4] but they are careful to do this out of the action, to themselves, out of earshot. For most people, a multiplication of syllables would seem ridiculous, even comedic. We tend to think it ridiculous to align *planned* moves with another person's with too much precision, unless what is being planned is a technical operation of great mechanical challenge: Robert DeNiro's character working with a mirror to guide Jean Réno and Michel Lonsdale in a surgery they perform—with him awake!—to extract a bullet from his side in *Ronin* (1998). A grave circumstance openly and

---

[4]For a truly charged exemplification, see the "rehearsal" scene—which involves a critical piece of cutting—between Meryl Streep and Jeremy Irons in *The French Lieutenant's Woman* (1981).

clearly signaled legitimizes talky detail, even as respite, and justifies the pattern whereby instruction helpfully precedes action and subsequent action is checked against that instruction. We see some of this in the amputation scene in *The Horsemen* (1971), primitive and urgent and notably contrasting with the elision-rich, thus dialogue free amputation scene of *Thirty Seconds Over Tokyo* (1944).

When we align ourselves, our position, with others in regard to a film, we avoid, as though by consensual arrangement, acknowledgment of status and relative position that could place us on a social/geographical map; we become for the moment, equals in posture. Also elided, or made tacit, is offering of permission, on both sides, to continue with the extension of a relationship posed upon that relative positioning. So, for example, the following sorts of pronouncements, entirely utterable, grammatical, and logical, will be taken for granted, if not entirely disattended, instead of being spoken explicitly, because "We just don't talk this way":

> A: Since I recognize myself as your friend, and since we have been friends in this way since childhood; and since I am standing here on the sidewalk in the North End of San Francisco with my face twelve inches away from yours, at twilight, I make bold to tell you that I don't like the way you speak so curtly about *Gravity,* one of my truly favorite films.
> B: Oh! Well,... standing with *my* face twelve inches away from yours, as twilight is now fading, and clearly also in the North End of San Francisco; and acknowledging our extraordinarily long friendship, which I believe began in third grade, in Portland, and notwithstanding that I am now, as always, one year and two weeks older than you, I mean, taking all that for granted, I now convey to you my apology, and also ...

We don't say what is obvious to us in the situation; it is a usefully silent component of the language already, so that pointing to it in any way makes for confusion. The same works with our film talk, when we intentfully neglect to point to many observable, even pungent details that don't at the instant seem pertinent. Thus, the "movie" we are talking about when we talk, is a gathering of momentarily useful fragments. The movie itself is indigestible as a whole.

Artful contraction and ellipsis, ways of packaging mutually acceptable presumptions, will also play a key role in alignments, as in:

> A: Wow! (So, I'm saying to you I loved that film.)
> B: Oh, geez!! (I hated it!)

Or in begging inappropriately for clarification:

> A: You hated it! What do you mean, "hated"? What do you mean exactly?
> B: Hated! You know, Love-hate. I hated it.
> A: Yes, but do you mean the "I" who was in the theater or the "I" who is standing here now talking to me? And do you mean "hate" as in "I hate anchovies" or hate as in "I hate people who say 'I hate'?"
> B: What's the matter with you?[5]

The point is not that commentary involves ambiguities we work to elide. It's that we all know commentary involves ambiguities that should be elided, and we work to elide them and act as though we know we work and have been working. *We talk as though there are surely ambiguities here but they are already resolved.* The film was the film. Yes, we should talk about it; but no, we shouldn't worry too much about what we say or about the fact that we are talking about it; or even about the fact that we are not talking about talking about it.

[5] *Understandings (Sub-stances)*
Can failure to fully and deeply understand another's commentary about a film become an obstruction of any kind?: to a friendship?, to a grasp upon what we saw, what was there to be seen?, to the ability to find full pleasure in the film-watching experience? Perhaps the words we utter are far less relevant than the campfire we build together by agreeing to have a conversation about the film, as though the film has moved us both, as though we are presently sharing enthusiasm's afterglow.

Take, as an extreme case, Rose and Jack's illicit orgasm in *Titanic* that "unexpectedly" coincides with the iceberg's tearing a hole in the side of the ship (talk about pathetic fallacy!). The way this irony is interpreted, post hoc, can imply a certain unavowed moral talk.

> They were so distracting as they panted and moaned, so very distracting, one didn't even see the Rolls Royce anymore, such a beautiful car! But heavens!: just as we were distracted by those bodies *so was the ship!* The ship was us. It was as distracted as we were, listening to the echoes of them. And so it bumped into the iceberg. Supposed to be a genius ship, but actually it's a dumb-dumb. But for certain, the collision was the ship's fault. The ship was paying too much attention to the sex.

---

[5]Inventing this little dialogue I am borrowing from Harold Garfinkel's study of the "technical mastery" of the "moral order without" focused on "commonplace scenes," where he asked his students to imagine expanding a propositional conversation (42–3).

Or,

> Here was a comment (from the filmmaker?; from the filmmaker's preacher?) about the forces of the cosmos, whatever or whoever they are, looking down upon extra-marital sex. The collision happened to disrupt the orgasm that was so very wrong. If these two had only kissed, *and nothing more,* the ship would have avoided the iceberg!

Or,

> It was purely happenstantial that two events happened more or less at the same time (and, speaking historically, this is probably what really happened and the filmmaker was trying to get the historical reality right). The moral message is: *no moral message.*

Or,

> James Cameron dreamed this up, thinking it would be a nifty dramatic moment to appeal to teenage viewers. Totally exploitative.

Or,

> Cameron knew we would be so distracted by the sex that we'd stop paying attention to the iceberg and then, at the collision, we'd be shocked, and we'd understand the shock on board, but in any event it would be a shock *in the movie* and this would make the movie especially exciting.

The happening inside the theater, inside the auditorium of whatever size where spectators watched, was more or less unitary in a crucial respect: *this thing* was there to be seen. A machine beamed light through a linear series of film frames containing composed images, and for each member of the viewing audience the film inside the projector is technically the same film. Scenes or moments play out in only one syntactical order, although it is possible for various people to receive the film, think of it, digest it, remember it in idiosyncratic ways. When we speak of a film to one another, we are speaking of our memory, after all; perhaps, dear reader, you have the misfortune of recalling all those nervous chatterboxes in the dark, who wouldn't shut up while the film was screening? Finally, who can claim real knowledge of what *this thing* is, or was, or can be, outside of a particular memory and view of it, as though in a black night and in different vessels spotted about a grand sea we take careful readings of a star and some monstrous vessel sinking into the black, beneath it. The vulnerability of seeing, of remembering what we saw, or even the blindness of sight: that when a film plays out before us we are caught seeing it, yet we do not see; or do not see enough.

Silence

The quality, duration, and styling of viewers' attention can be structured from without. Given the movie theater as a form—seats all pointing one way, projection booth hidden behind spectators; an extraordinarily high-beam projector making a brilliantly lit fourth wall—we have the attentive audience almost as a by-product. Audience attention is fostered and abetted by the brilliance of that light, which contrasts impressively with the overwhelming darkness of the viewing space. Another way to see this (the way children see it): the theater is in darkness except that light flickers into it from the screen. All the available light emanates from the film in its peculiar, incomparable way. Wolfgang Schivelbusch declares the 1750s the moment when auditorium lighting dimmed relative to the stage and the stage was "seen as an autonomous space for creating aesthetic illusions that was strictly separated from the audience" (*Night* 205). First, then, the brilliant stage, for opera and drama: Gluck's *Alceste,* 1776; Mozart's *Così fan tutte,* 1790; Beethoven's *Fidelio,* 1805; Drama by Congreve, Dryden, Wycherley … Later, after 1890, an especially illuminated fourth wall for cinema, first makeshift in a nickelodeon upon a stretched sheet but not so long afterward formalized on the stage of a legitimate theater. The theater as an arrangement of space brings out our attention by way of characteristic light. We are transfixed. Perhaps in being transfixed by a film we are also moved. But what is it that leads from the highly lit fourth wall, the special presentation, and feelingful attendance to the *expository* audience?

One can be frozen into silence after a screening—this happened with *Titanic,* and it did with *The Manchurian Candidate* (1962) and *Caché* (2005) and *Clouds of Sils Maria* (2014), among other films. In the early months of 1966 there was rapt silence in the audience when *Blow-Up* ended. The *notable* inability to talk is only itself a way of expressing by showing an impossibility, soundlessly pointing to the conventional use of words to carry sound. Dirk Bogarde recollects the Cannes première of Bertrand Tavernier's *Daddy Nostalgie* (1990): "The film was followed in utter silence. Not a cough, a whisper, only very soft sobbing!" (386).

Thinking about *Titanic:* I

Things of our world don't float in a vacuum, and the film *Titanic* is a thing of our world. Must one place it? Does the way one sees such a work depend on what is next to it in consciousness, already, in real space and time, or else in memory, or in hope, or in belief? A "set" of some kind has *Titanic* as a member.

Consider, (a) *the film as a theatrical event.* When it is onscreen it inhabits a particular theater. Is it comparable to another movie we saw on this same screen, and are now remembering having seen? Have we made a mental map of this theatrical territory, then?: the aisle leading away from the seat and into the lobby, the walkway through the lobby and the pavement and thence to the end of the block and the bus stop? We often see a film where the venue is a center of concern, overriding all else.

Or (b) *the film as an instance of distribution.* One's reception could be organized and understood in terms of how a particular movie circulates: what other films were out there to tease the public, in the same week, films one passed by in order to go to *Titanic* four times? Or, one might be interested in how *Titanic* worked with clearances: it could have been seen in a movie palace in the downtown of a major urban center (such as Balaban & Katz's Chicago on State Street, Chicago) or in a much smaller venue in a small town (such as the Norwood on Manitoba Street, Bracebridge). A film faces different competition in the big city, but the A-list theater gives it cachet, echo, "noise."

A viewer could think of a film (c) *in historical terms.* That is, in terms of a personal history of viewing, or indeed in terms of the history of Hollywood. *Titanic* could appear to a viewer who earlier read about the tragedy in several historical accounts of the events of 1912. Or to a viewer who a few weeks before had seen *Good Will Hunting* (1997).

This film, any film, is also seen in accordance with a viewer's (d) *"image" of the world* (Boulding 3ff). The locus of the sinking is about a thousand miles away from where I sit writing, and where I see the film screened. This R.M.S. Titanic onscreen: is it drifting out there in the ocean that I cannot at the moment see, or sunk at the bottom of that ocean; is it "nearby"? And what is the relationship between the ocean that the Titanic sailed in 1912 and this "ocean" I am seeing lavishly depicted onscreen? To make a case: I was standing in the lobby of the Elizabeth House Hotel in Southampton, England, not more than roughly half a mile away from the spot from which the Titanic sailed in 1912, and there in the lobby was a photograph of the ship at the pier at that time; how, in that place, do I think of the ship and of the film as related to the ship? Nor do we fail to know that onscreen was an *image* or *picture* of the ocean, not the ocean. But was it a picture of the ocean or a picture of a studio tank got up as the ocean? Is the film invoking an argument about realism and representation? About imagination and knowledge? In seeing, are we wondering through the issue of how a picture of water can produce drowning? Viewing *Titanic,* do we all drown in the picture in a particular, mystifying way?

How did Jack and Rose crawl into that Rolls-Royce anyway? Didn't people lock their cars, down in the hold?

Imagine another pathway, (e) *social portrayal.* What universe, what world, what social setting does this film occupy as a narrative account? England 1912? Upper-class England 1912? A wooden deck where classes mix and confound? If *Titanic* is historical, should I pay particular attention to props, settings, costumes, and manners intended to "replicate" authentic 1912 versions of same? (When I keep noticing that the ship's interior seems very, very freshly to have been built I remind myself that of course it is, this is the Titanic's maiden voyage!—yet I *do* have to keep reminding myself, because the freshness seems contemporary with my viewing, it seems persistently to characterize a freshly finished film set.) Should I study the shipping routes and the details of shipping in April 1912? Should I watch for details about shipboard crews and their hierarchy? Should I try to understand destitute poverty in Southampton, Jack's diegetic origin? Or should I ask what is going on "now" as a cue for invoking a sensible response? Or is the *Titanic* I see in the theater merely an outcropping of its own promotion? Many such considerations could shape the conditions in which the film finds itself (i) before viewers' eyes and (ii) coming out of viewers' mouths. If I should think to talk of a world pointed to by this creation, if I should consider *Titanic* as a window upon some cultural reality, how else, beyond James Cameron's address, might that world have been commented upon—in drama, in photography, in painting, even in dance, in journalism of the time, in memoirs, in historical accounts, in historical *records,* in autobiographies and biographies, in whatever social gossip one can dig up? By looking this way, one would be circling around the estimation of *Titanic* as "realistic" and perhaps wondering what select "reality" or "realities" it points to, and how it points, and how it fails to point.

(f) Genre can come up: *Titanic,* an "ocean film," like, say, *Jaws* (1975) or *The Poseidon Adventure* (1972) or even *I Love You Again* (1940). An "architectural disaster" film, like *The Towering Inferno* (1974) or *2012* (2009). A love story like *Romeo and Juliet* (1968) or *The Seventh Voyage of Sinbad* (1958). A social-class commentary, like *Saturday Night and Sunday Morning* (1960) or *The Out of Towners* (1970) or *Howards End* (1992). *Titanic* could be regarded, remembered, recollected as part of the oeuvre of James Cameron, a reflection of his methods; or as a Jon Landau production, in part; or an excuse for James Horner to write another score, or for Celine Dion to sing a song? When one considers the collaborations into which a filmmaker would enter—with money people and with performers and with technical experts—one might ask whether *Titanic* sets off not from a ship at a quay in Southampton but from Twentieth Century Fox and Paramount and their internal hierarchies of decision making and influence.

Parading through questions like these one could perhaps become ready to sail, or could feel the waters sloshing over the head.

Thinking about *Titanic:* II

But how about this?

Since *Titanic* is a (brave and exorbitant) recounting of the well-known ship disaster, the by now very, very well-known ship disaster, which is to say, the often referenced ship disaster about which most of those who reference it know virtually nothing … it asks the viewer to sit and untangle events that one already expects to find depicted, albeit events here decorated by tiny revelatory instances, possibly inventions, about character personality. The viewer has full knowledge of what is about to happen, broadly speaking, and knows, too, roughly when this will all be, *when* as measured against other rhythmically unfolding events depicted onscreen. As the film winds on, and we come closer and closer to the fatal moment, that moment not only gains expansive (and expensive) treatment onscreen but begs especially honed audience attention, since the content of the images at that point will assuredly be fleshly mortalities tinged with principled moralities. There will be, too, the undeniable spectacle of the mammoth construction smoothly slipping beneath the waves—nothing less than sublime—at first slowly but inexorably (a technical fact or a set-up for the viewer's thrill), then more quickly and with what can be felt as an immeasurably grand sigh. Waiting for this payoff shot as we build our way through the screen action, yet waiting for specifically *this* payoff, regardless of how it will be seen, we feel together a mounting excitement and a mounting desire for avoidance, call it shame. There is a building, a bursting, and a dénouement perfectly laced together, that can only be thought pornographic in the way the gawker's enthusiasm is toyed and tinkered with by a vivacity she cannot touch. Escorted by the camera *aboard* the ship in new and unheralded ways (all Titanic renditions get us aboard somehow but not in the dynamic way Cameron does), we are given to experience the awkward tremble beneath us and can imagine ourselves sensing, perhaps bodily, how horrible it would be—it will be?; it would be?; it will be?—to find oneself cast into the sea. To imagine sensing the sea before experiencing; yet, since we cannot experience, to *imagine in lieu of experiencing*. For all Cameron's daring camera angles, we remain dry.

But dry, we witness a kind of mass execution set in a floating palace.

Again, there is nothing here we did not already "know" (beyond the young lovers' moaning and the old lady's memory of long ago remembering that moaning), unless we are totally blind to twentieth-century history. Since everything that is here and now unfurling (spontaneous and fresh and present) is, we can grasp, in truth lost and gone, now merely a pale reflection of what nobody doubts happened, we are continually weighted with the feeling of seeing with unfettered eyes a spectacle that is at once only the record of a fact, if not, indeed, the "record" of a "fact." More: even before opening our eyes, we are made aware that we will be watching a record of an Already-Past (and I don't mean a film the scenes of which already happened before the camera). We're going to stare at "something that happened a long time ago," considered and reconsidered and reconsidered and reconsidered again, yet as we stare we are to permit the temporal narrative to convince us that this outplay is not an Already-Past but a Present, not a having-happened but a *happening,* right here, here where we are placed to observe at both an exact latitude and longitude in the Atlantic and an exact latitude and longitude before the screen. Indeed, we are seeing it happen *for the first time.* Here. Now.

As Tennessee Williams had it in *Camino Real,* we're under a full moon and the gypsy's daughter is getting her virginity back.

And we are seeing, as we properly should be, from the best seat in the house. Thank you, Mr Cameron.

Thinking about *Titanic:* III

Most viewers would shy away from thinking themselves hungry for pornography—that ineffably sweet release from the agonizing promise of sweet release—so that here, as in the cases of other movies that have luscious set-ups of similar opulence, a cover denial is in order, properly to soothe us: something a viewer can latch onto, something so very blatant and obvious, indeed something so mythic and supramundane, that one could preface spelling it out with an "of course." In this case there exists, and has since 1912, a *de rigueur* explanation or accounting, and this is the Tower of Babel analogy, fundamentally a claim that presumptuous, technological man boasted of himself that he had created the supreme machine, one that would float with an enormous mass, that would be as elegant inside as a palace, and that would speed from Southampton to New York faster than any ship ever built. Further, the puissant money men who not only shelled out for this floater but took the dare to ride it on that first, that fateful voyage—these men had hired engineers so capable, so utterly brilliant, so infallible that when they produced the boast that this one should be thought "unsinkable" they were to be heeded, indeed soon enough taken for granted. So here was the unsinkable thing sinking, a message from the gods that no *hubris* goes unpunished. The Titanic had to sink precisely because the lords of the universe claimed it couldn't, all this in order for the multitudes to learn that humans are not gods.

A lesson of incalculably tragic proportions for the masses on board.

Thus, of course, this tale is a drama in the Greek tradition, huge, powerful, encompassing, passionate, base, affronting, and human. That beneath every pyramid sits the punctured psychology of a wounded human being who had been, once, Ozymandias.

When, after a screening, the plot of *Titanic* is chatted over, when the curtain is raised on the Moral Outcome, *hubris* will be cited centrally. The irony "unsinkable yet sinking" will be found just too candy-coated to avoid. As with all ironies, the layers of this one need a little teasing apart. It is almost always read through a historical syntax. First the claim is issued that this newly Christened masterpiece is unsinkable (posters, newspaper accounts, bruited gossip, pompous official claims). *Then* it sinks, no doubt, through a divinely inspired accident. When read in light of the earlier pronouncement of unsinkability, the sinking has a sneer on it. God, the gods, the universe, the Forces We Do Not Know—are sneering at our pathetic boasts.

Yet it is also true that ascending the gangplank with merriment and excitement at the Southampton quay (I stood there one day, marveling at the very emptiness), folk didn't mutter to one another that they were entering an unsinkable paradise. Not the fated folk. They marveled, they oohed and aahed, they ran around as best they were permitted given their social class ... but the ship was a new and temporary world and they adored the experience of coming into it and being there. Possibly for most of the roughly 1,500 people on board, only a very small number, and those in the upper class, heard beating about the carpets the whispered provocation, "Unsinkable" but most passengers who survived could know the Titanic as unsinkable only after it sank. In Cameron's film, as in all accounts of this sinking in cinema, the whispering of that key word is made central in the drama, more central, to be sure, than it could have been in the hubbub of the affair. The sacred word was uttered publicly in news accounts after the ship was gone. In short, the irony worked backwards: the ship sank, and *then* people spoke about how it had been touted as "unsinkable." In the first case the sneer is for the thing itself, *der Ding an sich,* a defective ship twinkling like a strand of jewels as it sails to the western horizon. In the second case the sneer is for the touters, the braggarts who didn't know half as much about building a ship as they liked to think they knew; or who talked too much about a ship they hadn't themselves built.

Coming out of the theater—remember my chum's brother with *A Night to Remember*—if one doesn't want to talk about the personal involvement with the drama produced through the photography, or about the filmmaker's career, what does one sigh except *"Hubris!"* "How could they have been making love at that instant?" also means, "How could an act so quotidian be our focus when such a grand *hubris* is being challenged?"—teenagers will sneak off for a sexual fling whenever there is a waiting Rolls in a waiting hold, of course, so the scene itself is utterly perfunctory. Or: taking the idea of comeuppance totally for granted, so much that it need not be uttered because everyone alive knows this already (as with "There are icebergs in the sea"), one leaps to details made very relevant filmically yet possessing a relevance that can only be filmic: Kate Winslet's gowns, her red hair, her mother!, the new boyfriend so cute and so smooth or the old boyfriend so oily and so full of himself. Look at that bannister! Oh my, champagne and oysters! Of course this is all going to be about *hubris,* soon, but look at the costumes, the set design, the stars! Leo is so handsome. Forget that his character is fated. Leo is so cute. Leo is so desirable. Leo is so young. Leo is so out of his depth (!).

As a conversational topic in a society beset by rigid gender boundaries (still), Leo is easier for girls to talk about than for boys, and so most of the gab about *Titanic* is female gab. Adolescent girls were the most loyal customers.

Mouth

This discursion about *Titanic* as a case study of necessity avoids—or out of blitheness skirts around—a fundamental issue, stated as a riddle but not yet answered: why is it that after the eye has been so very frenetically stimulated, the mouth *must* be drawn into play? Why, having seen a film, especially a film like this with such daunting moments, moments that we experience, do we (need to) talk about it?

In *Permanence and Change,* the great Kenneth Burke remarks that we all sit, nervously loquacious, at the edge of an abyss. Nervously loquacious, not just loquacious. Is the talkiness an effect of the nervousness, an obvious side effect and symptom? Or does the nervousness, something broad and pervasive in us, produce something of an irritation, like an itch, one that we have come to believe the act of talking will scratch. This could be a primordial variant of what much later, with Freud, will be called the "talking cure," but in this case the "disease" is life. "Psychoanalysis begins where Wittgenstein ends," writes Norman O. Brown. "The problem is not the disease of language, but the disease called man" (71). Or are we nervous because we are facing the abyss, and who, presumably, is not nervous at the edge of an abyss (see *Vertigo)?* We can be thrown into utter confusion by the abyss—call it abysmal confusion—and it may be, actually, that we are talking to ourselves when we string words and sentences together to sort a way out. We surely believe in the divine power of Speech, articulated in the very first passages of Genesis and extended all through Western culture. That to name is to control,[6] and to speak is to name. No matter the ultimate form—cuneiform, papyrus, movable type, electronic pixels—the utterance produces the action, the action produces the event, the event ushers the future.

---

[6] I thank Rabbi Steven Paul for this insight regarding language and control.

We speak at the edge of the abyss to take control. We speak to find our bearings, to find footing, to find one another, to find what we can believe in as a truth, to find ourselves.

Now there is an obvious riddle that must be posed. Given all our spieling about it and around it, should we think of cinema as an abyss? We surely find ourselves nervously loquacious when we see it, when we find ourselves at its edge. Is there something about that presence on the screen that transcends story, character, actor, costume, lighting, framed picture, reference, implication, tangentiality, sequence, idea, memory, clue, hue, ambiguity, and thrust but that also incorporates all of these and more in a way that is ineffable, even wholly unspeakable—so very unspeakable that we are daunted to speak of it and therefore, in courage, raise our voices? It would seem that whatever cinema itself is, the cinematic experience is abysmal, that our view at the edge of the screen is just over the lip of the abyss, and that in seeing, in incorporating what film offers us to incorporate, in turning it around, we try to reach past the limit of our extensions, past the end of our knowledge, past the light on the screen.

Taste the film, so that summarily it is in the mouth. Hand it over. Hand it to the lips:

> Hands of the stranger and holds of the ships,
> Hold you poison or grapes?
> (Dylan Thomas)

to Matthew Solomon

12

A Claims Apartment

Bobby Darin (l.) and Sidney Poitier in Pressure Point *(Stanley Kramer, Stanley Kramer Productions, 1962). Digital frame enlargement.*

Very early in the 1970s, the celebrated social critic, poet, novelist, and utopian thinker Paul Goodman told me, most likely over a soothing cup of tea, that while with most people it paid to attend to what they did and not what they said, with writers it was the other way round and one should pay attention to what they said not what they did. For the writer, saying is an action. As we watch films, if not also in the everyday, saying is almost always offering a claim.

And at the edge of the screen we are barraged with a legion claims chummy and official, real prospecti for delirium (both effervescent and tormenting).

As a writer of fiction Goodman understood, as I do, that characters aren't people, not in the strict sense, not in any sense, notwithstanding that they are intended to be taken credibly as people. And so with the people of fiction we write a special kind of action, through saying about them. As to the folk of fiction themselves, those brave characters, they are all assertions: assertions of a novelist or filmmaker, assertions of our own as we agree to accept them. This, no matter the action that words attribute to them. Their action is in fact a claims statement: a writer's, filmmaker's, film watcher's claim. "Call me Ishmael": well, because Herman Melville told you this man was telling you to do that. To see a body move in film, cover space, extend itself, offer an angle—all this may be a giant leap away from words, yet it is still a claim, since the body as we are seeing it, isn't there. Or: the body that is there is not the body we see.

Given the narrative voice or presence belonging to a film—the "voice" of an unseen "figure" of sorts, one of Chion's *acousmêtres*, quite surely a being different than we are—there is no one to be met save through the agency of that voice and voicing, and of the perceptual scheme and bank associated with it. If a figure's physique belongs to a famous star whom we have seen many times before, say, pacing down a sidewalk in a great crowd (Dustin Hoffman recognizable in a 5th Avenue pedestrian hubbub in *Tootsie* [1982]) we hold it in suspense until a figural claim is made to "fit" it; until the narration "points out" the figure as somehow linked to the world of the film.

Yet we know, of course, that anybody might point out anyone or anything at any time without discernible reason.

Identity, action, attitude, intention, recollection, aspiration, withdrawal—onscreen these are all claims, whether in words or in actions supported by words through description, announcement, or feeling. The dramatic moment is what it is *claimed* to be—the claim being a kind of navigational marker. One could point to claims made not by a figure but on her behalf by the scriptwriter, by the camera, by other figures, by the occasion as defined and designed. We can constantly ask not "What does this mean?" but "What are we to take as being asserted for *this* creature at *this* moment?" Both creature and moment are what the film claims them to be.

Because the film's claim is so faithfully tied to the film's frame, it is possible with a very slight movement of the camera to radically alter a viewer's understanding of where she is and what is going on. In this light, it is quite wonderful to watch some of the painting sequences in Jean-Luc Godard's *Passion* (1982) or the Van Gogh sequence in Kurosawa's *Dreams* (1990), where various human poses take on new meaning depending on how the film frames them.

Next Stop, Truth

It is conventional and convenient to think of films as outplayings of action—adventurous, emotional, passionate, religious—but seen at the edge of the screen, films are claims played out. We enter a nightclub in Morocco where things are happily swinging, but no, this is not fully enough Morocco, not Casablanca, until a claim is made that this is Rick's American Café (an exterior marquee), and that we are there one typical night (it is dark outside), that the persons passing before us are visible *because they should be* (always some figure in focus, no matter the shot) not because we have been favored with a special position from which to see them (no evidence of the camera or the world in which the camera lives). We purchase and revel in the film's claims. A figure moves—Ilsa walking in with Laszlo, looking around with glittering eyes, finding a table: we take her to be just the person the film claims her to be (sometimes by scripting the character to name herself: this one is Ilsa Lund). Claims meant to be taken as authentic; claims meant to be understood as false (Strasser lying through his smile); claims tentative and claims definitive (UGARTE: "Help me, Rick!!!!"); claims uplifting and claims degrading: all these offered for us to accept, and we do accept them for what they (have been made to) seem to be. This acceptance is a signal part of the pleasure of being before the screen, of inhabiting the edge. You spiel, and I will follow along—without questioning or doubting what you say, because what I really want is to follow as you lead me to follow.[1]

Note especially figures who address or point to one another by name. There are no characters anywhere who know anyone, who know even themselves, not in the sense that we could say we know these characters. Figured characters do not know, but the script gives them claims of knowledge to articulate. Claude Rains as Dr. Jacquith meets Bette Davis as Charlotte Vail in *Now, Voyager* (1942) for the first time, calling her, "Miss Vail ...." Sensibly, she responds. But "Miss Vail" is a construct, and no construct actually recognizes "Dr. Jacquith," another construct, or anyone else. Davis and Rains use their expertise to play the scene with, on each part, a kind of hesitant willingness to meet, and the scene becomes truly exquisite; Rains's facial expressions in particular go straight to the bone. (We must stop thinking of him as a character actor; he was a star.) Our man Jacquith doesn't know anybody, however; in fact has borrowed the name Miss Vail from her mother who spoke of her before she entered; and the mother made the claim of being a Vail herself by lording it in a rich Boston home (as we are told) where outside the door a bronze plaque reads VAIL. It is the narrative that claims the "Vailness" of Mrs. Vail—and here appears the old lady herself (Gladys Cooper, in a stunning performance of brittleness and hauteur).

In *Catch Me If You Can* (2002), by making Frank Abagnale's claims and claiming essentially comedic Steven Spielberg leads one away from seriously considering the problem of claims by making claiming into a "game." We

---

[1] *Vertigo* (1958) can be watched as a film about a follower.

enjoy watching figures (claimed by the narration to be whom we agreeably take them to be) actually overtly make claims that are false, and enjoy, as much or more, watching other figures *believe* (claim to believe) those claims. How comical appears the person, then, who claims to believe the (patently empty) claims put up like cardboard fronts by another! (How comical are we!)

Once a character has been labeled, the outplaying drama will lead us variably to treat the labeling itself as authentic, inauthentic, or indeterminate and by this route we will be guided as to how seriously the identification claim should have been treated at the outset. Yet the progressive nature of dramatic construction enjoins the viewer from going back and correcting "errors." Once an identity claim is accepted, what viewers and other characters look for—expect to find—is behavior fundamentally consonant with it—and even a radical change of view is, in explicit denial, fundamentally consonant. It goes without saying that as we watch the screen we will find many unnamed folk, mere decoration, as it were, for whom the only claim made by the film is that in aggregate, and perhaps somewhat mindlessly, they are décor. The citizens in their dungarees ambling down the dirt street as the bad guys ride into town for a shoot 'em up.

And if an identity reveal is constantly (or emphatically) promised but neglected, one begins to look to the neglect as a tacit claim itself, as well as doubting the promise as much as one adopts the neglect. Consider this interesting example:

We are introduced (by a dignified-seeming man *with a British accent, no less*, to whom we have not been introduced) to Leonard (Martin Landau) in *North by Northwest* (1959). Leonard is indicated as the "close assistant" of this dignified-seeming man, who is himself notably well-suited and articulate but also, we will learn, nefarious (James Mason), and so we work ahead on the presumption that in his own right Leonard is sufficiently articulate and dignified and nefarious to deserve his position. Not long later, after all this nefariousness has been duly noted, Leonard helps force a bottleful of bourbon down the throat of an unwilling victim—behavior entirely consonant with the identity we have secured for him. Later still, he fires a gun at his master's chest: this brings a moment of stupefied shock until it becomes evident that—just as Leonard already knew it was going to be (and as we really could have suspected)—the gun was loaded with blanks, this being the servant's underhanded (read, sinister) way of demonstrating fidelity to the master, more dramatic than leaning over and whispering a secret. As a culmination, this Leonard makes to murder the victim of that bourbon, who is now dangling for his life from a precipice, by slowly pushing his shoe down on the man's hand. Leonard, it proves, is wholly, deeply, and ineradicably despicable; but from the start he was set up for this late moment and for his earlier moments, *by claim*, as a man ready—much too ready—to assist a mannered stranger we have been given no reason to like. Leonard is evil, but finally *unsurprisingly* so.[2]

Lie and Lie

Claims will be dubious when they come from liars, of course: that is, from persons bluntly and unequivocally claimed as liars. The establishment of a screen character as a liar is a work to be attended to in its own right. Gaston in *Trouble in Paradise* (1932) is surely one of them (and is discussed in the Interlude). A speaker may boldly assert something that is bluntly contradicted on the instant by background action (the finale of *Notorious* [1946]); or may claim at a distance (say, by phone) to someone unable to detect a very different truth that we, here, watching, see easily enough (*Wait Until Dark* [1967]). A character may claim in privacy to another, without revealing that the privacy is only "privacy" and that an audience at a distance is in on the conversation (*Stage Fright* [1950]). Claiming at a distance is kept in mind by writers when they script procedural stories involving cell phones where a GPS function can be made operative or inoperative, according to the writer's needs: a character on a cell phone tells another character where she is, but we can see this isn't true. There is a central telephone-based misclaiming in Cukor's *Two-Faced Woman* (1941), setting up tension in the love relationship between Greta Garbo and Melvyn Douglas. We can also watch, if not outright lying then, outright inaccuracy, as an identification is made (incorrectly) by a character who is not now and never was privy to information offered the viewer earlier. In *The Mark* (1961), an ex-con named Fuller (Stuart Whitman) makes himself known as a regular civilian to his new landlady and her husband (Brenda de Banzie, Maurice Denham). We know these two wrongly perceive him (following his lead that they should), but know, as well, that they have no means of getting it right, nor any particular motive for working at that. Here, a false claim does not lead to eventful circumstance. Claim arrangements work as

---

[2]The dynamics of claim alteration are interesting. In filmic narrative, it is no simple matter to begin with a character claimed to be decent and sweet and have the audience suddenly discover him covering a malevolent self. An early example of this trope is W. S. Van Dyke's *After the Thin Man* (1936). The problem is that considerable screen time and attention has already been given the claim of decency, and the contradictory claim of "secret, true evil" finally comes up spontaneously, not unlike a joke. The inversion, turning a character claimed as villainous into "actually a friendly, decent sort" is easier because the viewer's moral stance favors the decent, friendly sort and is happy (already) to find him buried inside the creep, no matter the time given to setting up the creep's creepiness. *The Spy Who Came in from the Cold* (1965) is a textbook.

nicely in animated cartoons as in live action; there the duping of one figure by another (Bugs Bunny is an inveterate false claimer) is a principal support of the form (and of the characterization).

With characters rapidly making claims—about themselves and about others, honestly or dishonestly, explicitly or inexplicitly—our ability to follow the complexity of a narrative depends signally on accepting, recognizing, remembering, and combining claims of identity, fact, possibility, threat, memory. A claim constitutes information, and the writer and director have to be thinking about how much information, current and past, a viewer can be assumed capable of holding (not to mention how, if he thinks we need to be told what we already know, a writer can seem incompetent). Further, claims of what purportedly happened before we came onto the scene must be weighed, and are generally given some truth value. When a character recounts a story of a past happening and a flashback serviceably takes us "there," supplying "direct" representation, we take all this at face value, without suspecting that the character is making it all up for a present strategic purpose we have not been positioned to gather; see *Rashômon* (1950). Even more chilling can be a past recollected in a present tale (say, a dream), which the recounter does not comprehend at all but which suddenly becomes transparently clear to someone else (this "clear" vision being a claim we accept as bona fide)—Robert Benton's *Still of the Night* (1982). In Curtis Bernhardt's *Possessed* (1947) almost the entire movie is a series of extended flashbacks meant to be seen as the sincere memory of a woman presently abed and, we discover only rather late, under psychiatric care (she appears at first to be receiving simply "medical" care). The story is written to make coherent sense when one flashes back, as it were, to all the material ostensibly leading up to the ending; but the film never gives any guarantee that the sick woman tells, remembers, or reconstitutes the truth. Perhaps the entire film is an artful lie, in no way less pleasant or intriguing for that.[3]

Unities

Whether it emerges from an oral assertion or from a visible action, what is fascinating about a figure's claim, temporary as it may seem in its circumstances, is a perduring underpinning unity, the origin and support for which may be elusive, ethereal, or even absent. Let me adduce a charming and bizarre little case, again from *Trouble in Paradise*.

---

[3] In *The Good Liar* (2019), this trope is taken a little further. The flashback "truth" proposed by one character to another's face is accepted by the second character because, in the first character's claim—that we fully accept—that second character was one of the people present.

The man self-identified as Gaston Monescu (Herbert Marshall)—a cute moniker connected intrinsically with both *MONE*y and *SCU*rrilousness—behaves and misbehaves in a large Venetian *hôtel de luxe* directly after the film begins. No *hoi polloi* here! Soon, and magically, we find him in Paris, where as Gaston LaValle he behaves and misbehaves—elegantly and with appeal—in a *mansion de luxe* (no *hoi polloi* here either) with scurrilousness and regarding money. We easily discern him amid the cluttering *objets*, because his is still the same embodiment, the same posture; he bears the same wisp of a smile (*I know more than you do; and doesn't that bring you delight!*) We are given no sense in the film that one of his claims—"I am Gaston Monescu"; "I am Gaston LaValle"—is more foundational than the other, that actually he is Monescu *only temporarily pretending to be* LaValle, or vice versa. Or even that (as happens to be revealed, but only later) he is an unidentified third who once pretended to be Monescu and now pretends to be LaValle. By a certain narrative regulation, once he has named himself LaValle in Paris this man is suddenly and easily called "LaValle" by everyone he contacts, and is considered actually to be LaValle—whatever "actual being" could mean; we take him to be the LaValle he regards in the mirror, and would be sorry to see him go, all because, and only because, he has claimed the name. We can even think his "previous existence" as Monescu was nothing but a mere foreplay to be dispensed with, once the action begins.

Yet we do see that the man begins as Monescu, becomes LaValle, and is Monescu again at the end. Even if this man should meet two lovely women at once in the same room, of whom one knows him as LaValle and the other knows LaValle is a pretense and his real name is Monescu, all he need do is hope against hope that the issue of his pretending should not come up in conversation; and the screenwriters of course oblige him. To the argument that all this simply means the man has taken a false name one would have to answer yes, certainly; but the issue is not *that* he has done this but *how*. How to take a name. And make it stick. How to take a real name, a false name, a masquerade name, a joking name, a former name, any name under the sun. Not that a screen figure shows proof *but that she can show proof*. In cinema, as long as one sports a name one is taken faithfully to be sporting it in good faith—that is, to be perceivably the person under that name, to all screen figures and viewers alike, until one is given a new name that is taken in better faith, that of a counterfeiter and a fake. We never stop believing what people who move on the screen are telling us they are. The best faith wins the day.

Two provocative factors:

- The figure could *be,* could have an existence in space and time—already always—without claiming to be; just as he *was* in the liminal zone before first announcing himself or being announced. Just a body, standing in front of us, saying what he says about life and doing what he does, but "of course" never bothering to say "I am here, I am myself, I am me." Yet many screen figures are abstract ciphers all along. Before the word "Gaston" and the word "Monescu" were tagged to him, this man always already was someone, a being without a name. The figure that existed already was *attributed with* a name, although there was, and remains, no existential connection between the thing and the name. As Wittgenstein made terribly clear, there is no existential connection between any thing and any name. Think how someone may apply a name out of thin air, and how the name might adhere, as with, say, Darth Vader or Adam and Eve. Bodies and names do not belong together, they are married by ceremony. As Gregory Bateson teaches us, a "c-a-t" doesn't scratch.

- In a crucial respect our named onscreen figure is not like any named member of the audience watching him. Any member of that audience might consider the name on his or her passport to be the only, true, genuine, and irrevocable name under which to be known, now and forever, or might just as well take on a series of other names for whatever purpose, names, like that passport name, believed and/or claimed by the holder to be true at the time of use. We take our names and the names around us in the space-time we call "reality" with seriousness; and unless people are engaged in covert activity (so many people are not) this is what they do, too. When we watch a screened figure whose name was invented we easily reflect, *But my own name was not invented; my name is my own name.* OWN: appertaining to me and only me now, always, and as ever was, as I assert it, ... as though no one sat on a bench under a spreading maple tree and came up with it one day. Not that with the little creature in the crib a name was not attached, and also on bureaucratic forms, which of course "realize" it. With films, the bureaucratic forms naming and preserving names are scripts and script revisions, contracts, hiring sheets, and cast lists which find themselves converted into screen credits everybody sees and believes (and which, as evidence, are not available for general inspection).[4]

---

[4]In studio practice, the proposed character names to appear in a script were all vetted by the Legal Department, which needed to make certain there was no other living person of that exact name operating in a similar fashion to the character in the location proposed; or, in some cases, more generally. With the Paramount Legal Dept. at work, in the case of Hitchcock's *The Man Who Knew Too Much* (1956), the names "McKenna" and "Drayton" eventuated after around a dozen proposed other choices.

"Trouty"

Imagine a narrative structure that is (built as) a claim game: a figure adopts a false name or makes a false claim regarding some action, this openly to us but (apparently) not openly to some other figures (Jerry Lewis's Homer Flagg in *Living It Up* [1954] is a paramount example). The conceit of figure-to-figure misinforming (involving secrecy, say) is easy enough to follow from where we sit at the edge of the screen, but only because unlike the onscreen dupe who is being taken in we are positioned to catch all sides of the claim performance, both the duplicitous surface and the backstaged trick of the duplicitousness.

   This issue becomes pleasurably riddling in a scene from *North by Northwest*. A dining car of a moving train, a table set with a thick linen cloth and flowers. A man introduces himself to a very pretty woman as "Jack Phillips, Western sales manager of Kingby Electronics." We have "sure" knowledge that he is not Phillips at all, but Roger O. Thornhill of Madison Avenue, here and now only briefly putting up a Phillips mask; and can believe in our knowledge because earlier we saw this same figure elsewhere, embodied with the Thornhill name tag. From our viewpoint, the man is either (a) amicably teasing the woman or (b) deluding her with a purpose. But just at this moment comes a joke. The woman knows what he's doing just as well as we do, she's a savvy one, she's "in the know" (quite as though, beside us here in the dark, she's been watching the whole movie so far, our seat mate). We know she's "in the know" because she now says, as a tickle, "No you're not, you're Roger Thornhill of Madison Avenue and you're wanted for murder on every front page in America. Don't be so modest." Note: her meaning is, "You're *in truth* Roger O. Thornhill," which is to say, a man who could be met that way by anybody; a man who always really, deeply, was Roger Thornhill and will continue to be Roger Thornhill in his figural lifetime; not to say one who is Roger Thornhill for me, Eve Kendal (Eva Marie Saint), right now in this dining car in the same way you were for the newspaper writers who captioned your photograph and—because of that photograph and that caption—will appear to be now to everybody else in America. Newspaper captions as imprimaturs for name claims. You are not Jack Phillips, you are Mrs. Thornhill's little boy, a claim substantiated several times over, including in a court of law. The implications of Eve's claim as to this man's *true* identity, her little lesson to him that she sees through his masquerade, go in many possible directions, and if neither Roger nor we can guess yet which direction best to follow we will at least have no trouble taking her claim to mean she's old enough to know better. You might be able to fool somebody, Buster, but you won't fool me.

   Or else: Listen to me—*I am telling you* what your name is.

Consider, too, our license to "step back" from the diegesis at will, to remind ourselves we are watching not Roger but Cary Grant: note that in the everyday world, this sort of stepping back very rarely happens, albeit it could. One could question the performance and identity of anyone, wondering what deeper organization of intelligence and energy was mobilizing what one could see—yet one doesn't. Just as we take the bank teller to be *really and truly* a bank teller, and the doctor to be *really and truly* a doctor, we take Roger to be *really and truly* Roger, as long as he and others keep claiming he is.[5]

Labyrinth

The claims and counterclaims put forward by Roger, Eve, and all the characters in *North by Northwest* make the film a labyrinth, one that works for viewers because they believe themselves able to see through all the falsities of truth and implication and find the bedrock of the real. Find the bedrock quite early on, even; and stand upon that bedrock while claims sally past in all directions pretending to be confounding. Pretending just expertly enough to spark wonder, doubt, suspicion, intuition, and hope.

But as a lesson on the structure of film claims, the predicaments of Roger and Eve are instructive exactly because we are led to be sure of them, against all odds. If we ask how it can be that we have such certainty, the answer, I believe, lies in yet one more layer of claims that for *North by Northwest* is powerful, regardless of how such a layer might work in other films. I refer to casting as claim. When the tag "Roger O. Thornhill" is affixed to Cary Grant, aged fifty-five, dressed in sleek gray silk and with notable salt-and-pepper hair, twinkly eyed Cary, of whom outside of cinema we know so little even though screened Cary we have known and loved so many times before, the affixing is unimpeachable. The same with "Eve Kendall" applied to Eva Marie Saint looking like a *Vogue* front cover, and to all the other meticulously cast actors, whose names may not be familiar but whose faces very surely were in 1959. Think, then, of the actor presentation of self as a semi-transparent foundational claim upon which all other claims rest and by means of which all other claims are made more or less sensible. This is why if without seeing the film you read James Naremore's continuity, if you found these figures as only words you would be confounded; reducing a claim to language alone opens special ambiguities. But when Roger is embodied by and spoken through Grant he becomes not only indelible but patriotic.

---

[5]In *An Eye for Hitchcock* I explore the interesting possibility of our self-claiming Roger *not* being Roger at all. Other discussions of the film have glowing value; see especially Cavell, *Themes* and Wood. On perceived "doctors" *really* being doctors, see Julio Cortázar's tiny story, "Instructions on or rather Examples of How to Be Afraid" (8–9).

Apple

This apple that sits in front of me without claiming to be an apple. In fact, to follow Wittgenstein, it is not an apple at all. But we have our words, and our words make claims, each nomination claiming, each gesturer a claimant. The images we see onscreen are on one hand narrative, full of claims and implications we take as guideposts; and on another hand like apples, there for the look of themselves and the inspiration we take: apples of the eye.

Hierarchy

We do not all interpret claims with equal speed, astuteness, or capability; nor is there widespread equality in the ability to make and deliver claims. When claims are made inside the diegesis to onscreen receivers who are part of the tale, those onscreen receivers can show variable interpretive expertise. And dramatic events can be structured to reflect or address such variation. In *Pressure Point* (1962), a benevolent white medical chief at a prison facility (Carl Benton Reid) has assigned a brilliant Black psychiatrist (Sidney Poitier) to work with a disaffected young white seditionist, full of bottled-up hatred, anti-Semitism, and racism against Blacks; and affiliated proudly with the American Nazi Party (Bobby Darin). The bulk of the film follows the psychiatrist's travails when, after hearing the patient recall his childhood memories he is repeatedly assaulted by the patient's virulent racism. (The film is noteworthy of its own accord for having been written by Robert Lindner, who also wrote the material from which Nicholas Ray made *Rebel Without a Cause* [1955], and for the stellar performances by Poitier and Darin, a leading popular singer of the time.) When the patient's parole hearing comes up, at issue is the final claim that will be made about his condition now, after lengthy imprisonment and subjection to regular meetings with the psychiatrist. The psychiatrist votes against parole. An outsider, the white chief medical officer, protected by his color from racist diatribes and by his Christianity from the power of anti-Semitic jibes, claims the patient is ready to return to the world, while the contradictory judgment of the psychiatrist, a man he assigned to the case, Black and, as far as we can tell, considerably more intelligent, is casually neglected. At a final head-to-head, the patient sneers and taunts the healer. The film implies that diagnostic claims are embedded in a hierarchy, those made by white Christian Americans taking precedence, automatically, over those made by non-whites and/or non-Christians. The telling irony is that during his long "therapy," the patient understood the racial dynamics more than his high-minded psychiatrist did. The film turns upon not simple claims and developments but a hierarchy of claims—in this case a racist hierarchy, although hierarchies could be based in any distinctive variation, such as social-class difference.

Michael Burnett's *Messiah* (2020) spotlights the Identity Claim as its central trope. Here and generally, flowing from identity claims is others' expectation as to how a person will comport himself, what sort of places he or she will be likely to inhabit, what actions he or she will straightforwardly take up, to whom he or she will bond in friendship, even, perhaps, what his or her politics will be. The case presented here is that of a soft-spoken young man of definite Semitic background—Israeli or Arab, it is manifestly impossible to tell—with very long hair and some facial growth, a notably pleasant, even beatific appearance, and a powerful educational background that has made him literate and sweetly oratorical. In the Middle East he has caused some political disruption—that is, acted in such a way that government authorities in various countries have "official trouble" with him, with his statements, and with his very existence. To wit, there are some witnesses who claim he is the Messiah reborn. He tends to phrase his speech as though God is using him as a mouthpiece, repeatedly invoking the presence of God as motivator for—as origin of—what he says. His messages are consistently about peace, love, harmony, enlightenment, and the "brotherhood of man." When, eventually, he comes to America, he blips the CIA's radar (of course). All through the multi-episode series, we are riddled with one repeating, finally vibrating question, "Who is this person?," by which any viewer could easily mean, "Who is this person *actually?*, this person who claims to be the Messiah ...." The question vexes characters widely placed, high and low, distal and proximate. And soon, "Who is he *really?*" becomes meshed with "Who do you want him to be?"

He is finally accorded completely private access to the president of the United States, who sits placidly in a chair and wonders aloud, like any chief executive officer, "What do you want?," our noble young man clearly having been read already as taking this meeting as prelude to some serious demands, "probably terrorist"; or to some economic transaction, as though a ransom will be demanded for the peace and security of the Western world. But no. The stranger doesn't want anything at all, nothing for himself. The issue is what God wants. And God—as described in the man's language and gestural attitude—never wants anything unreasonable, unpeaceful, unkind, uncharitable, unloving, or untrue. One way to watch the show is to take the hero as being exactly what he claims to be, mouthpiece of a merciful Almighty, and in this light to regard all the skeptics surrounding him as desperadoes advancing their own religious agendas, therefore unable to accept as divine anyone or anything that doesn't fit their preconceived (and iconic) ideas. With regard to these skeptics, one is continually awaiting a conversion of thought that seems impossible. Unsurprisingly (if also, one might feel, sadly), the hero's self-claim fails to match the preconceived claims of others for a Being such as he putatively puts himself up to be. A more cynical way to watch is to take the young man as a meticulously competent charlatan, whose every word is duplicitous, every action a thickly veiled threat, every human bonding a corruption of innocence and cooptation toward an as-yet-unspecified evil.

What is made palpable to the viewer of *Messiah* has, in the end, little to do with messianism or this particular young man or his odd situation. Instead, we face the human need for orientation and navigation in the face of a disarming, disabling, distressing unknownness, here finding an identity claim the acceptance of which calls for a huge, perhaps unbearable commitment of faith. That such a claim can be made is one thing. That such a claim once made, even substantiated by actions and sentiments, can wobble as it is buffeted by the winds of agreement or disagreement from (powerful) others is something else. One's claim needs to have coherence, which finally means the imprimatur of, and social acceptance by, relevant others.

Motive

Claims imply motive, motive reveals moral stature. When Sidney Poitier bellows at Bobby Darin, "I am a *doctor!*" much more than the name of the profession to which he is devoted he is saying and claiming a certain nature of devotion—that it surpasses even the religious kind; that he will strive against any odds and, if need be, until he expires to help his patient, and he will do this whoever his patient happens to be. He is saying that he has a *calling,* not an occupation, and that in taking up this calling he is following in a line of devoted acolytes who came before, and who knew, as he knows now, how cold, rational calculation is not enough. As Weber wrote, "Ideas come when we do not expect them, and not when we are brooding and searching at our desks"; and "whether we have scientific inspiration depends upon destinies that are hidden from us" (136). Poitier's psychiatrist has found and obeys "the demon who holds the fibers of his very life" (156). He promises not only confidentiality but unfettered truth, as far as he can know it—a claim of intent. But however eloquent he is, he has met a young man who has no intention of accepting his claims.

The problem of making and establishing claims, motor of this story, rests finally on a bureaucratic report of assessment, thus finally an agency of the bureaucracy the power structure of which reliably reproduces that of the society that grounds it. Always implicit is a search for motive. A claim of identity is a claim of intents.

In *The Spy Who Came in from the Cold* (1965), a greengrocer (Bernard Lee) is methodically slicing cold cuts when his doorbell sounds and Leamas (Richard Burton) straggles into the little shop, sopping wet from the rain and lingering at a distance. He looks bedraggled, and as the grocer steps away from his slicer and moves toward the cash register Leamas approaches. I give comment in square brackets:

> LEAMAS (trying, but not too hard, for conviviality): Wet night, Mr Patmore. [• Politeness to a functionary with whom he shops regularly. He himself needs kindness tonight. Yet if he does not mean to be fawning, no one will know that yet.]
>
> PATMORE (under his breath): Bloody dirty, Mr Leamas.
> [• Returning the greeting, but without effusiveness. This is not an offer of friendship any more than was Leamas's comment. But there is no good reason to hold back warmth on a dank night.]
>
> LEAMAS: Loaf of bread (*He stares at the grocer. PATMORE very slowly moves, takes a paper bag, puts a loaf in. LEAMAS turns his back to examine the shelves filled with tins.*) [• Patmore's very slow movement suggests that he is thinking hard, as if trying to guess what little scenario Leamas intends to trap him in, and he's seen it before. But don't be rude, walk along step by step. Patmore is self-protective, and he doesn't mind Leamas detecting that.] A tin of this corned beef (*LEAMAS seizes one, turns back, and puts it into the bag*) and some marmalade. (*PATMORE turns behind himself to fetch the marmalade.*) A tin of tomato soup. (*Patmore has to bend down to get the soup.*) [• The beef, the marmalade, and the soup Leamas demands in order, and without much pause. Once you have the ball rolling keep it rolling. But also, a little trick of which we will see the purpose only later: choose items no one will forget.]
>
> PATMORE (calculating): That'll be… uh…. 4/6', sir.[6] [• A calculating man, as merchants will be; but without any hope he'll see money. This is going to be a charade, and soon Leamas will go and he will empty that bag and put everything dutifully, if with disgruntlement, back on his shelves. It's awful outside, it doesn't hurt to talk with someone for a few minutes, but Leamas has always been a problem. That Leamas!]
>
> LEAMAS (curt): Shove it on the bill, Mr Patmore. [• Said by a "player" who knows he has used this line many times before, and knows that Patmore knows that.]
>
> PATMORE (drawing the line): Sorry, Mr Leamas, I told ye' last week. If you had a proper credit account.… You'd need a banker's reference.
>
> LEAMAS: Give you some cash on Friday.

---

[6]For the benefit of non-Brits (and even young ones today), this is four shillings sixpence, which comes to fifty-four new pence, roughly half a pound. At this writing, about US $1.20.

PATMORE (diffident): You c'n have the goods on Friday.
LEAMAS (leaning forward confidingly): I've got a job.
PATMORE (with a long, long stare, then a smile): Very well, sir.

A case study of tacit claiming. Leamas, we can notice without knowing—it is only later that things will be made clear—is working hard to set up two conditions at once, to make, by the most casual assertions, two broad and important claims—important for his secret job, in which he "protects England."

- He needs food, in fact has no money at present (not by accident), and also has given Mr Patmore troubles before, but tonight is not the night for that, and in the end he must not under any circumstances commit an actual crime. This is why the uncomfortable conversation must be seen by Mr Patmore to proceed all the way to the agreeable end. Leamas cannot have Mr Patmore making claims to the police. The scene is directed and photographed so that we position ourselves morally with Mr Patmore, though physically with Leamas. We don't want Leamas infringing on the law, and we surely don't want Mr Patmore to think he is. His legal cleanliness must be established carefully—in this scene through talk—because he surely does not look clean; as clean, say, as Mr Patmore looks.
- At the same time, Leamas *does* need and want Mr Patmore to speak to others about this encounter, others not the police, chit-chat not report, and so he makes the meeting memorable—corned beef with peaches and marmalade and tomato soup—and behaves just badly enough that an objective watcher (!) would conclude he'd given up civility. Of course, once one has given up civility one has given up London. And in Britain, once one has given up London one has given up The Throne.

Later we will learn what already here and now Leamas knows: that he will soon make to defect to East Germany, "disgruntled with" Britain, with his position in the British secret service, with the whole red-white-and-blue. He has no clue but Mr Patmore will be one of many who will tell the same sad story about this sad irredeemable man. Too much bad luck! Even with a job! If later we "gaze" back at this scene we will see Leamas's claim of disaffection planted here and carefully watered so that it will grow strong. The prodding is perfectly calculated. He is behaving uncouthly in one of those little *endroits* that for the Londoner is a haven of warmth in the cold, a retreat, a safe zone, the little corner greengrocer's where everything one needs is in ready supply as long as one is in good credit. Mr Patmore is the sort of person with whom one wishes to maintain cordial relations, one of those fabled British shopkeepers. Rile him at your peril.

Here, then, a delicious case of planting a complex false claim—I have found a job, I will pay you soon, I'm cold and wet and need some food, I'm uncouth but these are the items I want—artfully managed so that even to the looker-on (us, any other shoppers in this little place) it seems nothing but genuine. Espionage is the business of organizing "genuine" claims. In all, *Spy/Cold* is a symphony of claims, made in several countries by people who only pretend to know each other, directing life and death.

Attachments

Alone, a person tends to find it impossible to substantiate claims. Required for support and assistance are various attachments: clothing, settings, associated personnel, props. In *Spy*, Mr Patmore is Leamas's supporting player; the tomato soup is one of his props. In faking claims, it is by the use of such attachments that a claimant may change status, in cinematic stories almost always for strategic purpose. Take *The Fugitive* (1993), in which Dr. Richard Kimball (Harrison Ford), having found his wife murdered, is accused, tried, convicted, and imprisoned for the crime. We know better, as, of course, does he—although ironically we know differently than he knows: his knowledge comes from personal experience that we impute (because at the murder, seen in flashback, he does not appear to be present); but we already accept him before seeing the flashback of this experience, because he is Harrison Ford. Kimball escapes and is on the run for the bulk of the film, but here and there he is permitted to remind his audience of his legitimacy by way of a kindly, charitable, or humane act performed out of the air and strictly from the heart—the sort of thing a brutal murderer of the kind who slayed his wife just wouldn't—as one presumes—bother to do. In one interesting scene he has entered a major Chicago hospital to get some key information from the prosthetics records (he saw that, fleeing the scene of the crime, the murderer had a prosthetic arm). He ducks into a closet and changes into an orderly's blues, in this way radically demoting himself in one light and radically upgrading himself in another: doctors don't eagerly become orderlies, prisoners might. He pauses at a gurney where a young boy lies awaiting diagnosis, and glances at the chart. Then he asks the kid a few questions, quickly seizes the gurney, and races it into an elevator toward surgery. On the way he seizes the chart, crosses out what is written there, changes the orders and fakes a signature. When he runs into some nurses he barks that this kid needs surgery stat and stands to watch them speed the boy into the O.R. Kimball's fake "legitimate" claim to be present in the hospital corridor in the first place is bolstered by his orderly's outfit and the badge he has pilfered to put on it; nobody seeing people scuttling around in blues actually stops to check them in a busy hospital. But the change of diagnosis is something he manages in secrecy, with an illegible signature that will signal "some legitimate doctor" and procure attention. With the little boy he shows kindness and friendliness, and keeps his diagnostic questions short, amicable, and to the point. The doctor in fact has become a doctor in secrecy, but still a doctor. He is not making a claim *to* the boy, he is in effect using the boy—saving a life—to make a claim to hospital personnel and to us. The *fact* involved in Kimball's being a doctor *in fact* is his now-suspended license from the Illinois medical establishment—a license he hopes, and we hope with him, will be reinstated when the film is done. To earn that license, he claimed medical competence and substantiated that through a series of examinations. One can be who one claims to be by way of such certifying paperwork or by situating action in a context that will render identity obvious—a life saver is a life saver. But the film works outside Kimball and his dramatic concerns, as a manual on claims manufacture and strategy as both achievements and evasive tactics.

Since cinema can show the immediate relationship between a claim and the materials (attachments) being used to support it—Kimball's blues and his precise questions to the boy; his perfectly accomplished illegible signature—in this way making the practice of claiming visually dramatic in its own right (we can be shown the materials found or laid out before the claim comes down), it can also withhold such evidencing from the viewer so that a dramatic surprise can be in store. An identity claim that could be made is expressly held in reserve, even in secrecy. In *I Am Love* (2009), we meet an extraordinarily dignified woman (Tilda Swinton), matriarch of a large aristocratic Florentine family. Her comportment, her dress, her attitudes, her way of regarding life are all appropriate to her place if not, perhaps, a shade modest. But she falls afoul of the aristocracy in an ineradicable way, and we come to learn the history by which she came originally to be in this house. She is not from the ruling class at all but a merchant's daughter, and she is from far away. When her husband married her (into his rich family) she was compelled to change her identity claims, and, as we must presume, by careful study and attention managed this transformation with aplomb. *Do not say that, say this. Do not look this way at that person.* Here is a case of a character *elevating* a social claim early on, indeed before the film began, with her story keeping the elevation off-camera until a plot moment that is "too late," a point when, looking back with fresh eyes now, we can see for the first time just what the modesty was that we had been witnessing all along. Retrospective claiming of this kind tends to be central in adventure, police procedural, and contemporary sci-fi film. Always the issue is not what is happening but whom it is happening to, who people are to one another and to themselves. Even more: whom we will be ready to discover they are.

Interesting and somewhat peculiar about *I Am Love* is that our doyenne's class origins are not entirely unknown to at least some members of her family whom we see, but the masquerade is on us. A similar masking underpins James Ivory's film of Kazuo Ishiguro's *The Remains of the Day* (1993), a story of secret claims contradicting public faces. Fulcrum of the tale is the butler in a great house in England (Anthony Hopkins), whose life stands upon one great claim only, that his master is properly his master and regards him as properly the butler of the house. Could the master's claim fray at the seams?

Props

By a quirky convention of etiquette borrowed from the live theater and from literature, cinematic stories make a business of not merely presenting but expressly introducing central figures; by obversion, those who gain introductions are the central ones. We even sometimes hear a name bruited about before a body is attached, or sometimes meet someone without a name but with a function made clear (a formula with which *Saltburn* [2023] plays diabolically). Chekhov, for a case, is very careful about this kind of referencing; every reference is a claim. (Shakespeare is more playful.) Introduction can be spoken but also work—with no less effectiveness—by the mere placement of one figure next to others or in a particular setting (on which placement, for a limiting case, see *Wetherby* [1985]). A long shining table in a well-lit room, with a dignified Chairman of the Board at the head and twelve wise types sitting around: these are the members of the Board. We will know them as we see them, tag them as it were, notwithstanding that in the film story they take no action at all, speak no lines, have no purpose other than to be the materialized Board of which the man at the head, whom we do know, is the Chairman. In *The Errand Boy* (1961), Jerry Lewis satirizes this conceit by "dictating" in a board room to a thoroughly invisible Board. In medical movies a doctor will perform surgery, brightly lit, masked, and gowned, but around him will be nurses who merely stand, an anesthetist merely accompanied by canisters. All the postural introductions of these minor characters are played as mere half-introductions, without name or rank, and with none of them typically speaking a condition or self-indication. The argument is made generally that filmic scenes need to be set and played in "places" that will seem sufficiently real; "places" contain supporting players and props for them to use. Population of a setting by ancillary characters is managed in the name of this realism of place and moment. Yet we do not turn away from noticing the silence, the stillness, the ineffectuality of the many official working types all around. Ancillary types can abound, whereas in stage dramas there is limited space and far less money. In film, narrative space expands, and people can fill it.

Situated ancillaries effectively claim, "Here we are, filling out the room." Thus the orderlies, the privates on parade, the streetwalking public, the secretaries in the part of the office the heroine walks through every morning to get to her cubicle, the sailors in the engine room, the *corps de ballet*. All these clusters can be considered *corps de ballet* of one kind or another, however their discipline may be bought or forged. But there is another sort of figure, present without acting, with or without placement, and notably not doing: pointed to in someone else's claim but having no claim herself beside being in someone else's claim: the tacky real estate client's spoiled daughter, in *Psycho* (1960). This figure is an object, a prop. Figural props fill cinematic space, render a zone ostensibly habitable and in this way help focus belief.

As ancillaries are combined with protagonists in scenes and shots, a certain hierarchy is formed and given visual, compositional emphasis, since except in cases of meaningful dramatic subterfuge the star must always look the star, bright and twinkling enough to catch the eye. Design, costume, lighting, and cinematography must collaborate to bring the protagonist to our attention in a crowd. In *Living It Up* (1954), Homer poses in his shining scarlet silk bathrobe in the middle of a boundless hospital room/hotel suite, surrounded by literally dozens of buzzing, shifting, eager, muttering factota in gaily colored clothing, everyone there to "be with him" and "cater to his every need" and every single one negligible while Homer perpetually sticks out. Indeed, this identified being's making an identity claim while his surrounders are identity-free *is the claim* of the scene, that *they are not* and *he is*. Here is Ortega's "optical hero," a rounded, glowing presence around which the frame is composed. Where there is a bustling crowd—see the Grand Central Station concourse in which Judy Garland meets Robert Walker in *The Clock* (1945), or Waterloo Station with Bourne sneaking through in *The Bourne Ultimatum* (2007)—that crowd permits the spatial design, just as the spatial design calls for the crowd. But even more, the crowd *is* the space in which the protagonist's action culminates, the plinth beneath the hero.

Democracies

Experientially for actors onstage and actors on a movie set, whoever is present is no more and no less present than anyone else who is present. A democracy. It is insignificant as regards the working process of performers that there are dominant and recessive roles, that one character is a Lear and another is a Tom or even a page in court; insignificant, as the bodies must move and the voices must emerge or stay silent; insignificant, as there is action in front of the lens and it is the action, not the figures' egos, that counts. While in the culture of movie-making there are hierarchicalized groups, stars and extras, leads and choruses, and while this classed division is emphasized and preserved in publicity, in scholarship, in so-called truth-seeking journalism, still, when one is playing a scene with someone one is fully there to the other, and the other is fully there to you: person to person more than status to status. In the filmmaking *moment* all parties to the event are equal, are present together in amity and mutual respect. Off-camera or backstage there could be as much division of feeling and thought as one would find anywhere else in the world.

Effects Identity

Yet no CGI'd creature claims an identity in the same way that we do as we sit to watch. As collections of atoms and molecules we deem ourselves superior in status—at least for analysis such as this—to collections of pixels (regardless of the atomic nature of pixels). Beyond announcing itself as a wonder, CGI is silent. It not only doesn't show how its tricks are done—standard magical modesty—but at its most effective also doesn't show *tricks being done at all*, not, at least, to those with uninformed eyes. As it is brewed to do, the presentation looks reasonably substantive and "unachieved"; before one is puzzled as to how a trick works, after all, one must see the trick. Advances in CGI technology are like advances in any technology: (1) they are shocking >> (2) they are learned >> (3) they are customary; and >> (4) they are a bore. To look back on CGI of the past, even of a year or so ago, is to see through the claims curtain. So, while Harry Potter flying around on a broomstick may have brought summative delight on first screening, it has become very hard not to see the green screen poised "invisibly" behind him to ground his (and his performer's) claims.

Typically, in order that an effect be highlighted in all its power, the centrally involved figure is reduced in the frame, and the effect becomes the star. That an effect might seem vast owes to the vastness of cinematic space, that it is designed to be at its best in Cineplex or in super widescreen exhibition, and used in narratives involving wide-angle close-ups of colorfully dressed folk zooming through (interstellar) space by cavorting all around the screen. Effects work best when one moves through (and past) them. Thus, each figure who seems to be "here in this dramatic place" is actually only moving through. Where there is identity, it is formed as an identity tag, a superficial attachment to the moving form.

Investments

Since their lives are only "lives," and since they have an existence entirely bounded by the work in which they appear as figures, figured characters maintain with each other's claims only a temporary and apparent investment: they buy each other's claims exactly as, and only to the extent that, they are scripted to. (And tomorrow they will make their investment of belief over again.) If nearby claims raise their concerns, their worries, their delights, their excitements, their sorrows—all these disappear with the end credits, rather as though they had never existed, or had never been planted in fertile ground. The revels now ended are not those of living beings in a bounded space under light but those of cinematic forms engendered by living beings who remain only as phantoms. Cinematic figures are imprisoned with the swirling claims of those about them, as though the claims themselves box them in. There is nothing ultimate for characters in their figurations; and so claims can have no ultimate significance.

Final Claims

In the summer of 1946, when in progressive North America I was born, Wilfred Thesiger was traveling with the Bedu through the desert of the Empty Quarter, what is today the southeastern part of Saudi Arabia, "racked by the weariness of long marches through the wind-whipped dunes" (1). He was with a small party of camel riders, but, as he claimed, "I knew that if I traveled here alone the weight of this vast solitude would crush me utterly" (10). We have no evidence that David Locke, the protagonist of Michelangelo Antonioni's *The Passenger* (*Professione: Reporter*) (1975), read Thesiger; nor evidence that he did not; and he is a consummately educated journalist of international standing working in the rather demanding contemporary world of London. On assignment in Africa he drives a Land Rover. He sports a Uher tape recorder. There are "perfectly satisfactory answers" to all his questions but he probably "doesn't understand how little he would learn from them." Helpless and without prospect in an unnamed country where he has been hoping to encounter some resistance fighters, Locke has swamped his Rover in a wind-whipped dune with no one to help for an eternity around. The sun is blazing atomically, he is tired of Africa, tired of his career, tired of politics, tired of broadcasting, tired of his marriage, tired of himself, tired of life. Back at his hotel, after a long, parching trek, he wanders into the neighboring room of a chap he'd met and chatted with before, a British trader, and is surprised to find the man dead.

The body is stretched on the bed. Heart attack, no doubt. Locke leans over the corpse and stares into the unseeing eyes, trying in this strange wide desert of markers to find something, some nook to recognize. Looking to find himself. And then, as we watch him recollect an earlier conversation, which he apparently taped and is now playing on his recorder, he meticulously swaps out the two passports, turning the corpse into himself and becoming David Robertson. Goodbye, David Locke, wherever you are.

The man (Jack Nicholson) now at least possesses the passport, the datebook, and an airline ticket all in the name of David Robertson—evidence of accomplished claims—and in this respect is entirely secure in claiming a second life. Call it a life reclaimed. London, Munich, Barcelona, Algeciras, and into the future. As long as the man who was David Locke doesn't run into his wife or his television producer, as long as an entire social world is erased along with him, this new Robertson has a fighting chance. And especially when he meets a charming woman who loves architecture and won't say her name. A claim, "I am not claiming." What will happen as he works to decode the cryptic remarks in David Robertson's date book, what will he say and do as he meets the people Robertson is to meet and suffers the future that has been reserved for Robertson? Fittingly, the film takes its leave by sunset, at an old adobe structure called the Hotel de la Gloria. *Gracias por su visita.*

Does life insurance come as a bonus, when one makes a claim?

to Nick White

13

Speechless

Cyd Charisse with Fred Astaire in The Band Wagon *(Vincente Minnelli, MGM, 1953). Digital frame enlargement.*

Seeing and Seeing

Thinking of a child drawing a tree, Ernst Gombrich advises, "All art originates in the human mind, in our reactions to the world rather than in the visible world itself," adding, "it is precisely because all art is 'conceptual' that all representations are recognizable by their style" (87).

Gombrich's argument is that there is no sound basis for judging what the child *sees* as lacking in respect to, or different substantially from, what the adult *sees* when, for example, regarding a tree. *All art originates in the human mind,* and the person's indication of what she saw—child or adult—is the "art" in question. No representation will chauffeur us directly to *the thing* as perceived. Clearly, the art originating in the human mind, as it comes into the world, involves both vision and expression, since it is expression that *makes* the vision. The child's drawing of a tree may appear reductive and simplistic in comparison with, say, a landscape by Meindert Hobbema, but our access is not only to *what the young artist sees as she looks* but also to *the way she knows to express what she sees, given circumstances*; and "circumstances" include a great deal. The social situation and the press of demand. Expectation and normativity. The child's momentary desire. The child's expressive capacity. We show and see not what is there but what we are desiring and able to show and see. Every showing is a testament to the moment and to our expressive capacity just as much as to sight. Here is Rudolf Arnheim's way of putting this:

> We cannot hope to understand the nature of visual representation if we try to derive it directly from optical projections of the physical objects that constitute our world. Pictures and sculptures of any style possess properties that cannot be explained as mere modifications of the perceptual raw material received through the senses.

He goes on about children's drawings, "Children observe with an acuteness that puts many adults to shame; and no one who has seen the expression of breathless fascination in their eyes or the intense concentration with which they draw or paint will accept an explanation based on negligence or indifference" (163–4).

In any perceptual moment we may filter away what does not "belong"; but whatever we filter we first experience. Think of the Emperor's new clothes …

Competence

To speak a picture of the pictures one loves!

The relationship between the extensiveness of one's articulation and the extensiveness of one's capacity or tools to articulate, between what one perceives and the skills one has learned for expressing that, can help us understand the complexities of filmmaking in legion ways, since just as audiences perceive what is on the screen and may wish to talk about it so filmmaking collaborators perceive the world they work from and wish to make an expression of it onscreen. Take the screen actor. She must learn the tools of the trade before it becomes possible to seem competent in performance, but the tools of the trade develop, as cinema does, over time. By the early 1930s, actors already knew how their vocalizations, their delivery of dialogue, however clearly enunciated—and there was a tidal wave of clear enunciation, once the sound revolution skyrocketed—had, as well, an "interactive rhythm": the hesitation or pause after the last syllable uttered by A and before the first syllable uttered in conversation by B; or the time after A's line before A departs the room. They learned, too, how they depended for rhythm and speech effect, for the shape and length of a pause or delay, not only on their own powers of speech but also on a film editor who would be creating the rhythm of a scene. They came to know how to wait a few seconds after a dialogue take, to hold a pose, in order that a tail could be created long enough to give the editor flexibility in cutting. And they knew too that the pause for breath or consideration their character would endure before replying to someone was in another person's hands so that interactive elements like pensivity, hesitation, or even interruption would be managed editorially. If we look at the rather choppy talk in *The Jazz Singer* (1927) and compare it with the incomparably fluid rhythms of *His Girl Friday* (1940) or *Sullivan's Travels* (1942) we can see how deftly an editor could work and also what actors could have learned to assume about the editor's work. What this meant in practice was that the way one expressed a thought or feeling through speech had different features and demands once editing became more sophisticated. If for speaking the actor needed an expressive competence; now the requirements for that competence had changed.[1]

Or take expression by way of images; this also involves competence. Once three-strip Technicolor was in use as a camera and laboratory process, after 1935, there came onto the set a requirement for considerably increased illumination, this because the Kodak black-and-white recording film, that the Technicolor camera used for making the records which would be converted into color matrices later on, had an ASA of only 25, meaning lots of light was needed to get a solid exposure. Thus the fabled uncomfortable heat on sets. When with Technicolor filming a rear projection was involved as well—a diegetic window looking out on a field or precipice, a stormy sea—it was ideal to have the projection plates also shot in Technicolor (or the projected background would have been notably different from the foreground). But now the problem was that—since the front illumination on set was so intense—if the rear projection was not similarly bright, even if it had been produced out of doors, one would see the distinct incompatibility in light quality. In 1938 Paramount introduced its triple-head projector, which would take three identical copies of the rear-projection material and

---

[1] Jonathan Swift shows uncanny foresight inventing the Brobdingnagian "flapper" as a middler in conversations.

throw them simultaneously, one upon the other, onto the rear-projection screen, thus increasing the luminosity and density of the back image. Now a bright sunlit outdoor scene could be managed in a studio composite, because the Technicolor plate could be as bright as the Technicolor-shot foreground.

Dialogue and photography maneuvers like these are part of the expressive armature of studio filmmaking, and we can see how the diegetic "reality" that could be put onscreen, quite regardless of what was in a writer or filmmaker's mind, depended on how the technical facilities made certain renditions possible while blocking others. For example, in rear projections, no matter the image brightness a screen with good internal diffusion was required and such a thing was not immediately available in the early days of composite work.

There is a tendency of film watchers who look back to films from decades long gone, to regard the expressive intent as naïve or simplistic because, by comparison with standards of present-day filmmaking, the pictures seem so poorly conceived though they may have been made at the "crest of the wave." It never makes sense to pass retroactive judgment on the "innocence" of artists who were using all the tools they had at the time.

Impaired

One does not discover what one does not know how to look for, and one does not see what one does not know how to recognize. Gombrich notes how when we are confronted by an initially undecipherable drawing, in order to "understand" it or give it form we apply a schema already known; he cites an example of a figuration that some viewers thought of as an anchor, others as a winged creature, and still others as an ancient type of sword. Seeing was recognizing, placing into a known schema already normalized in the world. Directors, designers, and cinematographers are very careful in working out shots and scenes to prepare images that the audience will be able to grasp, and grasp quickly; in short, being viewers themselves they presume audiences' repertories of experience and abilities at recognition. In narrative, it is typically a specific interpretation that storytellers want to elicit, so ancillary clues to recognition are given in the surround, in the dialogue, and in dramatic figures' use of things. A shot is unlike a painting in a gallery in this critical respect, that it will fly by quickly, after other shots and before still others, and it must therefore be constructed to be not only visible but visible instantaneously. Godard's Louvre sequence in *Bande à part* (*Band of Outsiders*, 1964) plays with this differentiation somewhat hilariously.

But a circumstance can arise—does frequently, as I hope to argue—in which the film viewer becomes *impaired* in pointing to what has been experienced by way of the screen. In pointing to, not in seeing. Impairments in the viewing itself are quite another matter, a common experience in watching films from another culture since much of what the eyes catch may be undetectable if not unnameable. (One often notes signals of social class in British films gliding by American audiences, undetected.) Film audiences are in an especially precarious position as regards being able to use language, whether in a formal publication or in a casual encounter, to address what they see—*address* in the least complex way, not offer critique or evaluation but merely announce the experience of seeing. One does not see in a one-dimensional way, but it is not by seeing alone that we announce ourselves or that we make what was visual socially real.

For treating much that is seen at the edge of the screen, language, even used with expertise, puts only its most cursory forms at our disposal. The screen image, after all, is a matter of moving shapes, which is to say, unique contours traveling in peculiar ways and toward explicit directions (both diegetically, in narrative space, and supra-diegetically, upon the rectangle of the screen). Imagine contours indicating a human body (the bodies of animals import their own difficulties in description): whilst some viewers in the theater are equipped to "see" the bodies of screen figures *medically*— body types; typical or atypical movements; disfigurations—most watchers just see people, of whom, we all know, there are no two exactly alike. How many schemas would be employed in trying to spell out the way a particular body looked? How, for instance, would you use an untold thousand of words to give in language the face of Greta Garbo in *Anna Karenina* (1935)? Now considering body shapes, and all other shapes, too, note the variations that can be produced through the use of various lenses; or in the smallest gestural move; or by means of the slightest nuance of light hitting a face—countless exponentially magnified possibilities. The skin color or, for that matter, the color of anything at all, since our descriptors for color are woefully raw. Beyond color, tonal effects in black and white, lighting effects, forms and boundaries, subtleties of expression and movement—all this left in the care of a rudimentary language that at best offers gross categories in which items radically different must be worded the same. *He ran into the room:* ran like Lola in *Run Lola Run* (1998)?; ran like Gaston bounding Mme Colet's curling staircase?; ran like Tom Cruise in *Mission: Impossible – Ghost Protocol* (2011)?; ran like Cary Guffey trying to meet the alien light in *Close Encounters of the Third Kind* (1977); ran like the Scarecrow on the yellow brick road?

A still frame in which movements are helpfully frozen could exemplify some of these troubles. With stillness, the causes and weights, not to say the outcomes of the movement will fall out of consideration, and so will any particularity in the character of the mover, such as a limp or an elegant style. Left are graphic forms, implications. The image leading this chapter is taken from the ballet sequence of Vincente Minnelli's *The Band Wagon*

(1953), danced principally by Fred Astaire and Cyd Charisse. Michael Kidd choreographed it. Mary Ann Nyberg made the costumes. Preston Ames did the design under Cedric Gibbons's supervision. Of the two cinematographers on the picture, Harry Jackson and the uncredited George Folsey, one of them made this image. Instantly the conundrum (and, again, this faces us with only a single still image; imagine a whole film!): not *what to say?*, but *how to begin?* The eye jumps frantically over and across the frame, touching on a shoulder, a foot, a double bass (at extreme right) painted mauve-pink, a depth, a composition, a pair of expressions facial and also embodied; and there is some kind of suffusion of lavender mist; and the clothing is of another era, yet very swank (but what are the telltale marks of the swankiness?). What kind of place is this intended to be, with its colored glass and filigreed shutters? The people all around are not only gazing sternly at the principals, they seem ready to pounce: what would they be pouncing for? The long, long black (velvet?) gloves going all the way up Charisse's arms, as though to keep dust off her elbows. On a woman in the background one hand in the center of the shot (adjacent Charisse's left hand) covered in a banana-yellow glove: did this figure choose that glove? Why would Astaire have his pants hiked up some and his left arm a trifle crooked?

And on and on ...

Then we wonder, "What is this music we've been hearing (that is now paused)?" because surely all this poised placement and indicative movement is accompanied by, or is meant to accompany, some beat. How to describe the timbre, the tonalities, the amplitude, the harmonic combinations—not to say the crucial rhythm and the melody if there is one? *How to write the melody?* Or the sound of the voices if anyone is singing, for that matter, through the rest of the film in one after another moment of emotional annoyance? How to begin to get a tip of the tongue on all this? Extreme right, adjacent a black knee, a chartreuse fold of cloth.

Should we think it smart to make sense of the colors in their array, that is, the design? Should we look at the dancers' matching posture? Should we wonder about her red shoes? Is the spread of pink-lavender light on the floor emanating from her shod feet?

Should we think him a gangster and her a gangster's moll? Or an actor dressed to seem a gangster in a sequence meant to convey artificiality? Or even an actor dressed to seem an actor dressed to seem a gangster?

And this is only 1/24th of a second of the ballet.

Does she follow his every twitch as a cue for her next breath, her next phrase of meaning? Does he follow hers? Are both of them actually following Michael Kidd's breath in dancing their regard for one another?

Astaire's right knee is an inch or two forward of his left one and in either his dance step now or his immediate preparation for the step to come his heel is raised from the floor. There is a very slight discrepancy between the left and right shod feet of Charisse, just enough to intimate that perhaps her right heel is about to come up as well. Shall we take these little visibles as

(a) gestures, or (b) only parts of gestures, or (c) nothing significant at all? And if gestures, then what meaning is to be read (seen) and what thought associated with (told about by) them?

Yet it is also true that when we speak, when we recount, when we explain, when we lecture, we give some kind of a context to our commentary so that an audience can have reference to what we are pointing to. To grab this moment in *The Band Wagon,* would we not somehow contextualize it? One would wish to. But how? The tale inside the ballet leading up to this frame? The tale of the dramatic circumstances in the film leading up to the ballet? The relation between these characters as it develops in the film and is brought to this moment? I can say there seems to be a pink room, but how much do I need to evoke in order that not only the room *but also my pointing to the pinkness* can have some relevance to somebody else?

When one is speaking—of a film, of anything—one is not muttering to oneself, and the ability of a listener (or reader) to grasp the speech is no marginal feature of the activity. Why am I telling you about this?, and why might this moment be the right moment to pick? As for my going on about this image from the *Band Wagon* ballet, easy enough: I wanted something that would show form, posture, seizure, composition, nuance, and attitude *at least,* and that could intimate if not directly show flamboyant color (absent here because of the cost of publishing a paper book!) and also, one cannot go far wrong with Minnelli, or with Astaire, or with Charisse; and here we can have all three at once!

Yet, to say the truth: in trying to say all this, one is already breathless.

Sins of Omission

It would be an error not to mention that for most film viewers most of the time, in most places where most films are screened, at most edges of the screen, the solution to the riddle of how to say all that one receives and apprehends, how to word all the extraordinary richness, is: *don't bother.* Or, try any of these maneuvers instead:

- Say the name of the stars, comment freely on them. In this, assume that the star name is a code that can be counted upon to immediately bring up a preconceived file. Again in *The Band Wagon,* we are treated to a moment early on with Ava Gardner, when public use of just such a personality file—not only preconceived but known well enough to the star and her vast audience that it can be played and played to at will—is blatantly put on show.

- Say the genre of the film, "It's a great RomCom!" Generic nominatives represent the nth degree in linguistic generalization, call it schematization. We all already know what a Romantic Comedy is, and so in watching this film we can take our ease spying through the veil of previous knowledge. He kisses her, you know. She kisses him, you know, too. You know all of it. When they look at a double bed, they will wink.

- Compare the film to something else. "It's much better than *When Harry Met Sally* ... (1989)!" "If you liked *When Harry Met Sally* ... you'll love this!" Or, "Yechhh, *When Harry Met Sally* ... was *soooo* much better!" This nicely presumes a whole library filled and ready in the head of anyone current with the culture.
- Or, simplest and least taxing on the breath, advertise: "You hafta go see it!"

Opting for one of these pleasantries, one gets the film off one's chest, and one feels one has done proper duty not only as an avid consumer but as an astute evaluator of one's cultural materials and a well-intentioned sharer. But all those swirling effects for which one didn't trouble to find words, for which one didn't know words existed: they remain and mix with the residues of the rest of cinema as one knows it. One carries a kind of dreamworld on one's shoulder. What is central here is the power and richness of cinema compared with the poverty and impotence of language, not any viewer's mode of response as a personal characteristic. Even the commentator who speaks or inscribes at length about films, who stretches to be as descriptive and as clear-headed as possible in composing to the beat of the picture, even this adept lover of film will find language breaking off and the real traces of a picture lingering unspoken, unpenned, untold.

to Katie Gallof Houck

14

Don't Touch Me!

Above: "Noli me tangere" (Titian, c. 1514). National Gallery, London. Public domain. Below: Ida Lupino and Edmond O'Brien in The Bigamist *(Ida Lupino, The Filmakers, 1953). Digital frame enlargement.*

[1]

I have visited Titian's "Noli me tangere" several times, over a period of several years, astonished by the halted action of Jesus putting—intending to put, having just put—what seems a stop to the forward-going action of the woman, who is Mary Magdalene. John 20:17:

> Jesus saith to her, Touch me not; for I am not yet ascended to my Father; but go to my brethren, and say to them, I ascend to my Father and your Father, and to my God and your God.

She has recognized him after the Resurrection, and some students claim his statement to her, "Noli me tangere," means she should lay aside earthly habits that are physical and let it be only her spirit, or her heart, that touches him. Most of those who work to "interpret" this painting for its meaning do concern themselves with what the phrase *Noli me tangere* could be intended to say, in such a situation as this one or more generally. Even if there is a "general" meaning, we can see how Titian has taken pains to situate the conversational moment in real, call it everyday action. Her posture below Him suggests adoration and respect. The reach is that of the child eager to grasp what has appealed to the eye, eager, possibly, to verify the status of something as real. Jesus could be confounding his status in reality by forbidding the touch (see Ortega 111).

I remember distinctly how I was stunned by the grace, even dancerliness of His attitude. Leaping to mind was Titian soliciting the aid of a dancer or otherwise graceful man to pose for him. Note the *contrapposto*, the placing of weight upon the left leg and concomitant bending of the body, yielding an even arc running up the right leg, over the hip, and onto the back. This posture seems very speedily effected, as though while either standing quietly or being in forward motion past her, Jesus suddenly saw the woman's hand reach out and twisted His body to both avoid her contact and refrain from issuing any gesture of reprimand or feelingful withdrawal. Very much, "I am with you, but do not touch me."

Perhaps even, "I am with you to the degree that you do not touch me; as long as you agree not to touch me." Or, don't touch and I am here.

Her reach seems urgent, too, or at least did in these early inspections of mine. Not only to verify and identify Him but to bring the moment of experience to its fullness. The touch would gesture peaceful affection and receptivity, and there must be some primordial sense in which the standing male is saying, "Be done with gesture, ascend over it altogether. What you feel most deeply you cannot signal with your body." (One thinks of Hamlet having "that within which passeth show." Did Shakespeare gaze at this canvas, it was painted about ninety years before he wrote the Danish play?)

It is the way He lets His head follow the contour of the bending: graceful, polite, even submissive, as though her attentiveness has caught Him up. The use of the staff to keep balance. On the road far, far in the distance the solitary pedestrian, only other person visible: here's an inhabited, but at this instant lonely place. The delicacy of the brown oak leaves, each one fully being itself. That man has perhaps been tending to, or speaking with the sheep in the rear left. Now he is walking his dog. The clouds are as though in motion, one can feel the wind. In short, this is a brief instant in Jesus's presence and Mary's life, one of those wafer-thin slices of time in which paths can cross.

All this, and more, in my early viewings of "Noli me tangere," at any rate. I neither ceased visiting the beloved National Gallery nor kept my distance from this painting, which stands among a very small group of canvases I try hard never to miss sight of, to whatever brocaded wall they have been moved. I had further, even somewhat intriguing thoughts as I scanned my photographs of it in close-up, with "all the time in the world," as one says, and no sense of other viewers shuffling behind me. And what I saw was that, indeed, she is not touching Him … yet in the customary way that we speak the title of a painting while looking at it, I was saying "Don't touch me" while I saw her not touching. It was the—for me odd—conjunction between the phrase *Noli me tangere* and the actual pose of the instant that called out. Titian has caught, with notable precision, the openness of her thumb and stretch of the fingers of her right hand at the same time as affording her an open-handed, spread-fingered gesture with her left so that she can balance herself. They are both balancing themselves. This is a moment of balance. One can see how the (arbitrary) leftward cant of the tree behind Jesus works against the (necessary) rightward curvature of His body so that the attention of the viewer is not pulled one way or the other. His left hand, holding the staff, can be followed as a pale structure rightward as it "becomes" the pathway up to the town, and then the buildings of the town take on a weight that is balanced by the airy fluffiness of the sheep at the left, on their green.

She is not, at any rate, touching.

But then, staring and staring, I began to wonder about touch, and about the word "me" in that equation, since Jesus is imprecating her not to touch *Him,* the "me" of the context, and as we look we can ask what, in His view, she would have to be touching if she were touching Him. In short, what is going on here?:

- Is He making the claim that the cape, which has twisted around Him, is Himself? If she puts her fingers onto the fabric of the thing, has she committed that tabooed touch? Titian has made a fabulous ambiguity by way of the angling of her right hand as it reaches up, because we are now forced to remain entirely uncertain as to whether it is His hand or His cape she is or is not striving to touch. Were Jesus claiming the cape as being identical to Himself, He would be in effect asserting an identity between His garment and His being, as in, I am the clothes I wear; you cannot touch them without at the same time touching the Me who has them on.

- Or is He saying, in effect, "I" am whatever Presence is here by virtue of the body that you see beneath this cloak. There are, of course, two layers of cloaking, the bluish-white overcloak and the yellowish-white fabric tied around His loins, this latter a very considerably reproduced item in paintings of the crucifixion. I am He who is beneath the loincloth, which itself is beneath the overcape, but I give warning: if you touch one of these you will wish to touch the other, and then touch that body. Not touching the garments is a precaution, then, against the fingers hitting the skin, if there is skin to hit. The issue is fingering skin.

In either case, Jesus does not wish to be touched. Or: wishes to not be touched. I say "wishes" to indicate not that He has a desire but that He issues admonition for what He considers, and we should consider, a good reason.

We must try to understand the painting in its own terms, not as a simplistic illustration of a spoken or written account Biblical or otherwise. This woman *could be Magdalene after the Resurrection* but in the canvas nothing attests to that. She is there, she is eager, she is in a transport. We see this relation of bodies in depictions of fans trying to get at rock stars and movie stars, rock stars pinned to a stage in hot light and movie stars stepping ever so quickly down a ruby-carpeted path. Is it possible that, textual accounts aside, the *idea* of Jesus warning this Mary off, or of this man warning this woman off, is nothing other than a metaphor for another warning. It is not that the character in the painting makes the address, "Noli me tangere," it is the painting itself. And the recipient of the warning is not the female figure in the painting but the viewer of the canvas, just as it is me who feels the pressure to step back even though I wish to step forward when the movie star brushes past me.

If you touch me, you will rapidly discover that I am not what you took me to be.

You took me to be a holder, a kind of magical *etui,* in which a most valuable treasure is diligently kept. That treasure is a trace of Jesus (if we say, in His encounter with Mary after the Ressurection)—we are eyewitnesses to great sensitivity and brave fortune. You see a hill and a village, you see sheep in a meadow, you see the staff and the loincloth, you see the reaching hand and the beatific face of He who would not be known as mortal. In short, the viewer is believing him or herself to be gazing *through* the painting to its subject, and Titian's warning is that if our hand reaches out to touch Jesus's garment, following the inspiration provided by Mary, we will know that we are not looking *through* the painting at all, and also that we can never be looking through this or any painting. We are, and can only be, looking *at* a painting. And from afar. We are gazing at a prepared surface. And we are being told that our gaze is sufficient unto itself, whether we would choose to believe this or not.

Look, but do not touch.

Or else:

- Is the meaning of the visible body entirely different from the yearning to touch it? I am here, or at least I appear to you at this place and time, and my form—but only my form—is that of a human body dressed. The idea that, if you were to fondle my dress or even reach beneath my dress to my skin you would discover me, is without merit. The *here* in which I can be placed, the "place and time," is not coherent with the body as you see it. I am *in relation to* the body, which is to say, perhaps around it, perhaps above it, perhaps even inside it, but reach as you may strive to, you will find no way to contact me. I am beyond contact. *Noli me tangere = You won't touch me.*

And in this waits a revelation of the vanity of all those simplistic fumblings and embraces, those grapplings and massagings, all those supposed ways of getting past the carapace and into the flesh. The crowd lined up to watch the great Him or Her emerge into the street and walk to the limousine. The organization (call it the story) of the Titian painting is in relation to the canvas, within it, behind it, around it, just as the organization of the movie star is in the scene and the supporting guards, but it is not by touching the canvas that one can approach Jesus nor by touching the sleeve that one can touch the star. To allegorize by way of already-known religious figures was still, in the early sixteenth century, a method of communicating to a vast multitude in a straightforward and unimpeded manner—if also through ambiguity—and so the subject (to call it that) of Jesus and Mary and the Touch is convenient. Even if virtually every sixteenth-century viewer, and almost every viewer afterward, would have seen this picture by way of interpretation, seen it as being about Jesus, still one must gaze at the world through one's own eyes, and I gaze at *Noli me tangere* through eyes that no one else shares, eyes that cannot touch. Or: eyes that touch only in the strange way that eyes can touch.

[2]

Antonioni's *Beyond the Clouds* (1995) begins with a small story set in Ravenna. A young man meets a young woman at a small hotel. A tryst seems on the threshold, but each, for separate reasons, declines to take the step.

Some long time later, after a cinema screening one day, he meets her purely by chance. He visits her apartment and in silence, without the encumbrance of clothing, they encounter each other. The scene mounts to a climax but does not reach the top. He dresses and quietly leaves and she is left to watch after him through her high window. Noli me tangere.

The encounter on the bed has its own remarkable features, and represents something of a torsioned address to the problem of touch raised in the Titian (painted when the artist was only in his young twenties). Silvano (Kim Rossi Stuart) and Carmen (Ines Sastre) bear far less allegorical weight than Jesus and Mary; in this way, they are even more deceptive than certain clearly referential figures in visual art, who persist in seeming to claim a fictional identity worth the viewer's fixation. We find ourselves entirely convicted of the casual and eager freshness of these two, the spontaneity of their moments, the mounting desire and painful suppression involved in their not gaining fulfilment. And Silvano does not issue Carmen a warning about touch as prelude to some affair of involvement without touch. For long moments, he caresses her form (not her body) as she lies in expectation, with tender sinuous hands that by the most careful arrangement do not land upon the skin. She never for an instant makes to reach out to him, but his reaching out to her, guised as the erect passion of the young male, never reveals itself truly, and turns instead to a kind of abstracted philosophical play, far less with her—her breasts, her groin, her belly—than with her expectations. It is the address to, and the play with expectations that links this scene to the Titian canvas.

If we step back, we can wonder whether the refraint from touch is being:

- [a] addressed by Silvano to Carmen, a form of strange communication or potent non-communication, in a "language" he presumes she will understand, and that her gestures of hunger give us to believe she does; or
- [b] addressed by Antonioni, *by way of Silvano and Carmen,* to the viewer whose gaze at the screen is an adulterated form of touch.

The viewing gaze as a form of touch:

The light from the screen touches the eye, to be sure, and we are all both metaphorically and literally *touched* by cinema. Yet also, again to establish the reality of the thing, we tend to reach out with the eye to attempt touching the object we see. Reaching across the abyss at the edge of the screen. Run the fingertips over the surface of it. This is as true of the muddy ditch into which Roger O. Thornhill hurls himself to flee the strafing airplane as it is of the shimmering red eyeglasses that don't quite help Marilyn Monroe see the wall in front of her in *How to Marry a Millionaire* (1953). It is there, the Glory; we have it by seeing it; and in having it we work to approach touching. But at the same time, it is perhaps too evident that with eyesight we cannot effect touch, or at least not that peculiar touch we attribute to the experience of the hand. The eye is, therefore, both a hand and not a hand. We handle the scenario with the eye, but we cannot get a hand on it. It is very easy to imagine, as we watch his hand move, that Silvano would gladly fondle Carmen's body and enter it, yet the subjunctivity implied here, *would gladly,* is the whole story. He does not touch, however beckoning she is. Are we being shown a moment in a series of happenings between these two people—these two figures—in which he signals to her the delirium of touch by not effecting it? Is that what is happening?

Or is the film addressing a primordial impulse of the viewer's, to enjoy the sexuality implied in the picture, to experience directly rather than by way of appreciative vision? Are we brought by the peachy smooth skin of the two young people, by the soft light through the window, to a state of desire more or less matching the state of desire we so forthrightly apportion to Silvano? Is his "simulating" sexual contact a stand-in for our own "simulation" of sexual contact? This is about teasing. We pass the eye over the contours of the screen (the screen is flat, the shapes pictured there lend, but only lend, the idea of contours) without touching—because without being able to touch. All this is very much present for us, very directly here, in this bounded space, and we feel ourselves (incorrectly, of course) to be inhabiting the same space these two young people inhabit, with the sense that if we were to reach out to touch either one of them, or both, we would be entirely sensible, we would be acting in no other way than we act when, seeing a tennis ball, we pick it up from the green, green grass and heft it. The cinematic screen differs from the painted canvas in being photographic (even the photorealist painters begin with a photograph), yielding a sharper and more rounded sense of depth that seems to us to preferentially simulate the experience of the unaided eye.

"Don't touch me!" is being proclaimed by the screen, just in the way that Silvano is "saying" to Carmen, "I will not touch you" and that she is thinking, "Please touch me." There is nothing idiosyncratic about the proclamation, since every moment of cinema is one in which we are urged or exhorted or stimulated to touch that which we cannot possibly touch. Cinema is always saying, "Don't touch me," as in: *You don't touch me*; or *try as you might you will not touch me*. But at the same time, the feeling that one is on the cusp of touch, that touching is possible, that one's desire can be fulfilled through a touch, is never compromised. The screen never stops beckoning, nor do we ever stop being sensitive to its call. We do not stuff wax into our ears, do not lash ourselves to the mast that stabilizes our seats when the Siren Screen beckons.

Within the diegesis we can imagine—really, it is not difficult to imagine—outcomes, perspectives, plans, and attitudes intentionally or happenstantially not spelled out (we are always doing this, watching film and being alive). He is building up his desire until it is ready to explode, but he is a profoundly narcissistic individual; so he will dress and go home, and immediately on arrival satisfy himself with the still-pulsing memory of her breathing and the still-tingling imagination of her warm flesh. Or, he is somewhat crude, possibly sadistic, and walking away will forget all about the encounter and leave her to her own self-satisfaction, or to nothing. Or, he wants to hold the love interest just as long as possible, and in walking away he is storing his desire until a next time, say tomorrow (just over the closing boundary of the little film story), when he will return and give himself to her. Or else he has had a sudden moral awakening, come sharply to the realization that for one reason or another, what he has been doing with her is wrong; he stops himself, he leaves, he repents, and the irony is that she does not have the same moral sense at all, and finds nothing to repent for in this afternoon's escapade except, perhaps, her irritation that he took himself away to repent.

Another conceivable interpretation, since one feels interpretation is a must: Silvano has indeed completed his act of "embracing" to his full satisfaction; this little dance of the palms and fingers is his normal way of being with a lover's body; and nothing either untoward or strange has been happening here at all. When she looks out of the window at him disappearing down the street, Carmen may be satisfied, disappointed, tentative, sad, fulfilled, joyous, or querulous and we are left with the power to read her at will. But nothing stands in the way, either, of self-diagnosis, of looking back at the scene in terms of one's own proclivities toward or away from touch; thus, of seeing on the screen both oneself at work and a total stranger.

[3]

While it is often efficient and proper to take a touching (or pointedly non-touching) gesture with seriousness, to consider it as being a straightforward and direct communication, seriousness is not the only mode invoked by touch. A certain mocking-up of serious touch can find its place in play, as, for one example, in the game of Tag, where the point of executing a touch upon another player is the very opposite of a desire of proximity; as one tags a player and utters, "You're *it*," the first impulse is to flee as far away as possible, to avoid being touched back by *It*. In the age-old medieval custom—much frowned upon in modern society—of rubbing a hunchback's hump for good luck we have the reverse, recognition of the healing power of a bodily stigma, the particular "good fortune" on offer through the lucky touch being at least in part transference of a motile stigma away from the self. Play, as Goffman suggests generally a version of untransformed activity (see *Frame Analysis*), can be shaped in many ways, some of which are really or potentially lethal, offensive, unpleasant, or problematic just as likely as pleasurable.

Consider for its unpleasantness the knife fight in Nicholas Ray's *Rebel Without a Cause* (1955). Newly moved to the Los Angeles area where the film is set, Jim Stark (James Dean) has tried to befriend members of a West Hollywood gang led by Buzz Gunderson (Corey Allen). Sparring, challenging, taunting, and insulting are all *de rigueur* for them, but things do get out of hand finally, and Buzz and Jim find themselves caught up in a fight with switchblades. This takes place with the gang gathered eagerly to watch (for the most part to watch the new boy cut to pieces by their leader-hero) on the eastern parapet of the Griffith Observatory, panoramically overlooking Los Angeles on a bright, sunny day. The etiquette of an open-air gang fight of this sort, which is to say, the unwritten rules by which the players engage mano-a-mano, centers around a kind of stunting, in which mortal threat is artfully simulated at the same time as the production of death, or even serious wounding, is artfully avoided. Nobody is actually trying to kill anybody, but it must be played as though everybody is; the fighters are aiming to feel the effect. But this means the fight is itself a staged performance that Jim and Buzz are acting through, each knowing how to show zestful masculinity, prowess, strength, discipline, and reserve while at the same time respecting the other's dignity. What makes the action a stunt is the fact that the blades really can cut, and one player might, if not sufficiently careful in his choreography, actually hurt the other, an act that would "bring the curtain down." So it is necessary for each boy to play at (i) being dangerous and (ii) withstanding danger, all the while (iii) skirting the actual production of danger and (iv) not giving away the ploy.

The diegetic fight game as performance is of course doubled in the sequence by means of a scripted, in a way broader containment, "fight-as-performance," which is what James Dean and Corey Allen are engaged in as they move around for Nicholas Ray's camera. We watch the simulation of a "knife-fight-simulation," all set up for the lens, pose by pose, move by move, with both actors in full agreement about what they are trying to do and working in companionship. This gives a pleasing aura to the characters who also, as they hover and circle, seem to be feeling a warm camaraderie, their demonstrative growling aside.

What happens here diegetically, in this actors' outplay of a playing-out, is (a) threatened physical contact, amplified by (b) knives in the boys' hands so that this contact can become brutal, and (c) actual avoidance of contact in the proof of it. The whole symbolic point of this "knife fight," Buzz already knows and Jim is learning from him in this initiation, is putting up an entirely credible empty threat—all of which Dean and Allen are putting up. So, pretend you intend to touch (with the knife point). In fact pretend that nothing would give you greater pleasure than to touch, even to mar; but *don't touch*. The pornography of the scene for the eager onscreen audience would be vitiated the moment one boy actually damaged the other, so damage must be avoided that the figures' pleasure and ours may build and swell. *Noli me tangere.*

Avoiding or mediating touch can be as important as, or more important than, touching; can be a way of touching in itself.

Possibly we can imagine how during the shoot the situation was at once made hyperreal as "dangerous" and also profoundly confused, because Corey Allen's knife tip actually did touch James Dean. The two had been getting into the spirit of the action, actually becoming gradually more aggressive as actors. As tension grew in the crew, Lawrence Frascella and Al Weisel report, "there was a palpable sense of peril as both actors became more and more frenzied. Suddenly, Ray shouted in a frightened voice, 'Cut! Get a first aid man to Jimmy on the double.' Allen had nicked Dean on the ear and a trickle of blood had begun to run down Dean's neck." Dean was entirely cool about the matter, and was furious at the director: "Goddamn it, Nick! What the fuck are you doing? Can't you see this is a real moment? Don't you ever cut a scene while I'm having a real moment!" (115). As an actor, Dean was apparently using the story preeminently to contextualize his experience, "becoming Jim," as it were. Thus, from his point of view, the nick, the blood, and the aggression behind the movement were *real*, and Ray's interruption was trivially "fictional." Given that the overriding context for Dean was a knife battle ("to the death" if not to the death), a nick that drew blood was not only permissible but *de rigueur*. Nick Ray had made his own nick, too.

[4]

Some other contexts altogether, for outplay of the same ritual:

When the cantor reads aloud from the scroll of the Torah, in order to keep his place on the line of hand-sculpted glyphs, moving right to left upon the parchment, he makes use of a *yad* (the Hebrew word for "hand"), this being a device most typically fashioned of silver, long and thin as a quill, about a foot's length, very often beautifully ornamented and with a pointed tip or tiny fashioned hand of silver at the end. No living hand touches the actual parchment surface on which the Torah is inscribed. This is the administration of the ceremony. A respectful distance is maintained, or, the touch of respect is allocated not to the cantorial hand but to the cantorial hand's refraint from contacting the parchment directly, a touch of pureness and holiness achieved through not touching, which in this case is intermediary touching. The *yad* is a constantly evocative symbolic device, so that as it glides over the surface of the words, which are painted with ink by hand and not printed—the scribe touching the parchment with his quill or his brush and not with his hand—it announces its presence, announces its holding back from touch with each syllable that comes out of the cantor's mouth. Born in this usage is the idea and fact of a hand that is not a hand, a substitute with limited capability at the same time as it glows in purification.

It is interesting that in surgery the principle of medical transformation is put in play as a conceptual *yad*, a covering rationale that explains how, in the unique space of the living body, now mechanically opened to touch, any actual digital manipulation by the surgeon—holding back an organ, squeezing an artery—while producing an effect impossible without touch is also distanced from touch through a mapping of organic space and a physics that understands causes and predicts outcomes there. In this way a person's gall bladder, for example, becomes *the* gall bladder, positioned in such and such a way, functioning to complete a cycle, movable, removable, and so on, while the person whose bladder it is, or shall we say the person *of* the bladder, is abstracted away through anesthesia. The anesthesia works doubly, on the patient to obviate pain and on the surgeon to insinuate a withdrawal into "direct touch only at a remove."

The *touch figure,* stilled as pose, is to be found in the grace of Jesus's body curling around Mary's outstretched hand, quite as though she is understood and loved for her gesture while also guarded against, so that He be sanctified and she can be sane. In *Rebel* the touch figure is made very complex, beginning with the knife dance, arms circling in the air, but then vibrating through Dean's reaction, both professional and personal, when a contact—the switchblade is a *yad*—actually draws his blood and he is forced into a confrontation with the spirit by which he performs. In *Clouds,* Silvano uses an habitual method as *yad,* and the power of the touch figure is made evident in the still composure of his face, his observant—even too observant—eyes that both guide the movement of his hand, regulate its altitude over the planet of Carmen's skin, maintain vigilance over the actions he commits, and seek her response. Silvano may himself be nothing but Antonioni's *yad,* a way for the filmmaker in cantorial mode to read out a significant passage regaling the eager spectator with the tale of Jesus and Mary again, this time showing the extraordinary delice of the touch of avoidance as being, much more than natural, a devoted achievement. To watch people touch or stand back from touching is to touch by standing back from touching.

[5]

There is a gross form of touch, something sufficiently expansive that it describes a situation or stretches a relationship, as when we see two onscreen figures who are posited as being married or who by their ongoing behavior toward one another vividly suggest they are. Even if physically they do not touch each other, we can read the situation as though the sphere of action and feeling of one character touches, abuts against, perhaps even overlaps the sphere of the other. In separation and divorce tales, the distancing of spheres becomes a central dramatic issue to manage. For example, in *The Marvelous Mrs. Maisel* (2017), Joel and Midge do not much alter their emotions regarding one another after they separate, then divorce, but the distance is invoked graphically with Joel visiting Midge's domestic space with notably diminished frequency, for notably diminished spates of time, thereby showing diminished comfort.

But a peculiar and complex presentation of *not touching* is shown in Ida Lupino's *The Bigamist* (1953). Here, Harry Graham (Edmond O'Brien), a company manager living with his wife Eve (Joan Fontaine) in San Francisco, makes frequent business trips to Los Angeles to seek clients. Broader, less cloistered light there. The wife back home is very attached to him, somewhat insecure, and wholly genuine in her loving feeling. He is nothing but entirely warm to her. She carefully packs his bag when he leaves town (like the detective's wife helping him on with his holster before he goes to work, in *On Dangerous Ground* [1951]).

In LA, it comes to light—because he and his wife were aiming to adopt a child and Jordan, the adoption society investigator (Edmund Gwenn), relentless in his suspicion, has followed him there—that Harry is going by another name, Harrison Graham. Harrison is lonely, and one day on a see-the-stars'-homes touring bus he meets a woman who gains his interest, Phyllis Martin (Ida Lupino). They slowly come together over a period of time and he is finally living with her as his wife. The questions raised by the narrative, on the most simplistic level, are two: (a) how much will nosey Mr. Jordan tolerate, once he has witnessed both situations, before exploding the situation, and refusing to sanction the adoption?, and (b) for how long will Harry be able to maintain his second life as Harrison, his second home, his partner Phyllis, in the face of Eve's complete innocence? It is important for catching the taste of the narrative to see that Harrison is utterly genuine in his affection for Phyllis, genuine and honest and forthright; and Harris is the same way with Eve. He is not a guileful person, just one who is at first befuddled by his circumstances and then eager in a sincere way to make the very best of both worlds. But Eve does find out, collapses emotionally, and finally sues Harry for divorce. Phyllis walks out on him.

As she directs this film, Lupino establishes the distance between Harry and Harrison in terms of markedly different residential settings, differences in performative lingo, and mood changes that O'Brien executes brilliantly. Two secret worlds are being held away from each other, *Noli me tangere,* and as we toggle back and forth between them we are never in doubt about which world is currently in play nor in suspense about Harry/Harrison's behavior, which is uniformly and predictably civil and genuine. It is *only his name* that he puts on, not his self. When he is confronted by the much older Jordan, who just cannot fathom this reality, he confesses that he doesn't know quite how this happened, what he could have done differently, or what he should do. There will not be a structural problem showing a story of two worlds by bouncing back and forth, unless somehow the worlds collide, providing Harry/Harrison with a severe bout of what behavioral scientists call role conflict, and Jordan is of course the gravitational force making the worlds collide. As Eve becomes more and more involved in administering Harry's San Francisco business she moves further and further from him; and Harrison and Phyllis gain intimacy to the point where she becomes pregnant.

In the courtroom, Lupino stages a moment when, with Harry/Harrison facing the judge and both women sitting behind him in the chamber, the prosecuting attorney makes a small, extraordinarily pithy statement. This comes virtually at film's end, after the well-structured narrative gap has been posited, examined, re-examined, re-examined again, and finally spanned—the span being the poisonous touch that makes termination. What the lawyer says to the judge is this: that in a way he is sorry for all of this, because had Mr. Graham chosen to take an extra-marital mistress nobody would have batted an eyelash. Here, however, when he tried to be honest in both cases, and law-abiding, and responsible, he faces penalty. Harry/Harrison's two lives, then, were collaborating to execute an elaborate two-city ritual of touchlessness, and the touch that finally came about was provisional, unplanned, and awkward, rather like someone walking down a sidewalk and accidentally bumping into the wrong someone else. Accident is, of course, a frequently used and quite wonderful cinematic trope. The accidental touch here was a visible one, unlike all those surreptitious accidental touches with which, the film would have us believe, our culture was filled in the early 1950s (if not still today).

Lupino is careful in both situations not to show much emotive physicality beyond facial expressions, walking side by side, quietness of discourse, and shared conversational topics. Lovemaking is nowhere near the screen. But as their tour bus glides through the streets of Beverly Hills and Harrison gazes out the window, the guide through his sound system suddenly directs viewers to look at that large house with the tree: "That's where Edmund Gwenn lives!"

[6]

In Ingmar Bergman's *The Touch* (1971) one finds a not untypical story of clandestine love, family dynamics, and neurosis. Yet after seeing it—seeing it with some awestruck respect, for this is one of Ingmar Bergman's masterpieces—one might reasonably wonder what "touch" is being referred to. Whose touch? A touch when? A touch that does what?

Karin (Bibi Andersson) is a securely married woman with a professional husband, Andreas (Max von Sydow), living in a splendidly bright and spotless Scandinavian home, but we do not discover this about her until after we make our first encounter in an even more spotless hospital room, as she stands vigil over the just deceased body of her mother. Pristine silence, as some clock somewhere on earth is relentlessly ticking away the seconds of our lives. The mother was very old; Karin is not so young; and mortality feels at this moment like a large and heavy door swinging shut on her experience. Before leaving the hospital she meets a younger man, David (Elliott Gould), arrived from America to do some archaeological work in the vicinity. They meet again later and he tells her how he fell in love with her the moment he met her. Inexperienced at this sort of thing, but taken with him nevertheless, Karin enters an affaire de coeur with David, who lets her know that his family were concentration camp survivors. He is a pressing, urgently expressive, demanding, and sincerely passionate, if clumsy, brash, and boiling young man. They have a painful relationship as the film progresses, with Andreas in his own kind of pain outside it.

Are we watching the touch of the finger of death, near Karin?

Or the touch of affection, then love, between Karin and David?

Or, from a distance, the touch of the marriage of Karin and Andreas, now perhaps gaining a distancing diminishment?

Or the touch of conversation, that moves forward just as a clock does, and just as film does, defining and substantiating us in time?

Or David's recalcitrance to touch Karin more deeply, out of his own fears and concerns and out of respect for hers? There is a short visit to David's sister (Sheila Reid), whose hands are crippled with arthritis.

Or an angry, retributive touch of Andreas's hand upon David—held back, never taking place?

Or any other touch.

A wooden statue of the Madonna has been moved to a little local church and David has been studying it with a burning fascination. He brings Karin to see it, a kind of love offering on his part, we may think. But we have not plumbed to the abysm of David's agony yet. While she admires it with her eyes agape—it is slender, Modiglianiesque, elegant, worn to the smoothness of marble—he gently leads her to the side so that she can look behind. A fulsome army of parasites is at work eating this thing of beauty from within.

The Madonna's wooden face: tranquil, accepting, redeeming, and also moving toward an eternity of nothingness. Even a sculpture must touch mortality.

"It is the touch of life, everything," Elliott Gould said to me in January 2021. And it was possible to sense him still speaking as David, fifty years on, seeing the world for its charms and attractions with eyes that also look inward to a vast and unbounded plain of agony. "The touch is life. The life that our mind inhabits." As though, for the character and for the actor, life is greater, so much greater than the mind. And as to the greatness of the mind: when I was an undergraduate, Kenneth Boulding, the esteemed economist, showed me one day a rough mathematical proof to the effect that the human mind could comprehend the universe. If you take the measurements our greatest telescopes have provided of the radius of the known universe and calculate the diameter, and then sit with a pen and write down the number that expresses that diameter, at the rate of one digit per second and with no pauses, it would take some four a half years to write the number. Now if you assume every brain cell is either on or off, and this of course is a great reduction since things are not so simple in truth, and you take 2 to the power of the number of cells in the human brain, and you sit with a pen and write down *that* number one digit per second, you would not be able to complete the writing in the span of a human lifetime.

For Boulding, as I understood him, the brain which may seem to inhabit the universe is in truth the habitation of the universe. But for Gould and for David, David whose memory encompasses the Camps and the sculpture and Karin and even more, *life* is greater even than the universe, immeasurably greater, and is the habitation of the mind. Our minds, able, perhaps, even to comprehend the universe cannot understand life. The touch is all of what we live. Tangible, regardable, significant, but incomprehensible.

[7]

And then *E.T. the Extra-Terrestrial* (1982), about which only one small question:

The little creature, E.T., discovered and befriended on earth, takes a moment at one point to show his new friend Elliott (Henry Thomas) one of his alien powers. Elliott has fallen and scraped his head. The little fellow looks at him with his enormous eyes (that seem thirsty for knowledge and innocent rather than what they probably are, all-knowing), raises an index finger toward Elliott's head and, mimicking what Elliott has said, "Ouch!" (we learn language by mimicking), whispers "Ouuuuch" and touches his friend. The wound is healed. But this finger: the tip of it lights up and radiates, reddish orange like an ember in a fire, as though burning with intent from within. A kind of organic flashlight! A magical wand! And of course E.T. with his lit fingertip is one of the universally recognized icons of the film, a major aid to business.

That one character might heal another by the laying on of hands comes from a very old combination of practice and myth, in medicine the palpation; in magic the touch of the magician's special hand upon some inert substance; in revivalism the touch of the healer upon the sick, mimicking Christ (or, tales of Christ). We understand E.T. healing Elliott by touch easily enough remembering other renditions of therapeutic touch. The nurse applying a compress to the forehead of the ailing soldier. Patricia Neal nursing Brandon De Wilde in *Hud* (1963).

But why for this touch of the finger is E.T.'s fingertip illuminated? An obvious answer is, as a marketing ploy, since it establishes the idea of strangeness and superiority, these together working to construct our sense of the extra-terrestrial. Terrific as a design element for posters and other advertising. The little digital fire also makes for an easy notation on the viewer's part, since the creature is always already so sightworthy but in the healing scene it is necessary to follow a peculiar and very particular screen point. Inside the experience of watching the film, the lit finger does not advertise, it speaks. And, fire burning from within, sacred fire, E.T.'s fingertip speaks with a strange tongue. "Ouuuuuch!" The figure is showing that he is enthusiastic, that he has the enthusiasm:

> God in us: *entheos:* enthusiasm; this is the essence of the holy madness. In the fire of the holy madness even books lose their gravity, and let themselves go up into the flame: "Properly," says Ezra Pound, "we should read for power. Man reading should be man intensely alive. The book should be a ball of light in one's hand."
>
> (Brown 6)

Two connotations of the idea of divine presence in the "alien" hand:

First, that the same deity under whose hand little Elliott and his family live their lives in LA would protect and care for E.T., too; that E.T. is a godly creature, like us: godly/goodly:

> O, wonder!
> How many goodly creatures are there here!
> How beauteous mankind is! O brave new world,
> That has such people in't!
>
> *The Tempest* V.i.xx.182–5

(For the charming creature is both with mankind and part of mankind: we can detect the many instances in which Elliott works to give E.T. humanity, to complete his humanity, to be equal with him, and these include not least the startling moment when he leads a flight to save the creature from vivisection by government agents. Elliott is an example of the "white thinker" posed by Leslie Fiedler, on his way to becoming an anthropologist, à la Montaigne. "The invention of America implies the invention of a new science: the systematic investigation of the *other* man, the *other* culture" [41]. Anthropology as the alternative to racism. E.T. and Elliott civilize each other, their cultures touch.)

But in that touching healing hand is a lit life of its own, coming into play less as an extension (in McLuhan's terms, *medium)* than as a singular spirit. David Sudnow recognized the idiosyncrasy and personality of his own hand as he taught himself to play jazz piano. Sudnow personifies his hand. "My hand had ways with the keyboard that allowed repetitions of all sorts" (47); his hand had an "engagement with the terrain" (41); it finds itself "correspondingly configured to fit dimensions of [the] keyboard" (58); it "knew its ways" (132). The hand has not only a capacity to signal but a will. Frank Wilson discusses the interesting case of David Hall, who built strength for his rock climbing by "suspending his body weight with his fingers, sometimes even lifting himself with just the fingers of one hand" (124). Hall confesses that when, somewhat small for his weight, he engaged in the sport of wrestling he would use his hand to very quickly rap his opponent's head, in this way surprising, disarming the other, establishing his dominance. *Disarming. Unhanding.*

[8]

In Frank Perry's *David and Lisa* (1962), two emotionally disturbed teenagers (Keir Dullea and Janet Margolin) are cached away in a treatment home in the country. Each has, and in an idiosyncratic way shows, communicational difficulty. David cannot be touched by others, as though the touch of another person's hand would be acidic for him, contaminative, discomposing and decomposing. Lisa has been split in two: one self is silent and the other capable of speaking only in rhymes. In an inexplicable way—that feels a resultant from an intercession of divinity—these two manage to cross the border with one another, incomprehensibly for the staff and everyone else except, secretly, themselves. They are brought with the other residents on a day trip to the Philadelphia Museum of Art, not far away, and while the others drift through the caverns David and Lisa find a sculpture of two life-sized figures in iron, mounted on a large plinth. Lisa goes up and inserts herself into the form, cuddling in a partly fetal position between the figures. Perry gives a very clear shot of the entirety of the sculpture with Lisa embedded inside, sculptural.

It has become a cultural taboo to touch a galleried work of sculpture with the hand; in this restriction is permanently lost the pleasure and intelligibility that derive from a touch upon rendered materials. To eye Rodin's *Cathedral* (1908), moving around the joined pair of right hands in prayer formation, is a richness, but to feel that smoothed stone glisten under the palm would be something closer to the human; to insert one's living hand in between these two "living" hands. Unless we own sculptures we are not permitted to do that. Lisa is openly violating a taboo, and with David we gape at her cuddling into the sculpture, torn between a soothing sensation of settling into the Sacred Nook and feeling the eye of surveillance glaring upon us as preface to a rebuke—not to say, for this boy's part, terror at the physical contact. For Lisa, the innermost chamber of the self is put into a condition of rest and quietude while the moral surface bridles against, certainly recognizes, public complaint. Because of the positioning of Perry's camera here we cannot, like Lisa, experience these two polarities together in an agony of conflict, or even satisfactorily choose comfort and exclude shame, but must both (a) stand back as judgmental witnesses imbued with the force of the taboo, therefore perceiving her through a hypercritical stance; and (b) wish to move forward in association with, perhaps even in residence within, her characterological body in its need for soothing and salvation.

Perry's museum sequence presents touch as an accomplishment sensational and perduring and tormenting, bringer of an ambiguity that can never find satisfying resolution. Lisa's infraction will not be erased—only, perhaps, repressed so that any blissful feeling will be cut off inappropriately. We can think of this as slow touch, since even the repression extends and continues the touch, obverted.

The opposite, touch by glance, can be seen in several sequences in *Blow-Up* (1966) where a professional fashion photographer in London (David Hemmings) is seen using his camera on both models and landscape. Most telling, perhaps, is a scene between him and a slinky long-haired model (Veruschka), which he begins with his camera on a tripod, striding up and handing her some ostrich feathers. Then, after a contact that has been nothing but perfunctory, he steps back and snaps furiously. Soon, he is crouching beside her and, *coup de grâce,* kneeling astride and on top of her, pointing his 35mm camera, with its stubby long lens, into her face as she twists and contorts with "pleasure" and his release/rewind reflex is sped up to a delirious limit. She regards his posture atop her midriff as being outside the "stagelines" of the dramatic interaction, thus as not only invisible finally but unregardable in the process. All that counts for her is the eye of the camera, that device with the hungry personality through the agency of which he is touching her faces, every face she makes, every twist of the head, in its hungry rapidity. As for touch and hunger, hunger and touch, and the way the hand seizes what it is that, watching a film, we try to seize with the eye, see in *Empire of the Sun* (1987) the remarkable moment when young Jamie (Christian Bale), on the cusp of starvation, wolfs down a bowl of rice.

to Linda Ruth Williams

15

The Outcry

Cyd Charisse in Two Weeks in Another Town *(Vincente Minnelli, MGM, 1962)*. Digital frame enlargement.

Friends: in this day when cynicism rules I plead guilty to being sentimental.
KRUGER, IN *TWO WEEKS IN ANOTHER TOWN*

Brick Wall

The *European Magazine* for January, 1783 described some fashionable colors: "*Elliott's Red-Hot Bullets* and *The Smoke of the Camp of St. Roche.* It is manifestly impossible to identify exactly or to obtain authentic samples of such colors today" (Maerz and Paul 5). The idea: a color that exists, or that once existed and exists no longer, and the "manifest impossibility" of identifying or obtaining it. Color desired but unseeable. Color from a world which, itself, has disappeared.

In *Two Weeks in Another Town* (1962), his salute to Fellini, Vincente Minnelli is giving us the story of Jack Andrus (Kirk Douglas), a washed-up actor from the Hollywood studio days now working at Rome's Cinecittà to make a film under the aegis of the tempestuous tormentor Maurice Kruger (Edward G. Robinson) and his tempestuous tormentor wife Clara (Claire Trevor). Andrus is a wounded genius. His days of shining success are past, but he lived them in a bizarre cocoon with a siren named Carlotta (Cyd Charisse), who drove him to the point of attempting suicide. Now, far from Hollywood, he has run into her again, and she is no less seductive than before, albeit wedded to a man with insuperable wealth. Can our Odysseus steer his vessel clear of her deafening call?

It will be important to know that Minnelli worked here under the guiding hand of John Houseman for MGM, in collaboration with cinematographer Milton Krasner, who had in recent years shot for him *Home From the Hill*, *Bells Are Ringing* (both 1960), and *The Four Horsemen of the Apocalypse* (1962); set decorator Keogh Gleason, who had done *Gigi* (1958), *Bells Are Ringing*, and *Four Horsemen* (as well as *An American in Paris* [1951]), and the talented designer Pierre Balmain. If you are asking yourself, as Minnelli surely did, how to make someone look like she belongs in a picture: not, how to compose so that the person and the frame are coordinated and balanced, nor to select from a population of women the single one who could most beautifully pose, nor how to use technique to glorify her pictorially as she could not be glorified in the everyday ... if you want to cause a unification in which she is joined to the pictorial conceit with such delicacy, firmness, uninhibitedness, richness, utterness, and lambency that the picture would seem to be, for the moment anyway, all of her existence, even that she would not have existence outside of this picturing, if you are seeking an image such as this it will be useful to have nearby a person such as Krasner who knows how to light for color, a decorator like Gleason who knows what texture, color, shape, and radiance can do for enhancement, and a creative genius like Balmain who understands that whatever she does or says, a woman's character in cinema is bound to what she wears. This is going to be Carlotta. A scheming radiance.

She comes to know that Andrus has met an enigmatic and charming young girl, Veronica (Dahlia Lavi), who is secretly taking a temporary holiday from her boyfriend David (George Hamilton), star of Andrus's film; and now she wants to draw him back to her "island," very much against his desires. She turns on the seduction. Seemingly out of nowhere, we are catapulted to a view of this *femme* in full allure, on the telephone, coaxing. But what she says is entirely forgettable, indeed we can have no full idea of what Andrus could be thinking as he listens, unseeing, at the other end, because ....

Because the vision of Carlotta sweeps us away.

(The vision that Andrus cannot see. The vision that is entirely ours.)

Supine on her bed, she has phone in hand, lipstick in full attack mode, eyes made up, golden hair aswirl. But now even Carlotta the figure vanishes, because her *presence in* the situation has taken over. Medium shot, tranquilly gazing down. She is in a pale mint-green peignoir. The bedsheets and pillowcases around her, one could say sloshing around her, are glimmering pale mint-green satin trimmed with lace. The color mint-green, pale, candied, teasing and somehow questioning fills the screen, swathing Carlotta, encapsulating her, it wouldn't be misdirection to say flavoring her. Questioning? Questioning our very act of gazing at it; *I know I am attracting your gaze, right here, right now, but how do you permit that?* An aura projects upward toward us from the pale mint-green satin sheets, running over her pale mint-green body. Though she is narratively central at this point, her narrative existence has disappeared. She is color. She is a color that has vanished from our world.

This pale mint-green shine is not a color one is used to in cinema—in fact, this may be its first, or even only usage.[1] It is not a minor part of the construction, it overwhelms, it is the colored ocean floating around and over the bobbing soul. We are given no option but to swim in a pale mint-green shine, as it pulls us to some unimaginable destination in the mint-green universe *before* or toward another universe in the mint-green wonder *to come*. We cannot navigate, we are drawn.

This very green—no connection at all to forest green, grass green, Kelly green, sea green—is almost the color of certain lime sorbets from 1955, but also derives from the green pieces that in the 1960s could be found in the "lime" components of a package of New England Confectionary Company lozenge-shaped wafers, generally produced as Chase and Co. "hub wafers" between 1847 and 1912 and henceforward as "Necco wafers" until 2018, with the green variety disappearing as of 2009; it is the association with this wafer green that perhaps aligns Minnelli's green with its candy-shoppe sweetness, mintiness, and, for the child, truth. Pistachio ice-cream is pale green but it lacks the sprightliness, the tug of this green. Were it much more severely restricted in its display here—a wall; a gown; a cap—we might conceive it as medical, but here there is too much of it, spreading too eagerly, for that. It reverently calls up the earliest childhood memories of color, the soda fountain at which one swooned in abstraction as the world of the everyday slid toward the forgotten; the magical soap tinted somehow by the chlorophyll of a thousand gardens and then bleached in the sun; the butterfly's chrysalis brought into the classroom by the otherwise stern,

---

[1] As I learned visiting a show curated by Nadia Buick in Brisbane years ago, a green very similar to this, but not identical, was the color of a garment worn by Claudette Colbert in *The Ten Commandments* (1934), but in any event that film was black and white.

foreboding science teacher who would normally be swinging her yardstick in threat but today plans to delight the children in a special dream.

Even more than the nature of the color, more than its biology, is its very presence. Since we are in a medium shot, the edges of the bed have fallen offscreen and so the pale mint green is flooding over the entire image, puckering over the Charisse body, undulating away from her. Sloshing in mint green, that body is not even quite a body. Irony: she expresses herself on the phone, gestures facially, all in relation to the Andrus she is not seeing (while through intercutting we are) and is perhaps recalling some halcyon days the cataclysm of which has passed into her oblivion. Ah, this is *Oblivion Green!* She is talking, his is the voice she is talking to, and for her the pale mint green, Oblivion Green, is an essence that has no value. The value is for us.

One must look at this picture as a picture, of course. This is a woman pictured as though able to exist only in a picture. One somehow thinks of a curious sentence of Dashiell Hammett's: "Everybody was sitting very still, as if to call attention to how still they were sitting" (149).

Since we cannot manage to stray from Carlotta, we also cannot manage to find or increase our interest. Oblivion Green calls up an age and a history we must struggle to remember, or a future we contort ourselves to imagine. It is stunning as the sublime is stunning, defying ontology and tacking us into the present of experience. The pictorial frame is insufficient to contain or support it, it is staining every aspect of the universe that we have been imagining as Andrus's Rome. In this way Minnelli shows—*shows,* not says—that Andrus cannot get her out of his mind, Veronica's ineffable young charms notwithstanding. Veronica's charms, Davey's mischief as he acts out his despondency at losing his girl, Kruger's abject dictatorship and then collapse in what seems a heart attack. All of this pulsing in Rome—Fellini again, the Oblivion Green Rome of *La dolce vita* (1960) with its traffic-filled, panicked streets—the Rome stained over.

Naming

The power of color sensation to elude language is easily enough seen in perusing Maerz and Paul's *Dictionary of Color* (that I acquired thanks to Vladimir Nabokov) where, after noting that *Werner's Nomenclature of Colours* by Patrick Syme (1814) contained 110 color samples; that William Hallock's 1892 listing for the Standard Dictionary contained 388; that the French *Répertoire des couleurs* (1905) had 1,356; and that Robert Ridgway's *Color Standards and Color Nomenclature* (1912) had 1,113, they themselves index no fewer than 4,200 names (ranging from "Abbey" to "Zuñi Brown") and still come to the conclusion that "*it is urgently to be desired, and herein is earnestly recommended, that these names of pigments never be used as names for specific color sensations"* (139; emphasis original). With Carlotta we are having a color sensation; I am naming it Oblivion Green; Andrus is having merely a sensation. Maerz and Paul's "opaline green" (17.A.6 on page 57) comes close to mine, but only close. At any rate, they remind us that "color has no objective existence" (143). Tell Andrus about objective existence.

Color slips away from language, but language surely refuses to capitulate. Here is a fabulous description from Augustin Challamel's *History of Fashion in France* (1882), quoted in wonder by Maerz and Paul:

> A great sensation was caused at the opera one night by the arrival of a lady dressed as follows. Her gown was "a stifled sigh," trimmed with "superfluous regrets," with a bow at the waist of "perfect innocence," ribbons of "marked attention," and shoes of "the queen's hair" embroidered in diamonds, with the "*venez-y-voir*" in emeralds. Her hair was curled in "sustained sentiments," a cap of "assured conquest" trimmed with waving feathers and ribbons of "sunken eye," a "cat" or palatine of swansdown on her shoulders, of a colour called "newly arrived people" (*parvenus),* a "Médicis" arranged "as befitting," a "despair" in opals, and a muff of "momentary agitation."
>
> (140)

"Some of these," Maerz and Paul remark,

> are delicious... and the world would be the poorer without them. ... what profound significance they have for one who looks below the surface, and how exactly do they reflect the thought and conditions of their time. ... among the various groups into which words may be divided, that which concerns colors is not the least valuable. Some of its members are ludicrous, to be sure, but they are not the less instructive for that reason.
>
> (140)

Colors are magical, at any rate, in a way that color names are not.

What profound significance they have for one who looks below the surface.

Color wordings, like words generally, can both motor and decorate the illustration of a tale, as can descriptors for quantities of light (in black-and-white films), but in cinema words are never elemental to the form, or shall we say, never present before the experience. We can understand, then, Gorky's sensing cinema as a "Kingdom of Shadows" in the last years of the nineteenth century, and the strange, entranced reverberation of early (two-strip) color, say, in Chester Franklin's *The Toll of the Sea* (1922) with its garnet pink and chrysalis green. The green in *Toll of the Sea* is somewhat close to the green on Carlotta's bed, a little more factual perhaps, a little more attached to the things we feel we already know.

As image, Carlotta in her bed is also Style. Not the predilection or technique of observant Minnelli on the moment but his rich and well-aged sensibility to form and color, that were both with him long before. I would imagine him to have had not a preference leading to this green but instead a feeling for the greens presented to him. As style, the image speaks clearly and forcefully as a rendition of fictional detail—for example, that here we have a particular Carlotta choosing to lie upon sheets of Oblivion Green and wearing a peignoir to match and taking pleasure spreading herself out. All this "factuality" is both expressly clear and irrelevant to the sensation of seeing the image onscreen. We may commit the error of thinking that watching a film is tagging some hold on a story and going forward with the story elements to have access to some dramatic unfolding or turn of events or climax. This thought leads to fishing through the imagery, constantly, with the aim of locating and tagging out the plot-relevant aspects, enchaining them, stretching a storyline forward: finding film images decorating the tabernacle of the storyline beneath.

That kind of approach converts images to words.

Then without delay one begins interpreting a dramatic flow according to the serial pronouncements of characters: who said what before?, who will say what next? One begins to think people are going where they *say* they are going. We take it as read that they feel and intuit what *they say* they feel. We pick up the onwardness of an arbitrary *construction*; one could easily shut the eyes and let the soundtrack ramble us through. Think of Nicholas Ray's lesson to his young acting students—in *I Was Interrupted*—to work their way through a scene by what the character is trying to do there, not by what anybody says:

> Each character in a play has one overall action, one thing he wants to achieve more than anything else. Directors, you must know what the action of each character is, and still you must be receptive to whatever the actor brings to you, without changing your central idea, your concept. The actor's final choice of an overall action must be in terms of its contribution to the realization of the central idea.
>
> (93)

Two Weeks in Another Town can certainly raise interest dialogically; one can certainly feel the tensions created, measured, mapped, and plotted by virtue of the language. And, as my epigram here hints, by Kruger's language especially. But then we come to Carlotta in bed with her telephone, and it seems we have struck a kind of underground seam, because what she is saying into the mouthpiece, what she is meaning to say, what her listener (Andrus) is hearing .... all these fade to insignificance and nullity, a vapor that is lighter than air. There is so much now confronted by this Oblivion Green, this minty pallor and minty shimmering, this boundless spreading that we neither know nor seek to know. Our presence at the edge of the screen is not about knowledge. Where it comes from, that Oblivion Green—not as chemical coloration but as essence. Did this color simply appear? To what alluvial substrate in or around Carlotta are we being pointed, to what nuance of sentiment and memory? Even from Minnelli himself, what self-referential plasm of consciousness and desire has leaked out to surface here?

There are other supremely colored moments in the film leading us to considerations of this sort. Kruger has a temper tantrum with irate, dominating Clara in their Rome sitting room, and she paces back and forth toward and away from our static camera in a cherry-soda pink housecoat that speaks her power and motive and blazing frivolity. Davey is splayed morosely on Andrus's couch and a close shot reveals his chestnut-brown eyes, swollen, hungry: the "conker" of childhood is the perfect chestnut, just like these eyes, swollen, gleaming in sunlight, smooth as breath. But of all this detailing one can say that it is purely informative, that it works in an arrangement of conveyance whereby the film is understood as a delivery system for hypothesis (dramatic facts) and conjecture, a stimulus to decoding. As though we come to cinema to learn, as though cinema teaches or broadcasts. As though so teleological an approach could help us face a Vermeer or a Cézanne, or a Minnelli.

The Oblivion Green is not a (Lacanian) "excess," that is, an essence; it is a presence—in the Sartrean sense, that existence precedes essence. How very slight an admixture will tell a color. How very little poison need be in the wine.

Miracle

Miracle, from Lat. *Mirari,* to wonder. That which brings on wonder. It will be asked, what is gained by the artificial act of abstracting out a moment of color and fixing meditative attention on it? Much, I would argue, that is not so widely received as value:

- First, the momentous *shock* of Oblivion Green is no aspect of a dramatic presentation: that the color swells as we look, becomes the entire world of the screen. Dispensed with are the bed, the sheets laid upon it, the body wrapped in the sheets holding a telephone, the purpose of a telephone call, all this cultural heritage. All is come awash. Then,
- To experience an aesthetic moment such as this is to float, to bathe, to be within, where no simple, reductionist perspective waits.

Through one's sight one senses, and appreciates sensation, more than establishing space and navigating through it. Storyline (as map) is suspended. Further:

- Even asking the question, What is gained?, begs an answer couched only in the exact pathetic terms that this suffusion of color overwhelms; an answer only in the supramundane zone of calculated effect, costs and benefits, foci of attention and distraction. Whereas the aesthetic moment is truly, ineffably mundane: wholly, bluntly, and powerfully what is here now in itself. Mundane, instantaneous, come and gone before it is caught to be catalogued. One of the marvels of Carlotta's bed is the flash of a moment in which we see it, a passing miracle.

In such touching moments one leaves the narrative space. And having left it in *Two Weeks*, still gazing stunned, one notes that these are not sheets, these pallid minty opaline Oblivion Green essences, and this is not a bed. Carlotta is an indiscriminateness, too, her motive and desire unfathomable no matter what she says. It's all a gift, not a statement.

Molecule

If I meditate on a momentary aspect of a film (say Carlotta in the Oblivion Green bed in *Two Weeks in Another Town*) can I legitimately claim to have meditated upon the film as a whole, even upon film itself? How molecular might film be, in other words? Because if one examines a molecule, any molecule of a substance, one sees the structure of everything. What of the film's "building blocks" or "constitutive phrases," the "stuff" out of which the Andrus/Kruger world of Rome is built?

One helpful case:

Having watched the film and admired it, one feels bequeathed a single cinematic gesture, the Oblivion Green sheets. Nothing else stays in residue. And long afterward one carries the shifting, fading, strengthening vision of those sheets as experiential trace. Imagine, too, that one is without interest in the biographical history of Minnelli (his aesthetic development), of Charisse, of Douglas or Robinson or Trevor or Hamilton or Lahvi or any of them; and further, is willing to let the figures evanesce. Nor does Rome hold a special fascination, notwithstanding how excitingly Minnelli shows it. Or forget the film business itself, in many ways the subject of the picture: nothing other than a gaggle of workers doing skilled jobs together—Noah and his sons building the ark. Simply to argue: let us say that without antipathy one experiences no stimulation or attraction from event, story, or conflict and watches with a peculiar openness to anything as may provoke wonder (but not clutching at pre-arranged favoritisms). Opened this way, and leaning nowhere, one feels the thunderclap strike: Oblivion Green, pale, shimmering. There!, here!, the peignoir not covering the body but being the body, and the Oblivion Green action upon the viewing embodiment now incalculable, spontaneous, *bouleversant*. One tries pointlessly to hold onto it but already the vision begins to melt and pull away. One cannot go back. Or forward.

Every moment of cinema is and becomes gone this way—goes, perhaps, to a stratum so deeply buried no miner of the imagination could ever find its seams. If I cannot remember the actual green, can it have existed, should I now believe in it? This color, a palette of such colors, did exist before my time.

And if a cherished Oblivion Green is all that is left me of *Two Weeks,* am I obliged to find more?

Artificial

All of the *Two Weeks* that is mine knows Oblivion Green, *once I see it. Video:* Lat. I see. I mediate and meditate for the moving figures. While Minnelli's Andrus (*andrus = the man*; *the man who*; *he*) holds the phone, it is not Carlotta we encounter but the moment generated by, from, around her, which is Oblivion Green.

The moment of experience, integrated in time, comes as origin to all reflection; a constantly revivified origin, a beginning that never ceases being a beginning. The moment in cinema is a flash, and the reception of the flash is an experience of delirium and unimagined hunger. Flow and thrust affect one without pressure, even with an inversion of force, something like an exquisite invitation or even a voyage into that ur-memory of the past that is all pasts. One watches in wonder. The watching itself is wonder already.

There may be no clearer exemplification of the disconnect between the viewer's aesthetic sensitivity to the screen and the logical construction of a narrative, no more directly presented case of the power cinema has to override factuality, than Carlotta in Oblivion Green. It is not the formula of character that superimposes itself on our riding consciousness here, nor the figure's conflict, nor a set of pervasive clues for solving a mystery but something entirely artificial, that is, made of *artifice,* the light of the screen. For Stanley Cavell, in his recurring look at the remarriage comedies, that shimmering fascination for Cary Grant and Irene Dunne coming back together again in *The Awful Truth* (1937), an artifice inseparable from both luminosity and acting genius. One does not find more sensitive readings than his, yet for all the spectacle and ramification made possible by the ghostliness of black and white, all the vast array of delicacies and hopeless subtractions and echoing courage and all the loyalty to forthcomingness, still, something in Carlotta's Oblivion Green makes an override, even comes onstage to stand in like the brave understudy who magically senses in a breath that the star is about to collapse. This moving picture is a colored affair, and what we see is color moving—forward with eventuality and backward in nostalgia. The natural nourishing spring has given up this green radiance as a signal we are born again.

to Nellie Perret

16

A Crafty Screen

Ray Liotta in GoodFellas *(Martin Scorsese, Warner Bros., 1990). Digital frame enlargement.*

The fidelity of friendly interactions tends to rest upon gestural completeness, that in silence the body says everything not merely a part of it. By virtue of the principles of extension, turning, and rounding out, the beginning of a gesture—opening a sentence, stretching out a hand, touching the back of a chair before sitting—carries a tacit promise of continuation and completion—saying the whole sentence until its end, making a handshake and releasing it, taking a seat and settling in. Interrupted gestures have their own distinct uses and qualities, such as when, to indicate uncertainty, a speaker begins *but intentionally does not complete* an utterance or when, to indicate a change of mind, a person reaches out for a handshake but stops midway and withdraws. What is notable about such interruptions of gesture is that they signal themselves *in themselves* as interruptions; that is, they are themselves gestures, so that an interactional partner becomes aware of the break-off in alignment, intention, and movement, the shift from one gestural scheme to another. I was about to— ... but now I'm no longer sure. The expectation of gestural completion is so widespread and so pervasive in cultural matters high and low that it goes without notice unless "extrinsic" dramatic interruption brings it to the fore. In the absence of noteworthy interruption, interactants take each other to be offering complete gestures, that is, interpret the gestures they see and receive as being full and untrammeled.

When a figure says something, we presume that at this moment in dramatic time, *this is all that figure has to say.*

Bearing in mind that there is an interactional relation between the cinemagoer and the gesture-filled screen, between the watcher's seeing and the camera's; and also that typically in the act of cinema-watching watchers mostly refrain from expression, I want to explore some features of the camera's gesturing when gestural completion becomes an interpretive problem.

Camera Eye

Now more than thirty years after its release, it is perhaps permissible to discuss one particular narrative trope in Martin Scorsese's *GoodFellas* (1990) designed to instigate a very special confusion in the viewer. [Spoiler alert.]

At the film's beginning, white titles speed across a black field, right to left. Then we are behind a car on a highway at night, its tail lights gleaming. Inside, three men. And sounds ... rumbling from somewhere, disturbing to the driver, certainly provocative to us. The three pull off the road onto a shoulder. Robert De Niro climbs out along with Joe Pesci and Ray Liotta. They move to the rear, placing themselves in the ruby glow exuded by the tail lights. Liotta gapes forward like a witness, or a camera. Now we are watching them in profile view. The trunk is opened, the men peer in—we cannot see what they see—and De Niro and Pesci fire their guns several times into the secret space. The credit sequence ends and the film moves on with a jump elsewhere: no explanation of where we have just been, or who these men are, or why two of them would be shooting into the trunk of their car and why the third would be watching agape: the car has evaporated and another story has begun.

This other story: it describes a teenaged boy growing up under the protection of some gangsters. He takes a fall for them, does jail time, goes free, and is quickly adopted into their family like a beloved son who has lost his virginity. He becomes the youngest member of the gang (before the film's surprising conclusion). This is the biography of Henry Hill (Liotta), a figure with whom we bond from our first moment of seeing him (played by Christopher Serrone) look off through Venetian blinds and hearing his offscreen voice recollecting the story as now given. He is our child, too.

Much later in the turning, well after we have met the principal characters and seen many of their challenging, exciting, sometimes terrifying interactions—Pesci's Tommy DeVito is a psychopath; De Niro's Jimmy Conway is an Irish American thug—we find ourselves in a car with them, speeding down a highway at night, then suddenly pulling off onto the shoulder. Tommy, Jimmy, and Henry, tensed up (like actors in the wings waiting to go onstage), focus their concentration, go feverish with purpose. We move to the tail lights with them. With Henry, we see Tommy and Jimmy open the trunk. But now, using their point of view, we peer inside and see … what?, a deer run over on the road? No: a rat, that is to say a human being who has ratted out one of the gang's secrets, trussed and gagged. They execute him in a brutal flash, and move on.

What is it that becomes palpable at this instant?:

- That this is the same scene we saw excerpted at the beginning of the film, call the early scene A and this one AA. AA is shot from different camera angles but is otherwise narratively intact, indeed more complete. Looking back we note that A was a curtailed gesture.
- Now that we see AA, we imagine how from A one could perhaps have predicted it. This late, retroactive view may in fact be germinated by our sense of familiarity with A. That is, *from AA at this viewing moment now* A seems familiar; we transpose the "familiarity" we feel in AA backward onto the early scene and allow ourselves to suspect that in A we anticipated a "familiar" outcome there.[1] In the fact of it, however, we are remembering a curtailed gesture only retrospectively known as such.
- However, to be faithful to the experience of watching, we must admit that memory in AA—our "gazing" back to A—serves us more faithfully than did prediction—guessing forward—in A, a general case with cinema. We see an early scene more clearly looking back than we foresaw a later one back then. A was *not* familiar at all as we watched it, it became familiar only afterward. Therefore,
- The link in the opening scene with the flash-past credits, simulating motion down a highway, was a method, *as we can see only later,*

---

[1] The final movements of Beethoven's Third Symphony and Prokofiev's Piano Concerto No. 2 are both structured this way, with a preamble that after we have forgotten it returns in force.

of hinting about—even more than vehicular motion, speed, and travel—time's flight. Time's flight will be germaine to this story.

- By the time we watch it, AA is thoroughly intelligible in itself: not only the characters but the provocative situation that led to this execution have all been clearly spelled out by that point. In short, the scene plays out in a straightforward, even conventional narrative way, without its own rise. At the same time:
- We *are* surprised as we see that *this* is what the now-forgotten A was pointing to. In short, this violent moment was present, was implicit all along; was "in the cards"; and would have turned out this way no matter what, *even though in the form of A it was hidden from view, waiting in the wings*. Actions have consequences; consequences flow from provocations; but consequences are not fully imaginable until they are actions.

I am here laying aside details of the *GoodFellas* plot: what is "actually" happening in the trunk of this car; who is holding the pistols; the emotion in the shooting; the film itself as a whole. Look instead at the way Scorsese uses the A>>AA formula, foreshadowing>>revelation, as a way of catching and developing curiosity, postponing satisfaction, and then delivering a narrative punch in a way that is unanticipated when it happens yet entirely logical, even somewhat nostalgic given what viewers already know.

To be blunt: given that AA makes complete sense as it is framed, we know when we watch it that the narrative line of *GoodFellas* could have proceeded smoothly and efficiently *without* that preamble A, which, clear enough now, was nothing but an excerpt. What is offered by A at film's opening, then, isn't what will ultimately seem narrative logic (even if things seem to proceed logically enough), but something else:

- (a) a particular kind of suspense, gestured as fragment; that is, something that becomes understandable later on as an uncompleted gesture but that may not seem like an uncompleted gesture at the time; and
- (b) a way of tailing off a gesture by making the present incomplete moment stretch forward in a way, reappear for completion when we are fully prepared to see a gesture completed.

In the excerpt, we saw three men, De Niro's Jimmy, Pesci's Tommy, and Liotta's Henry—the last of whom, we will learn definitively only after many scenes have passed, was the teenaged boy we met right after A, now grown up. His observational discourse being retroactive, he now sees himself *back then* as observing while the other two committed action; indeed, generally he remembers himself as an observer. In the film, as we see, he turns out always to have been just that; the one with the narrative eyes (but the clean hands).

What, however, of the *camera eye* as it produces/experiences the filmic event A during that opening; and during any such scene as A, speaking generally? The eye of the camera not as a mechanical device but as representative of the production's intent-to-give but deciding suddenly not to at the moment, and of the viewer's willingness to see and not see at once. Camera as interruptor of gesture.

What is it to speak of a *camera eye,* since palpably it can do that interrupting?

We know that the camera records action on celluloid stock, and we grasp that acts of *seeing* and *catching* are invoked by it. This *caught* recording we *see* as we watch the screen; even partial seeing is seeing. As the camera *is seeing,* we *are seeing.* Further, in order that we will be able to see anything, the camera must have seen it first and retained it. Overlook all the many ways a piece of film "seen" by a camera can be adjusted before it is seen by audiences (tinted, re-cropped, blown up, optically printed, intercut, and so on) and merely focus on the fact that both the camera and the viewer "*see* the moment" but not simultaneously, that in our seeing we always mimic something the camera did beforehand. (Even were we standing on location watching the shooting, our eyes would not see what the camera sees.) Every nuance we pick up viewing was caught by and embedded "in" the camera earlier, so that our film experience not only owes to the camera but tacitly gives the nod to the camera, acknowledges blood-relationship to the camera's prior experience. It is because the camera as eye and the viewer's organ of concentration, the eye, are inseparable in the viewing that one can think of the camera as having, as being, an *eye.* In that shot of Henry staring out through the blinds, Scorsese floods his face with obscure light, shows the eyes bulging with desire and curiosity. Pirandello: "What he says and what his eyes say cannot correspond" (122).

Scorsese's preamble device (A) renders *GoodFellas* impossible to see twice. It has been employed often in film and television narratives since, sometimes with complication but always essentially the same: presentation of a scene that *only later* turns out to make complete (or more complete) sense, as it were a screen gesture that only later proves to have been incomplete, whilst our first viewing seems just cogent enough not to provoke doubts or confusions. The camera eye is both giving and not giving us a vision, and in the later moment we can feel that we have been told that. Every vision on the screen is *really* given, after all, but a camera might secretly give a picture in part that is given wholly only later.

We take the camera's offering as though it is ingenuous, laid before us by a faithful, entirely beneficent friend—the hand reaching out for a handshake, as it were, and reaching all the way out. More: a camera not only wanting to help, assist, encourage, and warm to us but also a hale and hearty camera, visually acute, turned on and happy to be turned on as far as any device can be happy, and in its helplessly rote way of working wholly unblemished and true. The camera does not wink or deceive or malfunction. The camera does not have narcolepsy. The camera is not bashful, the sort of entity prepared to modestly turn away from an action we would deem morally outré. Not shy, not daydreaming, not myopic, not intentionally concealing, in showing us loyalty (as we take it) the camera summons our loyalty. It will agree to reveal only insofar as we will agree to receive revelation.

Provisional Camera

Introduced for our consideration, then, as we look back, is the duplicitous (or wounded) camera, whose vision we ought perhaps not really have trusted, but whose wound we note only too late. Once one admits the possibility of one's failed or withheld trust, up jumps the notion of the "unreliable narrator," typified so famously in literature by *The Murder of Roger Ackroyd* (1926) and in film by *The Usual Suspects* (1995). But the camera is not the narrator of a film narration, the camera presence is rather like an ether in which the narration is suspended, the fluctuating embodiment that breathes out the narration. Were it possible to have a book on page 76 of which the type would instantly vanish when one turned to it; or a page 76 that would suddenly flake away in one's hand; or indeed a page 76 coming after not page 75 but page 74—or better still: a page 76 following from a page 75 surely enough yet also indicating through the continuity of its text that after page 75 and before itself something was missing!—all these might come close to approaching what can happen with our watching experience when the camera is known to have failed in its faith. It is one thing to be confounded reading a page of print and coming to the astute conclusion that the meaning is ambiguous, that there are two or more ways the words can reasonably gain interpretation; and quite another thing to come to a page where when the eye focuses the words actually dance around to new positions, constantly on the move, making stable syntactical reading (as one has been knowing it) impossible.

Take a moment in *How to Get Away with Murder* (2014): A camera shows a body lying dead on a floor, the head bathed in a pool of blood, and high above a person looking down at this from a balcony. We take the display as we see it: a murder, a witness discovering. Later, however, after considerable narrative development, we come back to this body image, perhaps even an identical shot (or the same one), now and only now catching the corpse as the tail end of an action scene in which a person fought with somebody else on that balcony, the somebody we saw gazing down, who pushed our antagonist up against and then over the balustrade so that he fell to the floor and was apparently killed. Meanwhile now, action intervening elsewhere... after which we return yet again to this scene, now with the body on the floor and a number of people gathered around staring at it anxiously. Still more intervening action somewhere else. Then, presto!, back to the body on the floor at still another moment (even, perhaps, another day); it has risen up, the body of a man strangling a young woman to death. Up steps another man with a solid object and bashes his head in. *Now* the bleeding body on the floor looks exactly as it did in the first instance I cite above. We would have no trouble understanding this as a bizarre way of playing out narrative continuity, call it "fracturing." And each visit to the murder scene draws back in time a little and goes a little further forward into the narrative future, so that *we see more*. Finally we can come to believe we *are seeing it all*, although of course this is a specious conclusion under these circumstances. The point is, that the camera can show a scene "fully" without showing it fully. It can show a reality, or series of realities, that fails to suggest what is true.

Even in the face of the image we are without grounding.

We decide upon the credibility of an image, and fashion our belief, in the context of continually shifting perspectives that make every moment tentative in retrospect. The provisional camera. And once we have the provisional camera we can construct believable (but either untrue or not fully true) moments of at least two kinds: (a) moments that will become more pregnant with meaning through later expansion; (b) moments that, as we see with *Get Away*, will through later expansion appear to have been false.

We work and breathe with an accretion of understandings.

For a good example of "provisional accretion"—the moment that grows into a greater and deeper truth, and never belies itself—look at a dream trope in François Truffaut's *Day for Night (La nuit américaine,* 1973):

[1] Ferrand (Truffaut), director of the film-within-the-film "Meet Pamela," has been having trouble sleeping, beset by a recurring dream cast in the tone of nightmare: a tap tap tapping sound (borrowed by the filmmaker from the mother on the staircase in *Marnie* [1964]) and black-and-white imagery inserted into a full-color film. Tiny street. Night. A little boy in a dark suit walking down an alleyway tapping a cane on the pave. He pauses and looks behind him.

[2] Later in the film, a recurrence of this nightmare: The boy walks down the alley and proceeds to a metal grating in front of a building, raps it with his cane.

[3] Finally a more equivocal version. As Ferrand turns his head in bed we see superimposed on his face a number of neon Cinéma marquees lit at night and hear hesitant orchestral chords

progressing. The boy runs to the alley, walks down it tapping his cane, comes to the grating which is protecting the entrance of a movie theater. He uses the cane to drag forward a wheeled stand on which about a dozen glossies from *Citizen Kane* are posted. He reaches in and pulls them down one by one, until he has collected nine or so, and runs off with them as the music comes to a (triumphant) harmonic climax.

    The boy is Ferrand in his childhood, we grasp; and this is, or was, the beginning of his love of film, the germ that made him grow into a filmmaker. The final nightmare sequence is more chilling, more moving, more provocative, and more exploratory than the first. Not a different vision of the narrative world, it is a curious zoom-in to fullness by "pulling back."

Detected by looking back, the "fallible" camera can make for a kind of narrative instability, a simulation of the purely textual ambiguity we experience when a figure picks up a secret note that appears as a fragment and strains to decode it, only later finding another piece[2] that changes the meaning altogether. We reinterpret scenes, finding "new meaning" in what we saw before because of the later, expanded, "more faithful" exposition. Obversely: we find ourselves taking a later exposition to be more faithful than earlier ones (rather than unfaithful in a new way) because we feel ourselves recipients of what seems like accreted meaning. Consider the wonderful, and peculiar, pleasure that comes with seeing a great film a second, third, fourth, fifth time, with both meaning and doubt increasing pleasurably as one goes through time with the thing—grows older; one sees something the younger eye had missed … What we deem pleasure could also be provocation for anxiety or self-doubt, since in each case where a second viewing increases our satisfaction (and appetite) we face the memory of ourselves at the first viewing, we who—as we know only now—*didn't see what was plainly there to be seen.* Every discovery is a memory of a blackout.

Frame and Fragment

The roadside in *GoodFellas* again. In sequence A, a beginning that is not quite a beginning for you now, reader—since you have swum through the preceding paragraphs albeit you knew nothing of what was to come until I pointed to it (try to conceive this: *un-read* what came before), knew nothing about the men we see, nothing about the car, the place, the moment, the red light, the highway … one casually (if also carefully) watches events

---

[2]Or, as in *Murder on the Orient Express* (1974), uses a chemical trick, a simulated toning.

happening before the eyes. Surely in believing A, we would be decoding through a weave of recognitions. Roughly:

- (a) a car trunk, something in the trunk involving danger, something that must be slain;
- (b) the men, burly, strong (whether tall or short), fiercely determined, perhaps hunters of some kind, although not dressed as typical hunters;
- (c) thus, some kind of creature that they have caught, in the trunk, that must now be killed, here, rather than in the place where they found it; killed and thoroughly killed; and killed ritually by all of them;
- (d) the suffusion of red light—red blood; the bloodiness of the kill, but also
- (e) killing by the road, or road kill, and urgent road kill, since the car pulls over so abruptly; and
- (f) a kill that flows evenly with the speeding-past of modernity, the cars on the road symbolized by the flashing horizontal shapes that turned into credit text;
- (g) not just three men but three friends who went hunting, now dispatching the prey by the side of the road at night, because
- (h) the prey is illicit in some way, and they must not be caught with it, yet also
- (i) they are not troubling to go far off the road, so perhaps this isn't such a busy road, or in the perfunctory nature of things any pulling off the road will do as well as any other …

… and so on.

Thoughts and half-thoughts, suppositions, proposals: nothing incoherent with what we see, which is sequence A.

Here as everywhere, we assemble meaning from the fragments that have been assembled for us and arranged pictorially. This is all happening so quickly, in the midst of such frenzied lateral action, and with such brutality, and in such saturated redness, that
- (j) we have virtually no consciousness of the limiting camera position and the fact that we are not given to look into the trunk of the car.

In essence we conclude that:

If we are being shown so very much, so tersely and energetically, and with such elegant precision, and in so deeply touching (stimulating) a place, why would we leap away from this presentation to some neutral point of view from which we could wonder, query, come to some doubt? The richness of any offering seems a guarantee of fulfillment because a guarantee of fullness. A guarantee, too, that the means by which the offering is made is a faithful, reliable means, the very fullness we take for granted being the collateral. We have what we can take as a very detailed, completed presentation, and we are committed to the notion that detail is truth; truth not in the sense of accuracy but in the sense of the unquestionable point of view—even if we're not seeing enough. Detail is full detail, not a fragment.

And whatever we are given to see we are given sufficiently; nothing is here—*nothing is apparently here*—to discredit our belief.

Our openness to adopting a fragmentary image as non-fragmentary is, in its origin, related to our desire to gather and arrange everything we see onscreen, fruit of the lens; all the pieces are apparently complete pieces. Invocation of the lens after Leeuwenhoek's advances in the early 1670s made it increasingly conventional to bound visual space distinctively *inside* a field of vision already made available to the eye, to accept on arbitrary terms the presentation of a fulsome world-within-the-world. We move easily to a new meaning of the frame, which had earlier served to hold and display the work of the artist's hand but which now could enter the artistic field itself, as a self-declaring limit to the eye. The "innerness," the boundedness of the diegetic world has come to seem natural, unaffected, and unachieved. A certain religious adherence to it seems called for, at least proper. Before the development of the lens, proximal approach to a subject required movement of the body, a kind of re-placement in social space. But the lens made possible a forward movement of the eye without a body, the visible world being imported to the eye's district.

Rarefaction of the Lens

The optics of the lens produced an image rarefied in a special way. Focal clarity could be achieved on a provisional basis at any plane in the field, and once something was in focus it could be perceived through an exceptional rendition of detail. Not only the close-up, which emphasizes the form of some *thing* residing (hiding) in the field but also the focused surface, which reveals blemishes otherwise obscure to the eye. The eye alone does not achieve the equivalent of f64 vision, that is, tight and crisp focus from a spot immediately adjacent the viewer's face and receding all the way to the back of the visual field. The eye is more selective, losing clarity in the far reaches if it gains clarity up close, and vice versa. Cinematic imagery, like photographic imagery, has the capacity for optical flatness if the subject matter is arranged properly, topologically, before the lens—everything bounded in the frame, no matter how far away it is, can be seen with what seems, well enough, to be thought equal clarity and sharpness.

Focal clarity and decisive framing both alter and augment unaided visual experience, flattering the body with an extension (as Marshall McLuhan noted it) of sense that can be detected, then noticed, then evaluated (as pleasure).

That roadside scene in *GoodFellas,* what I am calling A, appeals to belief because of its artful bounding and exceptional clarity—all this irrespective of the believable performances, the authentic-looking vehicle with its red tail lights, and isolated patch of highway (which looks like real highway, not back lot). We seem to be in a place seen articulately and housing interesting, if unexplained, behavior also seen without vagueness. If we are attracted to the vision, however—if its crispness and tightness lure us—what other features might make us revel in a cloud of belief rather than suspecting the scene of being irregular because unresolved? What would lead us to take the camera's gesture as finished rather than provisionally and temporarily portending some resolution still to come? Perhaps nothing but that we watch this film as we watch in general, by taking what we're looking at as whole in itself. A sense of engagement, involvement, entrancement, and participation brings us to achieve the acceptance that leads to belief. We believe what we are engaged in.

In making commitment to the scene A as first it is given, we use what might be called *hypersynecdochical* vision, straining far beyond taking the part for the whole in order to render the part *as* the whole (a whole that it fails to be). When a close-up is inserted inside a scene—in *The Lonedale Operator* (1911) the wrench in the stationmaster's daughter's hand—we extend its boundaries outward to embed themselves broadly in the scenic situation; in this way we come to know the centralized object as part of its surround. Here with A, however, is an excerpt never announcing itself as excerpt. It is more or less a "close-up" of something greater, that we neither recognize nor expand to, at the time: we act as though what we have, functionally a "close-up," is an entirety, the entire situation presented accurately and fully by this camera that is, we hardly need remind ourselves, seeing only a fragment.

Our engagement with the figures by the roadside brings on a crucial acceptance that shoos off that irritating hunger for "More!" spurred by the feeling one has not been offered the full handshake. Further, as a certain optical discipline in Western society eschews the idea of commiting one's sensory apparatus to distraction, it is natural to regard what we see as focally central rather than marginal. There is an action outplaying; our sensory array should be devoted to gathering it in. Were we to treat the business at the trunk of the car as *only part of* a greater, more significant something as yet unrevealed, we would be withdrawing from the full commitment of participation to which our screen experience beckons.

Also in play here, though I pay it relatively less attention at the moment, is the viewer's pre-ordained trust in, even fondness for the force creating the story, the writer and director giving generously, and not in order to establish yet another giving later; in short organizing syntactically. Committed by our faith and trust, we anticipate not a movement into drift but a charge into coherence—therefore a whiff of coherence already.

Time

Accepting what is given now as complete we consider it uninterrupted. We take ourselves to be seeing a scene from its beginning to its end—this even in films where a scene is bluntly put forward as a fragment. What we take as happening we see without searching for gaps, with a continuity that seems fluid even if it is achieved through spliced discreet shots. We move forward in time in a state of uniform alertness.

That generous "camera presence" handing over what we see, seems awake while shooting, awake and completely awake, without compromise, without daydream. As we could wish for ourselves the camera is never distracted, and so the framed composition becomes central as a locus of the attendable. When he made *Rope* (1948), this sense of continuous visualizing alertness is an aspect of filmmaking Alfred Hitchcock was seriously considering; he expected that his audience would watch the eighty-or-so-minute drama of the film as though it were transpiring in one spate of time, here and now, in a uniform and uninterrupted aliveness and as much as possible in one single shot.[3]

History records wakeful moments only.

The history of cinema has taught that scenes begin at a *beginning* and end at an *end*; that what we call a "beginning" and call an "end" are reasonably so considered. This thought of scenic completeness coupled with a belief in the camera and its powers, convinces the skeptic of seeing a scene completely, missing nothing. As far as we take it, then, in watching a film *we do not begin in a state of deprivation already having missed something*. And when the film ends, we do not feel deprived at not seeing what happens next—say, Louis and Rick living together in Brazzaville after they walk away from the airport at the end of *Casablanca* (1942).

History records events from the beginning through to the end—from what we believe ourselves quite legitimate in taking as a beginning through to what we believe ourselves quite legitimate in taking as an end. Matters deemed extraneous are *not included in* the present exposition; we feel strongly that they *should not be*. A film being taken as essentially moral,

---

[3]As is well known, the camera did have to "wink out" because the reels loaded in it could run for only eleven minutes; these would have to be spliced, in such a way that the camera could be taken never to have looked away.

what should not happen doesn't happen—at the filmmaker's hand, here, now, for our eyes. The present viewing experience is hermetic: all the elements contributory to it (a) are here, (b) always were here, (c) do not leak out to somewhere else, all of them or some of them, (d) are not interfered with by inward leakages from the outside, and (e) will find necessary resolution by the end. Regarding that highway scene A: we do not watch it wary of leakage inward from the rest of the film; later, looking back, we see how ruinous leakage would have been, although in that "later," we believe that already for us there has been no leakage.

Text and Hypertext

Hypertext provides an unlimited bridging structure allowing multiple discursive pathways to spring from any generative nodes in a master chain. As narrative goes, hypertext would make possible *n* variations on a story, since at every designated node (say, for one example, a noun) perpendicular alternative tales could grow.[4] Here is a casual but possibly helpful illustration. Take this apparent but also non-apparent sentence:

> Hypertext would make possible *n* variations on a Theme of Paganini performed by Dmitri Tiomkin's score was 202–84 in a brilliant test match for my shoes and socks and sealing wax museum guide because no other job was available that September Song.

Look again, this time with dots to indicate the launch points:

> Hypertext would make possible *n* • variations on a Theme of Paganini performed by Dmitri • Tiomkin's • score was 202–84 in a brilliant test • match for my • shoes and socks and sealing • wax • museum guide because no other job was available that • September Song.

All this could theoretically happen:

- Hypertext would make possible *n*:
    a—variations of text
    b—variations on a theme
    c—Variations on a Theme of Paganini (Rachmaninoff)
- variations on a Theme of Paganini performed by Dmitri:
    a—that is, Dostoevsky's character in *The Brothers Karamazov*

---

[4]This sort of operation was initiated in the Czech Pavilion at the 1967 World's Fair in Montreal.

- b—that is, Dmitri Shostakovich's pianist son Maxim
- c—that is, (movie composer) Dmitri Tiomkin, whose
- score
    - a—musical score
    - b—cricket score
- was 202–84 in a brilliant game where the match for my
    - a—match: that is, the game
    - b—match: the color coordination of
- shoes and socks and sealing
    - a—my shoes and my socks, considered colorwise
    - b—quoting Lewis Carroll: "shoes and socks and sealing wax"
- wax
    - a—sealing wax
    - b—Wax Museum
- museum guide because no other job was available that
    - a—(month of) September
    - b—Kurt Weill's "September Song."

And one could see how at each node, first a different story could spin outward—a different edit—and secondly, further nodes could also split off from the splittings-off. Given this (ridiculously simplistic model), a conventionally told story would be one where the hypertextual possibilities were rigorously managed, even made wholly probable.

Hypertext engenders the Internet, where for a programmer what I am calling "nodal points" are *hrefs*. But what hypertext also permits for any syntactically positioned indicator is a severing from the chain context in which it holds apparent position; for film, we might say the implication of a scene or shot in a narrative context now relieved, freed by a jumping away to some *other connection*. As to the grammar of film construction, it can be learned by the viewing audience that any vision can both (a) hold syntactical presence and grammatical relation, at least provisionally, and (b) alter its form to generate novel narrative conditions. The grammatical coherence of jumps would be in the hands of the filmmaker: Godard's *Weekend* (1967) contrasted with Max Ophüls' *La ronde* (1950).

To return to Scorsese, then, one concluding time:

roadside, red light, night …,two men operating on something in a car trunk …,the third, younger, standing with eyes wide open to watch. Camera moves into that gazing face, while a voiceover patiently spiels a personal history and we focus on the watcher's eyes (by the roadside) now cutting to a young boy whose eyes are wide open staring out through a Venetian blind and on the screen pointing in the same direction.

The eyes at the roadside become a hypertextual link to the eyes near the Venetian blind. Same eyes, same person, younger, a long time ago. But now utterly severed from the roadside, the trunk, the red light, the car, the other two figures, and repositioned in a new moment, new place, bright daylight, many years ago. This can be likened to a logical explanation of the editor's jump cut, but:

A jump like this is merely one facet of the strange viewer experience of the crafty camera: not only the camera that, filming something, makes it conceivable for us to leap forward to something apparently unrelated but the camera that in filming can give us the impression of showing a whole when it is only showing a fragment that has already been severed. If in *GoodFellas* Scorsese does not cut away here he will have to show too much too soon; or: the whole structure of the film depends upon this leap.

Much in decline today is the viewing audience that adopted the camera's view in a contract of respect and gratitude, as though something was being shown faithfully and would be connected to another thing shown faithfully, too, and ensuing in simple, logical, present-centered syntax. Aggregating now at the edge of the screen is an audience that has given up faith because it knows it is in the presence (enjoying the tricks/suffering the embrace) of a faithless camera. Since everything depicted is now both what we think it is and not what we think it is, we are in the age of the suspended judgment not only technologically and economically but also aesthetically. Scorsese performs the trick in bravura fashion, but also possible (and cheap, I think) would be replaying an original scene precisely, angle for angle, but then out of the blue pulling back to reveal a character who was "standing there all along but we didn't (couldn't) know." Watching becomes a losing of virginity. Consider the camera pull-back from the lovers' embrace to reveal the spying rifleman in an apartment nearby as he shoots at them, in *Little Murders* (1971).

I should add that *GoodFellas* is a film about a young man losing multiple virginities, one after another. Innocence lost. And the moment at the roadside, A, is both harbinger of this theme and preparation for a notably shocking moment for him, when, in AA, his friends remove their amicable masks allowing him to see their diabolical side. For this to happen at the beginning of the film would merely inform the viewer about a loss of innocence rather than causing the viewer to experience one and understand it, as it were, from within. Scorsese's use of the crafty camera is his way of mocking the deceitfulness of the older, experienced men he shows, who cover over what they are, especially in the face of the young.

to Scott Smith

17

Domain of Wraiths

Jacques Tati in Play Time *(Jacques Tati, Specta/Jolly, 1967). Digital frame enlargement.*

"Family" Ties

At the edge of the screen, one comes home.

Because cinematic narratives are human in their content, construction, and performance, they are presented to audiences, like stage vehicles, *sociably*. Imagery itself is human. Missing in cinema is the actor's actual breath; missing in theatre is the image of a moment. One watches film as a person, takes the figures one sees to be persons as well, and so our watching is in a *personal* mode. The viewer has no problem focusing on "somebody" he or she has never met before, no trouble *staring at strangers*, because we understand that strangers are in the human family. We huddle together, we converse (with cinema we think out our responses to speech), we interact (those figures look at us or near us; they know the family is there for them, that we gaze at them or near enough). We erect towers of understanding. Take a step further: an actor hired to play a character for the screen, turning that character into a figure before the lens, will relate to the figured character in a sociable way, too, feeling comfort, having knowledge, experiencing. Regarding an actor experiencing: I once had the opportunity to ask James Spader what it was like doing *Crash* for David Cronenberg. "Oh God," he said, with a tentative smile, "I couldn't work for a year after that!" And one senses his deep weariness, watching the performance. To the character beneath the figure on the screen and to the performer beneath that character we react and bring relation, morally, culturally, philosophically, emotionally, physically.

One of the intriguing differences between stage figures and those of the screen is that almost always, stage figures are given to vanish before our eyes at a curtain call, being replaced on the instant, as we take it, by the actors who gave them life (by way of the script and their own invention). One has an illusion: the living actors standing on the stage have now consented to present themselves directly, without trappings, without guise or guile—even for only a brief moment before the curtain falls to separate them from us (at which point they can really be real, or certainly realer, and head back off to their real lives—which are as real as our real lives, as we think about them having real lives). In film, things are different. With rare exceptions, the curtain call is elided, replaced by a final credits crawl in which if we are lucky (i.e., if we are not watching on Netflix) we see names flash by. Names are not people.[1] If in theatre our sense of presence during the show gains a radical alteration at the end, in cinema our view continues *not* bringing us close while stimulating us nevertheless to feel closeness. More than theatre does now, or ever did do, cinema charges us with hope about and conception of the performers in their world outside it, that world where, as we know or forget to know, we mingle with them.

Viewers will extend the boundary of figuration in order to make credible supposition of the actors in their work, more precisely the "actors"—the working performers (unknown) as cooked into glowing form by viewers following recipes provided in publicity. Outside the film, beyond it, forward from it, these folk have engagements waiting and we fantasize them not as they are and will be but as the kind of recognizable figures we would wish

---

[1] Sidney Lumet's *Murder on the Orient Express* (1974) has a smartly designed curtain call at film's end; *Citizen Kane* (1941) has a call with substitution by clip. Binge-watching serial TV dramas through streaming can be especially fraught, because seeing the characters for so many episodes seriatim one has particular trouble evacuating them from the mind as one leaves the screen.

for, moving onward in a scenario we care to invent: dressing and coiffing before the Academy Awards; having dinner at Musso's; visiting Tyrone Power's grave at Hollywood Forever; doing a photo shoot in Istanbul ….. This fantasy "life" that we accord these "members of our family," much as we can hope to know them, is a complex "movie" of performers' lives—lives in Hollywood where they drive, sit by swimming pools, chat on the phone, sign deals, meditate behind tall cedars and elegant wrought iron gates in Bel Air or high shrubbery in Brentwood or flower gardens in Beverly Hills. There is more. Beyond fantasizing where these people are now, today, at this moment—after all, being alive with us they have to be somewhere—a 24th floor hotel room in Toronto—we assume the power to dream-imagine them in retrospect, over a period of years or decades since our earliest encounters. The "Woodie" that Jimmy Stewart drove to his home on North Roxbury Drive in 1956, the steak Alfred Hitchcock liked to eat at Chasen's in the early 1960s, Alan Ladd posing for *Photoplay* around 1953 as nothing but another dad with his young kids by the pool; Charles Laughton, Jackie Gleason, Tallulah Bankhead, and Barbara Stanwyck playing fantasy canasta at the Garden of Allah around 1932; Nicholas Ray entertaining James Dean at the Chateau Marmont in 1954. Since a magical epoch all the way back then, and all the way until now, the performers in our family, those who have not died, have been constantly "here." We have witnessed and adored them; we have followed the "careers." We know who they are when they sit to our table.

One-Way Street

If in watching such strangers as the figurines on the screen, if in being struck by their work we make them our familiars, it is with a sense of openness and hospitality on our part: that the stranger can enter familial territory so swiftly, so easily, with such force, and be welcomed there. For all of us who would claim to love film, our very earliest days at the edge of the screen were filled with new people this way. In fact, we traveled to the theater in rapt anticipation of seeing faces we had never seen before, taking them to heart, inviting them in.

But we might strive to notice that the figures of the screen have not explicitly invited us. They act as though someone is expected to be watching them, as though in the minutest aspect of every gesture they are working to show themselves off to someone who is of course always already there, but we cannot certainly take ourselves to be the exact someone by explicit request. They did not say, "You, Virginia … you, Adam … come and watch us." It is true that when I watch, it is true that someone is watching, because in myself I am a someone; but it is not true that when someone is watching, therefore I am. I watch in an audience, and I take my watching seriously. But this audience is massive, and inside it I can speak for only myself.

No one of us is exactly "the watcher" the figures address and the performers under the figures know about; yet anyone can watch. We are not expected—by the actors, by the figures, by the screen itself—to open ourselves for inspection or imagination, beyond that we are knowably present surveilling their field. They speak to us by speaking toward us, in our hearing and in our general direction, even when what they say is secretly whispered. They speak as though our receiving their every word is vital to their own presence. But they do not judge us as we judge them, and judge them we surely do. Are they as estimable as we want them to be, or as we remember them having been before? Are we in any way made special by virtue of our current point of view upon them? Will they succeed or fail, and will this be because of their merit, their honor, their placement, their luck?

Or:

Look in, carefully, on a world where not one person is conscious of us. We are then peeping. Monsieur Hulot in Jacques Tati's *Play Time* (1968) on his balcony staring down at office cubicles filled with those who do not know he is there. And note the remarkable view-from-the-sidewalk sequence where he has been invited into an old acquaintance's apartment for a drink and through the modern building's plate glass façade we presume to watch the familial routines mimed out "unselfconsciously" in adjacent apartments that share a wall. This puts us on a one-way street, seeing but not being seen seeing, neither troubled nor even nudged since we watch by license and as though by vocation. No one has called upon us, of course, not upon you and me; only a vast and internationally based audience (with plenty of money) has been called, if called at all, and we may include ourselves at will. No voice comes to pique us or tap our shoulder: "Look here!"

In looking "here," we perform an actual reaching out, far beyond yearning or study, beyond mere fascination, beyond loneliness. Some arcane knowledge seems to be hiding in the screen world; we are entitled to seek it, and must do so, if we are to affiliate fully with our peers on earth, if we wish to be all that our sense can give us to be. At the edge of the screen we are especially conscious of this reaching out, its delicate strain.

Histories

Now, however, a signal complication:

The splendid (if in every geographical zone somewhat restricted) range of viewing opportunities given through multimedia platforms allows one to search in cinema's past, sometimes even through the agency of brand new, expensively restored prints that purport to look today, albeit on smaller screens, the way a film looked on the first day of its release (before projector wear entered the picture). Historical material has many benefits and side effects, including a chance to examine cultural artifacts and techniques of a bygone age. Yet, in one's familiarization with the screen, in our making the figures there part of a family, there is one signal chilling effect, namely, watching today and being entranced at one's present age by a figure, thus also an actor, who moved arms and legs long ago, long long before one was born. Because the images on one's screen, fresh as they may appear, come from far off, all the performers creating the figures one catches today are, literally, distant stars. The gestural nuances one picks up from them, their smiles, their elegiac waves at the horizon were given decades ago, on a soundstage, perhaps on a rainy afternoon. Given before the new year came. Given before death, sometimes.

It is true that when one looks at a current movie, the gestural nuances were done in the past, too, but not so far into the past, and the gesturer can be imagined alive and gesturing today, roughly embodied as we saw onscreen. With film rescreenings from the classical era, there are obstacles for us to jump as we race to connect these folk to our current sensibilities, as we try to befriend them, because we are seeing them in their relative youth. Seeing them, it may be, flailing, grimacing, gesticulating, hopping, and sailing through space in the flush of the days *before these days in which we live, before even our parents were there to watch*. We are reaching for what the world was before we made an entrance there.

Even if we think of these figures "of the past" as specifically cinema-historical—Anny Ondra in the age of silent cinema; Katharine Hepburn in the 1930s; Luke Skywalker fighting in early CGI—we find that in the moments of our actual engagement with them, when they pause to be seen and we pause to see them, in that nodal eclipse that is pure cinema, they are wraiths. We catch gestures at the edge of the screen, but the gesturers are not there, and *not there* in a quite different way than actors are generally "not there" while we watch them. These wraiths are not on the screen but also not in limousines bearing them to lunch; nor anywhere living folk might find them in the living crowd.

They shine for us not out of a life we can imagine outside the closure of the boundary, but out of an obscurity. Out of an entire secret universe of which we can only speculate. Thus, spectacles that are speculations; speculations that are spectacles. And they bring a reassuring certainty at the edge of the screen. That even out of the darkness their strange lifelikeness, this strange liveliness of the screen, with quivering edge and carnival population, is waiting for our touch even when we do not watch.

to Laura Mulvey

REFERENCES

Ackerman, Diane. *The Moon by Whale Light and Other Adventures among Bats, Penguins, Crocodiles, and Whales.* New York: Vintage, 1992.
Albee, Edward. *The American Dream and the Zoo Story.* New York: New American Library, 1961.
Alter, Robert, Trans. *The Five Books of Moses.* New York: W. W. Norton, 2004.
Antonioni, Michelangelo, Mark Peploe, and Peter Wollen. *The Passenger.* New York: Grove Press, 1975.
Arbuthnot, John. *An Essay Concerning the Effects of Air on Human Bodies.* London: Printed for J. Tonson, 1733.
Arendt, Hannah. *The Human Condition.* 2nd Edition. Chicago: University of Chicago Press, 2013.
Arnheim, Rudolf. *Art and Visual Perception: A Psychology of the Creative Eye.* Berkeley: University of California Press, 1974 © 1954.
Attali, Jacques. *Noise: The Political Economy of Music.* Trans. Brian Massumi. Manchester: Manchester University Press, 1985.
Austen, Jane. *Northanger Abbey.* Annot. and Ed. David M. Shapard. New York: Anchor Books, 2013.
Austin, J. L. *How to Do Things with Words.* 2nd Edition. Cambridge, MA: Harvard University Press, 1975.
Barrie, James M. *Peter Pan.* Wordsworth Editions. Ware: Hertfordshire, 1993.
Bateson, Gregory. *Steps to an Ecology of Mind.* Chicago: University of Chicago Press, 1972.
Baum, L. Frank. *The Wonderful Wizard of Oz.* Chicago and New York: G. M. Hill, 1900.
Bazin, André. "The Ontology of the Photographic Image," in *What Is Cinema?*, Vol. 1, trans. Hugh Gray, Berkeley: University of California Press, 1967, 9–16.
Benjamin, Walter. *Charles Baudelaire: A Lyric Poet in the Era of High Capitalism.* London: Verso, 1997.
Benjamin, Walter. *The Arcades Project.* Trans. Howard Eiland and Kevin McLaughlin. Cambridge, Mass.: Harvard University Press, 1999.
Benjamin, Walter. "The Newspaper," in *Selected Writings, Vol. 2, 1927–1934*, trans. Rodney Livingstone and Others, ed. Michael W. Jennings, Howard Eiland, and Gary Smith, Cambridge, MA: Harvard University Press, 1999, 741–2.
Benjamin, Walter. "Introduction" to Walter Benjamin's *One-Way Street.* Cambridge, MA: Harvard University Press, 2016, 1–20.
Benjamin, Walter. *One-Way Street.* Trans. Edmund Jephcott. Cambridge, MA: Harvard University Press, 2016.

Billington, David P. *The Tower and the Bridge: The New Art of Structural Engineering*. Princeton: Princeton University Press, 1983.

Bogarde, Dirk. *Ever, Dirk: The Bogarde Letters*. Ed. John Coldstream. London: Weidenfeld & Nicolson, 2008.

Bonitzer, Pascal. "Nous n'aimons plus le cinema (1949)," in *Le goût de la beauté*, Paris: Éditions de l'étoile, 1984, 41–6.

Bordwell, David. "Intensified Continuity: Visual Style in Contemporary American Film," *Film Quarterly* 55: 3 (Spring 2002), 16–28.

Bottomore, Stephen. "The Panicking Audience?: Early Cinema and the 'Train Effect'," *Historical Journal of Film, Radio and Television* 19: 2 (1999), 177–216.

Boulding, Kenneth E. *The Image: Knowledge in Life and Society*. Ann Arbor, MI: University of Michigan Press, 1961.

Brooks, Peter. *The Melodramatic Imagination: Balzac, Henry James, Melodrama, and the Mode of Excess*. New Haven: Yale University Press, 1995.

Brown, Norman O. *Life against Death: The Psychoanalytical Meaning of History*. Middletown, CT: Wesleyan University Press, 1959.

Brown, Norman O. *Love's Body*. New York: Vintage, 1966.

Brown, Norman O. *Hermes the Thief: The Evolution of a Myth*. New York: Vintage, 1989 © 1947.

Brown, Norman O. *Apocalypse and/or Metamorphosis*. Berkeley: University of California Press, 1991.

Burke, Kenneth. *Permanence and Change: An Anatomy of Purpose*. Berkeley: University of California Press, 1954.

Butler, Judith. *Gender Trouble: Feminism and the Subversion of Identity*. New York: Routledge, 2006.

Calvino, Italo. *Invisible Cities*. Trans. William Weaver. New York: Harcourt, Inc., 1974.

Carey, John. "Temporal and Spatial Transitions in American Fiction Films," *Studies in the Anthropology of Visual Communication* 1: 1 (1974), 45–50.

Cavell, Stanley. *The World Viewed: Reflections on the Ontology of Film*. Enl. Edition. Cambridge, MA: Harvard University Press, 1979.

Cavell, Stanley. *Pursuits of Happiness: The Hollywood Comedy of Remarriage*. Cambridge, MA: Harvard University Press, 1981.

Cavell, Stanley. *Themes Out of School: Effects and Causes*. San Francisco: North Point Press, 1984.

Cavell, Stanley. *Cities of Words: Pedagogical Letters on a Register of the Moral Life*. Cambridge, MA: Harvard University Press, 2005.

Challamel, Augustin. *The History of Fashion in France; or, the Dress of Women from the Gallo-Roman Period to the Present Time*. Trans. Cashel Hoey and John Lillie. London: Low, Marston, Searle, & Rivington, 1882.

Cogeval, Guy and Dominique Païni, eds. *Hitchcock and Art: Fatal Coincidences*. Montréal: Musée des Beaux Arts, 2000.

Coleman, Herbert. Memo to Luigi Luraschi, Aril 15, 1955, re character names, *Man Who Knew Too Much* Script File, Margaret Herrick Library, Academy of Motion Picture Arts and Sciences, Beverly Hills.

Corbin, Alain. *The Foul and the Fragrant: Odor and the French Social Imagination*. Cambridge, MA: Harvard University Press, 1986.

Cortázar, Julio. *Cronopios and Famas*. Trans. Paul Blackburn. New York: Pantheon, 1969.
Crary, Jonathan. *Techniques of the Observer: On Vision and Modernity in the Nineteenth Century*. Cambridge, MA: M.I.T. Press, 1990.
Darwin, Charles. *The Expression of Emotion in Man and Animals*. New York: D. Appleton, 1873.
Davenport, Guy. *Objects on a Table: Harmonious Disarray in Art and Literature*. Washington, DC: Counterpoint, 1998.
Davis, Mike. *City of Quartz: Excavating the Future in Los Angeles*. London: Verso, 2006.
De Beauvoir, Simone. *Le deuxième sexe*. Paris: Gallimard, 1949.
De Montaigne, Michel. "On Experience," in *The Essays: A Selection*, trans. M. A. Screech, London: Penguin, 1993, 364–426.
De Montaigne, Michel. "To Philosophize Is to Learn How to Die," in *The Essays: A Selection*, trans. M. A. Screech, London: Penguin, 2004, 17–36.
Dickens, Charles. *Oliver Twist*. Harmondsworth: Penguin, 1966 © 1837–9.
Didion, Joan. *Slouching towards Bethlehem*. New York: Washington Square Press, 1968.
Didion, Joan. *After Henry: Essays*. New York: Simon & Schuster, 1992.
Douglas, Mary. *Purity and Danger: An Analysis of Concepts of Pollution and Taboo*. London and New York: Routledge, 1966.
Dumas, Alexandre. *The Count of Monte Cristo*. Trans. Robin Buss. London: Penguin, 2003.
Durkheim, Émile. *The Division of Labour in Society*. Trans. W. D. Halls. New York: Free Press, 2014.
Epstein, Jean. "Magnification," in *French Film Theory and Criticism: A History/Anthology*, Vol. 1, ed. Richard Abel, Princeton, NJ: Princeton University Press, 1988, 235–41.
Festinger, Leon. *A Theory of Cognitive Dissonance*. Evanston, IL: Row, Peterson, 1957.
Fiedler, Leslie A. *The Return of the Vanishing American*. New York: Stein and Day, 1969.
Fiedler, Leslie A. *Freaks: Myths and Images of the Secret Self*. New York: Simon and Schuster, 1986.
Fjastad, Roy. Letter to Arthur Benjamin, February 11, 1955, re cantata rights, Alfred Hitchcock Papers, File 390, Margaret Herrick Library, Academy of Motion Picture Arts and Sciences, Beverly Hills.
Flaubert, Gustave. *Bouvard and Pécuchet with the Dictionary of Received Ideas*. Trans A. J. Krailsheimer. Harmondsworth: Penguin, 1976.
Foucault, Michel. *The Order of Things: An Archaeology of the Human Sciences*. New York: Routledge, 1989.
Fowles, John. "Poor Koko," in *The Ebony Tower*, London: Vintage, 2006, 143–84.
Frascella, Lawrence and Al Weisel. *Live Fast, Die Young: The Wild Ride of Making "Rebel without a Cause"*. New York: Touchstone, 2006.
Friedan, Betty. *The Feminine Mystique*. New York: W. W. Norton, 1963.
Garfinkel, Harold. "Studies in the Routine Grounds of Everyday Activities," in *Studies in Ethnomethodology*, Englewood Cliffs, NJ: Prentice-Hall, 1967, 35–75.

Gastineau, Benjamin. *Les romans du voyage: La vie en chemin de fer*. Paris: Dentu, 1861.

Gaudreault, André and Tom Gunning. "Cinema as a Challenge to Film History," in *The Cinema of Attractions Reloaded*, ed. Wanda Strauven, Amsterdam: Amsterdam University Press, 2007, 365–80.

Goffman, Erving. "On Cooling the Mark Out: Some Aspects of Adaptation to Failure," *Psychiatry* 15: 4 (1952), 451–63.

Goffman, Erving. *Frame Analysis: An Essay on the Organization of Experience*. Cambridge, MA: Harvard University Press, 1974.

Goffman, Erving. *Forms of Talk*. Philadelphia: University of Pennsylvania Press, 1981.

Goffman, Erving. *Stigma: Notes on the Management of Spoiled Identity*. New York: Touchstone, 1986.

Gombrich, Ernst. *Art and Illusion: A Study in the Psychology of Pictorial Representation*. Princteon: Princeton University Press, 1960.

Gomery, Douglas. *Shared Pleasures: A History of Movie Presentation in the United States*. Madison: University of Wisconsin Press, 1992.

Goodman, Paul. *Speaking and Language: Defence of Poetry*. New York: Vintage, 1972.

Gorky, Maxim. "In the Kingdom of Shadows" (July 4, 1896) repr. in *Lapham's Quarterly*.

Gould, Stephen Jay. "The Proof of Lavoisier's Plates," in *The Lying Stones of Marrakech*, New York: Three Rivers Press, 2000, 91–114.

Graves, Robert. *The Greek Myths*. London: Penguin, 1960.

Gunning, Tom. "An Aesthetic of Astonishment: Early Film and the (In)Credulous Spectator," in *Viewing Positions: Ways of Seeing Film*, ed. Linda Williams, New Brunswick, N.J.: Rutgers University Press, 1995, 114–33.

Hammett, Dashiell. *Red Harvest*. New York: Vintage, 2023 © 1929.

Henderson, Gretchen E. *Ugliness: A Cultural History*. London: Reaktion, 2016.

Herbert, Daniel and Constantine Verevis. *Film Reboots*. Edinburgh: Edinburgh University Press, 2020.

Hitchcock, Alfred. Letter to Sidney L. Bernstein, January 25, 1955, re musical rights to the Benjamin cantata, *Man Who Knew Too Much* production files, Margaret Herrick Library, Academy of Motion Picture Arts and Sciences, Beverly Hills.

Hitchcock, Alfred. Letter to Sidney L. Bernstein, February 10, 1955, re musical rights, *Man Who Knew Too Much* production files, Margaret Herrick Library, Academy of Motion Picture Arts and Sciences, Beverly Hills.

Howard, Jennifer. *Clutter: An Untidy History*. Cleveland: Belt, 2020.

Huhtamo, Erkki. *Illusions in Motion: Media Archaeology of the Moving Panorama and Related Spectacles*. Cambridge, Mass.: M.I.T. Press, 2013.

James, Henry. *The Art of the Novel: Critical Prefaces*. New York: Charles Scribner's Sons, 1934.

James, William. *The Principles of Psychology*, Vol. I. New York: Henry Holt, 1890.

Jung, Carl G. *Dreams*. Trans. R. F. C. Hull. Princeton, N.J.: Princeton University Press, 1974.

Kafka, Franz. "The Tower of Babel," in *Parables and Paradoxes*, New York: Schocken, 1961, 35.

Kafka, Franz. "In the Penal Colony," in *The Metamorphosis, In the Penal Colony, and Other Stories*, trans. Willa and Edwin Muir, New York: Schocken, 1975 © 1948, 191–228.
Keats, John. *Odes*. West Chester, PA: Spruce Alley Press, 2016.
Keynes, John Maynard. *Essays in Persuasion*. New York: W. W. Norton, 1981 © 1931.
LaBelle, Brandon. *Lexicon of the Mouth: Poetics and Politics of Voice and the Oral Imaginary*. New York: Bloomsbury, 2014.
Lawrence, D. H. *Studies in Classic American Literature*. New York: T. Seltzer, 1923.
LeCarré, John. *Absolute Friends*. New York: Viking, 2003.
Locke, John. *An Essay Concerning Human Understanding*. London: T. Tegg and Son, 1836.
Loughman, John and John Michael Montias. *Public and Private Spaces: Works of Art in Seventeenth-Century Dutch Houses*. Zwolle: Waanders, 2000.
Luraschi, Luigi. Memo to Alfred Hitchcock and Herbert Coleman, April 15, 155, re character names, *Man Who Knew Too Much* Script file, Margaret Herrick Library, Academy of Motion Picture Arts and Sciences, Beverly Hills.
Maerz, Aloys and Morris Rea Paul. *A Dictionary of Color*. New York: McGraw-Hill, 1930.
Mannoni, Laurent. *The Great Art of Light and Shadow: Archaeology of the Cinema*. Exeter: University of Exeter Press, 2000.
McCambridge, Mercedes. Personal conversation, September 1986.
Merleau-Ponty, Maurice. *Phenomenology of Perception*. Trans. Colin Smith. New York: Routledge, 2002.
Miller, Arthur. *After the Fall*. New York: Dramatists Play Service Inc., 1964.
Nabokov, Vladimir. *The Gift*. New York: Vintage International, 1991.
Nabokov, Vladimir. *Butterflies: Unpublished and Uncollected Writings*. Trans. Dmitri Nabokov. Boston: Beacon Press, 2000.
Naremore, James. *North by Northwest: Alfred Hitchcock, Director*. New Brunswick, NJ: Rutgers University Press, 1993.
Night Wire to Alfred Hitchcock, March 24, 1955, re Benjamin's agreement to write more music, Alfred Hitchcock Papers, File 379, Margaret Herrick Library, Academy of Motion Picture Arts and Sciences, Beverly Hills.
Ortega y Gasset, José. "On Point of View in the Arts," in *The Dehumanization of Art and Other Essays on Art, Culture, and Literature*, Princeton, NJ: Princeton University Press, 1948, 107–30.
Perkins, V. F. *Film as Film: Understanding and Judging Movies*. Harmondsworth: Penguin, 1972.
Piccolino, Marco. "Animal Electricity and the Birth of Electrophysiology: The Legacy of Luigi Galvani," *Brain Research Bulletin* 46: 5 (1998), 381–407.
Pirandello, Luigi. "Illustratori, attori e traduttori," in *Saggi, poesie, scritti varii*, ed. M. Lovecchio-Musti, Milano: Mondadori, 1973.
Pirandello, Luigi. *Shoot!* Trans. C. K. Scott Moncrieff. Chicago: University of Chicago Press, 2005.
Pomerance, Murray. "Finding Release: 'Storm Clouds' and *The Man Who Knew Too Much*," in *Music and Cinema*, ed. James Buhler, Caryl Flinn, and David Neumeyer, Middletown, CT: Wesleyan University Press, 2000, 207–46.

Pomerance, Murray. *An Eye for Hitchcock*. New Brunswick, NJ: Rutgers University Press, 2004.
Pomerance, Murray. *The Eyes Have It: Cinema and the Reality Effect*. New Brunswick, NKJ: Rutgers University Press, 2012.
Pomerance, Murray. "Burton Black," in *The Works of Tim Burton: Margins to Mainstream*, ed. Jeffrey Weinstock, New York: Palgrave Macmillan, 2013, 33–46.
Pomerance, Murray. "Vox Orson," *Sounding Out*, ed. Neil Verma, at Soundstudiesblog.com, January 2014.
Pomerance, Murray. "Looking Up: Class, England, and America in *The Man Who Knew Too Much*," for *The Cambridge Companion to Alfred Hitchcock*, ed. Jonathan Freedman, New York: Cambridge University Press, 2015, 180–93.
Pomerance, Murray. "Doing Dumbledore: Notes on Accretionary Performance," in *Cycles, Sequels, Spin-offs, Remakes and Reboots: Multiplicities in Film and Television*, ed. Amanda Ann Klein and R. Barton Palmer, Austin: University of Texas Press, 2016, 166–83.
Pomerance, Murray. *The Man Who Knew Too Much*. London: BFI, 2016.
Pomerance, Murray. *Moment of Action: Riddles of Cinematic Performance*. New Brunswick NJ: Rutgers University Press, 2016.
Pomerance, Murray. *Cinema, If You Please: The Memory of Taste, the Taste of Memory*. Edinburgh: Edinburgh University Press, 2018.
Pomerance, Murray. *Virtuoso: Film Performance and the Actor's Magic*. New York: Bloomsbury, 2019.
Pomerance, Murray. *The Film Cheat: Screen Artifice and Viewing Pleasure*. New York: Bloomsbury, 2020.
Pomerance, Murray. "The Sound of the Sound," *Film International* 93, 18: 3 (2020), 58–66.
Pomerance, Murray. *Color It True: Impressions of Cinema*. New York: Bloomsbury, 2022.
Powdermaker, Hortense. *Hollywood: The Dream Factory; an Anthropologist Looks at the Movie-Makers*. London: Secker, 1967.
Rancière, Jacques. *The Politics of Aesthetics: The Distribution of the Sensible*. Ed. and trans. Gabriel Rockhill. London and New York: Bloomsbury, 2004.
Rancière, Jacques. *The Intervals of Cinema*. Trans. John Howe. London: Verso, 2019.
Ray, Nicholas (with Susan Ray). *I Was Interrupted: Nicholas Ray on Making Movies*. Berkeley: University of California Press, 1993.
Rilke, Rainer Maria. *Ahead of All Parting: The Selected Poetry and Prose of Rainer Maria Rilke*. Trans. Stephen Mitchell. New York: Modern Library, 1995.
Rodowick, David N. *The Virtual Life of Film*. Cambridge, MA: Harvard University Press, 2007.
Sacks, Oliver. *The Man Who Mistook His Wife for a Hat and Other Clinical Tales*. New York: Simon & Schuster, 1970.
Saint Augustine. *Of the Citie of God*. Englished by John Healey. London: George Eld, 1610.
Saint Thomas Aquinas. *Summa Theologica*. Allen, TX: Christian Classics, 1981 © 1948.
Salt, Barry. *Film Style & Technology: History & Analysis*. 2nd Edition. London: Starword, 1992.

Sarris, Andrew. *The American Cinema: Directors and Directions, 1929–1968*. New York: Da Capo Press, 1996.
Sartre, Jean-Paul. *Being and Nothingness: A Phenomenological Essay on Ontology*. Trans. Hazel E. Barnes. New York: Philosophical Library, 1956.
Schafer, R. Murray. *The Book of Noise*. Douro-Dummer, ON: Arcana Editions, 1998.
Schefer, Jean Louis. *The Enigmatic Body: Essays on the Arts*. Trans. Paul Smith. Cambridge: Cambridge University Press, 1995.
Schefer, Jean Louis. *Question de style*. Paris: Éditions L'Harmattan, 1995.
Schefer, Jean Louis. *The Ordinary Man of Cinema*. Trans. Max Cavitch, Paul Grant, and Noura Wedell. South Pasadena, CA: Semiotext(e), 2016.
Schivelbusch, Wolfgang. *The Railway Journey: The Industrialization of Time and Space in the Nineteenth Century*. Berkeley: University of California Press, 1986.
Schivelbusch, Wolfgang. *Disenchanted Night: The Industrialization of Light in the Nineteenth Century*. Trans. Angela Davies. Berkeley: University of California Press, 1995.
Schivelbusch, Wolfgang. *In a Cold Crater: Cultural and Intellectual Life in Berlin, 1945–1948*. Trans. Kelly Barry. Berkeley: University of California Press, 1998.
Sebald, W. G. *Vertigo*. Trans. Michael Hulse. New York: New Directions, 1999.
Shakespeare, William. *The Tempest*. New York: Signet, 1963.
Shakespeare, William. *The Tragedy of Hamlet Prince of Denmark*. Ed. Edward Hubler. New York: New American Library, 1963.
Shepard, Sam. *Angel City*. Alexandria, Va.: Alexander Street Press, 2005.
Simmel, Georg. *Philosophie des Geldes*. Leipzig: Von Duncker & Humblot, 1907.
Sinclair, Iain. *Living with Buildings and Walking with Ghosts: On Health and Architecture*. London: Wellcome Collection/Profile, 2018.
Sobchack, Vivian. "Being on the Screen: A Phenomenology of Cinematic Flesh, or the Actor's Four Bodies," in *Acting and Performance in Moving Image Culture: Bodies, Screens, Renderings*, ed. Jörg Sternagel, Deborah Levitt, and Dieter Mersch, Bielefeld: transcript Verlag, 2012, 429–45.
Stadler, Joseph Constantine. *Exhibition of Water Coloured Drawings, Old Bond Street*, after Augustus Pugin and Thomas Rowlandson, London: Rudolph Ackermann, 1808, included in George Birkbeck Hill, ed. *Boswell's Life of Johnson including Boswell's Journal of a Tour to the Hebrides and Johnson's Diary of a Journey into North Wales*, Graingerized Edition, Oxford: Clarendon Press, 1887, Vol. 3 Part 4, 278.
Sternberger, Dolf. *Panorama, oder Ansichten vom 19. Jahrhundert*, 3rd Edition. Hamburg: Claassen & Goverts, 1946 © 1938.
Stewart, James. "James Stewart," *Saturday Evening Post*, 11 February 1961, 76.
Sudnow, David. *Ways of the Hand: The Improvisation of Organized Conduct*. Cambridge, MA: M.I.T. Press, 1993.
Swift, Jonathan. *Travels into Several Remote Nations of the World: In Four Parts. By Lemuel Gulliver, First a Surgeon, and Then a Captain of Several Ships*. Dublin: J. Hyde, 1726.
Teilhard de Chardin, Pierre. *The Phenomenon of Man*. New York: Harper & Row, 1965.
Thesiger, Wilfred. *Across the Empty Quarter* (excerpts from *Arabian Sands*). London: Penguin, 2007 © 1959.

Thomas, Dylan. "Ears in the Turrets Hear," in *Twenty-Five Poems*, London: J. M. Dent & Sons, 1936.
Tolstoy, Leo. *War and Peace*. Trans. Richard Pevear and Larissa Volokhonsky. New York: Vintage, 2008.
Trollope, Anthony. "The National Gallery," *St James's Magazine*, September 1861.
Tuan, Yi-Fu. *Space and Place: The Perspective of Experience*. Minneapolis: University of Minnesota Press, 1979.
Turner, Victor W. *The Forest of Symbols: Aspects of Ndembu Ritual*. Ithaca, NY: Cornell University Press, 1967.
Vasari, Giorgio. *The Lives of the Artists*. Trans. Julia Conaway Bondanella and Peter Bondanella. Oxford: Oxford University Press, 1991.
Vonnegut, Kurt Jr. *God Bless You, Mr. Rosewater or Pearls before Swine*. New York: Dell, 1965.
Weber, Max. "Politics as a Vocation," in *From Max Weber: Essays in Sociology*, ed. Hans Gerth and C. Wright Mills, London: Routledge, 1948, 129–56.
Weber, Max. *Economy and Society*. Trans. Keith Tribe. Cambridge, MA: Harvard University Press, 2019 © 1921.
Welles, Orson and Peter Bogdanovich. *This Is Orson Welles*. Ed. Jonathan Rosenbaum. New York: HarperCollins, 1992.
White, T. H. *The Book of Beasts*. Cambridge: Cambridge University Press, 1954.
Wilson, Frank R. *The Hand: How Its Use Shapes the Brain Language, and Human Culture*. New York: Pantheon, 1998.
Wittgenstein, Ludwig. *Tractatus Logico-Philosophicus*. Trans. C. K. Ogden. London: Routledge & Kegan Paul, 1922.
Wood, Robin. *Hitchcock's Films Revisited*. New York: Columbia University Press, 1989.

INDEX

Page numbers in italic denote images.

8 ½ (Federico Fellini, 1963) 17
20 Million Miles to Earth (Nathan Juran, 1957) 169
37°2 le matin (*Betty Blue*) (Jean-Jacques Beineix, 1986) 75
55 Days at Peking (Nicholas Ray, 1963) 14
1917 (Sam Mendes, 2019) 43
1984 Olympics (Los Angeles) 108
2001: A Space Odyssey (Stanley Kubrick, 1968) *25*, *26*, *27*, 40
2012 (Roland Emmerich, 2009) 186
20,000 Leagues Under the Sea (Richard Fleischer, 1954) 27

À bout de souffle (*Breathless*) (Jean-Luc Godard, 1960) 74
À nous la liberté (René Clair, 1924) 180
Abagnale, Frank 195
Abyss, The (James Cameron, 1989) 27, 30
Aeolian Islands 41
Aeolus 41, 42
Affleck, Casey 159
After the Thin Man (W. S. Van Dyke, 1936) 197
Age of Innocence, The (Martin Scorsese, 1993) 14
Albee, Edward 96
Albert Nobbs (Rodrigo García, 2011) 134
Alceste (Christoph Willibald Gluck) 184
Alice in Wonderland (Tim Burton, 2010) 14
Alien (Ridley Scott, 1979) 40, 96, 125, 127, 134

All Is Lost (J. C. Chandor, 2013) 41
All the President's Men (Alan J. Pakula, 1976) *12–13*
Allen, Corey 231, 232
Allen, Jay Presson 48; *see also Marnie*
Allen, Joan 123
Allen, Woody 14, 92
Ama Flix 108
Amazon entertainment platform 109
American in Paris, An (Vincente Minnelli, 1951) 56, 242
American Werewolf in London, An (John Landis, 1981) 124
Ames, Preston 220
Anderson, Chester 176
Anderson, Wes 170
Anderson Tapes, The (Sidney Lumet, 1971) 77
Andersson, Bibi 235
Andrews, Julie 34
Angel City (Sam Shepard) 107
Anglim, Philip 51
Anna Karenina (Clarence Brown, 1935) 219
Anna Karenina (Joe Wright, 2012) 96
Antonioni, Michelangelo 81, 166, 213, 227, 228, 233, 272
Aquinas, Thomas 97
"Archaic Torso of Apollo" (Rainer Maria Rilke) 99
Arendt, Hannah 8
Argenteuil, *see* Paris, *see also* Seurat
Ariadne and the Minotaur, myth 56
Aristotle 18, 95
Arnheim, Rudolf 98, 216
Arrival (Denis Villeneuve, 2016) 125

Asphalt Jungle, The (John Huston, 1950) 165
Astaire, Fred 14, *215*, 220, 221
Astronaut's Wife, The (Rand Ravich, 1995) 26
Attali, Jacques 164
Austen, Jane 53
Austin, J[ohn] L[angshaw] 111, 112, 177
Austin Mini 174
Avatar (James Cameron, 2009) 170
Away (Andrew Hinderaker, 2020) 26
Awful Truth, The (Leo McCarey, 1937) 249

Babette's Feast (Gabriel Axel, 1987) 43
Bacall, Lauren 16, 82
Bad and the Beautiful, The (Vincente Minnelli, 1951) 90
Bad Seed, The (Mervyn LeRoy, 1956) 132
Baisers volés (*Stolen Kisses*) (François Truffaut, 1968) 75
Balaban, A. J. and Sam Katz, *see* Chicago Theater
Bale, Christian 160, 240
Ball, Lucille 50
Balmain, Pierre 242
Balsam, Martin *103*, 111
Band, The, *see* Dylan
Band Wagon, The (Vincente Minnelli, 1953) 14, *215*, 219, 221
Bande à part (*Band of Outsiders*) (Jean-Luc Godard, 1964) 218
Bankhead, Tallulah 269
Barker, Robert 83
Basevi, James 14
Basilica Cistern, *see* Istanbul
Batalov, Aleksey 127
Bateson, Gregory 200
Bazin, André 40, 59, 123
"Being on the Screen" (Vivian Sobchack) 47, 49
Bells Are Ringing (Vincente Minnelli, 1960) 242
Ben-Hur (William Wyler, 1959) 14, 162
Beneath the 12-Mile Reef (Robert D. Webb, 1953) 29

Benjamin, Walter
  on appearance 8
  on Arabic architecture 12
  on arcades 62
  on the newspaper 179
  quoting Balzac 95
Bergman, Ingmar 235
Bergman, Ingrid 15, 64
Bernstein, Carl 12, 13
Bevan, Billy 167
Beverly Hills, 90210 (1990) 109
Beyond the Clouds (Michelangelo Antonioni, 1995) 227–30
Big Sleep, The (Howard Hawks, 1946) 166
Bigamist, The (Ida Lupino, 1953) *223*, 234
Birds, The (Alfred Hitchcock, 1963) 41–2
Black Narcissus (Michael Powell and Emeric Pressburger, 1947) 14, 15
Blade Runner (Ridley Scott, 1982) 134
Blair, Linda 34
Blanchett, Cate 51
Blonde (Andrew Dominik, 2022) 12n2
Blood Simple (Ethan Coen and Joel Coen, 1984) 97
Blow-Up (Michelangelo Antonioni, 1966) 13, 23, 52n1, 81, 137, 184, 240
Blu-Ray, *see* visual technologies
Blue Velvet (David Lynch, 1986) 23
Bogarde, Dirk, on *Daddy Nostalgie* at Cannes 184
Bogart, Humphrey 53, 140
Bogdanovich, Peter, on Lubitsch 146
Bong, Joon Ho [Joon-Ho] 170
Bordwell, David, "intensified continuity," 61, 75
Borgnine, Ernest 21
Boulding, Kenneth 185, 236–7
"Boulevard des Italiens" (Gustave Caillebotte) *71*; *see also* Caillebotte
Bourne Ultimatum, The (Paul Greengrass, 2007) 211
Bowie, David 51, 134
Box, John 14
Breathe (Andy Serkis, 2017) 32

Brief Encounter (David Lean, 1945) 96
Bringing Up Baby (Howard Hawks, 1938) 139, 157, 167
Brisbane 243n1
Brooks, Peter 10
Brown, Norman O. 28, 56, 116, 190, 238
  unity 99
Brute Force (Jules Dassin, 1947) 134
Buick, Nadia 243n1
Bullock, Sandra 32
Bunny, Bugs 198
Buñuel, Luis 54, 55, 63, 142
Burke, Kenneth 190
Burton, Richard 14, 35, 205
Butler, Austin 23
Butterflies and Moths of the Russian Empire, The (Vladimir Dmitrievich Nabokov) 106
Byzantine Empire, *see* Istanbul

Cabaret (Bob Fosse, 1972) 34
Caché (Michael Haneke, 2005) 184
Caillebotte, Gustave 71, 71, 72, 73, 74, 76, 79, 81, 82, 87
  and balconies 72, 73, 75, 87
Calvino, Italo 95
Cameron, James 30, 183, 186
Camino Real (Tennessee Williams) 188
Canaletto (Giovanni Antonio Canal) 76
Cape Fear (Martin Scorsese, 1991) 34
Carol (Todd Haynes, 2016) 12
Caron, Leslie 56
Casablanca (Michael Curtiz, 1942) 54, 195, 262
Catch Me If You Can (Steven Spielberg, 2002) 195
Catch-22 (Mike Nichols, 1970) 126
Cathedral (Auguste Rodin) 239
Catherine of Aragon 98
Cavell, Stanley 11, 68, 202n5
  on Ibsen 16
  and remarriage comedies 69, 249
Cavill, Henry 51
Cazale, John 142
Cézanne, Paul 247

Chaney, Lon 76
Chaplin, Charlie 35, 36, 180
Charge at Feather River, The (Gordon Douglas, 1953) 2–4
Charhi, Liraz 145
Charisse, Cyd, *215*, 220, 221, 241, *241*, 242, 244, 248
Charlie's Angels (1976) 109
Chase and Co., 243
Chekhov, Anton 210
Chekhov, Michael 64
Chicago Theater (State St., Chicago) 185
Chicken Run (Nick Park, 2000) 169
Child 44 (Daniel Espinosa, 2015) 20–1
Chion, Michel, *acousmêtres* 194
Chopin, Frédéric, death 127
Christie, Agatha 39
Christmas Carol, A (December 19, 1991, Eugene O'Neill Theatre, New York) 53n2
Church, Fredric Edwin 76, 87
  at Cotopaxi 76
Cinecittà Studios (Rome) 242
Cinema, If You Please (Murray Pomerance) 82
Cineplex 212
Citizen Kane (Orson Welles, 1941) 7 10, 19, 44, 160, 170, 176, 258, 268
Clark, Candy 134
Claude, *see* Lorrain
Clennon, David 134
Cleopatra (Joseph L. Mankiewicz, 1963) 43
Clock, The (Vincente Minnelli, 1945) 211
Clockwork Orange, A (Stanley Kubrick, 1971) 27n2
Clooney, George 32
Close, Glenn 134
Close Encounters of the Third Kind (Steven Spielberg, 1977) 41, 219
Clouds of Sils Maria (Olivier Assayas, 2014) 184
Colbert, Claudette 243n1
Color It True: Impressions of Cinema (Murray Pomerance) 27

Color Standards and Color Nomenclature (Robert Ridgway) 244
"Concerto for the Left Hand in D Major" (Maurice Ravel) 22, 82
Congreve, William 184
Conley, David 119, 123
Connery, Sean 59, 126
Contact (Robert Zemeckis, 1997) 27
Contempt (*Le mépris*) (Jean-Luc Godard, 1964) 144
Conti, Tom 4
Cooper, Gladys 195
Corbin, Alain 42, 177
Così fan tutte (Wolfgang Amadeus Mozart) 184
Cotopaxi, *see* Church
Cotten, Joseph, 7
Coutard, Raoul 75
Cox, Ronnie 140
Cranes Are Flying, The (Mikhail Kalatozov, 1957) 127
Crary, Jonathan 73
Crash (David Cronenberg, 1996) 268
Crawford, Joan *155*, 156, 157
Creature from the Black Lagoon (Jack Arnold, 1954) 125
Cronyn, Hume 134
Cruise, Tom 35, 141, 219
Crying Game, The (Neil Jordan, 1992) 134, 161
Curtis, Tony 30, 54

Da Vinci, Leonardo, and monster effects 178
Daddy Nostalgie (Bertrand Tavernier, 1990) 184; *see also* Bogarde
Dalí, Salvador 64
Daly, Tyne 121
Damon, Matt 17, 34, 51, 159
Darin, Bobby *193*, 203, 205
Darjeeling Limited, The (Wes Anderson, 2007) 170
Dark (Baran bo Odar, Jantje Friese, 2017–20) 171n4
Darkman (Sam Raimi, 1990) 44
Davenport, Guy, head as fate 97

David and Lisa (Frank Perry, 1962) 239
Davidson, Jaye 134
Davis, Bette 51, 159, 195
Davis, Mike 107
Davis, Viola 109
Day, Doris 109
Day after Tomorrow, The (Roland Emmerich, 2004) 31, 41
Day for Night, see *La nuit américaine*
De Balzac, Honoré 95
De Banzie, Brenda 197
De Caestecker, Iain 36
De Lavoisier, Antoine-Laurent 44; *see also* Gould, Stephen Jay
De Montaigne, Michel 9, 176, 238
De Niro, Robert 34, 180, 252, 253, 254
De Wilde, Brandon 237
Dead Zone, The (David Cronenberg, 1983) 44
Dean, James 230, 231–2, 269
Death Watch (Bertrand Tavernier, 1980) 165
Delta Theatre (Hamilton ON) 2
Denham, Maurice 197
Depp, Johnny 109
Detroit River 30, 31
Devane, William 51
Devil in the Flesh (*Diavolo in corpo*) (Marco Bellocchio, 1986) 135
DiCaprio, Leonardo 109
Dickens, Charles 53
Dictionary of Color (Aloys Maerz and Morris Rea Paul) 241, 244, 245
Dictionary of Received Ideas (*Le dictionnaire des idées reçues*) (Gustave Flaubert) 97
Didion, Joan 107–9, 176
Diner, Michael 156
Dinner at Eight (George Cukor, 1933) 167
Dion, Celine 186
Disney entertainment platform 109
Disney, Walt, cartoons 40, 73, 125
Dixon, W[illiam] K[ennedy]-L[aurie] 79
Doctor Dolittle (Richard Fleischer, 1967) 125n4
Doctor Dolittle (Betty Thomas, 1998) 125

Doctor Zhivago (David Lean, 1965) 14, 168
Dog Day Afternoon (Sidney Lumet, 1975) 142
Domergue, Faith, 39
Donnie Darko (Richard Kelly, 2001) 37, 56, 57
D'Onofrio, Vincent 140
Douglas, Kirk 242
Douglas, Mary, discussing the Azande 177
Douglas, Melvyn 168, 197
Dr. Mabuse, der Spieler (*Dr. Mabuse, the Gambler*) (Fritz Lang, 1922) 77
Dr. No (Terence Young, 1962) 59
DragonHeart (Rob Cohen, 1996) 126
Dreamers, The (Bernardo Bertolucci, 2003) 23, 92, 101
Dreams (Akira Kurosawa, 1990) 194
Driver, Adam 109
"Dry Salvages, The" (T. S. Eliot) 10
Dryden, John 184
Du rififi chez les hommes (*Rififi*) (Jules Dassin, 1955) 77
Duck Amuck (Chuck Jones, 1953) 165
Dullea, Keir, 25 27, 239
Dunne, Griffin 124
Dunne, Irene 249
Durkheim, Émile, and division of labor 180
DVD, *see* visual technologies
Dylan, Bob
  in Manchester 172
  with The Band 172
  with the Hawks 172; *see also No Direction Home*
Dynasty (1981) 109

E.T. the Extra-Terrestrial (Steven Spielberg, 1982) 237
E[xtra-] V[ehicular] A[ctivity] 25, 26
"Ears in the Turrets Hear" (Dylan Thomas) 191
East, Jeff 51
East of Eden (Elia Kazan, 1955) 14
Eastwood, Clint 21
Easy Rider (Dennis Hopper, 1969) 44

Elephant (Gus Van Sant, 2003) 41
Elephant Man, The (April 19, 1979, Booth Theatre, New York) 51
Elephant Man, The (David Lynch, 1980) 170
Eliot, T[homas] S[tearns] 10, 103, 122
Elizabeth House Hotel (Southampton UK) 185
Elvis (Baz Luhrmann, 2022) 124, 179
Empire of the Sun (Steven Spielberg, 1987) 240
Enemy (Denis Villeneuve, 2013) 134
Epstein, Jean 79
Errand Boy, The (Jerry Lewis, 1961) 35, 210
European Magazine, The (January 1873) 241
Evein, Bernard 14
Ex Machina (Alex Garland, 2014) 171
Exorcist, The (William Friedkin, 1973) 34, 132
Eye for Hitchcock, An (Murray Pomerance) 202

Fabelmans, The (Steven Spielberg, 2022) 96n2
Fair Game (Doug Liman, 2010) 145
Family Plot (Alfred Hitchcock, 1976), script by Ernest Lehman 51
Fantastic Four, The (Marvel Comics) 44
Fantastic Voyage (Richard Fleischer, 1966) 158
Father of the Bride (Vincente Minnelli, 1950) 13
"Father's Butterflies" (Vladimir Nabokov) 106
Feld, Fritz 167
Fellini, Federico 17, 242, 244
Ferretti, Dante 14
Festinger, Leon, cognitive dissonance 31
Fidelio (Ludwig Van Beethoven) 184
Fiedler, Leslie A. 1, 135, 238
Field of Dreams (Phil Alden Robinson, 1989) 42
Fifth Element, The (Luc Besson, 1997) 14
Fight Club (David Fincher, 1999) 10

Film Cheat: Screen Artifice and Viewing Pleasure, The (Murray Pomerance) 48
Film Quarterly 105
Fitzgerald, Geraldine 14
Five Books of Moses, The (Trans. Robert Alter) 98
Flaubert, Gustave 97, 106
Florence Foster Jenkins (Stephen Frears, 2016) 34
Foch, Nina 130
Folsey, George 220
Fonda, Jane 137
Fontaine, Joan 234
Forbidden Planet (Fred McLeod Wilcox, 1956) 16, 124
Ford, Harrison 141, 208
Forever Amber (Otto Preminger, John M. Stahl, 1947) 44n2
Foster, Jodie 19
Foucault, Michel 97
Four Horsemen of the Apocalypse, The (Vincente Minnelli, 1962) 242
Francis, Kay 146
Francis Covers the Big Town (Arthur Lubin, 1953) 125
Frascella, Lawrence 232
Freaks: Myths and Images of the Secret Self (Leslie Fiedler) 135
Freleng, Fritz, cartoons 125
French Lieutenant's Woman, The (Karel Reisz, 1981) 180n4
Freud, Sigmund 64, 99, 190
Friedenberg, Edgar Z., 95
Friedkin, William 132
From Russia with Love (Terence Young, 1963) 58
Fugitive, The (Andrew Davis, 1993) 140, 141, 208
Fuller, Samuel 11
Funny Games (Michael Haneke, 2007) 22
Funny Girl (William Wyler, 1968) 35

G[lobal] P[ositioning] S[atellite] 197
Gaines, George 13
Galatea, *see* Pygmalion and Galatea
Galvani, Luigi 75n3
Garbo, Greta 168, 197, 219
Gardner, Ava 221
Garfield, Andrew 32, 124
Garfinkel, Harold 182n5
Garfunkel, Art 126
Garland, Judy 211
Garrel, Louis 101
Gastineau, Benjamin 81
Gay Shoe Clerk, The (Edwin S. Porter, 1903) 79, 84
Gelson's, *see* Los Angeles, Pacific Palisades
George III 83
Gero, Martin 120n1
Gerry (Gus Van Sant, 2002) 159
Ghost Story, A (David Lowery, 2017) 171
Gibbons, Cedric 220
Gibson, George 16
Gift, The (Vladimir Nabokov) 106
Gigi (Vincente Minnelli, 1958) 242
Glass Menagerie, The (Tennessee Williams) 17
Gleason, Jackie 269
Gleason, Keogh 242
God Bless You, Mr. Rosewater (Kurt Vonnegut, Jr.) 119–20
Godard, Jean-Luc 22, 75, 78, 144, 194, 218, 264
Goff, Harper 14
Goffman, Erving 8, 121
  biographical reconstruction 135
  play 230
  the "say-for" 20
Gold Diggers of 1933 (Mervyn LeRoy, 1933) 34
Gombrich, Ernst 74, 215, 216, 218
Gomery, Douglas 1, 43n1
Gone for Good (David Elkaïm, Vincent Poymiro, 2021) 170
Gone with the Wind (Victor Fleming, 1939) 171
Good Liar, The (Bill Condon, 2019) 198
Good Will Hunting (Gus Van Sant, 1997) 34, 185
Goode, Matthew 140
GoodFellas (Martin Scorsese, 1990) 251, 252–6, 258–62, 264–5

Goodman, Paul 112, 173, 158, 193
Gorky, Maxim, as cinema viewer in Nizhni Novgorod 175, 245
Gosford Park (Robert Altman, 2006) 164
Gould, Elliott 53, 236, 237
Gould, Stephen Jay, on Lavoisier 44
Grand Budapest Hotel, The (Wes Anderson, 2014) 170
Grand Central Station, *see* New York City
Grant, Cary 15, 47, 68, 157, 167, 202, 249
Graves, Robert 41
Gravity (Alfonso Cuarón, 2013) 26, 32, 181
Greatest Show on Earth, The (Cecil B. DeMille, 1952) 14, 96, 121
Green, Eva 101
Greenwich Village, *see* New York City
Greenwood, Joan 23
Greer, Howard 157
Greig, Robert 148
Grint, Rupert 51
Guinness, Alec 53, 168
Gwenn, Edmund 234, 235
Gypsy (May 21, 1959, Broadway Theater, New York) 35, 121n2
Gypsy Moths, The (John Frankenheimer, 1969) 37

Hackman, Gene 21
Haight-Ashbury (district in San Francisco) 176
Hall, David 239
Halliday, John 47, 68
Hallock, William, color listing for the *Standard Dictionary* 244
Hamilton, George 242, 248
Hamlet (William Shakespeare) 8, 35, 60, 224
Hammersmith, *see* London
Hammett, Dashiell 244
Hands of Orlac, The (Robert Wiene, 1928) 165
Hanks, Tom 124
Hannah, Daryl 134
Harrison, Rex 125

Harry Potter and the Sorcerer's Stone (Chris Columbus, 2001) 212
Harry Potter film series 51
Harryhausen, Ray 169, 178
Heflin, Van 156
Hegel, Georg Wilhelm Friedrich 177
Hemmings, David 52, 137, 240
Henderson, Gretchen 90–1
Henry VI 177
Henry VIII 98
Hepburn, Audrey 57
Hepburn, Katharine 34, 47, 68, 157, 167, 271
Herzen, Alexander 172
His Girl Friday (Howard Hawks, 1940) 217
History of Fashion in France (Augustin Challamel) 245
Hitchcock, Alfred 19n4, 41–2, 51, 64–6, 87n14, 100, 114, 115, 130, 200n4, 262
    characterizations of 269
Hobbema, Meindert 158, 216
Hodges, Eddie 51
Hoffman, Dustin 12, 13, 194
Hogarth, William 156
Holiday (George Cukor, 1938) 34
Hollywood
    Academy Awards 269
    acting in 3
    Aromarama 43n1
    Cheyenne as character trope in 1950s 2
    Claymation, use of (*see* Harryhausen)
    C[omputer] G[enerated] I[magery] 120, 123, 124, 125, 212, 271
    convention for dramatizing public executions 32
    dramatized 231, 242ff.
    and facial close-up 97
    history of 185
    Hollywood Forever 269
    Musso & Frank Grill 269
    painted backings in 86
    pre-Code era in 148
    rear projection 217, 218
    SFX 170
    Smell-O-Vision 43n1

technicians 73
3-D 2
typical party in 176
Hollywood Studios
  camera rig for *Pinocchio* 73
  Disney 40, 109, 125
  MGM, John Houseman and Minnelli 242
  Paramount
    Legal Dept. 200n4
    triple-head projector 217
    united with Fox for *Titanic* 186
  Twentieth Century Fox 108
    united with Paramount for *Titanic* 186
  Warner Bros., cartoons 198
Holm, Ian 134
Home from the Hill (Vincente Minnelli, 1960) 242
Honey, I Shrunk the Kids (Joe Johnston, 1989) 158
Hood, Morag 57
Hopkins, Anthony 19, 210
Hopkins, Miriam 148
Horace Rackham Graduate School, The University of Michigan 1
Horner, James 186
Horsemen, The (John Frankenheimer, 1971) 181
Horton, Edward Everett 147
Houdini (George Marshall, 1953) 30
Houseman, John 242
How Green Was My Valley (John Ford, 1941) 170
How to Get Away with Murder (2014) 256–7
How to Marry a Millionaire (Jean Negulesco, 1953) 114, 228
Howard, John 68
Howards End (James Ivory, 1992) 186
Howitt, Barbara 34
Hud (Martin Ritt, 1963) 237
Hudson, Rock 109
Hugo (Martin Scorsese, 2011) 85–6
Huhtamo, Erkki 85
Hunt for Red October, The (John McTiernan, 1990) 37
Hurt, John 61, 127

Hussey, Ruth 47, 68
Hutton, Betty 14

I, Claudius (1976) 124
I Am Love, see *Io sono l'amore*
I Love You Again (W. S. Van Dyke, 1940) 186
I Married a Shadow (*J'ai épousé un ombre*) (Robin Davis, 1983) 96
I Was Interrupted (Nicholas Ray) 246
Ibsen, Hendrik, *see* Cavell, Stanley
Importance of Being Earnest, The (Oscar Wilde) 9
Incredible Shrinking Man, The (Jack Arnold, 1957) 13, 37
Independence Day (Roland Emmerich, 1996) 38
"Instructions on or rather Examples of How to Be Afraid" (Julio Cortázar) 202n5
Interiors (Woody Allen, 1978) 14
Internet 264
Io sono l'amore (*I Am Love*) (Luca Guadagnino, 2009) 43, 166, 167, 209, 210
iPhone 108
Irishman, The (Martin Scorsese, 2019) 97
Irréversible (Gaspar Noé, 2002) 23
Ishiguro, Kazuo 210
Istanbul 110, 269
  Basilica Cistern 58
  and Byzantine Empire 84n10
  Milyon Tasi 84n10
Italian Job, The (F. Gary Gray, 2003) 77

Jackson, Harry 220
Jackson, Peter 51
Jacobi, Derek 124
Jacobs, Jason 52n1, 163n1
James, Lily 57
James, William 99
Jaws (Steven Spielberg, 1975) 170, 186
Jazz Singer, The (Alan Crosland, 1927) 217
Jenkins, George 13
Jennings, Michael 57
Jezebel (William Wyler, 1938) 121, 159

Johnny Guitar (Nicholas Ray, 1954) 158
Johnson, Ben 21
Jonathan (Bill Oliver, 2018) 10
Jovovich, Milla 14
Junge, Alfred 14
Jungle Book, The (Alexander Korda, 1942) 159
Juno (Jason Reitman, 2007) *155*, 156

Kafka, Franz 31n5, 54, 122
Keats, John, and Arcady 100
Keith, Robert 82
Kelly, Gene 56
Kenya 32
Kidd, Michael 220
Kieling, Wolfgang 33
Killing, The (Veena Sud, 2011–14) 32n6
King Kong (Ernest Shoedsack and Merian C. Cooper, 1933) 114
King Lear (William Shakespeare) 211–12
Kings Row (Sam Wood, 1942) 170
Kingsley, Ben 53
Kitano, Takeshi 4
Klute (Alan J. Pakula, 1971) 137
Korsakov's (Sergei) Syndrome 18
Krabbé, Jeroen 140, 141
Kracauer, Siegfried, in Berlin, 1946 176
Krasner, Milton 242
Kubrick, Stanley 26, 28, 29, 55–6

L'ange exterminateur (*The Exterminating Angel*) (Luis Buñuel, 1962) 55, 142
L'arrivé d'un train en gare de La Ciotat (Louis and Auguste Lumière, 1895) 3
L'arroseur arrosé (*Watering the Gardner*) (Louis and Auguste Lumière, 1895) 78–9
L'heure d'été (*Summer Hours*) (Olivier Assayas, 2008) 80
La chambre verte (*The Green Room*) (François Truffaut, 1978) 23
La dolce vita (Federico Fellini, 1960) 244
La femme Nikita (Luc Besson, 1990) 43
La nuit américaine (*Day for Night*) (François Truffaut, 1973) 163, 257
La règle du jeu (*The Rules of the Game*) (Jean Renoir, 1939) 43
La ronde (Max Ophüls, 1950) 264
La vie en chemin de fer (Benjamin Gastineau) 81
LaBelle, Brandon 175–6
Lacan, Jacques 247
Ladd, Alan 269
Lady Vanishes, The (Alfred Hitchcock, 1938) 40
Land Rover, *see* Passenger
Landau, Jon 186
Landau, Martin 196
"Landscape with Railway Tracks" (Gustave Caillebotte) 81
Lansbury, Angela 50, 121n2
Lantz, Walter, cartoons 125
Latham, Louise 49
Laughton, Charles 14, 269
Laurier Palace Theatre (Montreal), 1927 disaster 30n3
Lavi, Dahlia 242
Law, Jude 17
Lawrence, D[avid] H[erbert], and spirit of place 159
Le Carré, John 112
Le grand bleu (*The Big Blue*) (Luc Besson, 1988) 27, 29
"Le Pont de l'Europe" (Gustave Caillebotte) 81
Lee, Bernard 205–6
Lehman, Catherine 156
Lehman, Ernest, *see* Family Plot
LeRoy, Mervyn 132
Letter from an Unknown Woman (Max Ophüls, 1948) 83n9, 165
Lewis, Jerry 23, 35, 201, 210
Life Lessons (Martin Scorsese, 1989) 22–3
Life of Pi (Ang Lee, 2012) *119*, 123
Lili (Charles Walters, 1953) 93, 94, 96
Lindner, Robert 203
Liotta, Ray *251*, *252*, *253*, *254*

Lipara, mythical 41
Little Murders (Alan Arkin, 1971) 265
Livesey, Roger 23
Living It Up (Norman Taurog, 1954) 211
Lloyd, Norman 105
Locke, John, Apollonianism and Dionysianism 99–100
London
   Hammersmith 174
   Leicester Square Panorama by Robert Barker 83
   National Gallery 91n1, 225
   Waterloo Station 211
Lonedale Operator, The (D. W. Griffith, 1911) 84, 261
Lonsdale, Michel 180
Lord of the Rings films (Peter Jackson, 2001, 2002, 2003) 51
Lorrain, Claude 158
Los Angeles
   audience preview screenings 174
   Bel Air 107, 108
   Beverly Blvd. 108
   Beverly Hills 235, 269
   Brentwood 269
   Chasen's 108
   Chateau Marmont 269
   downtown area 157, 185
   East Side 108
   Garden of Allah 269
   Griffith Observatory 231
   Holmby Hills 108
   Mandeville Cyn. 52
   North Doheny Dr. 108
   North Roxbury Dr. 269
   and the Owens Valley 107
   Pacific Palisades 108
   Pacific Palisades Gelson's 108
   San Fernando Valley 108
   Vernon 108
   Watts 108
   West Side 108–9
   Westwood 108
Loughman, John 74
Love Boat, The (1977) 109
Loved One, The (Tony Richardson, 1965) 167

Lubitsch, Ernst 144, 146, 147, 149, 152, 153, 168
Ludwig II of Bavaria 90
Lumière, Louis and Auguste 3, 78
Lupino, Ida 223, 234, 235
LuPone, Patti 121n2

MacMurray, Fred 109
Magnificent Ambersons, The (Orson Welles, 1942) 9, 19
Magnolia (Paul Thomas Anderson, 1999) 37
Malkovich, John 51
Malleson, Miles 92
Maltese Falcon, The (John Huston, 1941) 10
Man in the Gray Flannel Suit (Nunnally Johnson, 1956) 14
Man Who Fell to Earth, The (Nicolas Roeg, 1976) 134, 136
Man Who Knew Too Much, The (Alfred Hitchcock, 1956) 34, 167, 200, 275
Manchester (UK), Bob Dylan concert 172
Manchurian Candidate, The (John Frankenheimer, 1962) 50, 184
Manet, Édouard, and balconies 73
Manhunter (Michael Mann, 1986) 123, 124
Mannoni, Laurent 83, 84
Marais, Jean 80
Margolin, Janet 239
Marie Antoinette (Sofia Coppola, 2006) 43
Mark, The (Guy Green, 1961) 197
Marnie (Alfred Hitchcock, 1964) 170, 257
   writer's character description 48–9
"Mars" *see Planets*
Marshall, E. G. 14
Marshall, Herbert 146, 199
Marvel Comics, *see Fantastic Four*
Marvelous Mrs. Maisel, The (2017) 233–4
Mary Poppins (Robert Stevenson, 1964) 32
Mary, Queen of Scots (Charles Jarrott, 1971) 57

Mason, James 23, 196
Massey, Raymond 41
Matter of Life and Death, A, see Stairway to Heaven
Max Factor 14n3
McCambridge, Mercedes 34
McCormack, Patty 132
McLuhan, [H.] Marshall 238, 261
McMillan & Wife (1971) 109
McTeer, Janet 134
Megna, John 10
Méliès, Georges 26, 72
Melrose Place (1992) 109
Melville, Herman 194
Memento (Christopher Nolan, 2000) 19
Memoirs of an Invisible Man (John Carpenter, 1992) 37
Men in Black (Barry Sonnenfeld, 1997) 140
Merleau-Ponty, Maurice 129, 143
Merman, Ethel 34, 121n2, 132
Merry Christmas, Mr. Lawrence (Nagisa Oshima, 1982) 4
Messiah (Michael Burnett, 2020) 37, 41, 204, 205
Midler, Bette 23
Midnight Lace (David Miller, 1960) 166
Mills, Mort 113
Milyon Tasi, *see* Istanbul
Mineo, Sal 14
Minnelli, Vincente 219, 221, 242, 243, 244, 246, 247, 248, 249
Minority Report (Steven Spielberg, 2002) 40, 141
Mission: Impossible (Brian De Palma, 1996) 77
Mission: Impossible – Ghost Protocol (Brad Bird, 2011) 219
Mitchum, Robert 53
Moby Dick (Herman Melville) 194
Modern Times (Charles Chaplin, 1936) 35, 180
Modigliani, Amadeo 236
Moment of Action: Riddles of Cinematic Performance (Murray Pomerance) 48

Monet, Claude 74
"Money, Money" (John Kander and Fred Ebb) 34
Monroe, Marilyn 54, 114, 228
Montias, John Michael 74
Moody, Ron 53
Moonrise Kingdom (Wes Anderson, 2012) 170
Moore, Annabelle 79
Moreau, Jeanne 23
Morse, Robert 167
Mr. Holmes (Bill Condon, 2015) 43
Mt. Rushmore 61
Mummy, The (Stephen Sommers, 1999) 37
Murder of Roger Ackroyd, The (Agatha Christie) 256
Murder on the Orient Express (Sidney Lumet, 1974) 166, 258, 268n1
Murphy, Eddie 125
Musée d'Orsay, *see* Paris
Mutiny on the Bounty (Frank Lloyd, 1935) 14
My Name Is Julia Ross (Joseph H. Lewis, 1945) 130
My Three Sons (1960) 109
Mystery of Oberwald, The (Michelangelo Antonioni, 1980) 76

Nabokov, Vladimir 94, 106, 244
Naremore, James 202
Nash, Mary 68
National Gallery, *see* London
NC-17 (US "Adults only" film rating) 177
Neal, Patricia 237
Necco wafers, *see* New England Confectionary Company
Neeson, Liam 53
"Nessun dorma" (Giacomo Puccini) 23
Netflix 31n4, 109, 171n4, 268
New England Confectionary Company 243
New York City
  1860s displays of 85
  Grand Central Station 211

Greenwich Village 67
Statue of Liberty 105
Waverly Theater 67–8
Yankee Stadium 61
New York Times, The 90, 105
New Zealand 174
Newman, Paul 33
Nichols, Mike 96
Nicholson, Jack 214
Night to Remember, A (Roy Ward Baker, 1958) 171, *173*, 174, 189
Nightmare on Elm Street (Wes Craven, 1984) 109
Ninotchka (Ernst Lubitsch, 1939) 168
Nixon, Richard Milhouse, resignation of 13
Nizhny Novgorod, *see* Gorky
No Direction Home: *Bob Dylan* (Martin Scorsese, 2005) 172
"Noli me tangere" (Titian) *223*, 224–7
Nolte, Nick 22
North by Northwest (Alfred Hitchcock, 1959) 37, 44, 196, 201–2
North by Northwest Continuity Script (James Naremore) 202
Norwood Theater (Manitoba St., Bracebridge ON) 185
Notorious (Alfred Hitchcock, 1946) 15, 197
Notre-Dame (2022) 37
Now, Voyager (Irving Rapper, 1942) 195
Nutty Professor, The (Jerry Lewis, 1963) 14
Nyberg, Mary Ann 220

O'Brien, Edmond *223*, 234
O'Connor, Una 95
"Ode on a Grecian Urn" (John Keats) 17, 100
O'Donnell, Cathy 14
Old Walton Bridge (Surrey) 76; *see also* Canaletto
Oliver Twist (Charles Dickens) 53
Olympus, mythical 41

On Dangerous Ground (Nicholas Ray, 1951) 234
Ondra, Anny 271
Orphée (Jean Cocteau, 1950) 80
Ortega y Gasset, José
  optical hero 76, 211
  proximate vision 160
  reality 224
O'Sullivan, Timothy 87, 158
Out of Towners, The (Arthur Hiller, 1970) 186
Outland (Peter Hyams, 1981) 26
Oxford University 98
  Christ Church 99
"Ozymandias" (Percy Bysshe Shelley) 188

Pacino, Al 142
Pakula, Alan J. 12, 13, 137
Palance, Jack 21
Pandora's jar, mythical 28
Paris
  Argenteuil 76
  Boulevard des Capucines 3
  Boulevard des Italiens 72, 76
  Boulevard Haussmann 82
  City of Light 72
  Gare de Montparnasse train catastrophe (October 22, 1895) 86
  Les Champs Elysées 74
  Musée d'Orsay 80
  Quai de la Tournelle 74
  Rue des Italiens 72
  Rue Taitbout 72
  Salon Indien 3
  Seine 56
  Théâtre Robert-Houdin 72
  Tour d'Eiffel (March 31, 1889) 73, 84n10
Paris Street, Rainy Day (Gustave Caillebotte) 82n8
Pasolini, Pier Paolo 99
Passenger, The (*Professione: Reporter*) (Michelangelo Antonioni, 1975) 166
  Land Rover in 213
  Uher tape recorder in 213
Passion (Jean-Luc Godard, 1982) 22, 75, 82, 194

Paul, Steven 190n6
Pearl Harbor (Michael Bay, 2001) 43
Peck, Gregory 64
"People" (Bob Merrill and Jule Styne) 35
Perfect Storm, The (Wolfgang Petersen, 2000) 41
Permanence and Change (Kenneth Burke) 190
Personal Shopper (Olivier Assayas, 2016) 89
Pesci, Joe 252, 253, 254
Peters, Bernadette 121n2
Phantom of Liberty, The (Luis Buñuel, 1974) 63
Philadelphia Museum of Art, The 239
Philadelphia Story, The (George Cukor, 1940) 47, 68
Phoenix (Arizona) 111, 114
Photoplay 269
Piaf, Edith 101
Pillow Talk (Michael Gordon, 1959) 168
Pinocchio (Norman Ferguson, T. Hee, Wilfred Jackson, 1940) 73–4
Pirandello, Luigi 50, 52, 255
Pissarro, Camille 74
Pitt, Michael 92, 101
Planck, Robert 94
Planet of the Apes (Franklin J. Schaffner, 1968) 125
Planets, The (Gustav Holst) 32
Play It Again, Sam (Woody Allen, 1972) 92
Play Time (Jacques Tati, 1968) 267
Poitier, Sidney 193, 203, 205
Polglase, Van Nest 157
Polyphemus 113
Pomerance, Ariel 149n1
"Poor Koko" (John Fowles) 44n2
Portnoy's Complaint (Ernest Lehman, 1972) 43
Portrait of a Lady, The (Henry James) 99
Poseidon Adventure, The (Ronald Neame, 1972) 186
Possessed (Curtis Bernhardt, 1947) 155, 156, 198

Potente, Franka 35
Poussin, Nicolas 98–9
Power, Tyrone 269
Pressure Point (Stanley Kramer, 1962) 193, 203
Promenade des autriches dans Les Jardins Zoölogiques de Paris (*Parade of Ostriches in the Paris Zoological Gardens*) (Louis and Auguste Lumière, 1895) 79
Psycho (Alfred Hitchcock, 1960) 60, 103, 110, 111, 114, 161, 211
Puritanism 99
Pygmalion and Galatea (myth) 16

Québec, Province: film exhibition law after 1927 disaster 30n3

Radcliffe, Daniel 51
Rain, The (Jannik Tai Mosholt, Christian Potalivo, Esben Toft Jacobsen, 2018) 37
Rains, Claude 15, 195
Rains of Ranchipur, The (Jean Negulesco, 1955) 14
Rancho Notorious (Fritz Lang, 1952) 179
Rancière, Jacques 97
Random Harvest (Mervyn LeRoy, 1942) 95
Rashômon (Akira Kurosawa, 1950) 198
Ray, Johnnie 132
Ray, Nicholas 158, 203, 230, 231, 246, 269
Reade, Walter Jr., 43n1; see also Hollywood
Rear Window (Alfred Hitchcock, 1954), camera positioning for 87
Reason, Rex 39
Rebel Without a Cause (Nicholas Ray, 1955) 14, 56, 203, 230, 233
Red Shoes, The (Michael Powell and Emeric Pressburger, 1948) 16, 163
 Swan Lake routine 17
Redford, Robert 12, 13
Redgrave, Vanessa 137

Redmayne, Eddie 124
Reese's Pieces 104
Reeve, Christopher 51
Reeves, George 51
Reeves, Keanu 76
Reformation, Protestant 98
Reid, Carl Benton 203
Reid, Sheila 236
Remains of the Day, The (James Ivory, 1993) 210
Réno, Jean 180
Répertoire des coleurs (France) 244
Rilke, Rainer Maria 99
Rise of the Planet of the Apes (Rupert Wyatt, 2011) 125
Roadkill (2020) 36
Robinson, Edward G. 242, 248
Robson, Flora 14
Rodowick, David 93
Rogers, Ginger 34
Rolls Royce 182, 185
Romeo and Juliet (William Shakespeare) 40
Romeo and Juliet (Franco Zeffirelli, 1968) 186
Ronin (John Frankenheimer, 1998) 180
Rope (Alfred Hitchcock, 1948) 262
Routh, Brandon 51
Ruggles, Charlie 139, 148
Run Lola Run (Tom Tykwer, 1998) 35, 219
Russell, Kurt 134

Saboteur (Alfred Hitchcock, 1942) 105
Sabrina (Billy Wilder, 1954) 140
Saint, Eva Marie 201, 202
Saklad, Steve 156
Salk, Jonas, polio vaccine 32
Salon Indien, Boul. des Capucines (Paris) 3
Saltburn (Emerald Fennell, 2023) 33, 210
San Francisco 107, 181, 234, 235
Sarris, Andrew 178
Sartre, Jean-Paul 91, 101, 135, 247
Sastre, Ines 228
Saturday Night and Sunday Morning (Karel Reisz, 1960) 186

Saudi Arabia, *see* Thesiger
Saveleva, Lyudmila 57
Saving Private Ryan (Steven Spielberg, 1998) 37
Schafer, R. Murray 164
Schefer, Jean Louis 13, 23–4, 73, 75
Schivelbusch, Wolfgang
  and auditorium lighting 184
  and 1940s Berlin 176
  panoramic perception 75, 80, 83, 84
Schneewittchen, see Snow White
Schumacher, Joel 15
Sebald, W[infried] G[eorg] 71–2, 88
"Second Coming, The" (William Butler Yeats) 104
Segal, George 131
Serkis, Andy 32, 125
Serrone, Christopher 253
Seurat, Georges
  at Argenteuil 76
  and dots 172
Seventh Voyage of Sinbad, The (Nathan Juran, 1958) 169, 186
Shakespeare, William 40, 60, 98n3, 167, 210, 224
Shearer, Moira 17
"Shepherd with His Flock in a Woody Landscape" (Peter Paul Rubens) 158
Silence of the Lambs, The (Jonathan Demme, 1991) 19
Simon of the Desert (Luis Buñuel, 1965) 54, 55
Sinclair, Iain 17
Sixth Sense, The (M. Night Shyamalan, 1999) 162
Sloane, Everett 7, 9
Smith, C. Aubrey 148
Snow White (Jacob and Wilhelm Grimm) 39, 40
Snow White and the Seven Dwarfs (William Cottrell, David Hand, Wilfred Jackson, 1937) 126
Snowpiercer (Bong Joon Ho, 2013) 170
Sobchack, Vivian 47, 49

Some Like It Hot (Billy Wilder, 1959) 144
"Some People" (Jule Styne and Stephen Sondheim) 35
Somewhere in Time (Jeannot Szwarc, 1980) 171
Sous le ciel de Paris (Jean Duvivier, 1951) 74
Southampton (UK) 186, 188, 189; see also Elizabeth House
Spader, James 268
Spartacus (Stanley Kubrick, 1960) 43
Speaking and Language: Defence of Poetry (Paul Goodman) 112, 173
Spellbound (Alfred Hitchcock, 1945) 64, 65
Spelling, Aaron 108, 109
Spy Who Came in from the Cold (Martin Ritt, 1965) 35, 197n2, 208
St. Justin Martyr 97–8
Stack, Robert 16
Stage Fright (Alfred Hitchcock, 1950) 197
Stairway to Heaven (A Matter of Life and Death) (Michael Powell and Emeric Pressburger, 1946) 37
Stamp, Terence 76
Stanwyck, Barbara 269
Stapleton, Maureen 14
Star Trek (Gene Roddenberry, 1966) 40
Star Wars (George Lucas, 1977) 32, 44
Statue of Liberty, see New York City
Sternberger Dolf 75, 84
Stewart, James 47, 68, 269
Stewart, Kristen 54, 89
Stewart, Patrick 53n2
Still of the Night (Robert Benton, 1982) 18, 198
Strangers on a Train (Alfred Hitchcock, 1951) 114
Streep, Meryl 34, 109, 180
Streets of San Francisco, The (1972) 109
Streisand, Barbra 35
Stromberg, Robert 14
Stuart, Kim Rossi 228

Sturges, Preston 165
Styrofoam 158
Sudnow, David 238
Sullivan's Travels (Preston Sturges, 1942) 37, 217
Summa Theologica (Thomas Aquinas) 97
Sunset Blvd. (Billy Wilder, 1950) 59n3
"Supercalifragilisticexpialidocious" (Robert B. Sherman and Richard M. Sherman) 34
Superman (character) 51, 62
Superman (Richard Donner, 1978) 42, 139
Superman Returns (Bryan Singer, 2006) 61, 62, 66
Swan Lake (Peter Ilyich Tchaikowsky, 1875–6) 17; see also Red Shoes
Swift, Jonathan 217
Swinton, Tilda 209

Takeshi, *see* Kitano
Talented Mr. Ripley, The (Anthony Minghella, 1999) 96
Tarzan the Ape Man (W. S. Van Dyke, 1932) 36, 125
Taste of Honey, A (Tony Richardson, 1961) 11
Tati, Jacques 10, 267, 270
Taylor, Elizabeth 13, 129, 131
Technicolor
  ASA 217
  black-and-white recording film for 113
  British Technicolor 159
  camera used for 87, 217
  make-up used for 14n3
  matrices for 217
  popularity of 162
  and rear projection 217–18
  storage problems 94
  widescreen, use in 162
Teilhard de Chardin, Pierre 21
Tempest (Paul Mazursky, 1982) 41
Tempest, The (William Shakespeare) 41
Ten Commandments, The (Cecil B. DeMille, 1934) 243n1

Ten Commandments, The (Cecil B. DeMille, 1956) 171
Teorema (Pier Paolo Pasolini, 1968) 76
Thai Cave Rescue (2022) 31n4
Thatcher, Torin 169
Théâtre Robert-Houdin, *see* Paris
Theory of Everything, The (James Marsh, 2014) 124
There's No Business Like Show Business (Walter Lang, 1954) 132, 162
Thesiger, Wilfred, travels in the Empty Quarter with the Bedu 213
They Live (John Carpenter, 1988) 114
Thief of Bagdad, The (Michael Powell and Emeric Pressburger, 1940) 92
Thing, The (John Carpenter, 1982) 134
Third Man, The (Carol Reed, 1949) 162
Thirty Seconds over Tokyo (Mervyn LeRoy, 1944) 181
This Island Earth (Joseph Newman, 1955) *39*, 40
Thomas, Henry 237
Thoreau, Henry David 172
Thumbsucker (Mike Mills, 2005) 76
THX 1138 (George Lucas, 1971) 161
Titanic (James Cameron, 1997) 42, 179, 184–91
Titanic, R. M. S.
  1912 sailing 186
  sinking 171
Titian (Tiziano Vecelli) 228; *see also* "Noli me tangere"
To Kill a Mockingbird (Robert Mulligan, 1962) 10
Todd, Mike Jr., Smell-O-Vision 43n1; *see also* Hollywood
Toll of the Sea, The (Chester Franklin, 1922) 245
Tolstoy, Leo (Lev) 57–8
Tönnies, Ferdinand 85
Tootsie (Sydney Pollack, 1982) 194
Torn Curtain (Alfred Hitchcock, 1966) 33
Toronto 110, 269
Total Recall (Paul Verhoeven, 1990) 140

Touch, The (Ingmar Bergman, 1971) 235–7
Towering Inferno, The (John Guillermin, 1974) 186
Trevor, Claire 242, 248
Trip to the Moon, A (*Le voyage dans la lune*) (Georges Méliès, 1902) 26
Trollope, Anthony 173, 174, 175n2
Trouble in Paradise (Ernst Lubitsch, 1932) 144, *145*, 146–53
Truffaut, François 23, 75, 163, 257–8
Tucson (Arizona) 114
Turandot (Giacomo Puccini), *see* "Nessun dorma"
Turner, Victor, forest of symbols 161
Twister (Jan de Bont 1996) 41
Two-Faced Woman (George Cukor, 1941) 197
Two Weeks in Another Town (Vincente Minnelli, 1962) *241*, 242–50

Uccello, Paolo, *see* Vasari
Uher (Uher Werke), *see* Passenger
Umbrellas of Cherbourg, The (Jacques Demi, 1964) 14
Uncle Boonmee Who Can Recall His Past Lives (Apichatpong Weerasethakul, 2020) 23
University of Cambridge 98
Unknown, The (Tod Browning, 1927) 76, 165
US Geological Survey 158
Usual Suspects, The (Bryan Singer, 1995) 10, 256

Valentine, Joseph 157
Vasari, Giorgio, discussing Uccello 178
Veidt, Conrad 92
Venice 149
Vermeer, Johannes 247
Vertigo (Alfred Hitchcock, 1958) 14, 130, 190, 195n1
Veruschka, *see* Von Lehndorff
Victorian era, sitting rooms in 156
videotape, *see* visual technologies
Vinall, Olivia 36

Viridiana (Luis Buñuel) 55, 114
Virtuoso: Film Performance and the Actor's Magic (Murray Pomerance) 34, 48
visual technologies, *see also* Hollywood, Technicolor
  Blu-Ray 177
  D[igital] V[ideo] D[isc] 94, 177
  videotape 21, 177
Vitti, Monica 76
Vogue 202
Von Leeuwenhoek, Anton 260
Von Lehndorff, Veruschka 240
Von Sydow, Max 141, 235
Vonnegut, Kurt Jr. 119–20
Voyage with Hitchcock, A (Murray Pomerance) 19

Wait until Dark (Terence Young, 1967) 197
Waiting for Godot (Samuel Beckett) 143
Walbrook, Anton 17, 163
Walker, Robert 211
War and Peace (Leo Tolstoy) 57
  Moscow invaded by Napoléon 57
War of the Worlds, The (Byron Haskin, 1953) 44
Ward, Artemus, New York panoramas 85
Washington Post, The 12
Watchmen (Zack Snyder, 2009) 140, 166
Watergate Affair (1972–4) 12
Waterloo Station, *see* London
Watson, Emma 51
Watts, Naomi 145
Wavelength (Michael Snow, 1967) 74n2
Waverly Theater, *see* New York City
Way We Live Now, The (Anthony Trollope) 175n2
Weber, Max 85, 205
Week End (*Weekend*) (Jean-Luc Godard, 1967) 264
Weekend, see Week End
Weisel, Al 232

Welles, Orson 7, 10, 16
Welling, Tom 51
"We're in the Money" ("The Gold Diggers' Song") (Harry Warren and Al Dubin) 34
Werner's Nomenclature of Colours (Patrick Syme) 244
Wetherby (David Hare, 1985) 210
When Harry Met Sally... (Rob Reiner, 1898) 222
Whitman, Stuart 197
Whitty, Dame May 130
Who's Afraid of Virginia Woolf? (Mike Nichols, 1966) 13–14, 96, *129*, 131, 167
"Who's on First?" (Abbott and Costello) 167
Wilder, Billy 59n3, 144, 153, 178
Williams, Tennessee 17, 188
Willy Wonka and the Chocolate Factory (Mel Stuart, 1973) 14
Wilson, Frank 239
Winslet, Kate 189
Wittgenstein, Ludwig 23, 113, 190, 200, 203
Wizard of Oz, The (Victor Fleming, 1939) 21, 23, 37, 41, 82, 125, 126, 162, 179
"Wooded Landscape" (Meindert Hobbema) 158
Woodward, Bob 12, 13
Wordsworth, William 82, 113
World Trade Center (Oliver Stone, 2006) 37
Wreck of the Mary Deare, The (Michael Anderson, 1959) 31
Written on the Wind (Douglas Sirk, 1956) 16, 82
Wycherly, William 184
Wyman, Jane 109

Yankee Stadium, *see* New York City
Yeats, William Butler 104

Zabriskie Point (Michelangelo Antonioni, 1970) 42, 78